ROBERT WISE:
THE MOTION PICTURES
REVISED EDITION

by J.R. Jordan

Orlando, Florida

Robert Wise: The Motion Pictures (Revised Edition)
© 2020 J.R. Jordan. All Rights Reserved.

No portion of this publication may be reproduced, stored, and/or copied electronically (except for academic use as a source), nor transmitted in any form or by any means without the prior written permission of the publisher and/or author.

Published in the USA by
BearManor Media
1317 Edgewater Dr. #110
Orlando, FL 32804
www.BearManorMedia.com

Softcover Edition
ISBN-10: 1-62933-536-3
ISBN-13: 978-1-62933-536-0

Printed in the United States of America

for Joseph C. Jordan Jr.

Table of Contents

FOREWORD BY GAVIN MacLEOD — ix

INTRODUCTION BY DOUGLAS E. WISE — xiii

ACKNOWLEDGEMENTS — xix

PART I
RKO RADIO PICTURES — xxiii

1. THE CURSE OF THE CAT PEOPLE (1944) — 1
2. MADEMOISELLE FIFI (1944) — 17
3. THE BODY SNATCHER (1945) — 25
4. A GAME OF DEATH (1945) — 35
5. CRIMINAL COURT (1946) — 41
6. BORN TO KILL (1947) — 49
7. MYSTERY IN MEXICO (1948) — 57
8. BLOOD ON THE MOON (1948) — 67
9. THE SET-UP (1949) — 75

PART II
THE FIFTIES — 87

10. TWO FLAGS WEST (1950) — 89
11. THREE SECRETS (1950) — 97
12. THE HOUSE ON TELEGRAPH HILL (1951) — 107
13. THE DAY THE EARTH STOOD STILL (1951) — 117
14. THE CAPTIVE CITY (1952) — 129
15. SOMETHING FOR THE BIRDS (1952) — 137
16. DESTINATION GOBI (1953) — 145
17. THE DESERT RATS (1953) — 155
18. SO BIG (1953) — 163
19. EXECUTIVE SUITE (1954) — 171
20. HELEN OF TROY (1956) — 185
21. TRIBUTE TO A BAD MAN (1956) — 197
22. SOMEBODY UP THERE LIKES ME (1956) — 209
23. THIS COULD BE THE NIGHT (1957) — 227
24. UNTIL THEY SAIL (1957) — 239
25. RUN SILENT RUN DEEP (1958) — 251
26. I WANT TO LIVE! (1958) — 267
27. ODDS AGAINST TOMORROW (1959) — 279

PART III
PRIMETIME!   291

28 WEST SIDE STORY (1961)   293
29 TWO FOR THE SEESAW (1962)   309
30 THE HAUNTING (1963)   317
31 THE SOUND OF MUSIC (1965)   327
32 THE SAND PEBBLES (1966)   341
33 STAR! (1968)   361

PART IV
THE SCIENCE AND SURREALISM OF THE SEVENTIES   375

34 THE ANDROMEDA STRAIN (1971)   377
35 TWO PEOPLE (1973)   391
36 THE HINDENBURG (1975)   401
37 AUDREY ROSE (1977)   417
38 STAR TREK: THE MOTION PICTURE (1979)   427

PART V
TWILIGHT   443

39 ROOFTOPS (1989)   445
40 A STORM IN SUMMER (2000)   453

BIBLIOGRAPHY   465

INDEX   469

FOREWORD
by Gavin MacLeod

The book you are about to read is a testament to the hard work and dedication of its subject. *Robert Wise: The Motion Pictures*, meticulously researched and written by J.R. Jordan, covers a memorable period of over fifty years. Detailed plot synopses and commentary of many important films are provided. When I first learned Joe was writing a book about Mr. Wise, I was immediately compelled to share my memories of such a great man.

    I first met Robert Wise during the late 1950s when I was asked to do a screen test for *Run Silent Run Deep*. Upon the test's conclusion, he expressed his approval of my performance but ultimately confessed that another bald guy had been cast in the picture. "Who is it?" I asked. "His name is Don Rickles," Mr. Wise replied. I immediately thanked him for the opportunity and that was that. Later, when the casting of *I Want to Live!* began, I met with Mr. Wise again. This time, I wore a hairpiece while reading for the part of Henry Graham, the drug-addict husband of Barbara Graham. It went well, but Walter Wanger, the film's producer, apparently felt I was too young for the role. Mr. Wise ended up giving me the part of the police lieutenant. In the credits, I am the last performer listed. My character didn't even have a proper name, but the experience of performing alongside Susan Hayward was indeed memorable. We had one interrogation scene together. I wrote all about it in my book, *This is Your Captain Speaking: My Fantastic Voyage Through Hollywood, Faith, and Life*. During the film's production, I was in my twenties and very nervous about working with Miss Hayward, especially since the scene called for my character to pull her hair. A friend of mine who never worked but knew of everything going on in Hollywood approached me one day and said, "You gotta watch out! She can be really tough, so if you're gonna pull her hair, I would be very careful about it!" Miss Hayward and I rehearsed and spent the whole day working on that scene in the interrogation room. At one point, she came to me and said, "Gavin, there's a rumor that I could earn an Oscar for this. If you would really, really pull my hair, it will help my performance." I agreed but made it clear I would not hurt her in any way. I was just as nervous as could be. When it came time to film the scene, I ended up really yanking her hair. Then, about six months later, she won the Oscar, and I proudly told all of my friends that I helped her earn it.

My father died when I was thirteen years old, and nobody ever really took his place. Robert Wise was somebody I always looked up to. He knew what he was doing. Just working with him and being in his presence, I immediately sensed he was such a kind, creative man with a great sense of humor. Then, *The Sand Pebbles* came up. One afternoon, I got a call from him. He said, "Gavin, this is Bob Wise. I'm doing a movie with Steve McQueen. How tall are you?" "How tall do you want me to be?" I asked. As Mr. Wise considered me for a role in his film, he made it clear that I couldn't be any taller than Steve in order to be cast. Years earlier, Steve and I actually played brothers on Broadway. He was about an inch-and-a-half taller than I was. I informed Mr. Wise of the height difference, and much to my surprise, he said, "Okay, you've got yourself about an eight month job." For me, that was the beginning of *The Sand Pebbles*. With Mr. Wise in charge, we all knew things were going to be handled beautifully. He was everything I would try to be as a person and a leader.

Years later, after *The Mary Tyler Moore Show*, people started to know who I was. Then, we did *The Love Boat*, and it went through the roof. As a result,

I was presented with many special opportunities. One evening, an awards show took place and Robert Wise was to be one of the recipients. The show's producers contacted me ahead of time and requested that I be the person to present him with the award. I knew it would be an important moment for me to say what I had been feeling about the man since I first met him. As I introduced Mr. Wise to the audience on that particular evening, I said, "What can you say about all the work this man has contributed to the film industry? He has impacted millions of lives – including mine. The truth is, if I had a chance to pick my father, it would be Robert Wise." He then came on stage and we embraced as he accepted the award. It was a great moment for me because I finally had the chance to say what I'd been feeling all those years, and because of that ceremony, my wife, Patti, finally got to meet Robert Wise for the first time. I always spoke of him to her. He was a brilliant, kind, extremely creative, and organized human being. He inspired me in so many ways. Later in Mr. Wise's life, as his ninety-first birthday approached, I decided to send some flowers to his home in Century City. However, I didn't realize he was in the hospital at the time. Shortly after I sent the flowers, he passed away. I think it was just a couple of days later. Whether he knew those flowers were from me or not, the decision to send them remained important to me.

Robert Wise was a master. He was the best director I have ever worked with. I've worked with some great comedy directors, but they could only do comedy. Robert Wise could do everything. The interesting thing about acting in his films is that even though I couldn't actually see him while I was performing in a scene, he was always there. The same goes for today. Even though Mr. Wise is no longer around, he's still here, and as long as there's a motion picture, he'll be here. Robert Wise will always be in the memories of those who had the great fortune to be in his presence. For me, it all started with a screen test, and later, I was finally able to tell the world that I wish Robert Wise could've been my father. That's the greatest thing I could say about anybody I've ever worked with.

INTRODUCTION
by Douglas E. Wise

The story of Robert Wise's career in motion pictures is fascinating on many levels. My father, David Wise, came to California and got a job at RKO Radio Pictures working alongside a construction gang, sweeping stages and doing all kinds of grunt work. He ended up in the accounting department but had a desire to eventually become a film editor. On some afternoons my father would visit the studio's post-production facilities, as it was his desire to learn all about synchronizing sound with film in order to compose the sync rushes. Today, these rushes are referred to as dailies, meaning that all of the footage shot a day earlier is viewed by production personnel (i.e., the director, producers). The head of the accounting department had plans for my father. He considered him to be a valuable asset and wouldn't let him go elsewhere within the studio. As time passed, my father worked his way up the corporate ladder and ended up running RKO, the facility itself. His responsibilities had nothing to do with the movie making aspect of the business. He nevertheless ran the facility.

In time, Robert Wise followed in the footsteps of his older brother, my father. He bravely departed Indiana for California to seek a career in the entertainment industry. Not long after Uncle Bob's arrival, my father got him a position with the studio working on the film dock. My uncle's very first job was to basically carry film from one place to another. He eventually transferred to the editing department and of course became very successful right up through *Citizen Kane*. It was only a matter of time before he made his way to the director's chair. Uncle Bob didn't have a business manager at the time. He therefore sought the guidance of my father, who eventually left RKO and bought a restaurant called the Nickodell. It became a joint venture between the both of them. Gino Cantamessa, the manager of the RKO commissary, resigned from the studio to offer his support. His guidance was necessary in order to run the Nickodell since my father and Uncle Bob didn't know much about the restaurant business. The venture turned out to be quite successful. By the time Uncle Bob became an established film director in Hollywood, my father ran all of his production companies and investments.

When I was a kid, I fondly remember spending time with my Uncle Bob and Aunt Pat. She had been an actress some years earlier. They had one son, who of course was my cousin. He was named Robert, after his father, but we used to call him Robby. They all lived in Santa Monica, right on the beach. I still remember the address: 702 Pacific Coast Highway. Robby and I always played together. Sometimes, we'd swim in the ocean. My uncle's backyard consisted of nothing but sand. Uncle Bob and Aunt Pat frequently hosted barbeques. Friends of theirs, some of whom were actors, attended these gatherings. Almost every weekend, there'd be some kind of function going on at their house. It was a lot of fun. Uncle Bob eventually sold his house in Santa Monica and built a beautiful home just north of Malibu. He also constructed a detached studio apartment located down below the garage, and next to the studio, a sauna had been built. Uncle Bob sometimes hosted parties down there. He would even hire a masseuse! Partygoers could therefore enjoy a nice barbeque, massage, and relaxation time in the sauna all in one evening.

Introduction

I distinctly remember the day I went with Uncle Bob and Aunt Pat to the old Directors Guild building on Sunset Boulevard. It contained a movie theater and stood just down the street from the current location of the guild's headquarters. All of us, including my father and brother, took in a special screening of *The Haunting*. It was a great, yet scary, experience. A couple of years earlier, at a time when I was a young kid in high school, *West Side Story* premiered. It was the first film of Uncle Bob's I had ever seen and remains amazing!

Later in my life, during the production of *Star Trek: The Motion Picture*, I was hired as the second assistant director, thanks to my uncle. The first assistant director was a guy named Danny McCauley. He had been in the motion picture industry for some time. I think Danny may have wanted to use his own people for the film. Most first assistants prefer to use their own people, but Uncle Bob told him, "I've got somebody I'd like you to use." It was a great experience and later paved the way for me to work on an additional four *Star Trek* films, all starring the original cast. I ended up being on the Enterprise quite a bit. As it happens, when I served in the navy during the 1960s, I was stationed on the aircraft carrier of the same name. Watching Uncle Bob direct *Star Trek: The Motion Picture* was an experience in itself. Everybody loved him. He was evenly tempered and such a pleasant person. If he ever had a disagreement with somebody on the set, or if an actor didn't care for a particular line in the script, Bob and that person would then take a little walk around the stage to discuss the issue, and that usually straightened things out. The production of *Star Trek: The Motion Picture* was so difficult because the studio decided to begin shooting without a completed script. The movie had actually been pre-booked in theaters in order to provide an extra source of revenue for it to be produced. Paramount was facing a specific release date, but problems would arise on a day-to-day basis, whether it was an issue with the photography or some other aspect of the production. I remember receiving so many revisions to the script that it became necessary for me to label such revisions with the day and time received. Some of the actors reported that they weren't receiving these changes, so I ended up taking people's call sheets and stapling the changes to their sheets, and whenever I handed them these changes, I would always require a signature. Therefore, if anybody ever claimed that they didn't receive the revisions, I was at least cleared of any wrongdoing. At some points, we would actually stop filming because we were out of material. The cast and crew would then go to the stage next door. A table in the form of a big U-shape was located in the center of this stage, along with many chairs. Gene Roddenberry's people would occasionally bring any and all script revisions to the table and distribute these revisions to everybody present. The film's performers took some time to read and review the changes. Finally, we'd all go back to the main stage and start shooting the new material. The experience was bizarre. Uncle Bob had no time to prepare and basically did things on the fly, but that's where his experience came in handy. He was able to choreograph the scenes despite not having enough time to think things through. I believe my uncle relied on his previous experience of arranging his shots on storyboards.

As a director, Uncle Bob's demeanor and personality were quite even. There was no temper. There was no ego. There was no flexing of power or anything else. He was simply a nice guy and everybody, cast and crew alike, admired him. I don't believe this to be true simply because he was my uncle. I've worked in the motion picture industry for thirty years as a director, assistant director, and production manager. During this period of time, I have never encountered anybody classier than my uncle. Furthermore, everybody loved my Aunt Pat. They loved her just like they loved Uncle Bob. I remember she drove a seven-year-old Chevy Camaro. Uncle Bob continuously insisted on buying her a new car, but she kept refusing. "No, I like *this* car," she'd say. Aunt Pat could've had anything she wanted, brand new every year, but she was very happy with the things she had in her life and didn't want anything to change.

Sadly, Aunt Pat died of cancer in 1975. She preceded Uncle Bob in death by thirty years. On September 14, 2005, he passed away due to heart failure, and just four months later, his son and my cousin, Robby, died suddenly. The timing was unbelievable. Robby had actually suffered a heart attack some time prior to his death. He was just a year older than me and was not in the best of health. Robby found work in the industry as a camera assistant and actually served in this capacity during the production of *Star Trek: The Motion Picture*, but he later had to quit the film business because he was suffering from diabetes. Things became so bad that he gradually went blind, and Uncle Bob was still alive when all of this happened. It was clearly terrible for him to see his son in such pain.

When I worked on *Star Trek: The Motion Picture*, I was relatively new to the business. I had recently become a member of the Directors Guild, having spent about a year as a second assistant director on television's *Barnaby Jones*. My experience was limited, and I didn't know too many people in the industry. Since then, I've worked with all types of individuals, and I can now reflect back on the type of person Uncle Bob was both personally and professionally. On occasion, people discover that he was my uncle. I never say anything about it, but people learn of my relation to him just the same and then proceed to tell me how great of a person he was. Naturally, it's always nice to hear such compliments. Whenever I reminisce about my uncle, I keep going back to the beach house in Santa Monica. Many times, he directed his pictures on location, and on these occasions, especially during the summer, my father would arrange for us to move into Uncle Bob's place. I remember being in my early teens. It was a great experience, particularly because it got us out of the heat. Our house in the San Fernando Valley didn't have air conditioning. We'd therefore stay in Santa Monica for a while - about a month to six weeks. I loved the beach, and Uncle Bob was only too happy to let us stay at his home. Such an outlook was a testament to his selfless nature, and he will always be missed by those who were fortunate enough to have known him.

J.R. Jordan, author of *Robert Wise: The Motion Pictures*, has written a thorough account of my uncle's career as a film director. Throughout the course of his research, he conducted over twenty interviews with those who knew Uncle Bob and also engaged in multiple viewings of each film, forty total, so that no stone would be left unturned. I remain impressed with Joe's enthusiasm and dedication, and I am proud to acknowledge his book as a welcome addition to my uncle's legacy. It not only pays tribute to a true stalwart of the cinematic arts, but going forward, it will no doubt inspire generations of film aficionados for years to come.

ACKNOWLEDGMENTS

When I began an interview with Gordon Gebert regarding his appearance in *The House on Telegraph Hill* (1951), he immediately spoke of his parents. "My mother was an industry watcher, not so much a film buff as she was an industry watcher," he said. "It meant very little to me back then, but around the time *The House on Telegraph Hill* was being produced, she told me my father was in awe of the fact that Robert Wise edited *Citizen Kane*." Naturally, such an achievement was a defining moment of Wise's career as an editor, but prior to cutting films, he collaborated with the sound effects crews of famous Depression Era musicals, including *The Gay Divorcee* (1934) and *Top Hat* (1935). Where would American cinema be without the contributions of Ginger Rogers and Fred Astaire? Wise, a fortunate individual, was granted permission to work behind the scenes of such memorable musicals and therefore fine-tune his skills in the process. He then reached a milestone upon cutting *Bachelor Mother* (1939), his first picture as a credited editor. A selection of Wise's additional, edited films include, but are not limited to, *My Favorite Wife* (1940), *The Devil and Daniel Webster* (1941), *Seven Days'*

Leave (1942), and *The Fallen Sparrow* (1943). In time, he became a director of motion pictures, never for a moment forgetting the skills he acquired up to that point. For the remainder of his career, Wise relied heavily on his previous experience as an editor. To those who had the privilege of working with him, such experience was evident through his elaborate storyboards and also through the notes he often recorded onto the shooting scripts of his films. Wise was economical, preferring not to shoot extra footage if the opportunity ever presented itself. As a result, he knew exactly what was needed when the time came for the editors to cut the film, thereby simplifying the post-production of his pictures.

On February 19, 1998, Robert Wise was presented with the Life Achievement Award by the American Film Institute, and many dignitaries of the industry were in attendance to share their memories of a man near and dear to their hearts. Yet, of all the speeches given on that memorable day, the most significant was that given by Wise himself. "Early on, I realized the most important element in any film is the script. With screenwriters like Ernest Lehman, Nelson Gidding, [and] Robert Anderson amongst others providing such marvelous screenplays, I felt I owed it to the audience to faithfully bring their fine work to the screen to the best of my creative powers," he declared. Such a statement is the basis for *Robert Wise: The Motion Pictures*. Throughout his lengthy career, Wise directed a total of forty films, and within this book, I provide an analysis of each film in specific regard to its story while devoting equal attention to his treatment of such a story. The book, however, would not be complete without the contributions of those who kindly shared with me their memories of Mr. Wise. I would like to thank the following individuals for their time: Jacqueline White, Gordon Gebert, Billy Gray, Janette Scott, Jack Young, Michael Dante, Neile Adams, Ralph Votrian, Eddie Foy III, Earl Holliman, William Phipps, Heather Menzies-Urich, George Chakiris, Alan Oppenheimer, Sandra de Bruin, Lindsay Wagner, René Auberjonois, Marsha Mason, Alan Dean Foster, Troy Beyer, Gillian Barber, Douglas E. Wise, and Gavin MacLeod. I would also like to thank those who, at one time or another, contributed their support towards the completion of this book:

Acknowledgments

Joyce Taylor, Pat Cardi, Julia Brunton, Jacqueline T. Lynch, Jesse Fankushen, Jan Foy, C. Courtney Joyner, Marguerite Krause, Kari Nissena, Adam P. Wadenius, Kathleen Haggerty, Steve Moyer, Boyd Magers, Neal Anderson, Scott Anderson, Audrey Loggia, Peter Sobczynski, Dina Roth, Mary Jane Dante, Greg Moffett, Sandy Moffett, Sharon Moffett, Tim Considine, Steve Sauer, Derek Maki, Sean Quinn, Paul T. Kimura, Jarome Winesberry, David Maqui, Maddalena Acconci, Karen Stowe, Cathey Lizzio, Susan Munao, Lucy Chase Williams, Tony Kashani, Jake Hinkson, Tim Turner, Margie Straub, Allan Duffin, and Ben Ohmart.

In closing, I remain especially grateful to my wife, Jennifer, and my two children, Jocelyn and Justin. Their continuous support through the years has been the very thing to keep me going. Finally, I would like to acknowledge Joseph C. Jordan Jr., the individual to whom this book is dedicated. Through him, I became inspired to write about Robert Wise. It primarily began with a screening of *The Sand Pebbles* (1966). The rest is history. Those I interviewed for this book generally described Robert Wise as noble, patient, validating, and a class act. Such words, in short, apply to Dad. Had it not been for his moral guidance, I would not be the person I am today.

J.R.J.
Hidden Valley, CA
July 20, 2019

PART I
RKO RADIO PICTURES

1
THE CURSE OF THE CAT PEOPLE

(PRODUCED 1943, RELEASED 1944)

> "I would rather walk with a friend in the dark, than alone in the light."
> - Helen Keller

On September 10, 1914, Robert Earl Wise was born in Winchester, Indiana, to Earl W. Wise, a meat packer, and Olive R. Wise (née Longenecker), a homemaker. In time, the family moved to Connersville, Indiana, a small town located approximately forty-five miles to the southwest. A young Wise often visited the three movie theaters in the area and essentially became fascinated with motion pictures. Years later, his older brother, David, abruptly departed the Hoosier State for Hollywood and obtained employment with RKO Radio Pictures. When Wise was twenty-years-old, he bravely followed his brother to the West Coast. Coincidentally, it was not long before David found his young sibling a job with the studio. Shortly thereafter, Wise worked diligently to become a film editor with RKO. He was then granted the opportunity to collaborate with Orson Welles during the production of *Citizen Kane* (1941). Wise's prudent work ethic and unrelenting tenacity earned him an Oscar nomination for Best Film Editing, but the award ultimately went to William Holmes for his work on *Sergeant York* (1941).

Orson Welles with his crew. Robert Wise (second from left) acquired a vast amount of knowledge during his days as an editor at RKO.

Following *Citizen Kane,* Wise and Welles reunited during the production of *The Magnificent Ambersons* (1942). A scenario of the film's narrative concerns the relationship between a mother, Isabel (Dolores Costello), and her son, George (Tim Holt). She is recently widowed, and Eugene Morgan (Joseph Cotten), a successful automobile magnate, vies for her hand in marriage. George, however, is vehemently opposed to such a union. Welles, credited as the film's director, was not always present on the set, instead working on another project in Brazil. Wise, editor of *The Magnificent Ambersons,* was therefore offered the chance to direct a particular sequence set in Isabel's bedroom. "Initially, the studio believed the film was too long and requested that I edit approximately forty minutes from the first cut," he said. "But as a result of removing so much footage, we had continuity problems, so I was asked to direct a new scene." In the scene, Isabel has received correspondence from Morgan regarding George's emotional state. A son then calls on his mother to discuss the nature of the letter. The scene, although not as popular as others of the film, was well-received by audiences during test engagements. The following year, on August 26, 1943, RKO began production of *The Curse of the Cat People* and tapped Gunther von Fritsch to direct, but all sorts of problems arose and the production quickly fell behind schedule. Von Fritsch was therefore dismissed and replaced by Wise on September 20, 1943, and although it was unknown at the time, *The Curse of the Cat People* signified the beginning of a unique, memorable career in motion pictures.

Six-year-old Amy Reed (Ann Carter) struggles to interact with those her age, choosing instead to favor the company of insects and animals. Her father, Oliver "Ollie" Reed (Kent Smith), expresses deep concern regarding her antisocial behavior. Amy's demeanor reminds him of his late wife, Irena (Simone Simon), who was descended from the "cat people" of her Serbian village. Alice (Jane Randolph), Amy's mother and Reed's current wife, questions the possibility of a connection between her daughter and the deceased Irena. Meanwhile, Julia Farren (Julia Dean), a retired stage performer and neighbor of the Reeds, befriends young Amy. She lives with her daughter, Barbara (Elizabeth Russell), whom she oddly perceives not as her own child, but instead, an impostor. Amy receives a wishing ring from Julia. Shortly thereafter, Amy wishes for a friend and is then visited by what appears to be Irena's ghost. The two form a special bond. Reed becomes livid upon learning of his daughter's so-called relationship with his late wife, dismissing it as an "old dream life." Consequently, Amy is punished for her supposedly false claims. Later, she runs away from home in search of Irena. Her quest takes her to the Farren house, but the elderly Julia, delusional to the point that she becomes terrified of an age-old folktale, suffers a fatal heart attack. Barbara, believing Amy to be responsible for her mother's death, attempts to do away with the child. Fortunately, Irena's apparition intervenes before it is too late. Reed arrives on the scene and is reunited with his daughter. Remorseful over her punishment, he vows to henceforth trust Amy and put his faith in any relationship she chooses to have with Irena.

"I come from great darkness and deep peace."

The Curse of the Cat People was produced by the illustrious Val Lewton, head of RKO's low-budget horror unit. The film was originally intended to be a sequel to his first picture, *Cat People* (1942), but DeWitt Bodeen, the credited screenwriter of both productions, had several disagreements with Lewton regarding the story's continuation.[1] The latter had a reputation in Hollywood. Some regarded Lewton as a controlling individual. Others, however, believed him to be a cinematic genius with a keen eye for adaptation-worthy literature. Wise once said that Lewton always prepared the final drafts of his films' scripts but would never take credit for the work simply because the screenwriters themselves were the ones who deserved such credit. Bodeen, however, was not impressed. He and Lewton rarely saw eye to eye while crafting the script of *The Curse of the Cat People*. In addition, the executives of RKO, who interfered with the film's production whenever the opportunity presented itself, had their own ideas about how to write the story. Hence,

---

[1] Simone Simon, Kent Smith, and Jane Randolph appeared in *Cat People* (1942) and later reprised their roles for the production of *The Curse of the Cat People*.

very few similarities between *Cat People* and *The Curse of the Cat People* exist. Curiously enough, the character of Amy Reed and its addition to Lewton's feline saga is the primary reason for such difference. The profound connections she shares with the adult female companions in her life, individuals who are not entirely without flaw, control the story. Furthermore, cats, let alone cat people, are not central to the film's plot.

Midway through *The Curse of the Cat People*, a distinct transition from autumn to winter occurs. The setting is the exterior of the Reed home. As leaves fall from the trees, the onscreen image gradually dissolves to yet another of the same view, but a key difference immediately becomes apparent. Instead of leaves, a multitude of snowflakes glide through the air, thus indicating a change in the seasons. Shortly thereafter, the audience finds itself inside the family's living room as a Christmas tree undergoes decoration. A time of giving is imminent, and it is Amy's desire to present Miss Callahan (Eve March), her teacher, with a gift. She has also purchased a ring for Julia. Finally, Amy has set aside a special gift for Irena. All three women, in spite of their shortcomings, establish themselves as intimate companions of the young girl and subsequently set a specific tone for the narrative.

Sir Lancelot.

Miss Callahan is sympathetic to Amy's introverted nature and understands all too well the differences between her withdrawn pupil and the remaining students of the class, but she ultimately draws the hastiest of conclusions. Recurring parent-teacher conferences, both formal and informal, reveal much. Early in the film, Reed appears uneasy during a particular meeting. He expresses concern regarding a previous incident during which Amy struck a male classmate. Miss Callahan nevertheless puts the situation in perspective:

MISS CALLAHAN: Really, Mr. Reed. There isn't anything to worry about. After all, it was only a slap. Alice, also present, seizes the opportunity to interject her opinion.
ALICE: That's exactly what I told Mr. Reed, but he insisted upon remaining home from business to talk to you, Miss Callahan.
REED: I know it may seem stupid of me, but . . . it's not the slap I'm worried about. It's the reason.
MISS CALLAHAN: Something to do with a butterfly. They were quarreling about it.
REED: No, Amy slapped Donald because he hurt the butterfly and . . . it was her friend.
MISS CALLAHAN: Well, that seems a harmless fancy.
REED: Amy has too many fancies and too few friends, and it worries me. It doesn't seem . . . normal.
ALICE: You know these fond fathers with their only chicks.
MISS CALLAHAN: I can see that you're worried, Mr. Reed. And Amy is a very sensitive and delicately adjusted child. But part of the blame for that may lie with you. Perhaps, you're overanxious, watch her too closely, worry too much. The child's bound to feel it.

Miss Callahan's argument is relatively valid. In an attempt to better understand Amy, she later makes reference to Robert Louis Stevenson's *The Unseen Playmate*, a short poem about an invisible "Friend of the Children." In addition, Miss Callahan cites *The Inner Life of Childhood* (1927), a popular book pertaining to child psychology.[2] It features "a whole chapter devoted to children like Amy," but despite all of her research, derived from sources of both fact and fiction, Miss Callahan dismisses Irena as "a friend who doesn't even exist." The character of Miss Callahan, however, remains important. It is one of the first seen by audiences. Furthermore, as Miss Callahan addresses her students in a meadow during the film's opening scene, her words foreshadow what is to come as she makes reference to the "legends" of Tarrytown, but the village, in essence, is better known by another name.

Elizabeth Russell as Barbara Farren. She previously appeared in *Cat People* (1942) as the cat woman.

---

2 In actuality, the book is entitled *The Inner World of Childhood: A Study in Analytical Psychology*. It was written by Frances G. Wickes.

Sleepy Hollow and the tale of the Headless Horseman is clearly the favorite discussion topic of the delusional Julia, and as she recounts the village's well-known legend, she bonds with Amy. The character of Julia Farren, however, is purposely underdeveloped. DeWitt Bodeen's script discloses the reasons behind Julia's madness within a key conversation between her and Barbara, but the ensuing film adaptation reduces the exchange to only a few words. The original, uncut conversation between mother and daughter was written as follows:

JULIA: My Barbara was killed. I killed her. Yes, it was my fault. Everyone told me not to drive from the theatre. There was a raging wind that night, and snow and ice. All was well until we got to the Sleepy Hollow bridge. Barbara was singing a little song and then ... I don't know how it happened ... when I awakened, they told me the car was overturned and they wouldn't let me see Barbara. Barbara was dead.

Barbara comes close to her mother and leans over her.

BARBARA: But I didn't die. Don't you understand? It was you. Your mind was dead for nearly ten years after that accident. You didn't know anybody; you couldn't remember anything. And then, when memory returned, you called for me, and I came into your bedroom to see you. I was sixteen years old then, ten years older than when you last remembered me. You said I wasn't your daughter. I loved you ... I wanted you for my mother ... but you denied me. You said they were playing tricks on you, that your daughter was a little girl.

The peculiarities surrounding the accident simply add to a narrative full of suspense. By way of illustration, the scene in which Amy crosses the infamous bridge on a cold winter's night makes for a chilling moment of the film, both literally and figuratively. Because of the tale Julia earlier recounted, Amy convinces herself that the Headless Horseman is approaching. Rapid hoofbeats become audible. Yet, in a matter of seconds, the tension subsides as only a vehicle equipped with snow chains approaches and crosses the bridge.

Nevertheless, such a sequence would have been especially significant had the entire, aforementioned exchange between Julia and Barbara remained in the film.[3] The bridge is a key landmark not only because of its association with the Sleepy Hollow folktale, but also because it is the location of Julia's terrible accident. Through the years, film historians have questioned the omission of Bodeen's dialogue. The reason, perhaps, is Julia, whose character is simply not as important as yet another of the film.

Simone Simon received top billing for her reprisal of Irena, and although her onscreen presence is forceful and impressive, her character is simply that of a spirit and cannot offer Amy the full benefits of companionship. With the exception of the audience, all but one are unable to see Irena. During the holidays, Amy tells her, "I wish I could show you to mommy and daddy. I wish you could enjoy Christmas with us." The audience is initially afforded a glimpse of Irena's shadow as it is projected against Amy's bedroom wall, but later, as Amy tosses a ball in the family's front yard, we watch it sail behind a tree and do not hear it land. Irena then emerges from the other side of the tree with the ball in her hands. She is a spirit, but the scene reveals her uncanny ability to grasp tangible objects. Hence, Irena is presented as a woman of both shadow and substance. Every appearance of Simone Simon in *The Curse of the Cat People*, be it in the form of an apparition or not, is noteworthy. For example, photographs taken of Irena while she was alive appear in the film, and Reed is clearly agitated upon viewing such photographs. He also becomes frustrated with Amy, as he believes her to be lying about Irena's untimely visits, but only Amy can see what others cannot. Reed has not accepted the circumstances of Irena's death, which essentially date back to the first installment of the saga.

---

3 The Sleepy Hollow bridge scene was directed by Robert Wise. In the film, the scene precedes that of the noteworthy, yet edited, exchange between Julia and Barbara. Nevertheless, in the case of multiple viewings, Amy's encounter with the mysterious vehicle likely would have evoked more of an emotional reaction from audiences had Bodeen's omitted dialogue remained in the final cut.

Jane Randolph and Kent Smith.

Cat People, released two years prior to *The Curse of the Cat People*, transpires in New York City. In addition to the setting, several other differences between both films are apparent. For example, Simone Simon's appearances in *The Curse of the Cat People* are limited. She was unhappy about committing to the production and only agreed to reprise her role as Irena in order to appease Val Lewton. In *Cat People*, however, Simon relished her contribution to the picture. True to its title, the narrative evolved around the concept of people transforming into cats. Such is clearly not the case in *The Curse of the Cat People*. Cats, and cat people, have very little to do with the film's story. Lewton went so far as to lobby for an alternative title. In addition, random appearances of cats are not specific to the narrative. Furthermore, a well-known painting, intended to accentuate the feline species, is not presented in its full context.

Shortly after Simone Simon makes her first appearance in *The Curse of the Cat People*, she speaks the words "Amy and her friend," which compose Val Lewton's favored title of the picture. In regard to Reed, he is presented as an important character of the story, but his relationship with Amy, his own daughter and only child, is dwarfed by the connection between her and Irena. As the film's chilling climax unfolds at the Farren home, Amy's desperate cry for help initially goes unanswered. She finds herself on a staircase, confronted by an angry Barbara. Amy calls for her father, but it is a futile attempt. Reed is not in close proximity to the house, but his distance from the Farren home is irrelevant to some extent. Reed does not appreciate his daughter the way Irena does. Amy knows. Hence, after her initial cry for help goes unanswered, she calls on Irena, a true friend, thus averting a crisis. *Amy and Her Friend*, Lewton's preferred title, is therefore fitting. RKO executives, however, had the final say, figuring a title of *The Curse of the Cat People* would be more appealing to the general public, but such a title, among other elements, bears little relation to the story.

Julia Dean as Julia Farren.

Random appearances of cats, intended in part to remind viewers of *Cat People*, are not specific to the narrative of *The Curse of the Cat People*. Such appearances are merely unnecessary additions to a so-called sequel. Upon the film's beginning, as Miss Callahan arrives at the meadow with her students, a black cat is seen to be lounging in a nearby tree. A boy pretends to shoot it with an invisible firearm. The cat then drops from the tree and runs away, thus marking its only appearance in the film. The sequence was directed by Wise a month after the conclusion of principal photography. It was filmed at the request of studio executives, who sought a more appealing look to the picture's introduction. Later in the narrative, a fixture of the Farren living room stands out amongst the nearby furnishings, as the camera periodically reveals a dead, stuffed cat firmly clinging to an artificial tree branch. Similar to the live cat of the opening scene, it appears out of place and is not particularly significant to the story, but perhaps the most incongruous element of the film is a well-known portrait.

Alice and Miss Callahan pause to analyze the replica of Francisco Goya's painting.

Goya's painting in full view.

Francisco Goya's famous "cat" painting, first seen adorning the wall of Irena's apartment in *Cat People*, reappears in *The Curse of the Cat People* within the Reed living room.[4] An obstructed view of the picture, however, does not reveal its full significance. The portrait's inclusion of caged finches is arguably its most important element. Early in the film, as Alice gives Miss Callahan a tour of the Reed home, both women approach the painting and pause to study it. Alice asks, "It doesn't fit, does it?" Miss Callahan immediately shakes her head, thus confirming her host's suspicions. The exchange is ironic. Goya's painting is not only an unwelcome fixture of the Reed living room, but its limited appearance in the film has very little to do with the narrative.

---

4 The painting's official title is *Manuel Osorio Manrique de Zúñiga*.

The portrait, painted centuries ago, depicts the young son of the Count and Countess of Altamira. He plays with a pet magpie, which holds the painter's calling card in its beak. In addition, three wide-eyed cats lounge near the boy's feet, but more significant is a cage full of finches. Ordinarily, the birds can be seen opposite the cats. In *The Curse of the Cat People*, however, Miss Callahan obstructs the audience's view of the cage. Instead, an emphasis is placed on the three cats, as if to serve as a reminder of the film's prequel. Yet, mere speculation indicates that Goya intended for the finches to be the most important element of his painting. Critics have argued that the caged birds appear not only as symbols of the soul, but also as ones of innocence, and according to such critics, Goya, through the finches, wanted to represent the frail boundaries that separate a child's world from society's evil forces. Also illustrated is the fleeting nature of innocence and youth. Such interpretations are perhaps applicable to Amy, but only the cats, and certainly not the finches, were the only details of the painting that appealed to the top brass of RKO.

Ann Carter.

The Curse of the Cat People premiered in New York on March 2, 1944. True to its title, the film's production was cursed. Once the crew fell behind schedule, a snowball effect virtually became inevitable. Gunther von Fritsch was dismissed from the set. Simone Simon lost all interest in reprising her role. Val Lewton continuously clashed with DeWitt Bodeen regarding the structure of the story, and the RKO executives wanted everything done according to their standards. Nevertheless, Wise was able to see the project through to its bitter end despite having limited control over the production. In short, although very little connection between *Cat People* and *The Curse of the Cat People* exists, a viewing of the former makes for a more entertaining presentation of the latter. The original fared better with audiences, but the sequel became significant in the years following its theatrical release. College professors of the social sciences frequently screened *The Curse of the Cat People* for their students in order to illustrate important concepts of child psychology. Regarding Wise, his commitment to the film's production ultimately earned him a director's contract with RKO. Life was good, and the adventure, in essence, was just beginning.

The Farren home. Prior to being demolished, the mansion was located at 900 West Adams Street in Los Angeles.

2
MADEMOISELLE FIFI

(PRODUCED AND RELEASED 1944)

> "Patriotism is a kind of religion; it is the egg from which wars are hatched."
>
> - Guy de Maupassant, *My Uncle Sosthenes*

Following *The Curse of the Cat People* (1944), Robert Wise began work on *Mademoiselle Fifi*, another Val Lewton production. The film is based on a selection of short stories by Guy de Maupassant, a prominent French writer whose favored setting was the Franco-Prussian War. With *Mademoiselle Fifi*, Lewton was attempting to expand his canon beyond the horror genre. Filming commenced on March 23, 1944, but Charles Koerner, the production chief of RKO, was not at all pleased with the script's subject matter. The Franco-Prussian War, which lasted from 1870-1871, resulted in a Prussian, or German, victory. In early 1944, as Wise directed his adaptation of de Maupassant's works, much of France was under Nazi occupation. Resentment of the German government grew stronger with each day that passed, and Koerner feared *Mademoiselle Fifi* would alienate select theatergoers due to the script's portrayal of triumphant Prussian forces. Wise was nevertheless fully committed to the project and essentially became determined to tell the story his way.

The year is 1870. The place is Cleresville, France. Enemy forces have occupied the area. The town's priest (Charles Waldron), an elderly man known as the Curé of Cleresville, continuously refuses to ring the church bell as a means of protesting the Prussian invasion. Believing he is too old to continue his devotion to the people, he summons a younger replacement (Edmund Glover) from Rouen, a nearby city. The young priest boards a carriage en route to Cleresville and travels with an assortment of characters. Elisabeth Rousset (Simone Simon), a humble laundress, finds herself to be the outcast of the group, as most of the passengers, including a count (Alan Napier) and countess (Helen Freeman), are of the upper class. Prior to its arrival in Cleresville, the carriage stops at an inn located in the village of Tôtes. Lieutenant von Eyrick (Kurt Kreuger), a Prussian officer, oversees the disembarkation of passengers and later demands that Elisabeth dine with him. He is called "Fifi" by his comrades due to his frequent use of the French expression, "Fi, fi donc!" When Elisabeth refuses von Eyrick's dinner invitation, he orders for the carriage to remain in Tôtes, thereby stranding everybody at the inn. Jean Cornudet (John Emery), a fellow passenger and revolutionary, applauds her patriotism, but the wealthy passengers become agitated and accuse Elisabeth of detaining them with her notions of honor. Filled with shame, she eventually acquiesces to the demands made upon her.

The following morning, the carriage departs Tôtes. Shortly thereafter, Elisabeth, Cornudet, and the young priest disembark in Cleresville. Von Eyrick arrives on the scene and continues his oppression of the French people. Cornudet, in an act of rebellion, shoots a Prussian officer and subsequently goes into hiding. A repeat dinner engagement between Elisabeth and von Eyrick transpires. His ongoing aggression ultimately prompts her to stab and kill him. Elisabeth flees the scene of the crime and comes into contact with Cornudet, and together, the two evade capture. As Prussian troops parade von Eyrick's casket through town, the young priest rings the church bell as a means of celebrating "the first blow [to have] been struck by a French woman" in the fight for freedom.

Mademoiselle Fifi begins with Werner Heymann's musical score. As the opening credits conclude, the words "Based on the patriotic stories of Guy de Maupassant" are displayed. Heymann then integrates the familiar notes of La Marseillaise, the national anthem of France, into the featured track. Patriotism is clearly a dominant theme of Wise's film. Elisabeth, at one point, cites the differences between the social classes of France in specific regard to relations with the occupying forces, declaring, "At the laundry, [the Germans] always said it was much harder for the rich to be patriotic."

Some of the French are simply instilled with more pride than others, and it is Elisabeth's stubborn nature that intrigues von Eyrick. At the time of the carriage's arrival in Tôtes, he is very much aware of her dislike of Prussian soldiers and does everything in his power to humble her patriotism. The working title of Wise's film was *The Silent Bell*, and although the strained relationship between von Eyrick and Elisabeth is a significant theme of the narrative, *Mademoiselle Fifi* is not a particularly fitting title. *The Silent Bell* is more appropriate because the church bell, the most vital of the story's elements, is von Eyrick's ultimate goal. Furthermore, it defines the young priest's presence in Cleresville and empowers Cornudet to rise above his circumstances.

Simone Simon and Kurt Kreuger.

As von Eyrick is first presented to the audience, he appears in the steeple of the Cleresville church, standing next to a bell that has been locked with chains, thus symbolizing his difficulty in coveting what he desires most. Throughout the film, he is generally overcome with boredom and fraternizes with Elisabeth as a means of self-fulfillment, but it is in vain. Within a baron's vacated chateau in Cleresville, von Eyrick and his comrades defile the property. They pride themselves on their makeshift explosives. Boredom, however, appears imminent until the baroness's dresses are discovered. A dinner party is scheduled. Ladies from the Cleresville laundry, including Elisabeth, are invited, and von Eyrick ultimately becomes reunited with his dinner companion from Tôtes. Immediately prior to his untimely death, Elisabeth declares, "I'm not a good French woman, or I wouldn't be here. I'm only the kind of woman the Prussians would want!" Such a statement is sarcastic, yet powerful, thus prompting von Eyrick to slap her across the face. He understands all too well that he will never win Elisabeth's heart, as she is a true patriot who dines with him only so that others will not suffer. Her sarcasm serves as a harsh reminder that those who lack a patriotic spirit are more inclined to give in to the demands of the Prussian soldiers. Elisabeth's love and respect, as von Eyrick eventually comes to understand, are both unattainable. The bell, along with the opportunity to ring it, is a suitable goal for him simply because it is more realistic than any kind of future he can have with her. However, it does not ring until von Eyrick's casket is paraded through the streets of Cleresville. Furthermore, the ringing is intended not to symbolize a celebration of his life, but instead, an observance of his death, and the ringer of the bell is indeed significant. Approximately fifteen minutes into the film, as the carriage's passengers disembark in Tôtes, von Eyrick establishes his presence, and ironically, the only individual he chooses to engage in conversation is the one to later strike the bell at his funeral.

The young priest, who intends to relieve the Curé of Cleresville, is drawn to the village because of the bell. Wise depicts him as the most important occupant of the carriage who, although generally reserved in nature, is a ready conversationalist if the topic is worthy of discussion. In Rouen, upon the film's beginning, the young priest is the first of the nine passengers to be presented to the audience. He approaches a statue of Joan of Arc, a symbol of valor and sacrifice, and kneels at its base. The preceding scene, in which the Curé of Cleresville informs von Eyrick of a replacement, exists so the audience can be made aware of the young priest's journey from Rouen. The carriage departs and eventually comes to a stop at the inn in Tôtes. Very few words are spoken by the young priest during the first leg of the trip, but shortly thereafter, he lounges with Elisabeth and Cornudet at the inn. The subject of the bell dominates their conversation, and unlike his demeanor in the carriage, the young priest has much to say. Yet, it is his companion who will ultimately resort to extreme measures to fight for his beliefs.

Jean Cornudet becomes empowered with the will to rise above defeat in part because of the bell and his dogged determination to keep it silent. The wholesaler in wines (Jason Robards Sr.), a fellow passenger of the carriage, occasionally exposes Cornudet's weaknesses, thus triggering the latter to overcome such shortcomings. As the travelers depart Rouen, most are quiet, but in a time of war, the wholesaler demands to learn more of the carriage's occupants. Upon discovering Cornudet to be one of the passengers, he brands him as "the man who built the barricades to defend Rouen, then ran away at the first sight" of the Germans.

At the inn in Tôtes, the wholesaler becomes privy to Cornudet's feelings for Elisabeth and describes him as being "green" with envy. Under pressure from the wealthy passengers, Cornudet ultimately encourages Elisabeth's acceptance of vonEyrick's dinner invitation so that the journey may continue. She is appalled at such an action and appears to lose all faith in Cornudet. Following the disembarkation of Elisabeth and the young priest in Cleresville, the carriage departs for its new destination. Cornudet, who remains on board, listens to the hypocritical rhetoric of the wholesaler, who states, "We'd still be stuck in the inn in Tôtes if [Elisabeth] hadn't been such a good sort. A means to an end ... a means to an end."

During Elisabeth's time in the company of the travelers, she was intermittently praised and degraded. At one point, when the starving wholesaler accepted a piece of chicken from her, he said, "In moments like these, it is good to find people who are obliging." Prior to such praise, however, he spoke in jest about eating Elisabeth, "the poorest of the passengers," to satisfy his hunger. Later, as the carriage departs Cleresville and the wholesaler speaks of "a means to an end," Cornudet finds himself missing Elisabeth and feels guilty for humbling her patriotism. Hence, upon enduring the wholesaler's hypocrisy, Cornudet suddenly becomes instilled with a newfound courage to make things right in his life. He orders for the carriage to stop, then prepares to disembark. Upon exiting, he boldly declares to the wholesaler and company, "France is well rid of you!" The door is slammed, and the audience ultimately bids farewell to the six remaining passengers. Cornudet reunites with Elisabeth. He then offers a plausible explanation for his sudden appearance. Cornudet's decision to leave the carriage, in short, was warranted because of two important factors: Elisabeth and the bell.

Mademoiselle Fifi premiered on July 28, 1944, and world affairs had undergone significant change since filming commenced. Several weeks earlier, on June 6th, Allied forces invaded German-occupied France – an event that famously came to be known as D-Day. It not only led to the liberation of France, it also swung momentum in favor of the Allies. World War II was gradually nearing its end, but *Mademoiselle Fifi*, despite its overt theme of patriotism, did not garner much attention. Josef Mischel and Peter Ruric, the credited screenwriters of Wise's picture, crafted a script based specifically on two of Guy de Maupassant's short stories: "Mademoiselle Fifi" and "Boule de Suif". Several of the film's elements, including the carriage's journey and the character of Cornudet, were extracted from "Boule de Suif". The story of "Mademoiselle Fifi" focuses primarily on its title character. Although Mischel and Ruric assembled a fairly-balanced adaptation of both narratives, such an adaptation did not fare well with theatergoers due to a general lack of interest. The production of *Mademoiselle Fifi* was nevertheless quite different from that of *The Curse of the Cat People*. It marked the true directorial debut of Robert Wise, as he oversaw the project from the beginning of principal photography to the establishment of its final cut. During that period of time, the cast and crew shared several memorable experiences, including a trip to Big Bear, California, which doubled for France's snowy countryside. Val Lewton, however, was not at all content with his period piece, ultimately deeming it a failure. He therefore returned to the genre he knew best and essentially suggested that Wise do the same.

3
THE BODY SNATCHER

(PRODUCED 1944, RELEASED 1945)

> "When the body escaped mutilation, seldom did the heart go to the grave unscarred."
> - Virginia Woolf, *Jacob's Room*

"It was the most successful of the films I did for Val Lewton," Robert Wise later said of *The Body Snatcher*, based on Robert Louis Stevenson's short story of the same name. Principal photography began on October 25, 1944, and the events leading up to the first day of filming were indeed extraordinary. RKO landed Boris Karloff for the title role, but studio executives sought another big name to star alongside their lead. Karloff had earlier taken audiences by storm when he appeared in *Frankenstein* (1931) as the film's titular character. Bela Lugosi, in essence, accomplished the same feat with *Dracula* (1931). The executives of RKO therefore wanted both men to appear in *The Body Snatcher*, believing the combination to be a framework for success. Lewton eventually agreed to the idea, and thus, a part was written for Lugosi. Although Lewton is remembered primarily for the films he produced, he was also an experienced writer. Prior to his tenure with RKO, he had been a novelist and also served as a story editor for David O. Selznick, but Lewton traditionally refused credit for his writing while serving as a film's producer.

Regarding *The Body Snatcher*, screenwriter Philip MacDonald wrote a satisfactory adaptation of Stevenson's work. Lewton then crafted the script's final draft, and much of its previous content had been changed for the better. The Writers Guild therefore argued that MacDonald should not be the only credited screenwriter of the picture. Lewton, however, wanted to be listed as a producer and nothing more. Hence, to appease union executives, he relied on a pseudonym from the past. As the opening credits of *The Body Snatcher* were presented to audiences, the name Carlos Keith appeared alongside that of Philip MacDonald. Little did people know at the time, however, that Carlos Keith and Val Lewton were one and the same.

Val Lewton.

The year is 1831. The location is Edinburgh, Scotland. Donald Fettes (Russell Wade), a young medical student, is promoted to become the special assistant of the school's head, Dr. MacFarlane (Henry Daniell). Fettes gradually becomes suspicious of John Gray (Karloff), a local cabman. MacFarlane relies on Gray to acquire cadavers, often from the local cemetery, for medical research. The undertakings, however, are not performed legally. Fettes desperately wishes to cure Georgina Marsh (Sharyn Moffett), a young girl who suffers from paralysis. MacFarlane is the only physician skilled enough to operate, but action cannot be taken without additional research, which requires a fresh cadaver. Fettes seeks the help of Gray, who refuses to visit the cemetery due to increased security. Hence, the unscrupulous cabman resorts to murder. Fettes is aghast. MacFarlane accepts the circumstances and performs Georgina's operation, which appears to have no effect on the young girl. Joseph (Lugosi), a custodian of the school, confronts Gray over the recent murder and attempts to blackmail him, but the latter eliminates the would-be extortionist. MacFarlane, fed up with years of torment, challenges Gray, and a scuffle ensues. MacFarlane ultimately overpowers Gray and kills him. Later, Fettes prepares to disassociate himself from the school but then discovers Georgina has been cured, as she is able to stand and walk on her own. MacFarlane rejoices not only because the operation is a success, but also because he is rid of Gray. Fettes agrees to continue his studies with the doctor. As a means of conducting further research, the two unearth the corpse of a recently deceased woman. Shortly after departing the cemetery, MacFarlane becomes wary of his acquisition and stops the carriage to inspect the body. Fettes disembarks to retrieve a light. Further examination reveals the corpse to be that of the late Gray. The horses become spooked and the carriage departs without Fettes. It begins to travel at a dangerously high speed and subsequently crashes. MacFarlane is killed. Fettes races to the site of the wreck. Upon arrival, he discovers the corpse to be that of the dead woman, not Gray.

The theatrical trailer of *The Body Snatcher* refers to Boris Karloff and Bela Lugosi as "The Hero of Horror" and "The Master of Menace" respectively. It suggests a union between the two as they join forces to form "the unholiest partnership this side of the grave!" However, Karloff and Lugosi, as audiences have been quick to discover, are rarely seen together in Wise's film. Furthermore, the noteworthy scene in which only their characters appear transpires over the course of a brief five minutes, and it culminates with the murder of Lugosi's character. The scene, however, is significant in regard to a real-life, social tragedy of the era. As Karloff, or Gray, devises a plan to acquire new specimens, he declares to his ill-fated companion, "We will, so to speak, 'Burke' them." In 1828, William Burke, an Irish immigrant, committed a series of murders in Edinburgh. He then sold the corpses of his victims to Dr. Robert Knox, a prominent physician and lecturer in human anatomy. Burke and his partner, William Hare, ultimately murdered a total of sixteen people.[5] Robert Louis Stevenson briefly makes reference to the killings in his short story, but the film, unlike the original narrative on which it is based, daringly broaches the subject of Burke and Hare. The topic tends to evoke an alarmed reaction from MacFarlane. Moreover, the inclusion of Scottish ballads, in addition to the considerable attention devoted to the infamous Knox, is indicative of a vast difference between Stevenson's story and Wise's film.

Boris Karloff as Cabman Gray.

---

5 In the film, it is stated that Burke and Hare murdered a total of eighteen people.

Burke and Hare's crimes against humanity are rarely mentioned in the short story, but the ensuing adaptation broaches the subject, as MacFarlane's sensitivity to such crimes becomes evident. Some of the doctor's pupils, namely Fettes, take the murders more seriously than their fellow cohorts. Approximately fifteen minutes into the film, Richardson (Robert Clarke), a young student, dissects a cadaver. He then directs MacFarlane's attention to "a beautiful bicep" of the corpse:

RICHARDSON: Burke and Hare could never have got the best of him.
MACFARLANE: What did you say?
RICHARDSON: Well, I was just making a joke, sir.
MACFARLANE: It's a poor subject for jest, particularly for a medical student!
MacFarlane abruptly departs the classroom. Shortly thereafter, another student approaches Richardson.
STUDENT: What did you say to His Imperial Highness?
RICHARDSON: Nothing but a merry word about Burke and Hare.
STUDENT: There's nothing in that to get excited about. They're dead and buried.

The Burke and Hare murders took place circa 1828. To reiterate, Wise's picture is set in 1831, and although a considerable amount of time had passed since the killings, much of Edinburgh's common folk remained uneasy. Midway through the film, Fettes becomes gravely concerned as the school is supplied, courtesy of Gray, with a fresh cadaver. Fettes suspects foul play and declares to MacFarlane, "It's like Burke and Hare all over again." Shortly after such words are spoken, the musical notes of "When ye gang awa, Jamie", a popular Scottish ballad of the era, become audible within Roy Webb's musical score, and the timing is appropriate considering the identity of Gray's victim.

"Ignorant men have dammed the stream of medical progress with stupid and unjust laws. If that dam will not break, the men of medicine have to find other courses."

The street singer of Edinburgh (Donna Lee), a supporting character excluded from Stevenson's narrative, eloquently presents the aforementioned ballad to audiences prior to her unfortunate demise, but she is not the only "serenading" individual of the film. As Gray prepares to eliminate Joseph, he makes reference to the Burke and Hare murders, singing, *"The ruffian dogs, the hellish pair... The villain Burke, the meager Hare."* The verse is from "Elegiac Lines on the Tragical Murder of Poor Daft Jamie", another Scottish ballad. Similar to "When ye gang awa, Jamie", it, too, is absent from the short story. Daft Jamie is a pseudonym for James Wilson, a real-life victim of Burke and Hare. When Joseph questions the method in which the many murders were committed, Gray resumes his presentation of the ballad, crooning, *"Nor did they handle axe or knife to take away their victim's life. No sooner done than in the chest they crammed their lately welcome guest."* The ballad is met with confusion, but it does not matter to Gray, as it is his intention to kill Joseph, not educate him, and a short time before the latter's murder, Gray makes reference to the key individual responsible for Edinburgh's state of turmoil.

The historical Dr. Knox, designated only by the letter K in Stevenson's short story, is afforded considerable attention in Wise's film. Supporting characters, created by Val Lewton, facilitate such attention. Georgina's recent surgery becomes the subject of an argument between MacFarlane and Gray:

MACFARLANE: I set those blocks together, patched the muscles, put the nerves where they should be. I did it and I did it right! She won't walk.

MacFarlane uses a pair of drinking glasses to illustrate his point. Gray abruptly sends them crashing to the ground. He then antagonizes MacFarlane, addressing him as Toddy, a nickname used in earlier times.

GRAY: You can't build life the way you put blocks together, Toddy.

MACFARLANE: What the devil are you talking about? I'm an anatomist. I know the body. I know how it works.

GRAY: You're a fool, Toddy, and no doctor. It's only the dead ones you know.

MACFARLANE: I am a doctor. I teach medicine.

GRAY: Like Knox taught you? Like I taught you? In cellars and graveyards? Did Knox teach you what makes the blood flow?

As the argument continues, the audience learns that neither Knox nor Gray intended to provide the basics of a medical education to MacFarlane, who has continuously struggled to become "a healing man." Gray eventually seizes the opportunity to reveal a harsh truth:

GRAY: I stood up in the witness box and took what should have been coming to you. I ran through the streets with the mud and the stones around my ears and the mob yelling for my blood because you were afraid to face it! Yes, and you're still afraid!

MACFARLANE: No, I'm not afraid. Tell. Shout it from the housetops. But remember this: they hanged Burke, they mobbed Hare. But Dr. Knox is living like a gentleman in London!

MacFarlane's sensitivity to the subject of Burke and Hare suddenly becomes clear, and his association with Knox is unsettling. Later, the supporting character of Meg Cameron (Edith Atwater), MacFarlane's lover, presents Fettes with an ingenious analogy when she declares, "MacFarlane was to Knox as you are to him."

Cabman Gray descends on his target. The set of *The Hunchback of Notre Dame* (1939), a film edited by Robert Wise, was reused for *The Body Snatcher*.

Production of *The Body Snatcher* concluded on November 17, 1944. Regarding Boris Karloff, the picture provided a welcome opportunity for him to break free from being typecast in monster roles. Upon an initial reading of the film's script, he immediately became intrigued with the fictional John Gray. Karloff especially understood the importance of the relationship between his character and that of Henry Daniell's, and Wise relished the challenge of directing both actors as their onscreen personas clashed with one another. Karloff was rumored to have battled chronic back pain throughout the film's production but refused to let such issues get the better of him. As a result, he shined in his role, and much of the picture's success can be attributed to his stellar performance. *The Body Snatcher* premiered at Hollywood's Hawaii Theatre on May 10, 1945. Two weeks later, it debuted in New York and was eventually distributed nationwide. Although the film was well-received by a majority of theatergoers, some condemned the picture for being too graphic. A review in *The Hollywood Reporter*, however, offered nothing but praise as it proclaimed, "Robert Wise gives the picture distinctive direction. For Val Lewton, this is another top production credit." In addition, James Agee of *Time* magazine declared *The Body Snatcher* to be one of the best films of 1945, adding that it exhibited "some of the most sensitive movie intelligence in Hollywood."

Bela Lugosi.

4
A GAME OF DEATH

(PRODUCED AND RELEASED 1945)

"The fascination of shooting as a sport depends almost wholly on whether you are at the right or wrong end of the gun."
- P.G. Wodehouse, The Adventures of Sally

In 1924, *Collier's* magazine published *The Most Dangerous Game*, a short story by Richard Connell. Its simple, yet chilling, plot, laden with twists and turns, captivated the attention of many. In 1932, RKO produced an adaptation of the same name, co-directed by Irving Pichel and Ernest B. Schoedsack. It starred Joel McCrea and Fay Wray and easily fared well with theatergoers. However, in 1945, and for reasons that are not entirely clear, the studio produced a remake of its earlier version with a different cast and crew. Robert Wise was selected to direct the film, retitled *A Game of Death*, and although he willingly accepted his new assignment, he later commented, "I don't like to do remakes. Usually, for one reason or another, you have to see the original film. And it always rather bugs you when you find yourself doing a certain scene, and you keep being reminded of what it was like in the first film."

Don Rainsford (John Loder), an avid hunter and famed author, becomes stranded on a remote island when the yacht on which he travels is mysteriously destroyed. All of his sailing companions perish, if not from the boat's destruction, then at the jaws of bloodthirsty sharks. Shortly after making landfall, Rainsford discovers a single, brooding fortress. Erich Kreiger (Edgar Barrier), the owner, introduces himself to the newcomer as a fellow hunter. In addition, he proudly reveals that he has read Rainsford's books. Robert Trowbridge (Russell Wade) and his sister, Ellen (Audrey Long), are guests of the fortress. Like Rainsford, they became stranded on the island via shipwreck. Two crewmembers from their boat also survived the devastation but have recently gone missing from the fortress. Kreiger boasts of a new animal he has been hunting, dubbing it "the ideal quarry." Ellen confides in Rainsford, secretly informing him that they are all being held against their will. A "trophy room" of human heads is discovered shortly thereafter. Rainsford, aware that Kreiger may choose to hunt him as prey at any given time, sets traps throughout the island while Trowbridge and Ellen distract their demented host. Pleshke (Gene Stutenroth), a servant, becomes privy to the attempted uprising and informs Kreiger. Trowbridge is subsequently hunted and killed, and Rainsford challenges Kreiger to a "dangerous game" with specific conditions. Should Rainsford survive, he and Ellen will be returned to the mainland on Kreiger's honor. The hunt begins and eventually extends far into the night. At daybreak, Rainsford surprises Kreiger at the fortress. The latter concedes defeat, but then produces a concealed firearm. A scuffle ensues and Kreiger is shot. Rainsford and Ellen escape the island in a small motor boat. Kreiger, still alive, attempts to fire at the departing duo but is instead mauled to death by his pet canines.

When comparing the short story with the RKO films, several differences become evident. For example, the former is devoid of sharks, and the yacht on which Rainsford travels is not destroyed. Instead, while attempting to position himself on a railing of the vessel, he abruptly loses his balance and plunges into the sea.[6] The yacht continues to sail along its designated course, never to appear again. The 1932 and 1945 adaptations, however, feature a disastrous incident that entails a tragic loss of life. In both films, the yacht is destroyed, leaving most of the survivors to be devoured by sharks. From beginning to end, the 1932 version is somewhat similar to that of Wise's, but the latter is unmistakably different regarding the island's history. Furthermore, Wise's antagonist, an individual who harbors a weakness for the opposite sex, is relatively symbolic of Nazi Germany.

RKO films traditionally begin with the studio's logo, which consists of a radio tower atop the Earth emitting beams of light. During Robert Wise's days as an editor, part of his job was to synchronize the moving dots with the soundtrack's musical notes.

Differences between the two films regarding the island's name and history are evident upon further examination. Traces of Portuguese colonization contribute to such disparities. In the 1932 version, just prior to the boat's

---

6 Rainsford climbs onto the yacht's railing because he hears the sound of three gunshots coming from the direction of the island. He figures his elevated position will help him to better ascertain the source of such gunshots.

destruction, references to a place called Branca Island are made. The devastation transpires shortly thereafter and Rainsford subsequently finds himself ashore. He then encounters Zaroff, Kreiger's 1932 counterpart, who boasts of his mighty fortress and claims it was built centuries earlier by the Portuguese. Further explanation reveals the ruins were restored so that Zaroff could make his residence on the island. In Wise's film, Branca becomes Bran Cara, and Rainsford interprets the name as "Man Trap."[7] An approximate Portuguese-English translation, however, is "White Man," but regardless of the significance, if any, behind such naming, the island of *A Game of Death* features a different history than that of its predecessor. Instead of Portuguese colonists, the area is said to have been inhabited by "pirates" approximately 100 years prior to Rainsford's arrival. Furthermore, Kreiger's fortress features a series of windows with bars that "were left over in the rebuilding," and all but one are relatively insignificant in regard to the film's plot.

Unlike Zaroff, Kreiger offers his bedchamber, a room devoid of bars on its windows, to Ellen, thus exposing his inherent weakness for the opposite sex. The words of a Ugandan proverb, spoken in the 1932 version and later modified for Wise's film, are generally indicative of such lust. Zaroff prioritizes his desires as he quotes what might be perceived as a guiding motto, declaring, "First, the hunt. Then, the kill. Then, the woman." Kreiger, too, makes reference to the words of the Ugandan chieftains as he proudly states, "Hunt first the enemy, then the woman." Zaroff remains preoccupied with the hunt and spends very little time pining for his sole female guest. Kreiger, however, covets Ellen. He is willing to give up his bedroom so that she may live in luxury, and upon the conclusion of Kreiger's great hunt, he eagerly anticipates Ellen's submission. His actions, however, ultimately prove beneficial to her and the other captives. Rainsford, by escaping the fortress via Ellen's window, initiates a plan of escape from the island, but in order for such a plan to be successful, it is first imperative for the prisoners to overthrow their atrocious host, an individual who warrants disdain from audiences in more ways than one.

---

7 The setting of Richard Connell's short story is Ship-Trap Island.

In Wise's film, the short story's original character of General Zaroff, an antagonist with Cossack roots, becomes Erich Kreiger, a symbol of Nazi Germany.[8] *A Game of Death* was produced during the final months of World War II, a time when Adolf Hitler dominated headlines. The film's production transpired from February to early March of 1945, and during such a period, Allied forces had yet to defeat the Nazis. The character of Kreiger, a deranged individual, is relatively comparable to that of Hitler. Similar to the production of *Mademoiselle Fifi* (1944), the executives of RKO perhaps sought a villain who could identify with one of the most despised figures in human history. However, on May 7, 1945, several months before *A Game of Death* was released to the American public, the front page of *Stars and Stripes*, a United States Armed Forces newspaper, announced Hitler's death, and only five days later, Germany officially surrendered. Nevertheless, at the time of its world premiere in New York on November 23, 1945, *A Game of Death* was presented to a nation that continued to cope with the aftermath of victory. The war, although over, remained fresh in the minds of Americans, and Wise's film, an entertaining work of fiction in its simplest form, was generally well-received.

Prior to its theatrical release, *A Game of Death* was advertised to the public as a "Nightmarish Romance on a Tropic Paradise of DEATH!" John Loder and Audrey Long, in their portrayals of an upright hero and brave heroine respectively, were convincing. The same can be said of their 1932 counterparts, Joel McCrea and Fay Wray. To reiterate, both films are similar in some aspects. For example, in the 1932 version, as Zaroff pursues his prey through the jungle, a subjective-objective tracking shot is used to invoke suspense. The audience is essentially afforded the opportunity to see the world through Zaroff's eyes. Then, we watch as he treads through the undergrowth, directly towards the camera. Wise, too, photographed such action in a similar manner as Kreiger hunts Rainsford during the film's climax.

---

8 United Artists attempted its own adaptation of Richard Connell's short story with *Run for the Sun* (1956), a thriller starring Richard Widmark and Jane Greer. The antagonist, like that of Robert Wise's film, is a Nazi madman.

Despite his opinion of remakes, Wise respected the original direction of Irving Pichel and Ernest B. Schoedsack, especially in regard to a specific scene. Wise's unveiling of the horrendous trophy room, in which multiple human heads appear to seamlessly float in glass jars, is one of the most memorable moments of the picture. Such a sequence of the 1932 version was heavily edited upon faring disastrously with test audiences. Wise therefore sought to enhance the scene for the most avid of theatergoers. Through the years, Connell's short story has been adapted numerous times for film, radio, and television. When one attempts to produce a remake, a pleasant experience will sometimes follow, but such is not always the case. Sam Raimi, famed director of motion pictures, once said, "If a remake is not good, no one wants to see it." He also alluded to a theory that an original remains unaffected if an adaptation proves unworthy of critical attention. In regard to Wise, he did not direct another remake following *A Game of Death*. He was nevertheless pleased with its overall reception and set forth to continue his productive, fruitful career in motion pictures.

5
CRIMINAL COURT

(PRODUCED AND RELEASED 1946)

"It is a pleasant world we live in, sir, a very pleasant world. There are bad people in it, Mr. Richard, but if there were no bad people, there would be no good lawyers."
- Charles Dickens, *The Old Curiosity Shop*

Mel Tormé, the esteemed singer, made his feature film debut with *Higher and Higher* (1943), an RKO production directed by Tim Whelan. The film is perhaps noteworthy more for its music than its plot. In addition to Tormé, several other singers were able to showcase their talents through the picture, but one such performer stood out amongst the others. Prior to its theatrical release, *Higher and Higher* was dubbed THE SINATRA SHOW. Frank Sinatra, a performer not yet in his prime but clearly on his way to stardom, was beginning to establish himself in Hollywood and beyond. His mere presence in Whelan's film captivated the attention of many. "I Couldn't Sleep a Wink Last Night" and "A Lovely Way to Spend an Evening," two of Sinatra's featured tunes, were again made popular in 1946 when Robert Wise directed singer Martha O'Driscoll in the RKO production of *Criminal Court*.

Steve Barnes (Tom Conway), an ambitious lawyer, is a declared candidate for district attorney. His girlfriend, Georgia Gale (O'Driscoll), takes a singing job at Club Circle, a popular nightclub. Barnes, however, becomes dismayed because Vic Wright (Robert Armstrong), the club's owner, is affiliated with a crime syndicate. Barnes eventually comes into possession of scandalous photographs. One such photo implicates Wright's kid brother, Frankie (Steve Brodie). Barnes intends to use the pictures as leverage for the upcoming election. Wright therefore offers him a campaign donation of $50 thousand on the condition the photos are not made public. Barnes refuses, so Wright threatens to expose "a story so hot" that it will result in the former's disbarment. A determined Barnes attempts to ascertain the details of such a story. He discreetly leaves a party held in his honor and goes directly to Wright's office, located at the club. The so-called story, however, is denounced as a bluff. Wright threatens Barnes with a pistol, and both men subsequently struggle for control of the firearm, which accidentally discharges. Wright suffers a fatal gunshot wound. Joan Mason (June Clayworth), a secretary of Barnes's who secretly works for Wright, witnesses the entire exchange from a concealed location. Later, Georgia goes to the office in search of Wright but instead discovers his corpse. Frankie arrives on the scene and concludes that she killed his brother. Meanwhile, Barnes returns to the party unnoticed. He eventually learns that Georgia is sought as a suspect in Wright's murder. She surrenders to the police. Barnes admits that he was the one to kill Wright, partly in self-defense and partly by accident, but nobody believes his claim, primarily because of his supposed presence at the party. Barnes then learns of an eyewitness to Wright's killing but is initially unsure of who it is. Joan inadvertently reveals a crucial detail of the fatal exchange. She speaks of the pistol Wright retrieved from "a panel in the wall" just prior to his death. Barnes realizes that only an eyewitness would be privy to such a detail. He therefore manipulates Joan into disclosing such information to a judge and jury, thereby exonerating Georgia.

Martha O'Driscoll.

Criminal Court is based on a script by Lawrence Kimble, but most of his ideas were derived from screenwriter Earl Felton, who crafted the original story for Wise's film. As a young child growing up in the 1910s, Felton developed polio. More often than not, he was badgered by many to use a wheelchair. Felton's mother was in awe of his determination to overcome polio's obstacles, but she took it upon herself to cure him. Revival meetings quickly became commonplace. Felton later admitted, "Dragging myself up to the pulpit was embarrassing enough. It was the crawling back down the aisle that was so humiliating." Nevertheless, he was a tenacious individual whose personality was often reflected in his writing. *Criminal Court* is no exception. The character of Steve Barnes, like Felton, is determined to lead a successful life, but the man Barnes aspires to be (i.e., the ideal juror, an individual of perfection, or the district attorney) in comparison to the man he truly is becomes an underlying issue of the narrative.

As Wise introduces Barnes to the audience, he presents his protagonist as one who attempts to mirror the most prudent juror of an ongoing trial, but a clear difference between both characters soon becomes apparent. Only those within the eccentric attorney's close-knit group understand his true nature. The film's opening shot is of Barnes's high-rise apartment building. Wise's camera slowly pans upward to indicate the unit's approximate location. An interior shot then reveals Luther (Joseph E. Bernard), Barnes's butler, to be selecting a tie from the closet. He appears pleased with his selection, but Barnes exhibits disgust upon receiving the tie:

BARNES: I'm surprised at you.
Barnes heads for the closet in search of a replacement as Luther looks on in astonishment.
BARNES: You know you're slipping, Luther. I've suspected it for some time ... (selects another tie) ... but on the last day of the trial? Oh, Luther!
LUTHER: Well, if I may say so, you're gonna look like a richly-dressed undertaker.
BARNES: If I wore that loud creation you selected for me, my client would need a richly-dressed undertaker.
During the exchange, Luther retrieves a jacket for Barnes and takes notice of his employer's recently bound tie. It is uneven.
LUTHER: Not crooked.
BARNES: I want it crooked. This time, my good Luther, is especially for Juror #3, Mr. Otto Brubaker. Solid citizen ... married 30 years ... same wife ... wears nightshirts and plain ties, he's the tough man on the jury. But in his eyes, Luther, I am exactly like him. And if I am exactly like him, how could I defend anyone but an innocent man?

Luther disagrees, indicating that Barnes is not at all like the juror to whom he compares himself. A carnation then becomes the center of attention. Luther intends for it to adorn the suit of Barnes, who rejects the flower, again cautioning his butler to be mindful of Juror #3. Shortly thereafter, Barnes drives Georgia to Club Circle, and she is quick to remind him of his eccentricities, asserting that he is notorious for "turning the courtroom into a 3-ring circus" and winning cases "with bathing beauties and bathtubs." The audience soon discovers for itself that he is not at all similar to the refined Juror #3 (a character never seen), and although Barnes's antics prove beneficial throughout a majority of the narrative, he happens upon an unforeseen obstacle at the most inopportune of times.

Barnes is generally presented as one with a flair for perfection, but his surprise encounter with Joe West (Pat Gleason), henchman of the deceased Wright, reveals a significant weakness. Whenever the whim seizes Barnes in times of trouble, he acts without considering every circumstance of his predicament. Such actions do not always produce positive results. Late in the film, West trespasses into Barnes's vacant office and waits patiently as the night grows still. He purposely leaves the room lit. Although West intends to catch Barnes off guard, he does not wish to take him by complete surprise. Both men eventually come face-to-face. Wise then makes use of a clever shot. As Barnes takes a seat behind his desk, he pushes a hidden button. The camera pans left from the desk, accompanied by a slow zoom to a speaker's exterior. A faint whirring sound suggests the existence of a concealed tape recorder. As the conversation between both men progresses, West speaks of important information that will exonerate Georgia. Barnes advises that such details would be valuable if disclosed in a court of law. West nevertheless vows not to repeat the information. Barnes, believing he has captured such information on tape, smirks as he prepares to turn the tables on his opponent. However, just as West is about to depart, he reaches into his coat pocket, retrieves an unknown object, and says, "I'm allergic to these home recordings." He abruptly tosses the object to Barnes, and it is then revealed to be the cylindrical audiocassette of the concealed tape recorder. The event marks an unusual moment of the narrative. Barnes, a man who habitually outwits those who dare oppose him, is essentially beaten at his own game. West, who took full advantage of the ample time afforded him prior to Barnes's delayed arrival, planned ahead and anticipated what was to come. His removal of the audiocassette is surprising. Like Barnes, the audience underestimates West, and the episode is an unfortunate setback for our hero. Yet, throughout a majority of the narrative, Barnes frequently appears to have the upper hand in the face of adversity, especially in an election year.

Barnes aspires to become the city's next district attorney, but as the story progresses, it is evident that the position is not the best fit for him. His priorities lie elsewhere. From the beginning, Barnes tends to frustrate Bill Brannegan (Phil Warren), his campaign manager, who works tirelessly to ensure victory. Georgia and her incarceration, however, quickly become a central focus of the narrative. Barnes assures her that she will soon be exonerated. He intends to call off the campaign considering he is "doing all right with [his] private practice." Georgia then becomes aware of the sacrifice that is being made. Joe West will produce the mysterious eyewitness, Joan, on the condition that Barnes surrenders the disparaging photographs implicating Frankie. Furthermore, Barnes must also agree to end his campaign. Although the maladroit incumbent, District Attorney Gordon (Addison Richards), would rejoice at such news of his opponent's concession, Georgia does not. Yet, the election's outcome eventually becomes irrelevant. As the narrative comes to a close, Barnes and Georgia stand on a staircase of the courthouse immediately following the trial. Together, the two ponder their future and spontaneously decide to wed. They scramble up the stairs in search of the judge. Wise then presents a fitting conclusion. As Barnes and Georgia depart the scene, the words "CRIMINAL COURT," painted on the wall, become visible to the audience. Seconds later, the closing credits commence as "The End" fades into view, cleverly covering the title of Wise's fifth motion picture.

The production of *Criminal Court* began on March 6, 1946, and wrapped within a few weeks. The film's world premiere transpired later that year in

New York on November 15th. On November 20th, it was released in theaters nationwide. Martin Mooney, a screenwriter who penned much of his work for Producers Releasing Corporation, a Poverty Row studio, also worked in the industry as a producer. *Criminal Court* marked his RKO debut in such a capacity.[9] In addition to writing fiction, he was at one time employed as a crime reporter. Mooney's expertise proved invaluable during his collaboration with Wise, whose direction of *Criminal Court* is noteworthy. Several moments of the picture (i.e., the aforementioned tape recorder scene, the film's closing shot) are indicative of clever directing. Furthermore, at Club Circle, as Wise first presents Wright to the audience, he does so with an immersive tracking shot. Georgia begins her audition and then smiles at her soon-to-be employer as he enters the lounge. Within the space of approximately fifteen seconds, the camera moves from behind her shoulder directly towards Wright. It stops just feet from where he is standing. Wise then cuts to a shot of Georgia as she continues to sing. She is on the stage, but in the distance. The perspective is Wright's, and we, the audience, essentially watch the performance with him.

The following scene transpires in Wright's office. Bob J. "Brownie" Brown (Joe Devlin), a stool pigeon of the immoral Wright, is given explicit orders to lie during an upcoming trial, by falsely identifying a man's killer. Brown is instructed to approach the defendant, place a hand on the latter's shoulder, and declare, "This is the man I saw fire the shots." In an attempt to rehearse for his upcoming performance, Brown then proceeds to place his hand on Wright's shoulder, but as he does so, Wise immediately transitions to the courtroom. The action, in essence, begins at Club Circle and then quickly shifts to the trial. Brown is revealed to be standing in the same position. His hand, however, rests on the shoulder of the actual defendant and not that of Wright. For a brief second, the audience is tricked into believing Brown is still at the club, but such is not the case, and that is entertainment of the most ingenious kind. Later, just prior to Wright's untimely death, Wise clev-

---

9 Martin Mooney's true debut with RKO transpired when he co-wrote the script of You Can't Buy Luck (1937), a Lew Landers film.

erly photographs Joan's exit from Wright's office as Barnes is arriving. The camera captures two separate doors but slowly zooms towards the one that is the most significant. As the shot concludes, a knocking sound emanates from the other side of the door. It signals Barnes's arrival, and he misses Joan by mere seconds. The scene's direction therefore creates dramatic tension. *Criminal Court*, in essence, provided Wise with an opportunity to hone his craft. Within a short three years, he had begun to establish his presence in Hollywood, but despite such early successes, Wise believed the debut of his first big feature was yet to come.

6
BORN TO KILL

(PRODUCED 1946, RELEASED 1947)

"The coldest winter I ever spent was a summer in San Francisco."
- Mark Twain

In 1943, James Gunn, a man in his early twenties who aspired to one day become a screenwriter, celebrated the publication of his first novel. It was titled *Deadlier than the Male* and ultimately attracted the attention of RKO. Gunn's novel was a hit with the American public not only due to its appeal as a classic murder mystery, but also because it was praised by critics as an outstanding psychological thriller. Shortly after its publication, however, some became wary of its provocative narrative. Joseph I. Breen, director of the Production Code Administration (PCA) and former general manager of RKO, declared that *Deadlier than the Male* was "the kind of story which ought not to be made because it is a story of gross lust and shocking brutality, and ruthlessness." A script based on Gunn's novel was written by Eve Greene and Richard Macaulay. It was considerably less violent than its original source, and Robert Wise was eventually hired to direct the adaptation. He had no choice but to honor any and all requests made by the PCA, but the title of Wise's film, *Born to Kill*, indicated to potential theatergoers that the narrative was not particularly tailored for the faint of heart.

Isabel Jewell and Lawrence Tierney.

In Reno to obtain a divorce, Helen Brent (Claire Trevor) finalizes its proceedings and prepares to leave town when Laury Palmer (Isabel Jewell), her housemate from a local boarding home, is murdered. Helen happens upon the scene of the crime but does not report it, instead opting to catch a train to San Francisco. Coincidentally, she encounters Sam Wilde (Lawrence Tierney), the murderer, at the depot. Both share the same destination and become acquainted during the journey. Some time after their arrival, Wilde goes to Helen's home. He is taken by surprise when he unexpectedly encounters her fiancé, Fred Grover (Phillip Terry). Also present is Georgia Staples (Audrey Long), Helen's sister. Meanwhile, news of the homicide begins to spread. Wilde soon learns that Helen is a foster child. Furthermore, she is not biologically related to Georgia, whose father owned the city's largest newspaper prior to his death. As a result of his passing, Georgia inherited the business. Much to Helen's disappointment, Georgia and Wilde are eventually married. His priority, however, is to run the newspaper. It becomes clear that Wilde does not love Georgia and instead harbors feelings for Helen, who ultimately reciprocates. Grover senses trouble and calls off the engagement. Helen, aware that the police are closing in on Wilde, makes Georgia privy to the details of the Reno homicide. The latter is also exposed to the harsh reality that her husband does not love her. Police detectives storm Georgia's home. Wilde learns that Helen is responsible for the raid. He shoots her as she tries to escape. Shortly thereafter, Wilde is fatally shot by the authorities. Helen later succumbs to her wounds and dies.

"You can't just go around killing people whenever the notion strikes you. It's not feasible."

Born to Kill features a curious assortment of characters, but none perhaps is more intriguing than that of Albert Arnett (Walter Slezak), the private detective investigating the homicide. He is retained by Mrs. Kraft (Esther Howard), head of the Reno boarding home. She, too, is fascinating, as her curt demeanor provides comic relief at the unlikeliest of moments. Arnett initially attracts the attention of Mrs. Kraft simply because his name "came first in the classified phone book," and her choice of detectives is noteworthy. Arnett intrigues from beginning to end. Upon the introduction of his character into the narrative, he frequents a Reno coffee shop, cynically declaring, "As you grow older, you'll discover that life is very much like coffee – the aroma is always better than the actuality." Later, as Arnett and Helen meet for the first time, he euphemistically refers to himself as an operative instead of a detective, but she takes no interest in his "professional drolleries." Arnett is nevertheless well-read, and whether he is quoting the French or making reference primarily to the Old Testament, his rhetoric essentially warrants a careful analysis of the film's characters.

At the time of Arnett and Helen's initial meeting, he speaks the words, "Noblesse oblige," thus quoting a popular French phrase which suggests he must conduct himself nobly, but as the narrative progresses, a darker side of his character is subsequently exposed. At the time of their second meeting, transpiring late at night on San Francisco's Treasure Island, he quotes a hymn of the nineteenth century, which essentially sets the stage for the tense exchange that is to follow. Arnett does not begin the encounter with a formal greeting. Instead, he declares, "Where every prospect pleases, and only man is vile." "From Greenland's Icy Mountains", a missionary hymn first penned in 1819, was deemed to be as "honourable as the effusion of a Christian mind."[10] Arnett, however, cites the most "vile" of its verses, claiming, "That quotation occurs to me quite often in my profession." Helen then inquires into the status of the investigation. She is clearly prepared to protect Wilde from incrimination, but Arnett senses that Helen is weak, as he becomes privy to the feelings she harbors for her brother-in-law. He therefore intends to take advantage of such a weakness:

ARNETT: I am a man of integrity, but I'm always willing to listen to an interesting offer.
HELEN: Well, I'm prepared to pay handsomely.
ARNETT: Good. Obstructing the wheels of justice is a costly affair.

---

[10] The Bishop of Calcutta expressed his unequivocal praise of Reginald Heber, the hymn's writer, in a letter that was eventually published in *The Christian Observer*, a periodical of the nineteenth century.

The words "Noblesse oblige" also suggest that one must act according to his or her position in society, but Arnett is willing to abandon his morals for a certain price. Hence, he does not necessarily practice what is preached, nor does he completely understand such rhetoric.

Claire Trevor as Helen Brent.

Born to Kill concludes with a direct reference to the Book of Proverbs of the Old Testament as Arnett reflects upon Helen's demise, sadly proclaiming, "The way of the transgressor is hard. More's the pity. More's the pity." The verse, however, is also applicable to his evident moral shortcomings. Upon the film's conclusion, Arnett happens upon a San Francisco newsstand and immediately purchases a daily paper. A headline of "SOCIALITE SLAIN!" dominates its front page. Arnett then refers to Helen as "the transgressor," but as a so-called "man of integrity," he has also violated general rules and overstepped particular boundaries. At the time of the aforementioned meeting on Treasure Island, Arnett reneges on his commitment to Mrs. Kraft, instead succumbing to greed as he negotiates with Helen:

HELEN: Five thousand dollars should do it.
ARNETT: Fifteen thousand dollars should do it.

Arnett's primary objective in life instantly becomes the $15 thousand and will remain so until the narrative concludes. Similar to Helen, he, too, is a transgressor, and both ultimately fail to achieve their goals. Helen is unable to shield Wilde from the course of justice. Arnett, in kind, does not obtain the prized fortune he so desires. Somewhat dejected, he departs the newsstand, most likely with the intention of returning to Reno. Earlier in the narrative, Arnett asks Helen, "Has it occurred to you? Neither one of us looks like a scoundrel, do we?" Yet, both are undoubtedly immoral, one perhaps more so than the other.

Arnett alludes not only to Helen's sinful nature, but also to her sexual prowess as he quotes the Book of Ecclesiastes of the Old Testament, declaring, "I find more bitter than death, the woman whose heart is snares and nets. And he who falls beneath her spell has need of God's mercy." A turning point of the narrative transpires when, at the conclusion of the wedding reception, she abruptly kisses Wilde for the first time. He is clearly taken aback. Time passes, and Wilde and Georgia return from their honeymoon, but he remains frustrated with Helen, commenting, "I don't get her. I don't get her at all." Helen is the most enigmatic of the narrative's characters. Just prior to the aforementioned kiss, she indirectly supplies Arnett with vital information "about the visitors Mr. Wilde's had."

It essentially becomes difficult for audiences to determine Helen's motives, and for Wilde, the sexual frustration continues as he says, "She puts herself in my arms and tries to trap me! She feels and digs and looks inside of me!" Helen becomes empowered from the moment she initiates the kiss, later asserting to have "the keys to the city . . . right in [her] hand." Wilde remains flustered, as he cannot ascertain where her loyalties lie, but perhaps, even Helen herself is unsure and remains as such until the very moments preceding her unfortunate demise.

Walter Slezak.

Born to Kill, Wise's sixth film, underwent principal photography from early May to late June of 1946. It was released on May 3, 1947. Since then, Eve Greene and Richard Macaulay's adaptation of James Gunn's novel has continuously enthralled audiences through the years, as the narrative remains captivating. Its catalyst, the Laury Palmer homicide, precipitates a sense of tension and anxiety, but such a homicide is extraordinary. It is a double homicide. Danny Jadden (Tony Barrett), Laury's gentleman caller, also meets his demise at the hands of Sam Wilde. Just prior to being murdered, Jadden produces a switchblade as his desired weapon of choice. Ironically, Mart Waterman (Elisha Cook Jr.), Wilde's close friend and confidant, later follows suit as he prepares to dispatch Mrs. Kraft. She nevertheless turns the tables and escapes death, and the once switchblade-wielding Waterman, like Jadden, eventually falls victim to Wilde's homicidal tendencies.

In the twilight of his life, Wise fondly reminisced about RKO as well as the film's clever script. "It was just fine working at RKO," he said. "It was one of the smaller studios, but very good, and they got some good properties. It all depends on the property, on that script. If you've got the right script and you cast it right, and you get enough time and money to make it, it'll turn out. The screenwriters, Eve Green and Richard Macaulay, did a great job, and I was so happy with the script when I got it. [*Born to Kill*] was a step up for me; better script, better picture, better cast . . . everything was considerably up."

Helen awaits Arnett's arrival.

7
MYSTERY IN MEXICO

(PRODUCED 1947, RELEASED 1948)

"Learning another language is not only learning different words for the same things, but learning another way to think about things."
- Flora Lewis

RKO sent Robert Wise to Latin America for his next film. He traveled to Estudios Churubusco, located in the Churubusco neighborhood of Mexico City. The studio had recently been established by RKO and Emilio Azcárraga Vidaurreta, the soon-to-be television magnate. Approximately nine months prior to Wise's arrival, John Ford and his crew occupied the premises for the filming of *The Fugitive* (1947), an historical drama starring Henry Fonda. Very few American filmmakers had yet to visit Estudios Churubusco, and on September 29, 1947, as the production of Wise's film began, it became clear to those involved that an extensive use of the studio's sound stages and back lots would be made. *Mystery in Mexico*, based on a story by Muriel Roy Bolton and adapted for the screen by Lawrence Kimble, features a group of characters that are anything but stagnant, constantly moving from one location to the next. Wise was given a month to complete his project. He not only welcomed the opportunity to direct a picture outside of the United

States, but he also appreciated the challenge of making a fast-paced film on such a limited schedule.

Steve Hastings (William Lundigan), an insurance detective, ventures to Mexico City. He searches for Glenn Ames (Walter Reed), a colleague who has not only disappeared but is also suspected of stealing a priceless necklace. Hastings acquaints himself with Ames's sister, Victoria (Jacqueline White), who likewise travels to the Mexican capital. Hastings does not reveal his true identity, choosing instead to determine if Victoria is involved in the caper. In time, he loses track of her. Following a lead, Hastings asks Carlos (Tony Barrett), a local cab driver he has befriended, to take him to Versailles, a popular nightclub. Victoria is discovered to be the club's featured singer. Hastings questions Benny (Armando Silvestre), a bartender who reminisces about his brief acquaintance with Ames. Benny, however, appears frantic. Joe Norcross (Ricardo Cortez), the nightclub's owner, becomes enamored with Victoria. Later, Hastings seeks another meeting with Benny but soon discovers that the latter has been killed in a car crash. Norcross gradually arouses suspicion. Once Hastings comes to the realization that Victoria and her brother are innocent, he informs her that he is a detective. Feeling used, she abruptly leaves him in a fit of anger. Hastings, believing Benny was murdered, presents his theory to the authorities.

Meanwhile, a local boy comes into contact with Victoria. He claims to have seen a picture of her in Ames's wallet. The boy guides Victoria and Carlos to his family's farm, where Ames seeks refuge. Hastings, who searches for Victoria, goes to Norcross's home to question him and is subsequently knocked unconscious. Shortly thereafter, Hastings regains consciousness at the farm. Carlos is present and reveals himself as an associate of Norcross's. Ames, Victoria, and the occupants of the farm, in addition to Hastings, are all held against their will, but a local police detective arrives on the scene and shoots Norcross dead. The latter's associates are then taken into custody. Hastings and Victoria ultimately celebrate a new life together and make plans to be married.

Jacqueline White.

Prior to the beginning of principal photography, RKO announced that *Mystery in Mexico* was to be a bilingual release. Hence, some anticipated two separate versions, one to be in English and the other to be in Spanish, but the latter did not materialize. Nevertheless, the dialogue of Wise's picture features both languages, and translations are not provided. Monolingual audiences must therefore rely on their own interpretations when viewing *Mystery in Mexico*, especially for the first time. A majority of the film is presented in English, but on some occasions when Spanish is spoken, the dialogue is cryptic to those individuals, characters and viewers alike, who do not understand the language.

Early in the film, shortly after Hastings and Victoria arrive at the Hotel Reforma, the former is accosted by unknown assailants. A struggle ensues. Shots are then fired as the assailants flee. Carlos, who has appeared in defense of Hastings and Victoria, remains with them at the hotel. When a policeman arrives on the scene to assess the situation, he declares, "Quedan todos detenidos! Habido muchos robos por aqui y a la mejor ustedes son los ladrones!" Victoria seeks an interpretation from Hastings, who replies, "[The policeman] said there have been a lot of burglaries around here lately and .

..*you* look like a burglar." She becomes appalled at such an accusation. In reality, an approximate translation of the policeman's words states, "All of you are to be arrested! There have been many robberies around here and maybe you are thieves!" Hastings, in essence, feigned ignorance in order to get a rise out of Victoria. He perhaps acted in such a manner because he presumed her to be an accessory to the unexpected assault. Only seconds earlier, Victoria sent him to investigate a dark room, and he was ambushed shortly thereafter. However, regardless of Victoria's intentions, which later prove to be innocent, Hastings's actions make for a comical scenario. Yet, on other occasions, language barriers lead to trouble. Early in the narrative, cryptic remarks made by Swigart (José Torvay), Norcross's henchman, essentially heighten the film's suspense. Furthermore, during two separate incidents, Carlos takes advantage of such barriers to deceive Victoria.

Shortly after Victoria lands in Mexico City, Swigart offers to interpret a conversation between her and a cab driver who is fluent only in Spanish, but his remarks to the driver are cryptic. To viewers who do not understand Spanish, such an interpretation appears excessive. Immediately prior to the exchange, Victoria retrieves a telegram, previously sent by Ames, from her purse, and as she attempts to communicate with the cab driver at the airport's curbside, Swigart arrives on the scene to offer his assistance:

SWIGART: May I be of help, Miss?
VICTORIA: Ah, yes.
SWIGART: Where do you want to go?
VICTORIA (reviewing the telegram): Mmm . . . number five, Del Carmen.
SWIGART (to the cab driver): Lleve la señorita a la calle Del Carmen numero cinco. Siga siendo como que no habla ingles y no la espere aunque ella se lo pida.

Swigart then turns his attention back to Victoria and smiles. He gives the impression of one who has her best interests at heart, but when Swigart spoke to the cab driver, he appeared to be saying more than was necessary. The address of the hotel is essentially the only piece of information that should be featured during such an exchange. However, a rough translation of Swigart's words states, "Take her to the address she is requesting. Continue pretending that you don't speak English. And do not wait for her even if she asks you to do so." Shortly thereafter, and much to the confusion of select audience members, Victoria is stranded by the cab driver. Earlier, when she disembarked from the plane, Swigart watched her every move. Therefore, by the time of their meeting at the airport's curbside, a particular degree of suspicion has been cast upon Swigart, and his cryptic remarks essentially add to such suspicion. Hastings, like Victoria, departs the airport in a taxi, but the driver of his cab ultimately proves to be far more distrustful than that of hers.

In order to better illustrate both the passage of time and the distance traveled between Cuernavaca and Mexico City, Robert Wise frequently transitions from the vehicle's bickering occupants to the regularly posted road signs.

Carlos, as audiences come to discover just fifteen minutes prior to the film's conclusion, is an associate of Norcross. Following such a revelation, Carlos deceives an unsuspecting Victoria as she prepares to reunite with Ames. The boy of the farm, whose family awaits his return, seeks the help of the police in connecting a distraught sister with her missing brother. Yet, because of language barriers, some in the audience are led to believe otherwise. In Victoria's hotel room, the boy conveys Ames's wishes to Carlos as he says, "El señor dijo que su hermana tiene que ir conmigo a la Policia." An English translation of the boy's words states, "The gentleman told me that his sister needed to go with me to the police," but Carlos instead informs Victoria that the child and his family are afraid of being involved with the authorities. Naturally, audiences fluent in Spanish become privy to such deception. Carlos does everything in his power to keep the police away from Ames, and upon arriving at the farm, he resorts to his usual antics.

As Ames reunites with Victoria, he does not react positively to Carlos's presence. She immediately takes notice. "It's alright. He's been very helpful. We can trust him," Victoria assures Ames, but shortly thereafter, Carlos deceives her yet again. She is concerned about her brother's health and eventually asks, "Is there a doctor close by?" Carlos relays her question to the farm's owner, who replies, "Esta muy lejos. Hasta el pueblo, por la carreterra." An approximate translation states, "It is far. You need to go in town, by the highway," but Carlos, as deceptive as ever, tells Victoria that the closest doctor is in the nearby village. He volunteers to summon the doctor but instead seizes the opportunity to bring Norcross to the farm. To reiterate, on some occasions when Spanish is spoken during Wise's film, the dialogue is cryptic to viewers who do not understand the language. Those fluent in both English and Spanish, however, may perhaps relish the narrative to the fullest extent.

"Starring in Robert Wise's *Mystery in Mexico* was a lovely experience," Jacqueline White said. "I don't remember much about the Churubusco Studio itself. It was my first time in Mexico. We drove around the country and went to a number of different places. I remember the hotel. The address was Orizaba Dieciséis. Of all the things to remember, the address stands out in my mind. I don't speak Spanish, but when we were in Mexico, it was important for me to remember the hotel's address because anytime I got into a cab, all I had to say was 'Orizaba Dieciséis.' Every cab driver knew the address very well. On non-production days, we would drive around Mexico to see the sights and go shopping. I remember thinking how different this place was from anything I had ever known. I enjoyed visiting the town of Cuernavaca. Mr. Wise was always the one to suggest where to go, and as a result, we got to see some wonderful parts of Mexico. It was quite a trip. The company was great. The people with whom I worked were just charming. Ricardo Cortez, an old-time actor, was convincing in the role of the villain. I was amazed because he had been appearing in movies several years prior to *Mystery in Mexico*.

"When we were filming at the studio, there were certain requirements that needed to be met. For every American crew member, whether it was a director or a producer, the Mexican equivalent was expected to be present on the set. The cameraman was an American who was married to a Mexican woman, and as a result, he did not have a counterpart like the others. Quite a few of the local actors had been cast in the picture. The Mexican director and producer did nothing but arrive at the studio to observe what we were doing. I guess there was some protocol that needed to be followed in order for them to get paid, but everybody was very nice. Both my hairdresser and make-up artist did not speak English. Years earlier, I had taken French in high school; coincidentally, they had as well. We therefore communicated in French. As a result, we were able to convey our thoughts to one another on the most basic of levels. It was quite an accomplishment. We laughed our way through such a funny method of chatting with one another.

"Robert Wise was such a thoughtful person. His style of directing was relaxed. He was quite encouraging, never critical, and not difficult at all. Mr. Wise knew what he wanted when it came to the direction of his actors. If he ever believed that I should change up my performance based on the type of mood that was required for a specific scene, he communicated his intentions to me in a very easy-going manner. I remember *Mystery in Mexico* being one of Mr. Wise's first movies. At the time, I wasn't aware of the films he had earlier directed. Patricia Doyle, his wife, also made the trip to Mexico. She was delightful. Bill Lundigan, too, was great. He was a fun and charming person. Similar to the film's story, he and I flew down to Mexico together. Bill's wife, Rena Morgan, also accompanied us on the journey.

"During my first day in Mexico, shortly after the plane landed, we went to a bullfight. The matador was gored and I remember coming very close to fainting. Eventually, some people took me to an area where I could recover. The flight to Mexico was rather long, and this may have been a contributing factor in regard to the way I was feeling, but the goring of the bullfighter left a very weird impression in my mind and made me sick to my stomach. I was taken to a medical station, where I discovered the matador, moaning and bloody, to be in the very same room! The doctor who examined me wanted to administer some medication of which I was apprehensive. I did not want to be treated with medicine, but the doctor was watching me. So, as cleverly as possible, I pretended to comply. The doctor, however, did not realize I hadn't swallowed the medication.

"Overall, with the exception of the bullfight, the production of *Mystery in Mexico* was a very pleasant experience and I had a great time. Mr. Wise enjoyed it just as much as the rest of us. I've been asked several times to reveal my favorite of all the films in which I have appeared, and it is *Mystery in Mexico*. Although the production of *The Narrow Margin* was also a very exciting experience for me, traveling to Mexico was an adventure in itself."

Mystery in Mexico premiered on July 1, 1948. It marked Jacqueline White's first and only collaboration with Robert Wise. The on-screen chemistry between her and William Lundigan was considered by many to be the main highlight of the film. Yet, despite White's stellar performance, her career was ultimately short-lived. A few years later, she retired from acting and moved to Wyoming. Regarding Wise, however, his career as a director of motion pictures was just getting started, and much of his early success was attributed to the relationships he formed with those on the set. Pepe Romero, a Mexico City journalist, served as Wise's technical advisor during the production of *Mystery in Mexico*. He knew the area better than most and proved beneficial in times of need. The film's opening credits feature many names, some representing those who appeared in front of the camera and some representing those who remained behind the scenes. All were loyal to Wise and worked diligently to ensure an entertaining final cut. One of the featured names is that of Samuel E. Beetley, the film's editor. His work ethic was indeed reliable. Interestingly enough, Wise and Beetley shared a particular commonality in that the careers of both men began in the editing rooms of RKO. It is no wonder that, when the time came, Wise tapped Beetley to oversee the post-production of his next film.

Ricardo Cortez as Joe Norcross.

8
BLOOD ON THE MOON

(PRODUCED AND RELEASED 1948)

"When you begin a cattle drive you can't expect to say you are finished until you have visited a fancy woman and played some games of chance."
- James Butler "Wild Bill" Hickok

Luke Short, a respected author of Westerns, enjoyed success at an early age. He celebrated the publication of his first novel while in his late twenties. Several years later, in 1941, *The Saturday Evening Post* serialized *Gunman's Chance*, another novel of Short's. It essentially pertains to an aspiring rancher who becomes involved with the wrong crowd. RKO developed an immediate interest in the story and purchased the rights shortly thereafter. However, due to problems with the script, the project was shelved for an extended period of time. It was not until the late 1940s when Theron Warth, an editor-turned-producer, and Robert Wise took it upon themselves to adapt *Gunman's Chance* into a major motion picture. The executives of RKO were initially reluctant, believing the project to be dead in the water, but Warth and Wise remained determined to solve any existing problems with the script. Harold Shumate, an unknown of the industry, was hired to craft a literary adaptation, and Lillie Hayward, formerly a musician, penned the script's final draft. The tide began to turn, as Warth and Wise eventually earned RKO's approval, and on February 16, 1948, production of *Blood on the Moon*, the project's new title, commenced.

Jim Garry (Robert Mitchum) travels the West en route to the village of Sun Dust. He encounters John Lufton (Tom Tully), a cattleman who has been supplying the Native Americans with beef for years, but Jake Pindalest (Frank Faylen), a newly appointed government agent representing the natives, has an agenda. Pindalest rejects Lufton's beef and prepares to kick him off the reservation. The beleaguered cattleman considers returning to a nearby basin, formerly his property. However, homesteaders have drifted into the area, and Lufton expects a fight over the grazing land. Tate Riling (Robert Preston), a competitor, has organized the homesteaders under his control and is also "bringing in gunmen" as muscle. Lufton is unsure of Garry's intentions. The latter nevertheless continues towards Sun Dust. Along the way, Garry engages in a brief skirmish with Lufton's daughter, Amy (Barbara Bel Geddes). She trusts few and essentially believes Garry to be an unlawful competitor. Shortly thereafter, Garry arrives in Sun Dust and reunites with Riling, an old friend who discloses the details of an elaborate scheme. Lufton's cattle are to be seized by the government, unless he is able to beat the odds and transport his herd to grazing land outside the reservation. Riling intends to prevent such action by any means necessary. If he is successful, Lufton will ultimately be forced to sell his cattle at a cheap rate. Through Pindalest, Riling will then resell the cattle to the government at the full contract price. Riling offers a percentage of the profits to Garry but intends for him to be a hired gun. Amy later chides Riling for pitting his gunmen against her father's working riders. Garry gradually begins to question the motives of his old friend.

Lufton's other daughter, Carol (Phyllis Thaxter), is in a secret relationship with Riling and provides him with confidential information regarding the herd's whereabouts. A rogue operation to prevent the cattle from departing the reservation is subsequently launched. Kris Barden (Walter Brennan), a homesteader and former rider of Lufton's, suffers a terrible loss when his son,

Fred (George Cooper), is killed during an ensuing stampede. A disgusted Garry cuts ties with Riling. He then attempts to delay Pindalest so that Lufton can avoid losing his herd to the government. Feeling used, Carol leaves Riling. Pressing circumstances force Garry to hold Pindalest against his will, but during an ensuing scuffle, the latter is eventually freed by Riling. Barden reunites with the Luftons and offers his home as refuge to an injured Garry. Riling converges upon the dwelling and a lengthy shootout transpires. In the course of defending himself, Garry kills Riling, and much to the delight of Lufton, Pindalest is exposed as an operative of the deceased.

From beginning to end, the character of Jim Garry intrigues. Within the film's opening minutes, he deceives Lufton, who questions whether or not the former has any acquaintances in Sun Dust. Garry replies in the negative but delays prior to doing so. Such actions arouse suspicion, especially from an audience. Lufton then takes a chance and requests that Garry deliver a note to his "womenfolk." It contains the most vital of information regarding the herd's impending departure from the reservation. Later, during Amy and Garry's third meeting of the film, she questions him about the note:

AMY: You *did* read that note, didn't you?
GARRY: No.
AMY: You're a poor liar.
GARRY: Yeah.

Although it is initially unclear if Garry read the note, the preceding snippet of dialogue essentially confirms that he did. At such a point of the story, the audience has borne witness to his deception. In addition to not coming clean about the note, Garry does not reveal his true agenda when first encountering Lufton. His reason for traveling to Sun Dust is to meet Riling, his former partner. Lufton harbors suspicions, but Garry, although deceptive, is essentially a misunderstood character of the narrative, evident from isolated encounters with Riling's crew, Riling himself, and Lufton.

Robert Mitchum, Barbara Bel Geddes, and Tom Tully.

When Garry first steps foot in Sun Dust, those loyal to Riling are unsure of the former's motives and subsequently become duped into believing he might be an operative of Lufton's. Milo Sweet (Charles McGraw), a member of Riling's crew, is overzealous, and his attempts at exposing the newcomer's identity only lead to further ambiguity. He pesters Sheriff Manker (Robert Malcolm) as Garry rides into town:

MANKER (watching Garry): That him?
SWEET: Yeah! What do you think?
MANKER: Hmm ... maybe.
SWEET: Maybe? My foot, Manker! You gotta get hit in the head with it? Lufton threatened to get one, didn't he?

Without any insight from the sheriff, Sweet becomes convinced that Garry is a cattle detective on Lufton's payroll. Sweet enters the hotel and recruits Nels Titterton (Zon Murray), an associate, to take part in a certain scheme. He instructs Titterton to assume the role of Riling, their established leader, in order to determine where Garry's loyalties lie. The latter arrives on the scene as the gang is engaged in a game of poker. Garry initially appears as one who believes Titterton to be Riling, but it quickly becomes evident that the scheme is a farce, as the part has not been played very well. The true Riling soon enters the picture, and the audience immediately discovers that he and Garry are old friends. Following the revelation, however, the film's protagonist becomes even more ambiguous than he already is. It is questionable why Garry, well aware that Titterton is not Riling, goes along with the charade in the first place. He dupes the gang into believing he has never met their leader and that he may, in fact, be Lufton's hired gun. Perhaps, audiences might later reflect that Garry, prior to reuniting with Riling, has already begun to suspect his former partner of illegal activities. Furthermore, because of his earlier conversation with Lufton, it might be his intention to ascertain the modus operandi of Sweet and Titterton before becoming reacquainted with an old friend, another individual who, like the others, attempts to fathom the uncertainties.

As the film progresses, Riling comes to believe that Garry, a former partner and confidant, is not at all like the man he was in earlier times, but the reality is that he never really knew or understood his "friend" in the first place. Everything comes to a boil at a cantina in Commissary, a neighboring town of Sun Dust. Riling demands an explanation from Garry regarding the latter's demeanor:

RILING: On the level, Jim. What are you doing here?
GARRY: Runnin' out.
RILING: Any reason?
GARRY: Two. Shotten and Reardon.
RILING (chuckling): I never heard of you runnin' from a pair like that.
GARRY: No. You never did.

Joe Shotten (Clifton Young) and Frank Reardon (Tom Tyler), like Garry, work for Riling as hired guns. Unlike Garry, however, both men lack a conscience. Earlier, near the Bella Union Saloon in Sun Dust, the two make an attempt on Lufton's life. Garry is present and thwarts the attack. Later, at the cantina in Commissary, he makes it clear to Riling that he will not allow Lufton, an innocent man, to be murdered. Garry is privy to Reardon's inconspicuous presence outside of the cantina and deduces that an ultimatum has been presented. Should he choose to stay with Riling and see Lufton's demise through to its bitter end, he will depart Commissary alive. However, if Garry severs ties with the gang and departs the cantina, Reardon will shoot him dead. Garry exposes Riling's scheme and, in what is arguably the most memorable event of the film, old friends immediately become sworn enemies. A lengthy fistfight ensues, and just as Garry appears to have the upper hand, Reardon enters the cantina and attempts to kill him, but Barden, also present, intervenes and shoots Reardon dead. A grateful Garry then questions the motives of Barden, who replies, "I always wanted to shoot one of you, and he was the handiest!" An unconscious Riling remains on the floor. Garry departs, intent on making things right with the man he originally kept at arm's length.

Lufton remains cautious of Garry from the moment both men meet simply because the latter often appears fickle. Yet, only Amy can enlighten her father. The aforementioned attempt on Lufton's life represents a turning point in the narrative. Following the confrontation, Garry issues a warning:

GARRY: You won't be this lucky next time, Lufton.
LUFTON: I don't get it, Garry. I just don't get it.

Amy, who has borne witness to the entire exchange, begins to realize that Garry is not fully committed to Riling's cause. Hope, in essence, is on the horizon. Later, Garry devises his plan to stall Pindalest, but Lufton refuses to become involved, declaring, "I'm not hiring a gunman to save my herd or anything else!" A disgusted Garry walks away. Amy follows and attempts to placate him. Lufton misunderstands Garry, believing the latter will incorporate murder into the operation. Amy, however, recognizes the plan's true purpose, and primarily because of her support, Garry ultimately earns Lufton's trust. Amy is arguably the most astute character of the narrative, at one point confessing to the often misunderstood Garry, "I know you better than you think."

Nicholas Musuraca, a master cinematographer who specialized in noir films, served as the director of photography during the production of *Blood on the Moon*.

During an early stage of Wise's career, a period of time when he was directing pictures for RKO and no other studio, he often reported to Sid Rogell, a tenacious producer with very little tolerance for those whose competence was not up to par. The deadlines of shooting schedules were expected to be met and production budgets were not to be modified. If Rogell encountered a director who could not keep pace with the grueling demands of the industry, there would be hell to pay. One day, while visiting the set of an RKO picture that was two days behind schedule, a memorable event transpired. Rogell confronted the director, ripped out a fistful of pages from the film's shooting script, and said, "There, now you're two days ahead!" Fortunately for Wise, over the course of several years, he managed to avoid angering the infamous producer. Coincidentally, in April of 1948, his collaboration with Rogell came to an end as the production of *Blood on the Moon* wrapped. Although Wise would go on to direct one final picture for RKO, it was done under the supervision of another. Regarding *Blood on the Moon*, it premiered on November 9, 1948, to generally positive reviews. Multiple critics were in awe of Wise's direction, especially with respect to the cantina fight scene between Robert Mitchum and Robert Preston. *The New York Times* declared that the scuffle "ought to satisfy most savage instincts." Wise himself later commented that it was "the most distinctive scene in the whole film." Overall, he was quite pleased with the final cut and ultimately referred to *Blood on the Moon* as his "first big feature."

9
THE SET-UP

(PRODUCED 1948, RELEASED 1949)

"You don't have to be in a boxing ring to be a great fighter. As long as you are true to yourself, you will succeed in your fight for that in which you believe."
- Muhammad Ali

Richard Goldstone, originally a Metro-Goldwyn-Mayer (MGM) writer and producer of shorts, joined RKO in the 1940s. He became intrigued with Joseph Moncure March's *The Set-Up*, a poem about a "dark-skinned jinx" of a boxer down on his luck. Goldstone recognized its potential to be adapted into a motion picture and summoned Art Cohn, a San Francisco Bay Area sports columnist, to pen a script of the same name. He then tapped Robert Wise to direct the upcoming production and immediately scheduled a meeting to discuss the project further. Wise collected the script, read it, and eventually returned it to Goldstone with his enthusiastic approval. He appreciated the narrative and prepared to further research its background. Prior to the first day of filming, Wise immersed himself in the daily lives of third-rate fighters. He visited an old, run-down arena in Long Beach, California, and was afforded the opportunity to observe the highs and lows of typical "fight night" events. Wise spent some time in the dressing rooms and took note of how the fighters composed themselves prior to entering the ring. He also discerned the manner in which they returned, win or lose, and on October 13, 1948, a day that marked the beginning of principal photography, a confident Wise reported to the set to begin work on his ninth motion picture.

Audrey Totter and Robert Ryan.

In Paradise City, Bill "Stoker" Thompson (Robert Ryan), an aging has-been of semi-professional boxing, prepares for an upcoming bout against the younger, favored Tiger Nelson (Hal Fieberling).[11] His manager, Tiny (George Tobias), conspires with Little Boy (Alan Baxter), a reputed mobster, to fix the fight in order to make a profit. Stoker is expected to lose by a knockout sometime after the second round. Tiny, however, does not make him privy to the plan partly because he does not want to part with his own share of the winnings, but also because many figure Nelson to be the clear

---

[11] Hal Fieberling was born Hal Brittan on December 10, 1918. Following the production of *The Set-Up*, he eventually changed his stage name to Hal Baylor.

favorite. Julie (Audrey Totter), Stoker's wife, pleads with him to retire from the sport, citing his sporadic memory loss as a major concern. She ponders whether to attend the event or not. Stoker is confident that he can defeat Nelson. Julie decides against appearing at the fight. Stoker takes notice but is determined to emerge victorious. A concerned Tiny becomes skeptical of the set-up. Between rounds, he reveals its details to Stoker and instructs him to "lay down" so that an altercation with Little Boy can be avoided, but the orders are ignored and Nelson is unable to defeat Stoker. Nelson is knocked out during the bout's final round. Tiny flees the arena. Following the fight, Little Boy confronts Stoker, who attempts to escape but is outnumbered. During the ensuing fracas, Stoker's hand sustains permanent damage, thereby ending his boxing career. In the aftermath, Julie comes to his aid. The two ultimately rejoice not only in the victory, but also with each other as the prospect of a better life appears imminent.

The exterior shots of Paradise City were photographed at RKO's Culver City studio.

Robert Ryan was cast in the role of Stoker Thompson for two reasons. First, he was under contract to RKO in 1948. Second, and more significant, Ryan had been the intercollegiate heavyweight champion during his time as a student at Dartmouth College. Yet, he bore no resemblance to the protagonist of March's poem. "The main character was an African-American," Wise recalled. "But we didn't have any African-American actor stars at that time." James Edwards, a soon-to-be established pioneer of the performing arts, was nevertheless cast in the supporting role of Luther Hawkins, the main event's charismatic victor. Through the years, such a character has remained an instant crowd pleaser. Hawkins, who is Black, is supportive of the underdog Stoker from the get-go. Race relations, however, bear very little significance to the narrative. Instead, the issue of youth vs. experience becomes paramount. Early in the film, Stoker and Julie argue about the upcoming fight. His will to persevere is evident, but she has other ideas for the future. Stoker asserts that Julie does not understand the situation from his perspective. "I understand that [Nelson's] twenty-three and you're thirty-five, Bill," she retorts. "Thirty-five in this business . . . you're an old man!" Yet, it eventually becomes clear that age is not a factor. Experience, in short, builds character, and to audiences, Stoker is more appealing through the supporting characters (i.e., his trainer, an aging vendor, and a blind patron) that closely identify with him.

Red (Percy Helton), Stoker's trainer, understands his protégé all too well and frequently clashes with Tiny in regard to the set-up. A conscious deception becomes extreme, thus complicating matters. To reiterate, Tiny blatantly excludes Stoker from partaking in the scheme. Red, however, is also a victim. Tiny cheats him out of an appropriate share of the earnings. He is not completely forthcoming regarding the total amount of cash received from Danny (Edwin Max), Nelson's manager, as Tiny claims to have pocketed thirty dollars instead of fifty. Red, in turn, receives a meager "fin" for his role but nevertheless becomes more concerned about the match than the money.[12] He

---

12 A fin is slang for a five-dollar bill.

"Maybe you could go on taking the beatings. I can't."

believes in Stoker, a fighter who "can still punch." Tiny, however, remains ignorant:

TINY: Nelson will butcher him. It's a hundred to one.
RED: That's just it! There's always the one! I tell ya . . . you gotta tell Stoker!

Unfortunately, Tiny delays. As the bout progresses, he witnesses firsthand the damage Stoker is capable of inflicting. Tiny is eventually persuaded by Red to disclose the set-up's details. Stoker, however, is on the war path and refuses to take a dive. Tiny departs the arena. Red does not follow suit, instead remaining for a few additional seconds to witness Stoker's defeat of Nelson.

Early in the match, the affable trainer smiles frequently as both fighters appear to keep pace with one another. He perhaps appeases Tiny while secretly rooting for Stoker. The tide subsequently turns, and Red remarks,

"I don't like this," as the thought of crossing Little Boy suddenly becomes a reality. Red chides Tiny, declaring, "You wouldn't listen to me! I told you to tell him," and just a few feet from Red is another who essentially believes in Stoker from the very beginning.

As Robert Wise directed the climactic boxing match of his film, he relied on multiple cameras to capture all of the fight's details, especially the emotions of his performers (below).

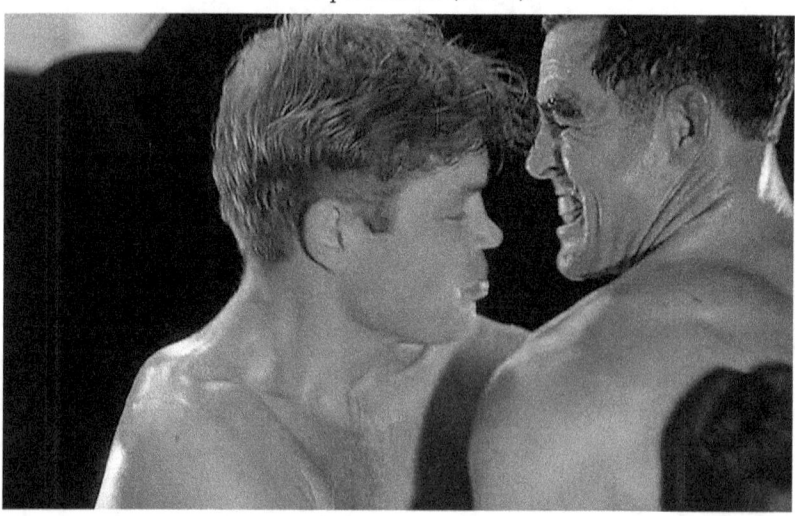

Bat (Frank Richards), an aging program vendor, eagerly anticipates Nelson's defeat while identifying with and rooting for the underdog Stoker every step of the way. Perseverance is essential. As the film begins, Wise presents the hustle and bustle of Paradise City. His camera slowly inches closer to the arena's exterior, and the first line of audible dialogue is spoken by a young newspaper vendor (Vincent Graeff) selling his "evening paper with the complete fight card." Like the camera, the newsboy makes his way to the arena. Bat is present, virtually a fixture of the venue's entrance. He sells *Knockout*, a program containing "all the fight news and pictures." Upon arrival, the newsboy abruptly positions himself in front of Bat in an attempt to garner more sales. The latter interjects, declaring, "I gotta make a buck, too," but the newsboy rudely dismisses his competitor, telling him to "go take a walk." Bat reluctantly leaves. Nevertheless, his role in the narrative becomes more significant than one may initially realize.

Unlike the newsboy, Bat makes frequent appearances throughout the film. He aims to persevere as he continues to sell issues of *Knockout* both inside and outside of the arena well after the event has begun. Furthermore, as Stoker prepares to square off against Nelson, Bat is there to offer words of encouragement. "You'll take him, Stoke!" he says. During the fight, Wise occasionally reveals an engrossed Bat to be fully transfixed on the action. In the ring, Stoker perseveres as he continuously withstands Nelson's determined onslaught, and upon the fight's conclusion, Bat is the only one ringside to congratulate the victor. Yet, unbeknownst to Stoker, he has the support of several others, including that of a most unusual gentleman.

Among the arena's patrons is a blind man (Archie Leonard) who, oddly enough, associates himself with Stoker based on the beating the latter sustains while fighting in the ring. A peculiar form of pleasure is elicited as Nelson attacks the eyes of his opponent with a series of jabs. During the second round, the blind man's companion (John Butler) offers a detailed account of the action:

COMPANION: Nelson's opened up his left eye. He's bleeding!
BLIND MAN (smiling): Good!
Seconds later, and much to the blind man's dismay, Nelson directs his punches elsewhere:
COMPANION: Nelson's pounding his kidneys!
BLIND MAN: Ah ... the sucker! Why don't he work on that eye?

As the round comes to a close, the blind man directs his comments towards the ring. "The other eye, Nelson ... close the other eye!" he says. Later, during the fourth and final round, Nelson knocks Stoker to the canvas. The blind man smiles. He perhaps yearns to identify with the underdog. As Stoker continuously sustains damage to his eyes, the blind man finds comfort in knowing that another can partially relate to his own plight. The fight's momentum then reverses as Stoker gains the upper hand:

COMPANION: Oh, what a switch! Stoker just landed one on Nelson's chin, knocked him right over at the ropes!
BLIND MAN (pleased): You've got him, Stoker!

It suddenly becomes clear to audiences that the blind man has been rooting for Stoker all along. Of the narrative's supporting characters, that of the blind man is arguably the most intriguing. Screenwriter Art Cohn's inspiration came from a visually impaired patron he observed while attending boxing matches in San Francisco, and similar to the film, a loyal companion was in tow to interpret the event's details one by one.

The Set-Up premiered in New York on March 29, 1949. Its events, which are set on July 27th of the same year, transpire within the actual running time of the film.[13] Immediately following the opening titles, and just prior to the

---

13 Alfred Hitchcock's *Rope* (1948), released approximately six months prior to *The Set-Up*, is an additional, yet rare, motion picture of the era that takes place within the actual running time of the film. Coincidentally, both conclude with the sound of blaring sirens.

closing credits, Wise presents images of downtown Paradise City. Furthermore, a clock is positioned in clear view to remind theatergoers of the exact time. Upon the narrative's introduction, it reads 9:05 p.m. Wise filmed several different versions of the film's closing shot that varied by only a few minutes, in regard to the clock's displayed time. *The Set-Up* was then previewed for select audiences prior to its theatrical release. Once the film's overall length had been determined, Wise used the version that most accurately reflected the final running time of the film. Hence, as the narrative concludes, the clock reads 10:16 p.m.

Arthur "Weegee" Fellig, a well-known photographer, appears as the timekeeper in *The Set-Up*.

Wise essentially made it a habit to remain on the set of his films as post-production transpired, especially when it came to the editing and rerecording of particular sequences. He was also a firm believer in sneak previews, often commenting that one never knows how a picture will be received if it is not tested with an audience ahead of time. The overall production of *The Set-Up* was exhaustive, yet memorable. Inside Hollywood Legion Stadium, the arena used for the film, Wise arranged for three separate cameras to record the action. One captured the entire ring. Another focused on the two fighters. Finally, a hand-held camera was used for various close-ups. Similar to Robert Ryan, Hal Fieberling had also been a boxer in real life, thus making it easier for Wise to photograph the match. Nevertheless, the production was not without its challenges. Rehearsals became necessary.

John Indrisano, a former boxer, choreographed the fight sequences, and Wise did some of the editing himself. In fact, *The Set-Up* marked the final time Wise would serve in such a capacity. He was on the verge of making a significant transition in his life. Only a few months earlier, as the beginning of the film's production drew closer, Howard Hughes purchased RKO and abruptly ceased operations. Wise decided that he wanted to leave the studio, but not until he was given the opportunity to direct *The Set-Up*. He loved the script and knew it would make for a successful picture. In time, Hughes reopened the studio. Wise then managed to get back on the payroll, direct his film, and depart RKO. The studio did not pick up his option for another term, so he "escaped." Such a departure, however, was bittersweet. "Of all the films I made at RKO," Wise once said, "*The Set-Up* is my favorite."

Stoker ponders his next move as he attempts an escape from Little Boy.

Audrey Totter and Robert Wise.

PART II
THE FIFTIES

10
TWO FLAGS WEST

(PRODUCED AND RELEASED 1950)

> "Nearly all men can stand adversity, but if you want to test a man's character, give him power."
> - Abraham Lincoln

April 11, 1950, marked the beginning of a new era for Robert Wise. On what would normally have been a typical Tuesday morning for the resolute filmmaker, he found himself far from the hustle and bustle of Hollywood and RKO Radio Pictures. Not only was Wise on location at the San Ildefonso Pueblo in New Mexico, he was also a newly-established contract employee of Twentieth Century Fox. The working title of his first assignment was *Trumpet to the Morn*. Frank S. Nugent, a writer responsible for a majority of the narrative, came up with his idea a year earlier while penning the script of John Ford's *She Wore a Yellow Ribbon* (1949). Such an idea addressed the state of the frontier as the Civil War drew to a close. Nugent researched the Confederacy's role as a potential watchdog of the West. Historians recorded varying accounts, believing some Confederate soldiers to be cooperative with the Union regarding western affairs whereas others were viewed as disloyal, instead conspiring to expand their political base deep into the frontier. In order to fine-tune his narrative, Nugent collaborated with Curtis Kenyon, a fellow writer and future president of the Writers Guild of America, West. A script based on their story was subsequently penned by Casey Robinson, and the film's title became *Two Flags West*.

During the Civil War in 1864, Colonel Clay Tucker (Joseph Cotten), a Confederate prisoner of war, is afforded the opportunity to be set free on the condition that he and his men join with Union forces to defend the frontier against Native Americans. He is demoted to the rank of lieutenant and travels west to Fort Thorn. Major Henry Kenniston (Jeff Chandler), leader of the outpost, looks after Elena (Linda Darnell), the wife of his late brother. She intends to one day return home to California. Tucker discerns Kenniston's hatred of the Confederacy upon meeting him. Preparations are later made for a wagon train to transport civilians west of Fort Thorn. Tucker and his troop are assigned to escort the departing caravan, but due to their displeasure with the Union, they plan an escape to Texas at some point during the mission. Unbeknownst to Kenniston, Elena departs with the group. Ephraim Strong (Harry von Zell), a Confederate agent posing as a merchant, approaches Tucker during a break in the trek. He proposes a plan to link Texas with the Pacific Ocean by forming a connection with the southern sympathizers in California. Strong, however, suggests that Tucker return to the fort on a temporary basis so not to arouse suspicion. The latter acquiesces but also reunites Elena with Kenniston against her will. The plan to defect is disrupted when natives attack the fort in retaliation for the death of the chief's son. Kenniston, responsible for the murder, surrenders himself to avoid further bloodshed. He is killed instantly. Tucker assumes command of the fort. News arrives that the city of Savannah, Georgia, has surrendered to General Sherman's forces, thus indicating the war's end is imminent. Elena chooses to remain at the fort as Tucker oversees its restoration.

As the film begins, Captain Mark "Brad" Bradford (Cornel Wilde) of the Union Army is presented to the audience. He speaks to a group of detainees, including Tucker, at an Illinois prison camp. For Bradford, the fighting has come to an end. Chattanooga swamp fever, coupled with a severe laceration near his right eye, has limited his ability to command. The eyepatch on Bradford's face becomes distinctly noticeable. Shortly thereafter, at Fort Thorn, Sergeant Terrance Duffy (Jay C. Flippen), Kenniston's confidant, ironically complains of "guarding the great American frontier [for a] bunch of one-eyed cripples." His frustration with those back East is evident. Curiously enough, as Bradford and company arrive at the fort, the patch is gone, and it immediately becomes clear that he is not at all similar to the Washington bureaucrats who command from behind a desk.

Later, as Kenniston chides a group of officers, including Bradford, he asks, "Am I to assume that each and all of you have lost your eyesight?" The rhetoric of Fort Thorn's overseers, however, does not always ring true. Bradford, perhaps, is more of a visionary than any other character of the film. He is the first to acknowledge that the Civil War is virtually at its end. Furthermore, much to Kenniston's surprise, Bradford foresees what others do not. The captain also instills in Tucker a reason for returning to the fort at the most critical of times.

Joseph Cotten.

Upon convincing the Confederate prisoners of Rock Island, Illinois, to join the Union Army, Bradford says, "This war is over for me," thus signifying his belief that, despite his physical limitations, the Civil War's outcome is essentially certain. He ultimately faults Kenniston for extending the conflict into the frontier. By way of illustration, a pair of renegades, detained in a Fort Thorn guardhouse, has been convicted of supplying whiskey and guns to the natives. Kenniston arranges for their execution and taps Tucker to oversee the job. Unbeknownst to the latter, however, the so-called renegades are Confederate agents, and following the execution, the truth is exposed. A livid Tucker storms into Kenniston's office to confront him. Bradford is present and also protests the atrocity:

TUCKER: A detail of my men has been required to shoot to death two Confederate citizens! We came here on the representation we'd never have to do anything against the South!
BRADFORD (to Kenniston): That's right!

Tucker eventually storms out of the office. Bradford then makes his thoughts clear to Kenniston. "You can't go on fighting the Civil War out here," he says. Kenniston, however, remains distrustful of Southern sympathizers in general, and more often than not, his hatred of Tucker is fanatical. "That man's a rebel to the core. He'll go over the hill first good chance he gets," Kenniston declares as the scene concludes. Arrangements are subsequently made for the wagon train to transport civilians off Fort Thorn. Hence, an opportunity for Tucker and his men to desert presents itself. Yet, all but one of the major's adherents become dumbfounded following an unexpected turn of events.

Bradford, the lone individual to anticipate Tucker's return to Fort Thorn, outwits a surprised Kenniston upon such a return, thereby gaining the upper hand in an oft-tumultuous relationship. The captain is criticized for his strategic thinking, but his general understanding of the rebels, in addition to such extraordinary patience, enables him to foresee the future without being privy to every circumstance of the caravan's westward trek. Earlier, when Tucker and company departed the fort, Bradford thanked Kenniston for trusting his "rebs" with the mission, but the major then admitted his belief that the group will head for Texas "the minute they smell rebel grounds." A heated exchange of sorts ensues:

BRADFORD: What on Earth are you thinking?
KENNISTON: Well, I hope I'm thinking with the brain of a soldier. That seems to require a bit of explanation to you. Alright, I . . . I don't mind giving you a lesson. You see, if I'm ever in a real pinch around here, I'd like to be sure that all of the enemy is in front of my guns . . . not some of it in my ranks. So, if they're going to desert, let them desert now. At least, I won't be any worse off than I was before they came here.

Meanwhile, during the trek, Strong reveals his true identity to Tucker and urges for him to be patient, as a return to Fort Thorn is of the utmost importance. Wise eventually transitions to Kenniston's office. The major is clearly livid as he dictates a letter pertaining to the "desertion of these rebels." Bradford waits patiently as Kenniston finishes the current paragraph. He then seizes the opportunity to speak his mind:

BRADFORD: Tucker will be back. I may be stubborn . . .
KENNISTON: You're not only stubborn, Captain. You're also asinine.

Bradford ignores the insult, instead looking out the window only to discover the arrival of Tucker's troop. A slight smile forms on his face as he anticipates Kenniston's reaction. The open-minded Bradford, without having any knowledge of Strong's influence, boldly predicts Tucker's return. Kenniston, in turn, becomes flabbergasted and requests that he be afforded the opportunity to relish his "moment of surprise." Tucker's arrival is indeed abrupt, but it is not the only time he will make an unexpected appearance at the outpost.

Kenniston later assigns a group of officers, including Tucker and Bradford, to investigate a series of wagon tracks beyond the fort. In the patrol's absence, hundreds of natives led by Satank, the Kiowa chief, attack the outpost. Miles away, Tucker prepares to finally rendezvous with Strong's wagon train and then proceed to California. Bradford, however, is an obstacle to such progress. Tucker subdues him but then arranges for the latter's safe return to Fort Thorn. Before such a return transpires, however, news of the siege arrives. Tucker then faces a dilemma. He ponders the future while resting alongside a dying campfire. Bradford, in close proximity, sits quietly:

TUCKER: What [sic] don't you say what you're thinking? Say we've got to go back. Tell me they're American. Say there are women and children there. Tell me if the fort is wiped out, it'll be because a troop of southern cavalry deserted its post.

BRADFORD: As a matter of fact, Clay, I was thinking of your home ... the South. Even though her battle is almost lost ... I know how much you'd like to help.

The conversation marks a turning point of the narrative; Bradford enlightens Tucker. The Civil War is virtually at its end, and a Union victory is imminent. Tucker is nevertheless persuaded to return to the besieged Fort Thorn and join the fight against the Kiowa, as his priorities have changed. In the aftermath, many lives are lost, including those of Kenniston and Bradford. Upon the film's conclusion, Elena and Tucker visit the cemetery. She expresses her firm belief that the deceased did not die for the North or the South, suggesting instead that their deaths were for a single cause: the quest for freedom.

On October 12, 1950, *Two Flags West* debuted in New York. The top brass of Twentieth Century Fox originally struggled to cast a contract player in the role of Clay Tucker. Some believed Victor Mature to be the ideal choice, but he eventually committed himself to playing the lead in Claude

Binyon's *Stella* (1950). Richard Basehart became another possibility until Joseph Cotten was ultimately loaned out to the studio by producer David O. Selznick. For Wise, the transition to Twentieth Century Fox was clearly for the better. Earlier in his career, upon screening the initial cuts of his films at RKO, studio executives constantly called for the prints to be modified. Select footage was either transferred to different reels or removed in its entirety. As the first cut of *Two Flags West* was screened for Darryl F. Zanuck, the head of Twentieth Century Fox, Wise prepared himself for all kinds of blistering criticism. Nevertheless, the picture was presented without incident. As the lights came on in the screening room, Zanuck lit a cigar and remained in his chair for approximately five minutes before speaking. Finally, instead of barking orders, he conferred with Wise regarding what could be done to perhaps make the film more appealing to the general public, but overall, Zanuck enjoyed *Two Flags West* and subsequently became instilled with the utmost confidence in his new director, and Wise was essentially well on his way to establishing a productive, long-term relationship with the studio.

11
THREE SECRETS

(PRODUCED 1949, RELEASED 1950)

> "My three Ps: passion, patience, perseverance."
> - Robert Wise

In San Marino, California, on a spring day in April of 1949, nine-year-old Barbara Fiscus and her cousin, Gus Lyon, left home to play in a nearby field. She brought along her three-year-old sister, Kathy, to join them in their afternoon of fun. Unforeseen in the field, however, was the opening to a deep shaft. It marked the site of an abandoned water well. Suddenly, Kathy fell into the shaft and became trapped many feet below the surface. A rescue operation was subsequently launched and involved the extensive use of drills, cranes, and even Hollywood floodlights, but tragically, when Kathy was discovered two days later, she was dead. Coroners concluded that she passed shortly after the fall due to a lack of oxygen. The rescue attempt had been broadcast live on radio and television, and in its aftermath, the nation mourned over the course of a lengthy grieving period. Within months, the tragic ordeal became the inspiration for *The Rock Bottom*, a new motion picture to be directed by Robert Wise. Production of the film began in early October of 1949, but prior to its theatrical release, which transpired a year later, the project's title had officially been changed to *Three Secrets*.

Patricia Neal.

Five-year-old Johnnie Peterson (Duncan Richardson) travels by air with his foster parents. Their plane abruptly crashes in the California mountains, and Johnnie is the sole survivor. As a rescue team scrambles to reach the boy, news reports surface that he was given up for adoption immediately following his birth. Susan (Eleanor Parker), a San Diego housewife, suspects Johnnie to be her long-lost son. She departs for Jackson's Lodge, an inn located at the base of Thunder Mountain; Johnnie is stranded near the mountain's summit. Upon arrival at the lodge, Susan meets Phyllis "Phyl" Horn (Patricia Neal), a woman she encountered five years earlier at the adoption shelter. Both gave birth to a boy on the same day, and shortly thereafter, they put their children up for adoption. Yet, neither Susan nor Phyl can be certain Johnnie is their son.

To complicate matters further, Ann Lawrence (Ruth Roman), another woman also present at the shelter five years earlier, arrives at the lodge. Determined that Johnnie is her child, she is frantic with worry. The three women anxiously await the outcome of the rescue team's mission. Susan sends for her husband, Bill Chase (Leif Erickson), to join her at the lodge. Upon his arrival, she confesses the details of a love affair that transpired before they met and suggests that Johnnie was conceived during the ill-fated relationship. Phyl, an adroit news reporter, uses her connections to investigate the details behind the adoption. She discovers Ann to be the true mother. Ann immediately becomes privy to the revelation, but the details are not disclosed to the others, including Susan. Following his rescue, Johnnie is transported safely to a hospital. Phyl and Ann ultimately deem Susan to be the most qualified of the three women to adopt the boy.

In Twentieth Century Fox's *A Letter to Three Wives* (1949), a sly seductress mails a letter to three ladies, declaring she has left town with one of their husbands. The trio's quest to identify the man then becomes central to the story. The film, directed by Joseph L. Mankiewicz, was released in theaters several months prior to the production of Wise's *Three Secrets*. Both directors essentially rely on flashbacks to support their respective narratives. The flashbacks of *Three Secrets*, comprising almost half of Wise's film, effectively divert the audience's attention from the stranded Johnnie to the three women, and Susan, whose flashback is distinct from the others partly because it is the only one to include all three female leads of the picture, is destined to adopt the boy. Her resolve to one day re-embark on the journey of parenthood is reflected in her determination to free herself from the clutches of a possessive mother. Furthermore, Susan's self-fulfillment is of the utmost importance to both Phyl and Ann.

Mrs. Connors (Katherine Warren), Susan's controlling and authoritative mother, triggers her daughter's impromptu road trip to Jackson's Lodge, thus evoking the latter's need to break free from a troubled past. The details are presented within the first flashback of the film. Paul Radin (Arthur Franz), a U.S. marine destined for overseas duty during World War II, proves to be a source of the conflict. Unaware Susan is pregnant with his child, he abruptly ends their relationship. Her suicide attempt follows, but Mrs. Connors intervenes before it is too late. Following the baby's birth, Mrs. Connors concludes that "living with an illegitimate child will be wrong and unnatural" for her daughter. The audience is not, at any time, afforded the opportunity to see Susan with her biological son. Instead, within a hospital's corridor, a nurse grants permission for Mrs. Connors to hold the baby, albeit briefly. Regarding Susan's father, he is notably absent from the film, never to be mentioned. Wise therefore infers that Mrs. Connors is a single parent.

Bill Welsh (right), the popular television announcer, interviews real-life members of the Sierra Club. Throughout the remainder of Robert Wise's career, he occasionally cast those of the media, particularly broadcast journalists, for a touch of added realism to his pictures.

Susan's predicament is relatively similar, but five years later, she is married to Chase, and he is not at all like her ex-flame. She earlier told Radin that she loved him, and he replied, "Don't say that. Supposing I don't come back to you." Later, during a similar moment of affection, Susan expresses her love for Chase, and he replies, "Don't tell me that now, Honey. I've got to go to Sacramento." Chase, however, is committed to his relationship with Susan.

Radin never was, and his effect on Mrs. Connors is lasting. She intends to continuously control Susan's life. As a result, the latter flees for Jackson's Lodge, only to be joined by the ever faithful Chase a short time later. Together, the two become Johnnie's destiny. Ann, the child's birth mother, is there to offer her undying support, and she is not alone.

Ruth Roman.

Phyl desires for Susan, the lone matron of the trio, to be Johnnie's adoptive parent simply because any other option is unsuitable. Phyl's short-lived foray into matrimony proves important. Through her flashback, Wise introduces the character of Bob Duffy (Frank Lovejoy), Phyl's soon-to-be ex-husband. At one point, she goes to Duffy's apartment to rekindle their relationship. The attempt proves successful when, following Phyl's promise to put her marriage before her career, he suddenly kisses her. In capturing the embrace, Wise's camera presents a curious find. Phyl is revealed to be wearing her wedding ring, but Duffy's is nowhere in sight. It eventually becomes clear that his faith in their marriage is lacking. The moment Phyl considers reneging on her promise, Duffy loses hope and their divorce swiftly becomes a reality. Later, at Jackson's Lodge, Susan decides to summon Chase to the area and dictates a letter to Phyl. Its contents are recorded, and upon completion, a precise confirmation is sought:

PHYL: Sure you want to send this?
SUSAN: Yes, I'm sure.
PHYL: Good.

A smiling Phyl then prepares to dispatch the message. She cannot undo the damage that has been done to her relationship with Duffy. Phyl nevertheless finds comfort in knowing that Susan will not follow suit. The latter essentially considers her marriage to be a top priority. As Johnnie is transported down the mountain to a waiting ambulance, the three women converge outside the lodge to discuss the boy's future:

SUSAN: Who is the mother? Did you find out?
ANN: We cancelled the call.
SUSAN: But why?
ANN: We thought it was better if we never found out. In a way, he belongs to all three of us and, since all of us can't have him, we decided that you're the one to try to adopt him.

Phyl, clearly caught off guard, deems it best to concur with Ann's sudden decision. She knows all too well that Susan's priorities are in order. Although Phyl is compelled to lie as she follows Ann's lead, both women understand the action that needs to be taken, one especially more so than the other.

Ann's sordid, murderous past ultimately leads to her support of Susan's quest to adopt Johnnie. Ann's flashback, the most unique of the three, accordingly draws a parallel to an uncertain future. As Wise transports audiences into her past, the film temporarily abandons its melodramatic overtones, instead providing a setting similar to that of the film noir genre. Theatergoers are exposed to techniques of German Expressionism, such as those of low lighting and an effective use of shadows. Wise presents his audience with a different Ann Lawrence, who at one time was an established ballet dancer for a prominent theater troupe. During the flashback, we learn of her affections for Gordon Crossley (John Dehner), a wealthy, powerful magnate and head of a lavish stage production. Their relationship appears "more and more perfect" with each passing day. Ann, however, gradually becomes suspicious of Del Prince (Ted de Corsia), Crossley's personal assistant and confidant.

For unknown reasons, Ann is not allowed to visit her beau, who suddenly becomes withdrawn. "The romance is over," Prince declares, but Ann is not easily deterred. Upon learning that Crossley is on a business trip, she makes the decision to travel three thousand miles to confront him. Days later, Ann arrives at her destination only to encounter Prince, and things consequently take a turn for the worse. She discloses the details of her pregnancy. Crossley, continuously elusive, instructs Prince to bribe Ann with enough money "to take care of everything and cover a lot of heartbreak besides." She remains undaunted. Shortly thereafter, Ann manages to confront Crossley face-to-face. He declares their relationship to be at its end. In a violent rage, Ann then murders her would-be lover with a bronze statuette. Again, elements of film noir (i.e., moral ambiguity, the doomed protagonist) are prominently featured in the flashback. Furthermore, Ann becomes a woman who would just as soon kill as love another, thus resembling a femme fatale. Upon the flashback's conclusion, the audience learns of her incarceration and subsequent exoneration, but more important is the parallel Ann draws to her future. Following Johnnie's rescue, a significant exchange between the women transpires:

ANN: Listen, Susan. You can get Johnnie. No court in the world would turn you [and Chase] down.
SUSAN: But, if he's yours?
ANN: Even if he turned out to be mine, I have nothing to offer him. Don't make me find him just to lose him all over again. It's much easier to tell myself that . . . maybe he's yours.

Ann traveled across the country to find Crossley, only to lose him a short time later. Although she has discovered Johnnie to be of her own flesh and blood, her future with the boy is one of uncertainty. Susan and Chase, on the other hand, represent stability and security. Shortly before the rescue, Ann overhears an exchange between the two, during which Chase expresses a profound desire to be Johnnie's adoptive father, proclaiming, "I couldn't deny him to you, not after the years of happiness you've given me." The conversation is significant, and it contributes to Ann's overall decision. As Wise concludes his film, a sense of joy is awakened in her as she stares up at Thunder Mountain. "You know? I just noticed something for the first time," Ann says to Phyl. "It's beautiful."

Ted de Corsia as Del Prince.

Three Secrets premiered on October 14, 1950.[14] A month earlier, Wise became thirty-six years of age. During the production of his film, the young director exerted himself tirelessly to ensure an entertaining work of fiction, and the final result remains a comparative triumph from beginning to end. As the

---
14 Two days earlier, Robert Wise's *Two Flags West* (1950) premiered in New York.

The aftermath of murder.

Robert Wise does not, at any time, provide his audience with Johnnie's perspective from atop the mountain. Theatergoers are instead kept in suspense.

opening credits of *Three Secrets* are displayed on the screen, Wise's subtle use of sound readily suggests to audiences that something is not right with the soon-to-be presented narrative. We listen as a plane's engine gradually loses power. The credits, meanwhile, continue to transpire before our eyes. *Three Secrets* then begins in full swing. The plane crash and reconnaissance mission come and go in a flash. Shortly thereafter, at a Los Angeles orphanage, the image of a spinning combination lock transitions to the rotating wheel of a paperboy's bicycle, and the latest issue of the *San Diego Herald* is then hurled onto Susan Chase's doorstep.[15]

Traditionally, when a city is first presented within a film's narrative, motion picture directors include a super of the city's name upon the screen to accompany the featured image. However, such a technique was seldom used by Wise, with *Mademoiselle Fifi* (1944) and *The Sound of Music* (1965) serving as rare examples. He instead preferred other methods of communicating with theatergoers. As the newspaper is delivered within the opening minutes of *Three Secrets*, Wise subtly makes his audience privy to the change in location from Los Angeles to San Diego. Sue Grafton, the novelist, once said, "Ideas are easy. It's the execution of ideas that really separates the sheep from the goats," and Wise's work ethic, always tenacious, essentially came to be reflected in his direction of motion pictures.

---

15 At the time *Three Secrets* was produced, the San Diego Herald was a defunct newspaper. Its circulation period transpired between 1851 and 1860.

12
THE HOUSE ON TELEGRAPH HILL

(PRODUCED 1950, RELEASED 1951)

> "American dreams are strongest in the hearts of those who have seen America only in their dreams."
> - Pico Iyer

In Italy during the 1940s, a young actress named Valentina Cortese (Cortesa) showcased her talents on the silver screen.[16] America gradually took notice. Near the end of the decade, Cortesa signed a contract with Twentieth Century Fox. It was not long before she was afforded the opportunity to star alongside Spencer Tracy and James Stewart in *Malaya* (1949), a World War II drama. Cortesa's life, however, was just beginning. Richard Basehart, an up-and-coming actor, was struck by tragedy when he lost his wife to a brain tumor. Barely a month had passed when he was required by Twentieth Century Fox to report to the set of his next picture, *The House on Telegraph Hill*. Basehart met with Robert Wise, the film's director, and assured him he was ready to move forward with the project, but yet another meeting would prove to be more significant. Because when Basehart encountered Cortesa,

---

16 Valentina Cortesa was born in Italy in 1923 as Valentina Cortese. Although she was not billed as the former until she began appearing in American films, both names were used at different times throughout her career.

his co-star, a special relationship began to form, and it was simply a matter of time before nature took its course.

Victoria Kowelska (Cortesa), a victim of the Nazi occupation in war-torn Poland, is sent to the concentration camp of Belsen. Over time, she befriends Karin Dernakova (Natasha Lytess), a fellow Pole who speaks of an aunt and infant son living in San Francisco. The war takes a turn for the better as the Nazis find themselves on the run from advancing Allied forces, but just prior to the camp's liberation, Karin dies. Victoria, lacking a family of her own, steals the identification of her late friend and assumes a new persona. Intent on moving to America, she sends a cable to Karin's aunt, a woman named Sophie. An attorney representing Sophie's estate, however, replies with a telegram bearing terrible news. Sophie is dead. Four years later, a determined Victoria sails to New York and, pretending to be Karin, meets with the attorney to demand custody of the boy. She encounters Alan Spender (Basehart), a man who is related to Karin's family by marriage. He is declared to be the child's legal guardian. Spender and Victoria become acquainted over the course of several days. She can sense his growing attraction to her. Victoria abruptly marries Spender as a means of feeling safe and secure. They travel to San Francisco, where Victoria meets Chris (Gordon Gebert), Karin's young son.

An opulent mansion on Telegraph Hill, Sophie's home for many years, serves as the family's residence. At a cocktail party, Victoria is introduced to Major Marc Bennett (William Lundigan), an old friend of Spender's. She recognizes Bennett as one of the liberating officers at Belsen, but he is unaware of her charade. Margaret (Fay Baker), Chris's caregiver, disagrees with Victoria in matters of opinion regarding the boy's best interests. Tensions come to a head, and Spender is not entirely sympathetic to Victoria. When she is almost killed in a car accident, suspicions abound. Victoria privately confesses to Bennett that she believes Spender wants her and Chris dead in order to acquire Sophie's estate. She also admits to not being Karin, thus evoking Bennett's compassion.

Victoria eventually discovers a newspaper clipping providing the exact date of Sophie's death. The aforementioned telegram of four years ago, however, was sent days prior to the incident. It essentially declares Spender, a manipulative individual, to be guilty of murder. Later, he serves Victoria a glass of orange juice, but she becomes suspicious and returns the beverage to its pitcher when he is not present. Shortly thereafter, Spender drinks the remaining juice and then reveals to Victoria that her glass contained a lethal dose of sedatives. When she explains to him that he was the one to drink the deadly juice, he becomes frantic and pleads with Margaret to call a doctor. Such orders, however, are not followed. Margaret, suspecting Spender has attempted to kill Chris on multiple occasions, lets him die. The authorities arrive and take her into custody. Victoria and Bennett agree to meet with the district attorney and disclose any information that will lead to Margaret's exoneration.

The House on Telegraph Hill was adapted from Dana Lyon's novel of the same name. The original story included a subtitle of *The Frightened Child*, which, during production, became the working title of Wise's picture. From the film's beginning, however, it becomes apparent that the narrative evolves around Victoria and her earnest, heartfelt desire for a better life. An opening narration in her voice states, "How the will to live survives in a place like Belsen, I do not know. But I wanted to live." Victoria's determination is later reflected in Barbara Graham, the main character of Wise's feature film, *I Want to Live!* (1958). Yet, the narratives of both pictures are entirely different. Regarding *The House on Telegraph Hill*, its opening minutes address the criminality of the Nazi regime, thus foreshadowing Wise's later works such as *The Sound of Music* (1965) and *The Hindenburg* (1975).

Victoria and Karin dream of a life away from Belsen. Aunt Sophie, a character frequently mentioned but never seen, represents freedom and prosperity. Upon Victoria's arrival at the house on Telegraph Hill, she remarks, "I like it just as it is. It's so old and beautiful." Then, as if controlled by an unseen force, she finds herself moving into an adjoining room in which a painting of the late matriarch adorns the wall. Spender follows, giving Aunt Sophie's portrait a brief once-over prior to speaking. "It's getting pretty late, dear. You must be tired. You can see the house tomorrow," he says to Victoria. Together, the two abruptly depart. Spender, however, again glances at the portrait upon exiting. His secret is deadly, one to which only Aunt Sophie was privy. Later that evening, Victoria cannot sleep. In narration, she confesses, "I had a strange feeling that Aunt Sophie saw through me." Spender eventually discloses a key attribute of the deceased's character, declaring, "She knew people inside out," and throughout the remainder of the film, timely appearances of Aunt Sophie, whether in the form of the painting or perhaps a conspicuous photograph, essentially guide Victoria on the path to salvation.

Valentina Cortesa and William Lundigan.

As Wise sets the stage for Bennett, a savior of Victoria's past, to be reintroduced into the narrative, he first presents an image of Aunt Sophie's painting to begin the scene. Bennett's subsequent comments regarding the portrait, in essence, facilitate the unforeseen reunion. A dinner party, complete with several guests in attendance, transpires at the house approximately thirty minutes into the film. The festivities serve a dual purpose – Spender's marriage to Victoria and her arrival in America. Dr. Burkhardt (Steven Geray), an esteemed guest, finds himself in close proximity to the painting as he proposes a toast, gesturing to both the painting and Victoria: "To the lady of the house, past and present. May your days in this house be as rich and rewarding as hers." Victoria, positioned next to the doctor, becomes appreciative. Another guest, Mr. Whitmore (John Burton), contributes his thoughts regarding Aunt Sophie. "Great character. Don't make 'em like that anymore." As Whitmore speaks, Bennett arrives on the scene, pausing in the room's doorway to observe Spender and the guests:

SPENDER: Nobody knows that any better than I do. She was a wonderful, wonderful woman.
BENNETT: She had a wonderful sense of humor. In fact, she'd laugh her head off if she could see this little votive group gathered under her portrait, drinking her vintage wine, growing mawkish over her memory.

Victoria immediately recognizes Bennett and turns away from him, pondering her next move. In time, Spender presents Bennett to his wife as the other guests disperse. Spender then exits the room to prepare a drink. Based on Bennett's recent, astute observation of the congregating guests, it is clear that he understands and respects Aunt Sophie. Victoria takes notice, and although she has no intention of revealing her true identity to Bennett at such a point of the narrative, she is nevertheless comfortable presenting herself as the embattled woman from Belsen. Following their reunion, her affection for him grows stronger with each passing day. Yet, an uneasy feeling regarding Aunt Sophie and the house persists.

Days after the party, Victoria innocently enters Margaret's room in search of her, only to discover a striking photograph of Aunt Sophie, and such a photograph subsequently leads to the most significant object in the house. A mysterious scrapbook and its mere existence ultimately justify the retention of an outdated telegram. Earlier, in New York, an important exchange transpires between Spender and Victoria as they dine in a restaurant:

VICTORIA (pretending to be Karin): If [Aunt Sophie] were alive, I would have been with her long ago. I sent her a cable.
SPENDER: Yes. I know.
VICTORIA: You know?
Victoria is clearly caught off guard. Later in the narrative, as she and Bennett are together on the dance floor of a San Francisco night club, the subject of the telegram sent in response to her original cable is raised:
VICTORIA (still pretending to be Karin): I realize now there was something wrong from the beginning. The way they tried to keep me from coming to America. The cold, heartless cable some lawyer sent me that Aunt Sophie was dead and not a word about Chris.
BENNETT: What lawyers?
VICTORIA: I don't know. I don't remember their names. Why? Is it important?
BENNETT: No, I...I just wondered.
VICTORIA: I can show you the cable. Alan doesn't know, but I still have it.

The following day, the two meet privately at the marina, where it is determined that the telegram is not authentic. A confused Victoria then decides to come clean with Bennett and expose the charade, thus marking a significant turning point in their relationship. Later that afternoon, she infiltrates Margaret's room with the intention of reviewing the scrapbook. Again, Aunt Sophie's photograph beckons Victoria to press forward in search of the truth. The newspaper clipping is then discovered, and it ultimately contradicts the contents of the suspicious telegram, thereby incriminating Spender.

In the aftermath, as Victoria departs the house on Telegraph Hill for the last time, she is once again drawn to the painting of Aunt Sophie, as the beginning of a new, promising life appears imminent. Although the scene is somewhat reminiscent of her initial encounter with the portrait, a major difference is noticeable. Victoria first comes to the house with Spender, and he does not openly acknowledge the existence of Aunt Sophie's painting. Upon the narrative's conclusion, however, Victoria is with Bennett and Chris, and an expression of sorrow becomes evident as she glances at the painting one last time:

BENNETT: You don't have to apologize to [Aunt Sophie] anymore.
VICTORIA: Do you think she'd understand?
A part of Victoria feels guilty for all that has transpired. During an earlier conversation with Bennett, she declares, "It is wrong for someone to lie, to cheat, even if only to find happiness and safety," but upon the film's conclusion, as they gaze at the painting, everything becomes clear:
BENNETT: [Aunt Sophie] would approve. I know. She might even approve of me.
VICTORIA: Then, all I can do is to thank her for everything.
BENNETT: Let's go.

Victoria marvels at the painting and ultimately departs the mansion similar to the way she first entered it, as her brief occupancy in the house on Telegraph Hill, in short, begins and ends with the image of a "kind and wise" matriarch.

"My mother was an industry watcher, not so much a film buff as she was an industry watcher," Gordon Gebert said. "It meant very little to me back then, but around the time *The House on Telegraph Hill* was being produced, she told me my father was in awe of the fact that Robert Wise edited *Citizen*

Kane. I was only about nine years old and questioned how an editor could be a director and vice versa. If you're a truck driver, you're a truck driver. How can you be a truck driver and later be a supervisor? That was my line of thinking at such a young age. Although I was puzzled about Robert Wise being an editor and then later becoming a director, I knew my parents were very impressed with him. When I was older, I saw *Citizen Kane* and considered it to be one of the greats.

"Regarding my contribution to *The House on Telegraph Hill*, the experience began early one morning when a studio limousine took my mother and me from our house to the train station in downtown Los Angeles. We then departed for San Francisco, arriving later that evening. The cast stayed at the Palace Hotel. Coit Tower served as the location for the mansion. Wise shot it cleverly. The grassy area surrounding the tower was presented as the mansion's yard. In fact, my favorite memory of the entire experience is playing catch near Coit Tower. Even when the cameras weren't rolling, a lot of time was spent throwing the ball around on the flat surface of the hill. Not only did I do this with Valentina Cortesa, but with my stand-in as well. I remember playing catch for hours, even though it was only reflected within a minute of screen time. San Francisco features rather variable climatic conditions, and natural lighting is apt to frequently change. Therefore, a fair amount of time was spent waiting for such lighting to facilitate the filming of the scene.

"Valentina Cortesa and Richard Basehart were clearly in a relationship at the time of the film's production. I'd occasionally see them walking on the lot hand in hand. My mother picked up on it, too. She read the trade papers, and there may have been some mention of Cortesa and Basehart's relationship in these papers. I just remember the both of them were very much together and it certainly wasn't undercover. Cortesa was extremely affectionate with me. She was warm and motherly. I have a feeling there was a bit of latent nesting taking place. Perhaps, the romance with Basehart spurred these motherly, matronly feelings. And some of the scenes, in turn, were sort of fueled by such feelings. Although, according to the script, my onscreen persona wasn't really the son of Cortesa's character. But as a nine-year-old, the plot was a little complex and beyond me.

"Robert Wise was a good director and knew how to handle child actors. There were varying approaches to dealing with such performers in those days. A director would mostly tell the actor to be natural and take steps to preserve such naturalness. Some directors were not very forthcoming about the whole story, plot, and so on. I can remember in some cases not obtaining the entire script and instead only receiving scenes. It was not just an attempt to save paper, or to save costs on the shipping or delivery of the script. It was more a matter of keeping actors, especially the young ones, isolated from any theorizing or unnatural thoughts. There was certainly no encouragement of learning the whole story, whether it meant reading an original source, such as Dana Lyon's novel.

"In some respects, *The House on Telegraph Hill* was a milestone. It was the fourth or fifth decent role that I was offered within a couple of years. The film gave me a sense that my career was definitely established, and that it wasn't just a flash in the pan. I remember Wise's picture very distinctly from all the others. The set was very professional, and the cast was fairly close with one another. The RKO production of *Holiday Affair* was also a memorable experience. I worked with Robert Mitchum, Wendell Corey, and Janet Leigh. The three of them were always hanging out and kidding around together. I saw the same thing on Wise's set with William Lundigan, Richard Basehart, and Valentina Cortesa.

"During a break in the production, I rejoined my classmates at my elementary school. On one day in particular, I sprained my ankle on the playground. When the cast and crew eventually returned to Wise's set to film more shots, problems began to arise. Some of these shots took place on the stairway of the house. And I can recall some difficulty with moving up and down the steps because of my ankle. I then distinctly remember Robert Wise consoling me and saying, 'That's okay, it's okay. Just take it easy on your foot. Save the foot for when we really need it.'"

Principal photography of *The House on Telegraph Hill* commenced on September 6, 1950, and wrapped over a month later on the thirteenth of October. The cast and crew reconvened on October 24th to complete additional sequences. Richard Basehart and Valentina Cortesa's romance eventually reached full bloom, as the happy couple wed on March 24, 1951. Wise's film premiered in New York on May 12th of that same year. It garnered an Oscar nomination for Best Art Direction of the "Black and White" category but ultimately lost to *A Streetcar Named Desire* (1951). *The House on Telegraph Hill* is nevertheless remembered by some for its inclusion of an important initiative of the era. Early in the film, as Victoria departs war-torn Europe for New York, Wise presents authentic footage of real-life refugees boarding an ocean liner in preparation for their transatlantic journey to the land of opportunity. The International Refugee Organization (IRO), a specialized agency of the United Nations, sought to transport displaced persons to IRO-affiliated nations in order for such persons to begin new lives, and Wise, in short, welcomed the opportunity to raise awareness of the initiative.

However, when Wise was first provided with the script of *The House on Telegraph Hill*, he did not find the story to be of particular interest. Nevertheless, the executives of Twentieth Century Fox sought one with enough patience to direct the young Cortesa, as she had yet to become acclimated to an entirely new language and culture. In time, Wise accepted the assignment primarily because it enabled him to return to San Francisco, the setting of his sixth motion picture, *Born to Kill* (1947). He enjoyed filming on location, especially if the featured city was to his liking. Later in his life, however, Wise admitted that his greatest memory of directing *The House on Telegraph Hill* was not San Francisco, but instead, Cortesa, as the opportunity to nurture her budding career was one he came to embrace with open arms.

13
THE DAY THE EARTH STOOD STILL

(PRODUCED AND RELEASED 1951)

> "A wise man changes his mind. A fool never will."
> - **Spanish Proverb**

Darryl F. Zanuck, a founder of Twentieth Century Fox and well-known film producer, telephoned Robert Wise one day with a direct request. Julian Blaustein, another producer with the studio, was in possession of an intriguing screenplay. *The Day the Earth Stood Still*, written by Edmund H. North, is based on the 1940 short story, "Farewell to the Master", by Harry Bates. Zanuck requested that Wise review and consider North's script for motion picture production. It explored the concept of world peace in the nuclear era but also presented audiences with the probability of extraterrestrial life in the universe. Wise went to Blaustein's office, introduced himself, and collected the script. Upon reading it, he immediately notified Zanuck of his unconditional approval.

The narrative's protagonist is Klaatu, an alien being who travels to Earth on a critical mission. Wise's first objective was to cast the ideal lead for his picture. Although Claude Raines emerged as the frontrunner, he ultimately committed himself to a Broadway production in New York, thus leaving Wise and company to search elsewhere. Zanuck, who had earlier vacationed in London, remarked about a stage actor he discovered while attending a West End play. The performer, Michael Rennie, was relatively unknown to the general public in the early 1950s. A confident Zanuck nevertheless offered him a contract with the studio shortly thereafter, and Wise in particular considered Rennie to be perfect as Klaatu, believing that one with an unfamiliar face, as opposed to the popular Raines, would be much more convincing in the role of a being from outer space.

A large, saucer-shaped spacecraft approaches Earth and lands in Washington, D.C., thus captivating the attention of the entire world. Representatives of the U.S. military, heavily armed, cordon off the area. Two hours later, a lone figure, claiming to be on a mission of peace, disembarks, but an edgy guardsman shoots and wounds the being. Shortly thereafter, a tall, intimidating robot emerges from the spacecraft and melts all military weapons using a high-powered laser beam. The wounded being, known only as Klaatu (Rennie), is transported to a hospital and eventually demands a meeting "with representatives from all the nations of the Earth." Due to political tensions, however, many will not oblige. Klaatu becomes curious about the "strange, unreasoning attitudes" of the earthlings and abruptly escapes from the hospital. In disguise, he seeks refuge at a boarding house and becomes acquainted with Helen Benson (Patricia Neal), a fellow boarder, and her son, Bobby (Billy Gray).

Klaatu later reveals his true identity to Professor Jacob Barnhart (Sam Jaffe), an esteemed scientist with great knowledge. Klaatu speaks of atomic energy and warns that if the people of Earth apply such energy to their spaceships, it will "create a threat to the peace and security of other planets." As a demonstration of his power, he temporarily neutralizes the electricity of the entire world, inadvertently trapping Helen and himself in an elevator. Klaatu then makes her privy to his identity and intentions. Helen is empathetic, but Tom Stevens (Hugh Marlowe), her significant other, has an agenda. He eventually exposes Klaatu for his own personal gain.

Gort (Lock Martin), the aforementioned robot, has meanwhile been instructed to wreak havoc on the Earth should anything happen to Klaatu, who is eventually shot and killed by military forces. Helen becomes frantic. Using a code phrase given to her by Klaatu, she is able to thwart Gort's attack. Barnhart schedules a meeting to discuss the political unity of nations, with dignitaries from all over the world in attendance. Gort resurrects Klaatu, but only for a limited period. The military calls for Barnhart's meeting to be cancelled. Yet, before such action can be taken, Klaatu makes his presence known at the gathering and emphasizes the importance of living in peace "without arms or armies." He presents a simple choice. The earthlings can either join Klaatu and live in peace or pursue their present course and face obliteration. Klaatu and Gort subsequently depart in their spacecraft, leaving the people of Earth to ponder their future.

Robert Wise prepares Billy Gray and Michael Rennie for the filming of an upcoming scene.

Production of *The Day the Earth Stood Still* began on April 9, 1951, and concluded on May 23rd of that same year. The experience of making the film was an opportunity Wise embraced from start to finish. Throughout his life he was a firm believer in the existence of UFOs despite any controversy surrounding such existence. Although some have refuted theories of extraterrestrial life in and beyond the solar system, others have remained convinced that the human race is merely a dot in the universe. Harry Bates capitalized on such speculative mania when "Farewell to the Master" was first published in 1940, and Edmund H. North merely followed suit a decade later with his ingenious adaptation.

"Farewell to the Master" curiously features the word "tragic" in its opening sentence. Upon the story's beginning, the original Klaatu is deceased, having met his demise at the hands of a "mentally unbalanced" human assassin. In addition, he is rarely mentioned throughout the story. Through North's script, however, Wise elevates Klaatu to the central focus of the picture and, in addition, modernizes Bates's narrative. Unlike the ensuing adaptation, "Farewell to the Master" presents a futuristic setting to its readers. Furthermore, in Wise's film, the character of Klaatu is afforded a noteworthy introduction to audiences and subsequently wastes little time exposing society's shortcomings.

The setting of Bates's "Farewell to the Master" is not at all reflective of the mid-twentieth century world in which he lived. Aeronautical advancements are conspicuously evident. The narrative evolves around Cliff Sutherland, a freelance photographer and reporter. Early in the story, he is transported via "aircab" to Klaatu's idle spaceship. Although Bates does not elaborate on the details of such a vehicle, readers are generally compelled to conclude it is a flying taxi. Shortly thereafter, Bates writes, "Every child knew that only two spaceships had ever been built on Earth, and none at all on any of the other planets and satellites; and of those two, one had been destroyed when it was pulled into the sun, and the other had been reported safely arrived on Mars."

The society depicted in Bates's story is clearly futuristic not only in comparison to that of Wise's film, but also to that of his own world. Two years following the publication of "Farewell to the Master", German scientists created the V-2 missile. It was the first rocket capable of flying high enough to reach space, and many years would pass before the advent of the space shuttle. Hence, the inclusion of futuristic elements into Bates's story, particularly the two spaceships, indicates he was ahead of his time, and such a story remains a noteworthy contribution to the genre of science fiction. North's script, too, entertains from beginning to end, but his adaptation features a major revision to the original story.

On the silver screen, the character of Klaatu is afforded a noteworthy debut. Instead of one introduction, however, Wise presents the audience with two. Klaatu's arrival on Earth is a spectacle as it dominates the opening minutes of the film. Regarding "Farewell to the Master", a much different scenario is described as Bates writes that the spaceship "just appeared" and "did not come down from the sky," but Wise, in unveiling his protagonist to theatergoers, worked with a special effects team of experts in order to present an elaborate landing. Furthermore, when Klaatu initially emerges from his ship, it is a grand introduction. Although he is subsequently wounded and transported to the nearest hospital, the chain of events paves the way for yet another debut.

As Klaatu arrives at the boarding house of Mrs. Crockett (Edith Evanson), the home's occupants are informed of a special alert broadcast on television. Drew Pearson, a real-life reporter appearing in the film as himself, attempts to urge calm as he addresses the nation in regard to Klaatu's whereabouts. Pearson declares "that though this man may be our bitter enemy, he could be also a newfound friend." Wise's direction of the scene is noteworthy. Unbeknownst to the lodgers, Klaatu has entered the home. As the broadcast continues, Pearson presents a picture of Klaatu in full cosmic attire, stating, "The only photographs we have are similar to this one, and do not show the man's face." Wise immediately cuts to an image of the newcomer, who stands in the shadows of the home's entryway. True to Pearson's words, Klaatu's face is not visible. The startled lodgers see only a figure in shadow. Courtesy of Wise, the mood is tense and remains as such until Mrs. Crockett engages the newly arrived stranger in search of an explanation. In retrospect, Klaatu's second introduction is arguably more significant than his first. It essentially confirms that he is always, at the very least, several steps ahead of the unsuspecting humans.

In Wise's film, Klaatu is quick to expose society's shortcomings. His meeting with Mr. Harley (Frank Conroy), secretary to the president, foreshadows the earthlings' ignorance in the midst of a crisis. Klaatu makes it clear that he is "impatient with stupidity. [His] people have learned to live without it." Harley then retorts, "I'm afraid my people haven't." Later, Stevens meets with Mr. Bleeker (Wheaton Chambers), a jeweler, and selfishly attempts to exchange the gems Klaatu has offered Bobby. The would-be transaction occurs as the world's electricity is neutralized. Eleanor (Elizabeth Flournoy), a clerk of the jewelry store, attempts to exit amidst the chaos, but she is stopped by Bleeker:

BLEEKER: Did you call the electrician?
ELEANOR: I tried, Mr. Bleeker. But the phone doesn't work either.
BLEEKER: Well, call the phone company.
ELEANOR: But the phone doesn't work!

Meanwhile, the president, unseen by the audience, prepares to declare a state of national emergency. World leaders remain reluctant to work together, and because of such ignorance, a crisis has developed. It is not until Klaatu is finally afforded the opportunity to address Earth's people that the narrative's conflict is resolved, albeit partially.

"Robert Wise's set of *The Day the Earth Stood Still* was very amicable," Billy Gray noted. "I don't think there was ever any dissension among the cast and crew that I ever noticed. We didn't, however, receive any cooperation from the U.S. government regarding the use of soldiers or equipment. They apparently looked at the script and said, 'We'll pass.' But the California National Guard was very cooperative. They let us use their tanks, jeeps, and more. And again, Wise's set was very amicable. In fact, it was more than that. Michael Rennie was quite enthralled with my mother. He was apparently somewhat of a ladies' man and was very solicitous of her, getting her a chair from which to observe the production, and getting her coffee. I don't know if his actions ever got him anywhere, but there was definitely some attention paid to her.

"The location shooting at the nation's capital consisted of stand-ins for Rennie and me. I didn't travel to Washington, D.C. The furthest I traveled was to the back lot of Twentieth Century Fox, which wasn't too far from the studio. It was like an open field. Now, it's Century City. The scene in which I secretly follow Klaatu to his spacecraft was also shot on the back lot. On the day when that particular scene was filmed, I distinctly remember receiving instructions that stated, 'His eyes were as big as saucers.' It didn't seem right that Wise would have given me directions such as those. But as Gort comes to life, the eyes of Bobby, my character, were supposed to become as big as saucers.

"Much later, Wise was honored at a special event. These types of festivities happened on a regular basis towards the end of his life, and at this particular gathering, a screening of *The Day the Earth Stood Still* took place. Patricia Neal and I were invited. Following the film, we answered questions for the audience. I then asked Wise about the scene in which my eyes were supposed to figuratively become as big as saucers, and he didn't recall giving me those kinds of instructions. But then, following the event, somebody sent me one of the original scripts, and as I was going through it, I noticed that the phrase was listed as part of the screen direction. Edmund North, the screenwriter, had written that 'Bobby's eyes were as big as saucers.' I guess it was his way of being a director.

"I didn't have much interaction with Lock Martin, but I was there when he was getting in and out of his latex suit. It was a particular chore for him. He was a big guy but not a very vital person. Actually, he was kind of frail. He could only be in the suit for about ten to fifteen minutes. If the conditions ever became too hot, he would then request to be released from the suit. The crew had him on a watch list, so to speak, in order to prevent him from fainting or toppling over. Aside from being a latex suit that was probably about a quarter of an inch thick, it was big and heavy. Being in somewhat close proximity to Martin, I was quite aware that the suit was an issue for the crew.

"I have a nice onscreen interaction with Patricia Neal that I think comes off very well. It is the scene in which I tell her that I have seen the spaceman and that he just happens to be our houseguest. Then, of course, she insists it's my imagination. 'I wouldn't call you a liar,' I reply. The scene is memorable. Neal was a super lady who was wonderful to work with. She fondly remembered the scene during which her character and that of Michael Rennie are in the backseat of the cab. The process projector displayed an image of the road behind them. They weren't in an actual taxi. Instead, the exchange was filmed on a sound stage. In the scene, Klaatu alerts Helen as to what should be done in case anything happens to him. It eventually came time for the famous words of 'Klaatu barada nikto' to be spoken. Klaatu demands that Helen say these words to Gort in order to prevent the attack. And when the time came for Neal to repeat 'Klaatu barada nikto,' she would start laughing. During rehearsals, she would make it about halfway through the line before she started cracking up. It happened several times. Rennie finally asked her if that was the way she was going to do it when the cameras started rolling. Neal assured him that she'd keep it together. She thought the whole thing was kind of a joke. I don't think she realized at the time that *The Day the Earth Stood Still* was destined to become an important film. She may have instead seen it as just another job for all of us. I certainly didn't realize it was going to be a special film until later. In addition to Neal, Michael Rennie couldn't have been more professional during the production. He was an absolute gentleman the whole time. There was never anything untoward about him. Regarding Hugh Marlowe, I don't recall any interaction with him at all. We did have a couple of scenes together. I liked the work he did. He was a terrific 'Judas' and played the part very well.

"At one point, when the crew was shooting the scene in which Klaatu is brought back to life, the question 'Does Gort have the power of life and death?' became an issue. The dialogue was written so that Klaatu's answer was, 'No, it's only a temporary thing.' North skirted the issue, or at least diffused it a little bit. It was a strategy to maybe avoid resistance from the Church.

"My favorite and least favorite memories of performing in *The Day the Earth Stood Still* transpired around the same time when we were shooting the spaceship scenes on the studio's back lot. I forget what time of the year it was, but it was bitterly cold. A favorite spot of the cast and crew was a 55-gallon drum in which a fire had been started. When people weren't working, they were always around that drum with their hands held out over the fire in order to stay warm. I enjoyed that part of filming, but it spoke to how uncomfortable the set could be at night. Despite the cold weather, I have pleasant memories of the production.

"Another memory pertains to an old friend of mine. Like me, he was a child actor. His name was Anthony Mazzola. He was part of the crowd that was standing around the saucer after it had landed. I had previously worked with Mazzola on other projects. Although he was an extra in Wise's film, he was featured in a close-up shot. Whenever I watch the film and see that image of him, I reflect back on the experience and it seems quite recent. Later in our lives, on the set of *Father Knows Best*, we did a scene in which our characters were fighting each other in a boxing ring. That, too, was memorable. Mazzola died in a plane crash in 1974.

"There's one scene in *The Day the Earth Stood Still* that is somewhat ironic in nature, and maybe it was intended to be as such. It may have just slipped by the audience in 1951. But since then, when people watch *The Day the Earth Stood Still* in theaters, this particular scenario always gets a giggle out of the crowd. In the scene, Klaatu has been captured and is taken to the hospital. Outside his room, a couple of doctors are having a conversation. The upshot of their discussion is that Klaatu is healing very rapidly considering the wounds he has sustained. They're astonished. Then, one doctor offers the other a cigarette and they both light up during the conversation. The mere sight of doctors smoking while talking about a healing patient gets a giggle out of the audience in present times. I don't believe people laughed in 1951.

At the time, the general public was aware that cancer was a probable result of smoking. I'm not sure whether Wise intended for the scene to be comical or not.

"I've worked with scores of directors. Early in my life, I was working all the time and was around a lot of sets and a lot of industry people. I never ran across anybody who was as genuinely pleasant a person, without any effort, as Robert Wise. All of my interactions with him just couldn't have been more uplifting and appropriate. He really stands out in an industry that draws people, especially actors, who are somewhat problematic in their psychology. Wise had no sharp edges that I detected. He did not try to be a nice guy. His kindness was genuine."

The Day the Earth Stood Still premiered in New York on September 18, 1951. Throughout the history of motion pictures, a select group of films have accomplished the feat of elevating science fiction as an art form. The trend arguably began with Fritz Lang's *Metropolis* (1927). The following decade, William Cameron Menzies's *Things to Come* (1936) took audiences by storm. The 1950s, too, were significant. In addition to *The Day the Earth Stood Still*, theatergoers flocked to sold-out screenings of *The Thing from Another World* (1951) and *When Worlds Collide* (1951). Wise's film, however, received unstinted praise from critics across the globe, and *Time* magazine declared it to be "the best of Hollywood's recent flights into science fiction." Wise later confessed that although *The Day the Earth Stood Still* was a highlight of his career, the film's production was not without its challenges. He particularly had a difficult time designing the interior and exterior of Klaatu's ship. Fortunately, a skilled team of professionals worked tirelessly to ensure a quality layout of the spacecraft.

In regard to music, Wise specifically recommended to studio executives that Bernard Hermann compose the film's score. A decade earlier, the two had worked together during the productions of *Citizen Kane* (1941) and *The Magnificent Ambersons* (1942). Hermann's contribution to *The Day the Earth Stood Still* has been hailed by critics through the years. Also noteworthy is

Wise's inclusion of real-life reporters in the cast, thus adding a touch of realism to his picture. In addition to the aforementioned Drew Pearson, commentators Elmer Davis and H.V. Kaltenborn appear as themselves.

In short, because of Wise's unremitting diligence, *The Day the Earth Stood Still* became a cinematic masterpiece and remained one of his most cherished accomplishments for the rest of his days. On February 19, 1998, he was presented with the Life Achievement Award by the American Film Institute, and upon the conclusion of a memorable speech in which he paid tribute to several of his treasured colleagues, Wise declared, "On behalf of that young man from Indiana, I'd like to say, 'Klaatu barada nikto,' which, roughly translated tonight, means, 'Thank you very much from the bottom of my heart.'"

14
THE CAPTIVE CITY

(PRODUCED 1951, RELEASED 1952)

> "I have built my organization upon fear."
> - Al Capone

Mark Robson, an apprentice with RKO, worked as an assistant to Robert Wise during the editing of *Citizen Kane* (1941). Ten years later, as established directors of motion pictures, both men entertained the possibility of a joint venture. They were in favor of greater independence regarding the production of their films. Similar to Wise, Robson's directorial debut was made possible by Val Lewton.[17] B pictures, however, were a thing of the past, as Wise and Robson essentially strived for something better. Theron Warth, an editor best known for his work on Alfred Hitchcock's *Notorious* (1946), joined forces with the duo in order to form Aspen Pictures. Their company aimed to produce quality films using the finest source material. Enter Estes Kefauver, a United States Senator from Tennessee. A tenacious politician, he headed a special committee whose sole purpose was to investigate organized crime. Kefauver's objective eventually became widespread news. Alvin M.

---

[17] Mark Robson made his directorial debut with *The Seventh Victim* (1943), a Val Lewton production.

Josephy, a war correspondent turned screenwriter, penned a script based on the shady underworld of organized crime and its serious threat to domestic America. Wise considered Josephy's story to be a suitable debut for Aspen Pictures, and when Kefauver received word regarding the film's production, he set forth to offer his full support.

James "Jim" T. Austin (John Forsythe), the editor of *The Kennington Journal*, a small-town newspaper, is approached by Clyde Nelson (Hal K. Dawson), a local detective, with a story that will "bust [the city] wide open." Murray Sirak (Victor Sutherland), an insurance magnate, is suspected of racketeering. Upon launching an investigation, Nelson suddenly endures constant harassment from the city's police. He figures they are accepting bribes from Sirak. Nelson's license is revoked, prompting Austin to meet with Gillette (Ray Teal), the chief of police, in search of an explanation; the latter blames the state government. Two weeks later, Nelson is murdered. A search of the deceased's office produces a listing of local bookies. Austin questions a majority of those on the list, but none are particularly forthcoming. Furthermore, as he makes his inquiries, the police appear to be watching his every move. A surprised Austin discovers Krug (Paul Newlan), a sponsor of the newspaper, to be on the list. He identifies a tenant of Krug's warehouse as Dominick Fabretti (Victor Romito), a reputed mobster. Sirak visits Austin and proposes a generous sponsorship of the newspaper on the condition that the investigation is put to a stop. The proposition is rejected.

Margaret (Marjorie Crossland), Sirak's ex-wife, informs Austin that Fabretti orchestrated Nelson's death. However, she pleads for the safety of her ex-husband. Margaret still cares for Sirak and divorced him only because of his ties to organized crime. She agrees to partake in a deposition that will incriminate Fabretti, but later turns up dead. Austin appeals to Reverend Nash (Ian Wolfe), the police chaplain, for a stop to the violence and corruption. A harsh truth states that Gillette can only run the sort of city that his "superiors" tell him to run. Austin concludes that if there is to be reform, he will need to take the matter to Senator Kefauver's newly established committee. He and his wife, Marge (Joan Camden), flee town. The next morning, they discover Fabretti's men to be in pursuit. Austin stops at the nearest police station and waits for an escort to safely deliver him and Marge to the Capitol, where he is afforded the opportunity to present his entire testimony to the committee.

As *The Captive City* begins, Wise presents viewers with the first volume of the committee's aforementioned investigation. The cover page turns to reveal a compelling message from Senator Kefauver, which states, "Ordinarily, Americans don't think much about the existence of organized crime; they know vaguely that it is there, and they let it go at that…UNLESS PRODDED BY SOME UNUSUAL CIRCUMSTANCES." Jerome Moross's score, at the moment serene, suddenly becomes unnerving as Wise transitions to a car racing along a desolate highway. Its occupants, a man and a woman, appear frantic as they are pursued by a vehicle in the distance. Their car eventually comes to a stop at the police station of an unknown locale. Shortly thereafter, the audience is introduced to Austin. He has, in essence, been prodded by the unusual circumstances of which Kefauver writes. The flashback and narrative begin as Wise presents the city of Kennington. It is not long before Don Carey (Harold J. Kennedy), Austin's business partner, is introduced to the audience. Both men are clearly motivated by differing agendas. Carey desires what is best for the newspaper. Austin, however, is driven by his morals.

Early in the film, Carey reviews a proposed advertisement with Coverly (Glenn Judd), a major sponsor of the paper. Also in the shot, courtesy of Wise, is an observing Austin. A phone rings and is immediately answered by a printing press operator who enters the frame, thus blocking Carey and Coverly from view. Austin remains in the shot, and Carey, although unseen, tells his client, "We have to convince you guys that advertising pays," but Wise places more of an emphasis on Austin and the incoming phone call, revealed to be made by Nelson. The image, albeit brief, foreshadows what is to come. The importance of advertising becomes secondary to more serious issues. Austin demands justice for the murdered Nelson, even if it results in a loss of business. Much to Carey's disappointment, Coverly eventually cancels his advertising. A frustrated Austin then declares, "I'm sick of walking a tightrope! See no evil, hear no evil, speak no evil . . . just because it might be bad for business!"[18] Wise's film essentially presents the concept of advertising as a double-edged sword. It has the potential to produce positive results (i.e., prosperity, headway, and instant rapport), but a price, monetary or not, must always be paid.

The talented Lee Garmes served as Robert Wise's cinematographer during the production of *The Captive City*.

As Wise transports discerning audiences into the Austin residence for the first time, his protagonist is revealed to be taking pride in a full-page advertisement of the journal, thus prompting Marge to comment about the two of them becoming "richer and richer," but social obligations, often demanding, accompany prosperity. The Austins join a local country club along with

---
18 The film's working title was *The Tightrope*.

Carey and his spouse, Sally (Patricia Goldwater). Associations with fellow members are supposedly "good for business." One evening at the club, Anderson (Jess Kirkpatrick), a used car salesman and sponsor of the newspaper, prowls the establishment in search of Sally, and when she emerges into view with Marge in tow, the latter forewarns her companion of what is to come:

MARGE: Uh-oh, here comes your dreamboat.
SALLY: Oh, no. I can't. Not again!
MARGE: Sally, now wait! You just can't . . . he's an advertiser!
SALLY: I don't care what he is! What about my feet? Tell him I. . . .
Sally attempts to retreat from whence she came, but Anderson arrives on the scene.
ANDERSON: Hiya, Sugarpuss! Hey, how about us givin' the folks another dancing lesson? Do you mind?
SALLY: Of course, Mr. Anderson. I'd be delighted.

Sally reluctantly accompanies Anderson to the dance floor. She does so in support of her husband and the newspaper. It is, in essence, a sacrifice that is expected of a person in her position, and Marge understands the conventions all too well. Wise then shifts the focus to Austin, who is clearly concerned about Nelson. News of the latter's death is received shortly thereafter. Austin therefore begins to rearrange his priorities. Later in the film, Anderson chides him, declaring that a "one-horsed newspaper" will not stop the syndicate. Some of the paper's sponsors, however, are perhaps less antagonistic than others.

Krug, one of several advertisers, indirectly leads Austin to Fabretti, thus providing much needed headway in the case, but as the investigation deepens, so, too, does the distress of the innocent. Phil Harding (Martin Milner), the young and somewhat naïve sports editor of the newspaper, goes to extremes in order to bring the killers to justice, and upon putting himself in harm's way, a snowball effect becomes imminent. Not only does he daringly capture a photograph of Fabretti as the latter exits Krug's warehouse, he also insists on processing the negative film immediately following the encounter. Austin advises against such a course of action, suggesting they wait until daybreak, but an ambitious Harding, not entirely aware of the dangers involved, presses forward. As a result, he is beaten by Fabretti's associates, and in the aftermath, a distressed mother (Frances Morris) chides Austin and Carey for "exposing a mere boy to a thing like that." Harding attempts to shift the blame to himself, but to no avail. The newsmen are abruptly shown the door. Outside of the Harding residence, a concerned Carey suggests to Austin that Fabretti be left alone. Differences of opinion abound, and a practical partnership suddenly appears unstable. Harding, however, bears no responsibility, as the spiral of decline had already commenced in the presence of another.

During their first meeting, Sirak uses advertising as a means of establishing an instant rapport between him and Austin, who exposes the former's actions as an act of bribery. Carey witnesses the exchange and becomes dismayed upon its culmination. He seizes the opportunity to confront Austin as Sirak exits:

CAREY: Laid it on kind of strong, didn't you?
AUSTIN: Why waltz with him, Don? He knows every move we've made.
CAREY: Look, Jim. I've never interfered in the editorial end and I don't
    intend to now, but can't you take it just a little easy.
AUSTIN: Thought we were in on this together.
CAREY: We were ... and we still are. But ... well this business has gotten a
    whole lot bigger than just putting the needle to Chief Gillette.
AUSTIN: How?
CAREY: How? Why you practically accused Sirak of murder!
A phone call from Harding briefly interrupts the conversation, as news of
    Fabretti's arrival at the warehouse is delivered. Shortly thereafter, Austin
    prepares to depart and addresses Carey in the process:
AUSTIN: Fabretti just pulled in!
CAREY: Jim, I hope you know what you're doing.
AUSTIN: Well, I've got some kind of an idea.

CAREY: I know, but ... what's all this gonna get us except a big headache, maybe.

AUSTIN: Don, would you rather take that ad from Sirak?

CAREY: I didn't say that. I ... I only ... Well, take it easy. Will ya? That's all I ask.

AUSTIN: Stop borrowing trouble! Will ya? Look, before I do anything, before I run one line of type, we'll talk about it. How's that?

CAREY (smiling): Fair enough.

Carey, however, slowly begins to lose confidence in his partner. Later, his suspicions are confirmed. Austin, without consulting Carey, prepares an open letter to Gillette, stating, "Kennington has not merely been threatened by gangsters, it has already been taken over by gangsters." The partnership between the two reaches a boiling point when an ultimatum is presented. "If you're gonna go on beating your head against a brick wall, somebody is gonna have to buy somebody out," Carey declares, but Austin's battle is not with him. Shortly before Austin departs town with Marge, he encounters Sirak one last time, and again, an attempt to use advertising as leverage is made. Sirak is intent on making his point. Austin then concludes, "I can take your advertising, or I can deal with the hoods that Fabretti's got parked outside my house." It does not take long for Austin to reach a decision, as he ultimately flees the captive city.

Maurice Zuberano, an illustrator and storyboard artist, collaborated with Wise on multiple occasions. Zuberano's industry debut, albeit uncredited, transpired during the production of *Citizen Kane* (1941). He was partly responsible for developing the film's sketches and graphics. *The Captive City*, however, marked the first time Zuberano became a credited crew member of a Robert Wise film. As a result, the two went on to enjoy a special camaraderie, which lasted professionally until the production of *Star Trek: The Motion Picture* (1979). *The Captive City* is also noteworthy due to Senator Kefauver's contribution. He was compensated handsomely but requested that his entire salary be donated to the Cordell Hull Foundation for World Peace, an organization named after the former U.S. Secretary of State.

Wise's film of corruption and organized crime premiered in New York on March 26, 1952. Kefauver remained in office until his death in 1963, and although he left behind quite a legacy, it was his brief cameo within the closing minutes of *The Captive City* that became ingrained in the minds of theatergoers. Kefauver's moving speech to the American public essentially underlined that "stamping out crime is not just a national problem; it is largely a local matter, a local responsibility. Cut off the crime dollar at its source in your own town, and the syndicate will shrivel and die. But it's up to you."

The Captive City was filmed entirely on location in Reno, Nevada.

15
SOMETHING FOR THE BIRDS

(PRODUCED AND RELEASED 1952)

"Love yourself first, and everything else falls into line. You really have to love yourself to get anything done in this world."
- Lucille Ball

Less than a month after the nationwide release of *The Captive City* (1952), Robert Wise returned to Twentieth Century Fox to begin production of *Old Sailors Never Die*, a comedy later retitled *Something for the Birds*. Alvin M. Josephy, a newfound colleague of Wise's, took part in crafting the film's original story, which pertains to an attractive conservationist and her enduring resolve to withstand a smitten Washington lobbyist by any means necessary. I.A.L. Diamond, the writer and producer who would one day become famous for his collaborations with Billy Wilder, also contributed his ideas to the script. Yet, it was the casting of the esteemed Edmund Gwenn as a major character of the narrative that made headlines. Two years earlier, he captured the nation's attention with his portrayal of The Skipper Miller, a clever swindler, in Twentieth Century Fox's production of *Mister 880* (1950), and Gwenn's role in *Something for the Birds* was expected to be very similar in nature. Hence,

Wise's film was advertised with a tagline that declared, "MR. 880 IS BACK – 881 times phonier!"

In Washington, D.C., Johnnie Adams (Gwenn) serves as a devoted engraver of Foster and Sons, a stationery business. He frequently receives orders to print invitations for lavish events. Sometimes, Adams will purloin duplicate copies in order to attend such events posing as a retired naval commander. He is affectionately referred to as "Admiral" by all of the partygoers who have grown accustomed to his presence through the years. One evening, Adams encounters Anne Richards (Patricia Neal) at a reception. She, too, is an uninvited guest of the party. Anne represents the Society for the Preservation of the California Condor (SPCC). Her objective is to mingle with the guests in hopes of making a connection with the Department of the Interior. Natural gas has recently been discovered on the nesting grounds of the species, and a bill in congress aims to enact a law that will allow for drilling to take place on such grounds. Anne is determined to ensure the bill's defeat. She is introduced by Adams to Steve Bennett (Victor Mature), a well-connected attorney and lobbyist who becomes quite taken with her.

The Continental Gas Company is discovered to be the sole organization to benefit from such drilling. When Anne discovers the organization to be a client of Bennett's, she prepares to return to California, but Adams intervenes and convinces her to stay. Together, the two work to garner votes against the bill. Mr. Taylor (Wilton Graff), the vice president of Continental Gas, becomes privy to Adams's intentions and, following a brief investigation, exposes him as a fraud. Bennett appears before the senate committee on lobbying and calls for the testimonies of both Adams and Anne. The latter seizes the opportunity to promote the condor, a symbol of vanishing natural resources, as the greatest challenge to the conservation of the country. Bennett subsequently warns a variety of bird societies against the bill's passage. Much to Anne's delight, Continental Gas agrees to drill outside of the condors' sanctuary. She learns of Bennett's involvement and, with the help of an exonerated Adams, proposes marriage to the otherwise enamored lobbyist.

Victor Mature.

Immediately following the opening credits of *Something for the Birds*, Wise presents an image of the Washington Monument, thus revealing the nation's capital to be the setting of the narrative, but perhaps unbeknownst to those viewing the film for the first time, the locale will not change. "Washington makes a man pretty jumpy," Bennett tells Adams shortly after their characters are introduced to the audience, and his words essentially set the tone for the growing turbulence that is to come. At one point, a congressman questions Anne in regard to her objective:

CONGRESSMAN: Now, tell me just one thing. What good are these, uh, these birds doing?
ANNE: Well, what good is the Washington Monument doing? But you wouldn't suggest tearing it down, would you?

She is quick-witted in the face of adversity. It is no wonder that Bennett and Adams take a liking to her as the three are initially together at the home of Della Rice (Gladys Hurlbut), a Washington socialite known for her lavish parties. The guest lists of such parties are always composed of the city's elite, especially politicians, but one such guest is Roy Patterson (Larry Keating), a radio journalist with a knack for making trouble. He comes face-to-face with Bennett and blatantly refers to him as "a pernicious influence around Washington." Adams observes the exchange and cannot make sense of the situation. Bennett nevertheless remains undeterred by Patterson's remarks; the latter eventually departs the scene. Bennett then proceeds to change the subject and demands to know why Adams has never asked any favors of him, but the request for "a good secondhand refrigerator" is subsequently made. Adams is not looking for anything fancy. Bennett therefore prepares to fulfill the request. Enter Mr. Lund (John Brown) of Northern Electric, an appliance manufacturer. He is a client of Bennett's firm and is willing to donate a dozen refrigerators on the condition "they get in the hands of the right people." Adams soon receives what he desires. His request, however, ultimately triggers an unfortunate chain reaction of events fueled by Patterson, Taylor of Continental Gas, and the United States Senate.

As Roy Patterson's radio program exposes Bennett as a "pressure boy" who distributes free refrigerators around town, a listening Anne is taken aback by a revelation of the broadcast. It is at such a point of the narrative that she becomes privy to Bennett's affiliation with Continental Gas. He attempts to rectify the situation, claiming he was unaware of his firm's connection to the merciless corporation. Anne, however, believes Bennett is simply out to protect his own interests. Ironically, Continental Gas became affiliated with the firm while he was out of town. A colleague, Bill Caldwell, originally obtained the account. Upon Bennett's return to Washington, a reversal of sorts transpired. Caldwell departed for Florida, and as a result, Bennett inherited the Continental Gas account along with a series of additional problems. Anne begins to lose faith and desires to be free of the "Washington rat race." She intends to return home to California. Consequently, Adams comes to Bennett's defense and convinces Anne to stay. His loyalty is naturally unquestioning, but around the time of Patterson's aforementioned revelation, Adams shows remorse for making the request of Bennett for the refrigerator.[19] Curiously enough, such a request was made on behalf of another.

Edmund Gwenn.

Mrs. J. L. Chadwick (Madge Blake), a neighbor of Adams's who desires to own a refrigerator, intrigues Taylor of Continental Gas, thus prompting the latter to act on his suspicions and subsequently reveal a harsh truth. A man many believe to be a prestigious admiral of the U.S. Navy is unmasked as nothing but a humble engraver of invitations, and such exposure is attributed to his support of Anne's cause. The trouble begins when Taylor, in search of an explanation, confronts Bennett at the latter's office:

---

19 Although Adams claims to have not heard the radio broadcast, he nevertheless remains uneasy.

TAYLOR: What's going on here, Bennett? I thought you had this drilling bill sewed up!

BENNETT: Well, you never know until all the votes are counted.

TAYLOR: We've been getting some very disturbing reports in New York. Who's Admiral Adams?

BENNETT: He's one of our more solid citizens. Why?

TAYLOR: My sources in congress inform me that he's lined up a dangerous number of votes against us!

Taylor becomes intent on investigating Adams and seeks the help of Bennett, who wants nothing to do with the matter. Mr. Duncan (Camillo Guercio), a partner of the law firm, suggests that Mac (Joan Miller), a secretary, should be able to provide a lead:

DUNCAN: Oh, Mac. Where does Admiral Adams live?

MAC: Aw...let's not start on that again! After what I went through trying to get a refrigerator to him....

DUNCAN: Was he in on that refrigerator deal?

MAC: Well, it wasn't for himself. It was for some woman he knew. I can give you her address.

TAYLOR: Ah...lady friend, eh? Now we're getting someplace. Where there's smoke, there's fire.

Later, as Adams arrives home, Mrs. Chadwick emerges from her room to greet him. An inquisitive Taylor has come and gone, and Mrs. Chadwick has innocently exposed Adams's true identity, declaring to Taylor that her longtime neighbor could not be a retired admiral due to his employment with Foster and Sons "for over thirty years." Alas, the damage is done, but Taylor is simply the beginning of Adams's problems.

A special committee, composed of select members of the United States Senate, upgrades its otherwise quiet investigation of lobbying to a full-scale probe upon learning that certain people have been receiving free refrigerators from Bennett. The scenario is somewhat reflective of an America of the 1950s. Senator Beecham (Emmett Vogan), an outspoken member of the committee, becomes intent on exploiting the imperfections of lobbying while addressing his colleagues:

BEECHAM: This is too grave a matter to be handled in the routine way. Now, I suggest we exercise the utmost discretion until everyone concerned has been subpoenaed. Then, we blow the lid off and go straight on television!

Throughout Wise's film, lobbyists are often portrayed negatively. At one point, Bennett amusingly makes reference to those who have declared lobbying to be "a parasitic occupation." Nevertheless, it was legalized with the enactment of the Federal Regulation Act of 1946, but Beecham intends to press his accusations. Joseph McCarthy, a United States Senator from Wisconsin, became notorious for his investigations into communism. Beginning in 1950, he engaged in the practice of making allegations, without substantial evidence, against prominent figures. Like the fictional Beecham, McCarthy relished the opportunity to conduct his congressional hearings on national television, and although lobbying and communism are completely separate concepts, a distinct similarity between the personalities of both individuals is clearly evident. By 1954, the general public began to lose faith in McCarthy. In regard to *Something for the Birds*, Beecham, too, is unable to win the support of the people. Adams eventually testifies before the committee to plead his case. In the aftermath, all is forgiven, but more important, perhaps, is that Anne accomplishes what she desires, as the bill is ultimately defeated.

Something for the Birds premiered in October of 1952. It is the first comedy to be directed by Wise. In addition to Alvin M. Josephy and I.A.L. Diamond, Joseph Petracca and Boris Ingster contributed their ideas to the film's story. Comedy is the most difficult of genres in regard to writing fiction. Fortunately for Wise, he had the opportunity to collaborate with some of the industry's finest. Ingster, in particular, had been a Hollywood stalwart for years.[20] Along with the film's script, the onscreen performances of Victor Mature and Patricia Neal are indeed memorable, but special attention must also be granted to the narrative's supporting players. Archer MacDonald, appearing as T. Courtney Lemmer, one of the "outstanding authorities" on bird calls, occasionally steals the show with his impressions of mockingbirds, swallow-tailed kites, and the like. Sadly, he did not live a full life. On November 4, 1955, MacDonald, depressed over his recent divorce, checked himself into the famous Hotel del Coronado near San Diego and committed suicide with an overdose of sleeping pills. At just thirty years of age, a promising life and career was tragically cut short. MacDonald's performance in *Something for the Birds* remains one of his most inspiring, and as far as Wise was concerned, his time with the young actor, although brief, was particularly worthwhile.

---

20 Boris Ingster's direction of *Stranger on the Third Floor* (1940) remains an extraordinary achievement in the annals of film noir. In modern times, however, Ingster is remembered primarily as a screenwriter and television producer.

16
DESTINATION GOBI

(PRODUCED 1952, RELEASED 1953)

> "My soul is full of longing
> for the secret of the sea,
> and the heart of the great ocean
> sends a thrilling pulse through me."
> - Henry Wadsworth Longfellow, *The Secret of the Sea*

On July 23, 1952, Robert Wise began production of his first Technicolor film. *Collier's*, the popular weekly magazine, had earlier featured a story pertaining to the Gobi Desert and World War II. The writer, Edmund G. Love, declared his narrative to be based on real-life events. Meteorologists of the United States Navy, stationed in the desert during the war, offered ninety saddles to a Mongolian tribe as a gesture of good will. Consequently, the natives offered to support the Americans in their fight against Japanese forces. Twentieth Century Fox acquired the rights to Love's story and established a working title of *Ninety Saddles for Kengtu*. The studio, however, encountered problems. Rumors suggest the working title was changed to *Sixty Saddles for Gobi*, as Twentieth Century Fox was unable to acquire ninety saddles. The production gradually transpired over the course of several weeks, and as Wise prepared his film, ultimately titled *Destination Gobi*, for its release to the public, he included a foreword which states, "In the Navy records in Washington, there is an obscure entry reading 'Saddles for Gobi.' This film is based on the story behind that entry - one of the strangest stories of World War II."

The *USS Enterprise*.

Sam McHale (Richard Widmark), Chief Bosun's Mate of the aircraft carrier *USS Enterprise*, is sent to the Gobi Desert in Mongolia as part of a weather unit for SACO (Sino-American Combined Operations).[21] Following the passage of several months, he and his men encounter Kengtu (Murvyn Vye), the chief of a Mongol tribe. The natives take an avid interest in several of the goods belonging to the Americans. McHale arranges for the U.S. Army to ship a generous supply of saddles to the area. Upon the arrival of such saddles, he offers them to Kengtu's tribe in exchange for protection from the Japanese cavalry, which lurks nearby. Shortly thereafter, however, an air raid attack by enemy forces destroys most of the camp, and Lieutenant Commander Hobart Wyatt (Russell Collins), head of the unit, is killed. McHale assumes command. Kengtu and his followers disappear from the

---

21 *Star Trek: The Motion Picture* (1979) is another of Robert Wise's films to feature a vessel known as the *USS Enterprise*.

area without notice. Figuring Japanese planes will return to finish the job, McHale decides to lead his men on a trek to the Pacific Ocean. They encounter Kengtu en route and demand that he provide some form of compensation for the saddles, but the goods are abruptly returned to the Americans. Yin "Nose Ring" Tang (Edgar Barrier), a merchant, trades four of his camels for the saddles. He then accompanies the men on the following leg of their journey. One night during a layover, Nose Ring attempts to rob the Americans, but Kengtu comes to the rescue and foils the attempt. McHale returns the saddles to the Mongol chief as the latter ensures safe passage to the sea.

In China, however, Kengtu reluctantly turns the unit over to Japanese soldiers. McHale and his men are then taken to a prison on the shores of the Pacific. They are nevertheless able to escape with the help of Wali-Akhun (Leonard Strong), Kengtu's underling. The Americans commandeer a Chinese junk but are pursued by the Japanese. A battle at sea ensues. Although McHale's navy emerges victorious, Wilbur "Coney" Cohen (Darryl Hickman), a younger officer, is wounded and dies. American planes successfully locate the junk, and days later, the war concludes.

As *Destination Gobi* begins, Sol Kaplan's score features a medley of traditional music of the Far East, but not before it presents the opening notes of "Anchors Aweigh", the theme of the U.S. Navy.[22] The patriotic tune recurs on several occasions throughout the narrative. At one point, "Anchors Aweigh" introduces a noteworthy series of events, as arrangements are made for the saddles to be shipped overseas. During the sequence, as Wise transitions from the Navy Department in Washington to the U.S. Army's Office of the Quartermaster General, a change in music is evident as "The Army Goes Rolling Along" becomes the featured tune. The saddles eventually arrive in Mongolia, and to accompany the cargo plane's approach, the familiar notes of "Wild Blue Yonder", the theme of the U.S. Army Air Forces, are heard.[23]

---

22 Sol Kaplan shared certain responsibilities with Alfred Newman, who is credited with the film's musical direction.

Through his montage, Wise sets the stage for perhaps the most important aspect of the narrative. Upon delivery of the saddles, a rapport between McHale and Kengtu is established, but their relationship undergoes several crises of trust. Nevertheless, McHale's faith in his Mongolian counterpart ultimately proves beneficial, as Kengtu's abandonment of the camp, rejection of the saddles, and capitulation to Japanese forces inadvertently leads the Americans to the sea.

Following the Mongols' desertion of the camp, McHale is reminded that his true destination is not the Gobi Desert, but instead, the Pacific Ocean. A sudden vision becomes reminiscent of an opening image of the film. As the men sleep in the camp's sole remaining tent, a restless McHale emerges at sunrise to ponder the unit's next move. The so-called 1st Mongolian Cavalry has disappeared, and the Navy's presence in the area appears futile. McHale stares at the horizon as yet another rendition of "Anchors Aweigh" becomes audible. Lieutenant Commander Wyatt's makeshift grave dominates the foreground, and beyond the burial site is a cloudy, blue sky.

As Kaplan's score continues, McHale experiences a revelation. The path to prosperity lies to the east. Earlier in the film, following the opening credits, Wise begins his narrative with the image of a bluish-grey sky occupied by massive clouds as the *USS Enterprise* sails into Pearl Harbor. "Anchors Aweigh" is presented, and the on-screen image essentially defines McHale's purpose in life. "I ain't worth two cents unless I got a deck under my feet," he declares to Captain Gates (Willis Bouchey) at SACO headquarters. Later, upon McHale's aforementioned revelation in the desert, he returns to the tent to awaken his men. Orders are then given to pull out of the area, and confusion abounds. Walter Landers (Casey Adams), a member of the unit, openly questions McHale's intentions:[24]

---

23 The events of Destination Gobi transpire from November of 1944 to September of 1945. When the U.S. Army Air Forces became the U.S. Air Force and was therefore established as a separate division of the armed forces on September 18, 1947, "Wild Blue Yonder" remained as the branch's cherished theme.

24 Casey Adams was born Max Showalter in 1917 in Caldwell, Kansas.

LANDERS: For Pete's sake, Mac! Are you crazy? Where are we going?
McHALE: Where sailors belong! To the sea!

Shortly thereafter, the unit departs. An arduous trek through the desert follows. McHale and company eventually encounter the Mongols at an oasis. Kengtu does not offer much of an explanation regarding his tribe's desertion. "You didn't forget to take the saddles with you," McHale chides, and similar to the Mongol chief's earlier abandonment of the camp, his following actions are altogether unexpected.

Kengtu abruptly returns the saddles only to again desire the coveted goods shortly thereafter, during which time McHale seizes the opportunity to seek safe passage to the sea. Nose Ring's eventual appearance ultimately works to the advantage of both the Mongols and the Americans. Upon arrival at the oasis, McHale seeks horses, supplies, and guidance from Kengtu. The latter appears with Tomec (Rodolfo Acosta), a subordinate with particular disdain for the Americans. Kengtu then opts to confer with his fellow tribesmen, as the decision to help McHale and company is pondered. The Americans wait as "congress [remains] in session." Jenkins (Don Taylor) and Elwood Halsey (Martin Milner), two of McHale's men, along with Landers, attribute the delay to Tomec:

HALSEY: What's taken 'em so long?
LANDERS: Probably a filibuster from Tomec.
JENKINS: I'm gettin' a bad case of Tomec poisoning!

A decision is eventually reached, and the Mongols express their feelings not through words, but instead, through the return of the saddles. Most appear reluctant to discard the treasured goods, but Tomec thrusts his saddle towards the feet of the Americans in disgust. McHale prepares to strike but then thinks better of it. Perhaps, Tomec was the one to influence Kengtu's decision. Yet, despite such influence, the Mongol leader takes notice as Nose Ring happens upon the scene to propose a trade with the Americans. The saddles are subsequently exchanged for four camels and safe passage "to the next water hole." A visibly concerned Kengtu, who has observed the transaction, eventually leads his men from the area.

Later, Nose Ring makes the poor choice of robbing the Americans as they sleep, but Kengtu returns to thwart the attack, declaring to McHale, "Yin Tang, bad man! Cheat Mongols! Cheat Navy! Sell camels many times over! Same camels!" In proving that his judge of character is far superior to that of Tomec's, the chief redeems himself with the hopes of reacquiring the saddles for his tribe. "Kengtu, you just help us reach the sea, you can have the saddles! And sixty beautiful saddle blankets to go with 'em," McHale says. Prior to departing for the coast, the Mongols provide the Americans with clothing as a means of avoiding further detection by the Japanese. Imperial forces, however, prove difficult to deceive.

As Kengtu capitulates to the Japanese upon arrival in the Chinese village of Sangchien, the Americans are sent to a prisoner-of-war camp and, coincidentally, the Pacific coast. McHale becomes angry with the Mongol leader, but the circumstances leading to the former's imprisonment are not indicative of any form of betrayal. Prior to entering China, Kengtu issues a stern warning that danger lies ahead, as the nation is full of Japanese soldiers. The Mongols and Americans then arrive at the outskirts of Sangchien, and McHale, optimistic because the Chinese are allies of the United States, wishes to enter. Kengtu, however, is hesitant and deems it best to travel around the city. He nevertheless respects McHale's request and presses directly forward with the group. It is not long before Japanese troops are discovered to be permanently stationed in Sangchien, and the saddles, bearing the imprint of "USA," are uncovered. It then becomes a matter of time before McHale's unit is caught.

Kengtu again appears as one with malicious intentions as he leads the Americans into a trap, but he is a step ahead of the others. The American uniform of the late Wyatt was earlier taken by the Mongols, and as McHale's unit endures its incarceration along the shores of the Pacific, Kengtu orders Wali-Akhun to wear the uniform. Japanese forces subsequently encounter Wali-Akhun and believe him to be an American soldier. He is then transported to the same camp as McHale's unit, but unbeknownst to the Japanese, Wali-Akhun has smuggled wire cutters into the prison. McHale and company seek an ideal opportunity to escape. Rain ensues, and a dumbfounded Landers, who considers himself to be one of the foremost experts in the field of meteorology, claims, "Now, how could Kengtu have predicted it? I didn't even know it would rain." At the time of the so-called jailbreak, McHale has twice been deceived by Kengtu. Nevertheless, he continues to have faith in the Mongol leader, partly because he is desperate to escape to the sea. Later, following a key conversation aboard the junk, their relationship reaches a turning point for the better:

McHALE: We thought you tricked us.
KENGTU: No trick friends. Trick Japs.

Throughout the narrative, Kengtu appears fickle, but he usually has an ulterior motive. In time, McHale becomes privy to Kengtu's agenda. There is conflict in all relationships. Consequently, McHale and Kengtu are able to determine an agreeable pattern for how to resolve such conflict, and hence, Wise's picture concludes shortly thereafter.

"The role of Frank Swenson was the first actual part that I ever had in a film," Earl Holliman said regarding his appearance in *Destination Gobi*. "I had done one line in a picture called *Scared Stiff* with Martin and Lewis, having played an elevator operator. That was my introduction into film. I also appeared in *The Girls of Pleasure Island*. My agent, Phil Gersh, handled Robert Wise and a lot of other big directors. One day, Mr. Gersh took me to Twentieth Century Fox, and I was cast in Mr. Wise's film a short time later. The casting people liked my haircut. They didn't even ask me to read for the role.

"Bob Wise was a wonderful guy. I've worked with some great directors, from George Stevens to John Sturges. With Mr. Wise, we were on location, staying in Reno, Nevada. Most days, the cast and crew was transported over thirty miles to the Paiute Reservation. The natives filled the roles of the

Mongol extras. We also went to Fallon, Nevada, because of the sand dunes located there, but our time on the reservation was particularly memorable. At the end of each successful take, Bob Wise would say, 'Get a lily.' It referred to an object used for the printers, so that the editors would have proper standardization of color when cutting the film. Therefore, whenever the cast and crew heard Mr. Wise use the term 'lily,' we instantly knew the take was a success. During one particular moment of the film, the unit is bombed by Japanese planes. It was a very complex scene to shoot, and after one of the takes, I remember overhearing a Paiute teenage girl remark to her friend, 'I hope someone's getting a lily!'

"Dick Widmark was the first movie star who ever offered words of encouragement regarding my acting style. He took me aside one day and suggested what I should and should not do when performing in a take. Widmark said some really nice things, at one point remarking, 'Just don't become a night club actor.' After *Destination Gobi*, we ended up playing brothers in *Broken Lance*. Then, a few years later, Widmark prepared to do a picture for Paramount called *The Trap*. His on-screen brother was to be played by Arthur Kennedy, who bowed out for unknown reasons. Widmark then arranged for me to fill the vacant role, which marked the second time I played the part of his brother, and the third time I worked with him.

"One day back at the studio, we all had lunch at the Fox commissary. After the meal, I offered Bob Wise a stick of gum. He politely declined, claiming to be on a diet. I openly questioned his decision. Mr. Wise then proceeded to tell me that there were eight calories in a stick of gum and it wouldn't be right to accept a piece. I suppose he was watching his weight, but overall, Bob Wise was a gentleman. He was easy to work with, and he was also very helpful throughout the entire experience."

Approximately one hour into the film, as McHale and his men proceed to don the clothing of the Mongols in order to elude Japanese forces, Paul Sabatello, an outspoken member of the unit, refuses to comply, declaring, "Anybody wants this uniform, they gotta take it off of me!" Physical force therefore becomes a necessity. Wise then dissolves to a shot of the defeated Sabatello, whose face is not immediately visible. As the camera slowly pans upward to reveal the raw look of anguish, Sol Kaplan's score undergoes a departure of sorts, as the featured track resembles the two-and-a-half octave solo clarinet glissando opening of George Gershwin's "Rhapsody in Blue". The scene, however, is memorable more for its featured performer than it is for its music. Ross Bagdasarian, the actor cast in the role of Sabatello, enjoyed great fame in the years following the production of *Destination Gobi*. He is best remembered as the creator of *Alvin and the Chipmunks*. Through his revered animated musical trio, Bagdasarian reaped the benefits of the group's successes from its inception in 1958 until his death in 1972.

In regard to *Destination Gobi*, Bagdasarian's character, as well as several others, is a welcome source of comic relief. Humor, in essence, became a necessity even when the cameras were not rolling. While on location, the weather was unbearably hot. Transporting the massive Technicolor cameras from one location to the next, in addition to keeping the cast and crew at ease, often became challenging. Nevertheless, Wise and company saw the production through to its end. In retrospect, he was quite satisfied with his film, suggesting that it "was intended more as a comedy than an overly serious drama, trying to tell another part of the war that went on globally." Principal photography wrapped on September 2, 1952. The production of additional sequences began the following month. At the time, however, Wise began to mentally prepare for his next feature, which, similar to *Destination Gobi*, takes place during World War II, but instead of the Pacific Theater, the story is set against the backdrop of the war's North African campaign.

17
THE DESERT RATS

(PRODUCED 1952, RELEASED 1953)

> "Courage is the price that life exacts for granting peace."
> - Amelia Earhart

The title of Twentieth Century Fox's *The Desert Fox* (1951), a World War II drama directed by Henry Hathaway, is a reference to Erwin Rommel, the popular German commander whose advanced desert warfare tactics earned him the clever moniker. Despite his affiliation with the Nazi party, he was regarded by some as a humane individual. Rommel spent most of the war in North Africa, leading German and Italian forces against the British and Australians. His Afrika Korps often took prisoners but was relatively fair regarding its treatment of such prisoners. Hence, Hathaway sought an emphatic depiction of Rommel, a portrayal of which select critics were not appreciative.

The following year, Twentieth Century Fox responded to the criticism by announcing its upcoming production of *The Desert Rats*. The film's script, written by Richard Murphy, was loosely based on the Siege of Tobruk. During the conflict, Tobruk, a Libyan port, withstood months of bloodshed. German forces were unrelenting in their quest for control of the city, but a significant percentage of Tobruk's defenders, the Australians, were just as tenacious. Their enemies, often flustered, ultimately referred to them as rats. Hathaway set forth to direct *The Desert Rats* but withdrew during the project's early stages for unknown reasons. Fortunately for the studio, Robert Wise was available and ready to work.[25]

In 1941, in the Libyan Desert of North Africa, a majority of British forces retreat from the Germans as Field Marshal Rommel (James Mason) sets his sights on the Suez Canal, the key to the Middle East. Standing in his way is a tiny garrison of Allied soldiers isolated in Tobruk. Captain Tammy MacRoberts (Richard Burton), along with a reserve group of Australian troops, is sent to the area. He discovers Tom Bartlett (Robert Newton), his former schoolmaster from many years ago, to be among the infantrymen. The garrison is committed to holding Tobruk for two months, but some anticipate Rommel will overtake the port within a week. MacRoberts and company are therefore ordered to go on the offensive. A plan to attack an enemy ammunition dump is devised. Bartlett requests that he accompany the squad on its mission, but MacRoberts, intent on keeping Bartlett out of harm's way, decides against such a course of action. Using captured Italian trucks, the Allies pose as enemy forces in order to infiltrate the dump.

MacRoberts is subsequently wounded and captured during the attack. He eventually comes face-to-face with Rommel, who downplays Tobruk's significance. MacRoberts, however, reminds his counterpart of the prized Suez, as it cannot be taken without crushing such a "rathole." As MacRoberts is transported to his cell, Allied warplanes strike. Amidst the chaos, he is able to escape and return to Tobruk. Rommel resumes his attack with heavy shelling of the area. The garrison withstands the siege, ultimately holding the port for an additional two months. An army of Allied forces is rebuilt in Egypt, and it advances towards Tobruk. When the relief column does not arrive at the expected time, many grow impatient. MacRoberts considers pulling the men out of the area. He and Bartlett spar over the issue, but relief eventually arrives, and after two hundred and forty-two days, the siege comes to an end.

---

25 Michael Rennie, star of Robert Wise's *The Day the Earth Stood Still* (1951), narrated both *The Desert Fox* (1951) and *The Desert Rats*.

Richard Burton.

Upon escaping from the Germans, Sergeant Blue Smith (Chips Rafferty), who along with MacRoberts managed to break free following the attack on the ammunition dump, declares, "I'd give my stripe for a mouthful of water." The scene is similar to the opening minutes of *Destination Gobi* (1953), Wise's previous film. Chief Bosun's Mate Sam McHale struggles to acclimate to the vast desert. In narration, he remarks, "I'd have given half my retirement pay for just one whiff of salt water," but it gradually becomes clear to audiences that *Destination Gobi* features a relatively lighthearted narrative which is not at all similar to that of *The Desert Rats*.

Wise begins *The Desert Rats* with an extraordinary battle sequence set to Leigh Harline's triumphant score, and as the film's background music continues, Wise adds a touch of comic relief as soldiers in foxholes toot select instruments of the brass and woodwind families. Following the opening credits, however, the narrative assumes a tone more serious than that of *Destination Gobi*. *The Desert Rats* features many casualties, one of which is the death of Harry Carstairs (Charles Tingwell), a well-liked Australian lieutenant. The character, albeit a supporting one, is the most important of the narrative. Carstairs is one of the few Aussies to support MacRoberts's command. Furthermore, his overall impact on the captain is extraordinary, but it is perhaps the impression he makes on Bartlett that is most significant.

Lieutenant Carstairs supports MacRoberts's order to establish a complete field of fire against Rommel's army and defends such a strategy in the captain's absence. Unlike most other Australians, he is not hasty in his criticism. As the Allies prepare for battle, MacRoberts seeks an update from Carstairs:

MacROBERTS: What's your field of fire, Mr. Carstairs?
CARSTAIRS (gesturing ahead with a sweep of his arm): 480, sir.
MacROBERTS: Better clear back here for a full circle.
CARSTAIRS (pointing in opposite direction): Behind us?
MacROBERTS: Behind you. The Afrika Korps is not committed to frontal attack.
CARSTAIRS: Uh ... yes, sir.

MacRoberts departs shortly thereafter. A soldier's complaint pertaining to the "rough side" of the captain's tongue follows, but Carstairs pays no attention, instead suggesting that MacRoberts is correct about the Afrika Korps "getting in behind us." During the ensuing battle, Captain Currie (Michael Pate), an Australian officer, is wounded. Stranded in the open field, he finds himself directly in the line of fire. Carstairs takes notice and leaves his entrenchment to attempt a rescue. Alas, it is futile, as Currie succumbs to his wounds and dies, but MacRoberts, livid because Carstairs left his position exposed to the Germans, arranges for the lieutenant to be court-martialed upon the battle's conclusion. However, he eventually withdraws the charges. Later, Carstairs approaches MacRoberts to express his appreciation:

CARSTAIRS: I wanted to, uh, thank you for dropping those charges.

MacROBERTS: Don't thank me. Thank the general. I had nothing to do with it.

CARSTAIRS: The copy of your letter's in the company files.

MacROBERTS: Oh. Well, I could have made a mistake.

CARSTAIRS: Maybe, you did. But the thanks still goes.

Carstairs departs. MacRoberts, in general, stresses that those who are killed or badly wounded in battle must be left behind. To do otherwise would simply endanger the patrol. Mick (Ben Wright), an Australian, questions such a strategy, remarking, "If a bloke cops one, you flaming well leave him there. You reckon [MacRoberts] would be so free with English troops?" Yet, Carstairs, in contrast to most of his fellow Aussies, is not quick to jump to conclusions about the captain.[26] Instead, he is patient and keeps an open mind. Regarding the dismissed charges, Carstairs took the time to seek evidence, a letter to the high command, proving that MacRoberts was responsible. Oddly enough, in light of recent events, the captain later does the unexpected.

As Allied forces raid the ammunition dump, MacRoberts is compelled to aid the wounded, thereby contradicting his own philosophy while simultaneously following the example of Carstairs, who also remains on the scene to offer his help. Of the two, one is perhaps more fickle than the other. Explosives are planted throughout the dump and then wired to a dynamite detonator. A soldier prepares to push the detonator's handle in order for an electrical current to finish the job, but he is shot as the Allies prepare to escape in their captured Italian trucks. MacRoberts takes notice and leaves his vehicle to not only help the wounded soldier, but to also detonate the explosives. He, too, is shot. A loyal Carstairs then leaps from a moving truck, races to the captain's position, and begins shooting at the enemy as a means of providing cover.

---

26 Upon dismissing the charges against Carstairs, MacRoberts assumes the temporary rank of lieutenant colonel. Nevertheless, to avoid confusion, he will continue to be referred to as his original rank of captain.

MacRoberts chides him for disobeying orders, but Carstairs, in the heat of the moment, tells the captain to "shut up and push the ruddy plunger!"

The objective is immediately fulfilled, resulting in multiple explosions throughout the dump. MacRoberts resumes his escape, only to discover that Carstairs has been killed by enemy fire. The captain's earlier attempt to save the wounded soldier contradicts his general beliefs, and as a result of such measures, he is captured by the Germans. Yet, MacRoberts's actions are an act of desperation, as it is imperative for the explosives to be detonated. Although it is out of character for the captain to leave his position when fellow soldiers are in need, such is not the case with Carstairs. The latter has no intention of being disloyal to his superiors. Such motives are instead attributed to a characteristic of much greater significance.

The attribute of courage becomes a topic of conversation between MacRoberts and Bartlett, who describes Carstairs as "honest, fair to his men, and for a young man, very understanding." A background tune, emanating from the harmonica of an unseen soldier, offers a candid reflection of the former schoolmaster's demeanor. As MacRoberts and Bartlett converse, the musical notes of "Greensleeves", a song pertaining to the primary color, are heard. Through the years, scholars have sought to understand the tune through various interpretations, some of which are more far-fetched than others. The word "green," however, occasionally refers to inexperience, and in *The Desert Rats*, examples are evident.

Upon the film's beginning, the general (Robert Douglas) makes reference to a reserve company of soldiers, declaring, "Green or not, I've got to put them into the line," and at one point, MacRoberts tells him, "These troops have been bloodied, but they're still green." Regarding the aforementioned conversation between MacRoberts and Bartlett, the latter speaks openly of his own consternation and inexperience. "You don't know much about real fear, Tammy. Maybe, it comes with age or…the bottle. You don't know what it is to be a coward, really a coward," he says. Bartlett essentially admires Carstairs because the lieutenant is everything he is not, and because of such admiration, in addition to the power of persuasion, MacRoberts surprisingly dismisses the charges that call for Carstairs to be court-martialed. The episode bears the utmost significance to the narrative's outcome. Had Carstairs been court-martialed, he would not have been present during the attack on the ammunition dump, and MacRoberts, in short, most likely would have been killed.

Production of *The Desert Rats* began on November 11, 1952, and wrapped approximately six weeks later. It then premiered in Los Angeles on May 6, 1953. James Mason was hailed by critics for his portrayal of Erwin Rommel. With *The Desert Rats*, he was reprising a role first originated in *The Desert Fox*. A difference between both performances, however, quickly became evident to audiences upon the release of Wise's film. In *The Desert Fox*, Mason's familiar British accent is featured throughout the narrative. Yet, in *The Desert Rats*, his onscreen persona speaks with a thick, German accent. In addition, for a majority of his scenes, all dialogue is presented in Rommel's native language.[27] An exception transpires approximately one hour into the film. As Rommel finally encounters MacRoberts, English is the featured language of their conversation.

Due to the backlash of some critics over *The Desert Fox* and Henry Hathaway's emphatic depiction of Rommel, studio executives most likely demanded that a majority of Mason's dialogue, as presented in Wise's film, be comprised of the German language. Nevertheless, despite any controversy, both films ultimately appealed to audiences worldwide.[28] Furthermore, to add a touch of authenticity to *The Desert Rats*, newsreel footage of World War II is featured throughout the picture, but perhaps a scene of the utmost significance transpires approximately a half hour into the narrative. Following the death of Captain Currie, the Australians, positioned in their entrenchment, express

---

27 Wise avoids English translations of German dialogue, a technique later used when presenting the Japanese characters of *Run Silent Run Deep* (1958). Many years following the release of *The Desert Rats*, a DVD edition of the film enabled viewers to display "forced English subtitles during German language sections."
28 Henry Hathaway sought an emphatic depiction of Erwin Rommel primarily due to the general scenario of his film. *The Desert Fox*, although released prior to *The Desert Rats,* is set after the events of Robert Wise's narrative and evolves around Rommel's plot to assassinate Adolf Hitler.

frustration over the leadership of MacRoberts. A wooden beam becomes visible in the background, and the name of "MARIA" has been written across it. Through the scene, Wise coincidentally foreshadows not only the heroines of *West Side Story* (1961) and *The Sound of Music* (1965), but in addition, two of the greatest films of his motion picture career.

18
SO BIG

(PRODUCED AND RELEASED 1953)

"I am not afraid of storms, for I am learning how to sail my ship."
- Louisa May Alcott

In the Netherlands during the mid-nineteenth century, Antje Paarlberg, a mother of eight, sought a better life for her family. Living conditions were deplorable, tragically resulting in the death of one of her children. Paarlberg and her husband, Klaas, therefore set sail for America, but he died of a severe lung infection en route. The ship's captain offered to return the family to the Netherlands. However, a determined Paarlberg refused. Upon arrival in the United States, her youngest child, less than a year old, perished from disease. Paarlberg and her remaining six eventually settled in a Dutch community outside of Chicago. She started a farm, which grew significantly over time, and additional farms of the family were subsequently established through the years.

At the time of Paarlberg's death in 1885, the legacy bequeathed by her was of priceless value. Her life story became the basis for Edna Ferber's 1924 novel, *So Big*, which was ultimately awarded the Pulitzer Prize. Paarlberg's courage and determination inspired the development of the narrative's main character, Selina Peake DeJong. A silent film adaptation, produced by First National Pictures, Inc., was released several months after the novel's publication. Then, in 1932, William A. Wellman directed a Warner Bros. remake starring Barbara Stanwyck. Twenty years later, however, the studio opted to revisit Ferber's novel with plans for yet another adaptation, and on February 16, 1953, Robert Wise, no longer under contract to Twentieth Century Fox, began production of his first film for Warner Bros.[29]

Selina Peake (Jane Wyman), the student of an all-girls boarding school in Chicago, begins a new life upon learning of her father's death. She travels to New Holland, a rural community on the outskirts of town. Klaas Pool (Roland Winters), a truck farmer, offers Selina room and board. She is to be the teacher of his younger children at the local school. Roelf (Richard Beymer), a teenage son of Pool's, becomes enamored with Selina. The two share similar interests such as reading and music, but when Selina develops a relationship with Pervus DeJong (Sterling Hayden), a local widower, jealousy stirs. She explains to Roelf that they both share a special love for beauty, whereas her love for DeJong is "just of the Earth." Selina and DeJong eventually wed. Shortly thereafter, she gives birth to a boy. He is named Dirk but given the nickname of "So Big" in hopes that he will figuratively grow tall enough to one day touch the stars. Roelf leaves New Holland to pursue new endeavors following the death of his mother, Maartje (Ruth Swanson). A few years later, DeJong succumbs to fever. Selina inherits the many responsibilities of running a farm, becoming more independent in the process.

As he comes of age, So Big (Steve Forrest) pursues a degree in architecture. He eventually finds work in the city as a draftsman, but much to Selina's dismay, So Big loses interest in designing, opting instead for a career in sales and promotion. He later encounters Dallas O'Mara (Nancy Olson), an artist commissioned by his firm to design some murals. So Big falls in love with her, but she is not attracted to his wealth and power. He discovers Dallas to be friends with a middle-aged Roelf (Walter Coy), who has become a noted

---

29 Robert Wise did not return to Twentieth Century Fox until the 1960s.

composer. Together, the three go to New Holland to visit Selina. Upon their arrival, a joyous reunion of sorts transpires, but Dallas announces that she will be traveling to Paris indefinitely. So Big comes to the realization that he "deserted beauty." Selina assures him that beauty is never lost. In the future, anything can happen.

Jane Wyman.

As the film begins, Wise presents the arrival of So Big and Roelf, both grown, at the DeJong farm. Dallas accompanies the two as they all eagerly anticipate their reunion with Selina, but it is not long before Wise transports his audience back in time to a Chicago of the 1890s. The setting is Miss Fister's Select School for Young Ladies. A youthful Selina, clearly jubilant, plays a piano while chatting with her fellow classmates. The topic of conversation is Selena's father, a prominent businessman and stockbroker. One girl refers to Mr. Peake as "the smartest man in the Chicago wheat pit." As the discussion progresses, everybody appears cheerful and lively, but such harmony is suddenly disrupted when Mr. Bainbridge (Grandon Rhodes), the business associate of Mr. Peake, arrives with terrible news, declaring, "To the very last, [your father] stood there in the pit with a fortune slipping through his hands, bidding, maneuvering, dying on his feet of fighting to save what he could for you. He couldn't. He tried, but he couldn't." It immediately becomes clear that Selina has undergone the most drastic of transformations. In the blink of an eye, she is suddenly without a father and has also become penniless. Despite his untimely passing, however, Mr. Peake posthumously instills in his daughter a will to persevere not only with a sense of adventure and independence, but also by virtue of a notable analogy.

Through the memory of Selina's father, a reference to the special quality of life is made, thus awakening her adventurous character in the aftermath of his death. In a quest for self-fulfillment, she ultimately comes full circle. Upon the narrative's beginning, as select goods and valuables are removed from the Peake estate, Selina pauses to acknowledge the most important item of the lot. An oil painting of her late father hangs above the empty, lifeless fireplace. "It's all adventure, Selina, finding a new treasure," his voice commands. "It's all adventure, the whole thing you call life. Watch closely. You'll see all the wonders of Baghdad."

Following an extended period of time, Selina grows accustomed to New Holland. Selina's marriage, however, becomes relatively ambivalent upon her husband's declaration that "a DeJong woman does not go to Haymarket!" He refers to it as the "Chicago thieves' market." Following DeJong's untimely death, Selina takes it upon herself to return to the city of her youth. As she and So Big depart New Holland en route to Haymarket, the locals take notice. Pool's second wife, formerly known as the Widow Paarlenberg (Dorothy Christy), openly questions such a journey. Nevertheless, the quick-witted Selina reflects upon her father's choice words of wisdom:

MRS. POOL: Where are you going this fine day, Mrs. DeJong?
SELINA: To Baghdad, Mrs. Pool.
MRS. POOL: Well, where's that? What for?

SELINA: To sell my jewels, Mrs. Pool. And see Aladdin, Ali Baba, and the forty thieves.

Selina's adventures at Haymarket, however, do not go as planned, as she and So Big are unable to sell their produce. Furthermore, a subsequent strategy of door-to-door sales along Chicago's Michigan Avenue, the location of Selina's childhood home, initially results in trouble. A policeman, Officer Riley (David McMahon), threatens to arrest her for peddling without a license. Julie Hempel (Elisabeth Fraser), a childhood friend, then comes to the rescue. Her father, August Hempel (Jacques Aubuchon), is a successful wholesaler of hogs, and Selina is welcomed into his lavish home. As an overjoyed So Big is served a generous portion of ice cream in the finest of bowls, Selina encapsulates the experience in one word. "Baghdad," she says, and nothing more. Later, Selina returns to New Holland in an automobile driven by the Hempel family chauffeur (Kenner G. Kemp). The locals, including Mrs. Pool and her husband, bear witness to Selina's arrival and are dumbfounded:

MRS. POOL: Sell her jewels, she said!
POOL: Yeah, to some fellow in Haymarket I never heard of: Ali Baba.

A delighted Selina takes pride in becoming reacquainted with Julie and her family, as there is strength in numbers, but the voice of her late father suggests an alternative path to success.

As the opening minutes of the film transpire, Selina faces the aforementioned painting and is reminded of the benefits of independence. "Remember, Selina," the voice of Mr. Peake proclaims, "Always remember that the more kinds of people you see, and the more things you do, the richer you are; especially the things you achieve by yourself. That's the hidden treasure…that knowing that what you've done, you've had the strength to do alone." To her, a future without So Big later becomes inevitable as he consequently comes of age. Upon his graduation from college, he prepares for his new life as an architect. A celebration is held at a nearby fraternity house, and parents are invited. So Big desires for Selina to attend, but she remains committed to priorities on the home front. "It's my busiest season at the farm," she says. Shortly thereafter, Selina departs for New Holland to resume her life of solitude, and much transpires in So Big's absence. She works diligently to harvest her choice produce, especially the DeJong asparagus, as it is continuously and "eagerly sought by the Chicago markets."

Eventually, Selina travels to the city to visit So Big. He casually suggests that she leave New Holland to live with him, but such an idea is out of the question, as Selina would "lose touch with life." Hence, the words of her late father ring true. She has accomplished much on her own, and as Selina's reunion with So Big transpires in his office, the celebration of a major milestone is ultimately revealed, as DeJong asparagus is to be featured on the menus of The Drake, Chicago's premier hotel. "I wanted to see it in print," Selina says with pride. The narrative eventually culminates with the arrival of So Big, Roelf, and Dallas at the DeJong farm, as Wise reminds viewers of the initial setting of his narrative. Within the film's opening minutes, the three wait for Selina, who toils alone in the field. In the home's living room, Roelf opens a chest in eager anticipation of its contents and discovers a picture of a young Selina, subsequently remarking, "She should've been emerald." Wise's flashback appropriately begins shortly thereafter.

At Miss Fister's Select School for Young Ladies, Selina makes reference to an analogy frequently cited by her father, claiming, "There are only two kinds of people in the world that really count: one kind is wheat, and the other kind is emerald. The kind with creative talent that makes the world prettier to live in, they're emeralds. And the people who feed us and give us all the necessary things, they're wheat." In addition to other characters of the narrative, such as August Hempel, she is "wheat," but the aspirations she harbors for So Big to one day become "emerald" are instead fulfilled by Roelf. Approximately forty-five minutes into the film, as Selina works in the field, she pauses to lift her infant son towards the sky, declaring "You're going to be emerald, So Big." Later, following DeJong's death, the two cruise down Michigan Avenue in their horse-drawn carriage. So Big, a youthful eight years of age, comments in regard to the fancy homes. He makes his aspirations clear to one day design houses himself. "You are emerald," a proud Selina replies. Yet, following So Big's graduation from college, it is not long before Paula Hempel (Martha Hyer), his girlfriend, instills in him her own ideas of success.

As the daughter of Julie Hempel, in addition to being the granddaughter of August Hempel, Paula has grown accustomed to a life of luxury and wealth. Furthermore, much to Selina's consternation, Paula steers So Big away from his creative aspirations. At the same time, Roelf establishes his presence in the world as a famed composer. Earlier, in adolescence, his "emerald" qualities are evident as he determines a dual use for potatoes. Aside from being consumed, the tasty vegetables "can make music." Roelf essentially uses the potatoes to stretch his fingers and ultimately master the intricacies of the piano. In time, Selina's impending marriage to DeJong has a devastating effect on the troubled teen, but Roelf departs New Holland to follow his dreams, which eventually come true. As the film concludes, So Big becomes disheartened upon learning of Dallas's departure for France. Perhaps, he will learn from Roelf's example and one day become "emerald" yet again.

The production of *So Big* transpired from February 16th to April 1, 1953. Wise's film debuted later that year. His retelling of Antje Paarlberg's tale, although considered by some to be relatively outdated, was well-received by the general public. The critics, too, were impressed. Bosley Crowther of *The New York Times* wrote, "For the better part of the picture, we are largely indebted to Jane Wyman...remarkably strong and effective in every forthright little bit she does." In addition, a reviewer from England's *Radio Times* cited the "nicely honed performances from big Sterling Hayden and lovely Nancy Olson." Without question, Wise was surrounded by individuals of natural talent throughout the production of his film. Vera Miles, just twenty-three years of age, appears briefly as a schoolgirl, and Richard Beymer's performance as the young Roelf Pool is especially noteworthy. Within years, he and Wise would reunite on the set of *West Side Story* (1961).

Yet, of the entire cast of *So Big*, Jane Wyman attracted the most praise from critics and theatergoers alike. She was thirty-six years old at the time of production. Both Gordon Bau and Edward Allen of the Makeup Department did an outstanding job in regard to the aging of Wyman's character. It was indeed a most challenging role for her to fill. Edna Ferber, however, came under criticism for her portrayal of Antje Paarlberg as pushy and flirtatious. The latter's family, in addition to the Dutch descendants of South Holland, Illinois, essentially cited an inaccurate depiction of the young widow.[30] The ensuing adaptations nevertheless sought to paint a better picture, and due to the hard work and dedication of Wise's cast and crew, his film became an instant crowd pleaser.

---

30 Edna Ferber centered the events of *So Big* on the real-life Dutch community of South Holland, Illinois. In the novel, however, it is known initially as New Holland and later as High Prairie.

19
EXECUTIVE SUITE

(PRODUCED 1953, RELEASED 1954)

"As I've always said, pre-production is so important. When you cast the actors, you've done much of the work. Now, you may need to guide them a little, take it up or down, have them go faster or slower, but the casting process is crucial."
- Robert Wise

In 1953, Robert Wise departed Warner Bros. for MGM to direct *Executive Suite*, a corporate thriller based on Cameron Hawley's novel of the same name. John Houseman, the film's producer, served as the editorial supervisor of *Citizen Kane* (1941) years earlier. He vividly remembered Wise's unrelenting commitment to detail and had the utmost confidence in his newly hired director. Ernest Lehman, a journalist who would later become one of the greatest screenwriters of the twentieth century, was commissioned to pen the adaptation of Hawley's novel. With *Executive Suite*, Lehman was making a debut of sorts. Earlier, he contributed his ideas to *The Inside Story* (1948), a Republic Pictures production starring Marsha Hunt and William Lundigan. The script of *Executive Suite*, however, was an accomplishment Lehman could proudly call his own.

Although Houseman did not foresee any collaborative issues between his writer and director, the casting of the film's actors proved to be a challenging endeavor. Houseman desired an all-star group of performers but sought many who were under contract to other studios. In time, he accomplished his objective. Nevertheless, it was not done without complication. Prior to the film's production, which began on August 24, 1953, *The New York Times* reported that "for the first time [in the history of MGM], an arbitrary inflexible starting date was set two months ahead." Houseman faced the unenviable task of coordinating multiple schedules to avoid the postponement of his production. Wise would later comment that Houseman was very similar to Val Lewton in regard to his creativity and sensitivity towards every detail of a film.

"It is always up there, close to the clouds, on the topmost floors of the sky-reaching towers of big business. And because it is high in the sky, you may think that those who work there are somehow above and beyond the tensions and temptations of the lower floors. This is to say that it isn't so."

Avery Bullard (Raoul Freeman), the chief executive of Tredway Corporation, a furniture manufacturer, sends a telegram from New York to the company's headquarters in Pennsylvania. His message calls for an executive committee meeting to take place. Seconds later, however, Bullard dies of a stroke on a busy Wall Street sidewalk. His wallet and identification are subsequently removed by a stealthy pickpocket. George Caswell (Louis Calhern), a Tredway board member, bears witness to the incident. He then arranges for a massive sale of the company's stock, figuring the corporation will "break wide open" when the Street eventually learns of Bullard's death. With the exception of Caswell and Julius Steigel (Edgar Stehli), a member of the New York Stock Exchange, nobody is aware of the dead man's identity. Erica Martin (Nina Foch), Tredway's executive secretary, follows the telegram's instructions and summons the committee of vice presidents. Naturally, Bullard fails to appear at the meeting. News of his passing, courtesy of Caswell, is later made public. Loren P. Shaw (Fredric March), the company's controller, orders the immediate release of Tredway's increased earnings, intending to counter the blow of such a tragic revelation. He believes his actions will ultimately send the company's stock up "quite handsomely." Frederick "Fred" W. Alderson (Walter Pidgeon), Tredway's treasurer, and McDonald "Don" Walling (William Holden), Vice President of Design and Development, suspect that Shaw desires to replace Bullard as chief executive. Julia Tredway (Barbara Stanwyck), a principal shareholder and daughter of the company's late owner, is distraught over the death of Bullard, with whom she was at one time romantically involved.

The following day, Caswell meets with Shaw regarding well over a thousand shares of unissued Tredway common stock in the company reserve. Caswell wishes to immediately purchase the shares at the closing price of the previous day. Shaw, however, exposes Caswell's unethical tactics and will only approve such a transaction in exchange for the latter's vote when a new president is to be elected. Walling decides to throw his hat in the ring. When he attempts to earn Julia's vote, she speaks of possibly selling her many shares at Shaw's suggestion; the voting process begins. Walling makes it clear to the board that Tredway should not focus primarily on paying the maximum dividends to its stockholders, as an obligation to use profits for the company's growth is of the utmost importance. The board members, especially Julia, are moved by Walling's rhetoric, and he is unanimously elected as the new president of Tredway Corporation.

Avery Bullard, one of the first characters introduced into the film, is never seen by theatergoers. The audience is instead afforded the brief opportunity to see the world through his eyes. Upon the narrative's beginning, Bullard shakes hands with Julius Steigel as George Caswell looks on.

Upon the film's beginning, Caswell, not yet privy to Bullard's death, speaks negatively of Tredway Corporation to Steigel. Caswell is not necessarily appreciative of his position as a board member. "The only reason [Bullard] put me on was to wrap up Steigel and Company for bond issues," he declares. Caswell cannot fathom how Tredway Corporation has gone so long without an executive vice president. He initially seeks to fill the vacancy. "It is my opinion, Mr. Caswell, that at lunch today you were crossed off the list," Steigel proceeds to tell him. Hence, a resentment of the company grows, and when Caswell happens to glance out the window and notice Bullard's lifeless corpse on the Wall Street sidewalk, the wheels begin to turn, as plans for a massive sale of the company's stock are immediately devised.

An imprudent phone call is subsequently made on a whim, thus prompting Steigel to remark, "There are some ways that don't seem right to make money." In the end, Caswell pays the price for his actions both literally and figuratively, but he is responsible for his own demise in more ways than one. Caswell's decision to include Julia in his scheme is questionable. Furthermore, his prior relationship with Shaw and initial abstinence from voting in the climactic election are also contributing factors.

Shortly after Bullard's death, Caswell instructs Julia to sell her own shares and later repurchase them at a lower price, inadvertently attracting Shaw's attention and therefore causing further problems. Her untimely appearance at Tredway Tower just prior to the initial executive committee meeting of the film sets in motion an unusual chain of events. As Bullard's vice presidents await his arrival, the clock strikes six. Erica enters the board room and summons Alderson to the outer office. Shaw takes notice. Alderson is then privately informed of Julia's arrival and immediately meets with her in Bullard's office. "I had a phone call a while ago, a rather strange call from someone in New York. This man said he had information that was highly unfavorable to the future prospects of the Tredway Corporation," she declares to the company's beleaguered treasurer. Alderson eventually discovers the caller to be Caswell. Time passes, and Bullard fails to show at the meeting. Julia ponders whether or not to follow Caswell's advice and sell her stock. From atop the high tower, she peers down into the street below, reminiscing of her late father, who leapt to his death from the very window at which she stands. The sale of her shares "would end a lot of things."

Shortly thereafter, as the vice presidents depart for the weekend, Alderson casually asks Shaw if he has recently been in touch with Caswell. Tredway's controller, already suspicious, answers in the negative. Caswell's initial phone call to Julia triggers her unexpected visit to the tower. She expects to meet with Bullard. Yet, for obvious reasons, Erica instead directs her to Alderson. Following a brief discussion with Julia, Alderson does not mention

Caswell's telephone call to the others. Shaw's curiosity, however, is piqued. As a consequence, he works diligently to expose Caswell's scheme, subsequently arranging for the immediate release of Tredway's earnings report, an affair that would have been avoided had Julia not been contacted in the first place. Following the meeting's cancellation, Julia attempts to reach Caswell at the Stork Club, but he appears generally unconcerned with her. Caswell severs ties with his associates under the most peculiar of circumstances, which is originally how he happens upon such associates.

Years earlier, when Caswell endorsed Shaw, an old acquaintance, for a position with Tredway Corporation, he was ironically contributing to his own downfall. In the aftermath of Bullard's death, Caswell understands all too well Shaw's profound desire to become president. "It's the kind of set-up you've been dreaming about . . . ever since you came on the Street with that

William Holden.

Barbara Stanwyck as Julia Tredway.

night school CPA in your hand," he says. In comparison with the other four vice presidents of Tredway Corporation, Shaw is quite different. Early in the film, as Erica shifts from office to office to spread the word of Bullard's impromptu meeting, she relies primarily on the men's secretaries in order to fulfill her objective. Upon entering Shaw's office, however, she encounters him and nobody else. He is alone with nothing but his Dictaphone and "Material Rejection" charts. Shaw is essentially without any form of companionship throughout the course of the film. Jesse Grimm (Dean Jagger), Vice President of Manufacturing, in addition to Walling and Alderson, appears with his spouse on at least one occasion during the narrative. J. Walter "Walt" Dudley (Paul Douglas), Vice President of Sales, is seen arguing with his wife via telephone, but he relies on his devoted secretary, Eva Bardeman (Shelley Winters), for female companionship. Shaw, however, is instead married to the company.[31] Interestingly enough, Wise omits Shaw's reaction to

---

31 Although a wedding band on Shaw's ring finger is occasionally visible to viewers, his spouse is neither seen nor mentioned throughout the entire film.

the news of Bullard's death. As word of the tragedy begins to spread, Shaw works behind the scenes, doing everything in his power to assume the presidency, and he comes rather close to accomplishing such a milestone until the unexpected transpires.

Despite nominating Shaw for the presidency, Caswell abstains from voting during the first round of the climactic election, thus leading to dire consequences. Caswell's discreet conduct ultimately affects Julia's vote. The opening round comes to a close when Erica declares "no decision on the first ballot." Shaw has earned a total of three votes and mistakenly assumes Julia has abstained. Caswell and Shaw subsequently adjourn to an adjacent washroom to discuss the round's outcome:

CASWELL: Well, Loren, how does it feel?
SHAW: What?
CASWELL (washing his hands): Not getting it.
SHAW: I had her. I know I had her.
CASWELL: Oh, you still do.
SHAW: It was you! Why? Why?
CASWELL: 3,700 reasons.
SHAW: I told you I was g- . . . I told you I was gonna do my best for you, didn't I?
CASWELL: I didn't realize this afternoon how much bargaining power I really had. It's not just that my "no" keeps you out and my "yes" puts you in. Loren, I want the delivery of that stock guaranteed.
SHAW: You blasted idiot. I have it for you right here. (gestures to his coat pocket) Julia Tredway's pulling out of the company and I'm handling the sale of her stock. (produces an envelope) Here's your 3,700 shares, right here. A letter of transfer signed by me, as president.

"Improve the profits but never the product...that's Shaw's philosophy! To him, the whole company's just a curve on a chart!"

At the time of Shaw and Caswell's brief absence from the board room, however, a key interaction transpires between Julia and Walling, both of whom were previously involved in a heated discussion during which hurtful comments were made. Yet, the one to apologize first is the bravest. "Miss Tredway, I don't know how you just voted, but I wanted to tell you how sorry I am for what I said. No matter how I feel about the company, I had no right to do that," Walling says. Although Julia does not respond, it eventually becomes clear she is moved by such an apology. Shaw and Caswell, meanwhile, are absent from the room because it was the latter's idea to break from the voting process. In their absence, Walling seizes the opportunity to essentially make things right with Julia.

Following the brief recess, Caswell attempts to nominate Shaw a second time, but before the board has a chance to vote, Walling stalls. The arrival of Alderson and Grimm, two individuals who do not support Shaw, is imminent. Walling envisions a new future for Tredway Corporation and therefore seizes the opportunity to appeal to its key players. Dudley will one day be able to sell merchandise with "beauty and function and value," and Shaw will be able to budget such merchandise "to the nearest hundredth of a cent because it'll be scientifically and efficiently designed," but Walling perhaps says it best when he declares to Julia that the new line of furniture will be a product "[she'll] be proud to have [her] name on." Immediately following the ultimate round of the election, Caswell approaches the defeated Shaw regarding the 3,700 shares. The aforementioned envelope is promptly torn in fourths, and as Shaw thrusts its remains into Caswell's hand, remorse becomes excruciatingly apparent.

Fredric March as Loren P. Shaw.

"Robert Wise almost cost me a finger during the production of *Executive Suite*," William Phipps said regarding his appearance in the film. "We were shooting at night on the back lot of MGM. I played the part of Bill Lundeen, the assistant to Bill Holden's character. Production costs were high when crews filmed at night. During one scene, Bill Holden is sitting in the driver's seat of an automobile, and June Allyson is in the passenger seat. As we were performing, I was leaning against the area where the door was hinged, but the door was closed. In the scene, I'm talking to Bill Holden. Robert Wise then approached intending to give further direction. He opened the door, changed his mind, and immediately shut it. Well, when Wise opened the door, my weight carried my hand into the gap, and then he shut the door on my finger. Wise immediately saw what he had done and opened the door. I told him I was okay because I had gone into shock and could not feel any pain. I soon collapsed. Robert Wise caught me before I hit the ground. Since the scene was shot at night and a lot of money was being spent, the crew wanted to continue filming because more needed to be done. I went to the infirmary, where my hand was bandaged. Bill Holden got out a bottle of King's Ransom scotch, which was his brand. I then drank a few shots to kill the pain.

"For the rest of the night, my wounded hand was in my coat pocket, even when the cameras were rolling. In one scene, Bill Holden and I are walking down some steps. He's actually holding me up by his shoulder and helping me down those steps. I don't know how obvious it is to viewers, but that's what happened. My hand had a bandage on it, and had it been shown, the image probably would have appeared unusual to audiences.

"The next day, John Houseman told me I did fine considering I had been drunk. Robert Wise never said anything more about it. He never apologized, never followed up to determine if I was okay. I was seriously hurt and thought I was going to lose my finger. The show must go on. Robert Wise and I barely had any conversations. He didn't talk to me about the part or my performance. I don't think he even introduced himself to me. This didn't happen probably because he didn't hire me. Houseman did, but *Executive Suite* turned out to be a great picture. It won the Special Jury Prize for ensemble acting at the Venice Film Festival. That was a great cast."

Upon its release to the American public, *Executive Suite* was advertised with the tagline, "Behind the lighted tower windows the conflict of love and power is reckless and daring!" Despite its intense narrative, Wise's picture is completely devoid of background music, a rarity for films of the era. Some elements, such as Ernest Lehman's dialogue, essentially take precedence over others. Prior to filming the concluding scene in the board room, Wise and John Houseman decided to close the set for an entire day and focus their attention on what they deemed to be the necessities. Both men spent time rehearsing with the actors. In addition, Wise worked with cinematographer George Folsey to review various camera angles. The extra effort paid off, as theatergoers quickly discovered the film's climax to be the most memorable of the picture. William Holden's stellar performance especially remains significant in the annals of cinematic history. "The force behind a great company has to be more than the pride of one man; it has to be the pride of thousands," his character boldly proclaims to the captivated members of the board. Interestingly enough, as Wise was directing *Executive Suite*, Lehman spent most of his time at Paramount Pictures working with Billy Wilder on the script of *Sabrina* (1954). Holden happened to be close friends with Wilder and would later perform in his film. Usually, following a typical day on Wise's set, Holden would visit Wilder's home, where Lehman was frequently present. More often than not, Holden had much to say about what transpired during the production of *Executive Suite*. He would customarily take Lehman to the side in order to fill him in on the details of the day's shooting. It supposedly drove Wilder crazy, but Lehman was appreciative, as Holden often provided daily reports pertaining not only to the set of *Executive Suite*, but to MGM as well.

The following year, Wise's film premiered in Los Angeles on April 15, 1954. Nina Foch earned a Best Supporting Actress nomination for her outstanding performance as the loyal Erica Martin. Furthermore, *Executive Suite* garnered three additional nominations: Best Cinematography, Best Costume Design, and Best Art Direction (all of the Black & White category).[32] Wise's picture, in short, made an everlasting impact on an America of the 1950s, as theatergoers were afforded the opportunity to see "THE CAST OF THE YEAR IN THE PICTURE OF THE YEAR!"

---

32 A CBS television series of the same name aired from 1976 to 1977.

Robert Wise cleverly presents an eavesdropping Caswell through the image of a conspicuous shadow.

The ultimate, decisive board meeting.

Mimi Doyle, Robert Wise's sister-in-law, appears in a brief cameo as a telephone operator of the Stork Club.

20
HELEN OF TROY

(PRODUCED 1954, RELEASED 1956)

> "A heart that loves is always young."
> - Greek Proverb

In the early 1950s, a significant rise in the domestic use of televisions transpired. As a result, movie theaters were not as appealing to the American public as they had been a decade earlier. Enter Bausch & Lomb, the popular manufacturer of eye care products. The company developed what came to be known as the CinemaScope lens, enabling studios to produce motion pictures almost twice as wide as those photographed with standard lenses. Twentieth Century Fox's *The Robe* (1953), a biblical drama starring Richard Burton and Jean Simmons, marked the debut of the CinemaScope format and ultimately took audiences by storm. Spyros P. Skouras, the president of Twentieth Century Fox, championed the new phenomenon as an absolute victory over television. Many of the other studios took notice. In March of 1954, Warner Bros. commenced production of *Helen of Troy*, an epic of The Trojan War, at Cinecittà Studios in Rome. Loosely based on Homer's ancient poem, *The Iliad*, it was to be the first CinemaScope film directed by Robert Wise.

Rossana Podestà as Helen.

Troy is a prosperous city and, to the Greek nations, a tempting prize of war. Nevertheless, Paris (Jack Sernas), Prince of Troy and son of King Priam (Sir Cedric Hardwicke), sets sail for Sparta to propose a treaty of peace. He is unfortunately thrown from his boat during a tumultuous storm. Paris washes ashore on the Greek mainland, only to be discovered by Helen (Rossana Podestà), Queen of Sparta. A mutual attraction develops, but she does not reveal her true identity. Paris is taken to Sparta shortly thereafter. King Menelaus (Niall MacGinnis) and company, however, do not believe the newcomer to be a Trojan prince. As a test, Paris is pitted against Ajax (Maxwell Reed), Prince of Salamis. He emerges victorious. Menelaus therefore prepares to hear the treaty's terms but senses Helen's attraction to Paris, who eventually discovers that she is the queen. Paris is provided with living quarters. Two soldiers stand guard outside such quarters. Menelaus privately confronts Helen and speaks of the harm he may do to the Trojan prince. She then helps Paris to escape and arranges for a Phoenician ship to return him to Troy. Under the threat of Spartan soldiers, however, they subsequently flee together. Not long after their arrival in Troy, Priam declares the quest for peace to be futile, and the city's inhabitants prepare for battle as a thousand Greek ships loom on the horizon.

War begins, thus leading to an ongoing siege. Helen, wishing to put an end to all of the fighting and bloodshed, decides to return to Menelaus, but the Greeks are not satisfied and demand half the treasury of Troy; the fighting continues and Paris kills Achilles (Stanley Baker) in battle. The Greeks later devise a feigned retreat and present the Trojans with a gift in the form of a massive wooden horse. Unaware that enemy soldiers are hidden inside such a horse, Priam has it transported into the city. At night, the Greeks emerge from their position and storm the palace, and Menelaus and Paris engage in battle. During the exchange, the latter is unjustly wounded by a Spartan guard. Helen comes to Paris's aid, but he dies. Menelaus then demands that Helen return to his ship. As she sails back to Sparta, she reflects on her love with Paris, concluding that what has been lived and shared is never lost.

"You are two women, both wise and good."

Helen of Troy is a tribute to the mythology of ancient Greece. Such lore features an extensive selection of moral tales and countless legends. Wise's film provides viewers with only a minute fraction of that which encompasses Greek mythology. Particular attention, however, must be granted to its heroes. *Helen of Troy* periodically features the character of Ulysses (Torin

Thatcher), or Odysseus. At one point, he speaks of a desire to one day reunite with his wife, Penelope, thus foreshadowing the long journey he will undertake in order to do so.[33]

Yet another featured hero of the film is the mighty Achilles, but following his slaying of Paris's brother, Hector (Harry Andrews), a horrendous act of shame transpires. Achilles ties the corpse of his vanquished opponent to his chariot and parades it outside the walls of Troy. Paris and the Trojans immediately reach for their bows and begin their attack against the hated Greek. Achilles appears to miraculously withstand the onslaught. Paris then looks to the gods for help. "Mighty Zeus, help me find a weakness," he says. Seconds later, Paris's arrow connects with the heel of Achilles. The latter, ejected from his moving chariot, is instantly killed when his head collides with a large stone. It is a defining moment of the narrative, especially to those familiar with the mythological origin of an Achilles heel.

Sir Cedric Hardwicke.

Shortly thereafter, Agamemnon (Robert Douglas), brother of King Menelaus, declares, "Defeated by men, deserted by the gods." The gods and goddesses of ancient Greece are of central importance to the film's narrative. At times, they are both praised and condemned by Greeks and Trojans alike.

---

33 Odysseus's journey to his home of Ithaca is depicted in Homer's *The Odyssey*, an epic poem set after the events of *The Iliad*.

King Priam, however, remains steadfast in his support of the gods. "The great god, Zeus, would never let [Paris] die, and with him our hopes of peace," he says as Paris, following a lengthy absence, returns to Troy midway through the film. Of course, upon the narrative's conclusion, it is painstakingly clear that Priam's prayers have gone unanswered. With the exception of the king and a few others, the most elite of Trojans (i.e., Paris, his sister, and the Queen of Troy) remain uncommitted to a firm belief in the gods, exhibiting instead some degree of uncertainty.

Paris admires Aphrodite, the goddess of beauty, more than any other supreme being, but he does not necessarily appear to worship her. His regard for such a being affects his overall demeanor towards Helen. At the king's palace in Troy, as Paris prepares to set sail for Sparta upon the film's beginning, he declares, "I'm not sure I worship anything. No. Admiration is the better word." He approaches a large statue of Aphrodite. "Admiration for the beauty of a marble image," Paris finishes. Following the storm and subsequent encounter of Helen, he appears disoriented and mistakenly addresses her as Aphrodite. Their love affair begins shortly thereafter. Much to his chagrin, Paris continues to associate Helen, a mere mortal, with the goddess of beauty. Following their escape from Sparta, a dilemma ensues. The island of Pelagos is Helen's preferred destination, but Paris wishes to sail for Troy. In the midst of their disagreement, he comes to a sudden realization. "Forgive me," he says. "I forget you're a woman, not a goddess." Later, as the Greeks establish their camps along the outskirts of Troy, Helen again speaks of Pelagos as the ideal place to be. Paris replies, "Oh, goddess, come to Earth. Make me immortal with your kiss, and we'll live on nectar and ambrosia." He briefly kisses her, and then pauses:

PARIS: But I'm not sure I like being so ethereal.
HELEN: Nor I.

Paris, however, cannot shake the feeling that Helen is, in some form, the goddess of beauty. Despite his sincere admiration of Aphrodite, he eventually confesses to "living in a world of fables" and does not appear to share the unwavering faith of his father. Yet, King Priam is more concerned with another of his children.

Cassandra (Janette Scott), Paris's sister and "troubled priestess of the temple," deems it necessary to pacify the gods not out of respect, but instead, out of fear. As she comes to develop a relationship with Helen, her disdain for Aphrodite is consequently redirected at Athena, the goddess of wisdom. Upon Paris's return to Troy, his beautiful yet mysterious companion is greeted with warmth and genuine affection. Polydorus (Robert Brown), Paris's brother, then seizes the opportunity to pose a most important question:

POLYDORUS (to Helen): By what name, my lady, shall we know you?
HELEN: My name . . . .
CASSANDRA: Her name is death!

Cassandra's sudden appearance in the king's court catches everybody off guard. Helen's true identity as the Queen of Sparta is subsequently exposed. "The goddess of beauty, Aphrodite," Cassandra declares, "come down to Earth in mortal form. She will bring the disaster I have prophesied. Her name will be written in letters of fire! Helen! Helen of Troy!" In time, however, as the war intensifies, such anger towards the queen subsides.

Cassandra foresees a different future. "New storms shall ride the sky, but the guilt will be Athena's, not Helen's," she says. Upon the film's climax, the wooden horse is delivered to the gates of Troy, presented as a gift from Athena. Cassandra pleads with Priam to refuse the offering, but he ignores her warning. "We must not be ungrateful to a goddess who has proved herself our goddess," he tells her, but Cassandra knows better. She is succinct and direct when, in the aftermath of Prince Polydorus's death at the hands of the Greeks, she proclaims, "We, the living dead of Troy, shall pay his debt in the years of siege to come." Many mourn the fallen prince, particularly a grief-stricken mother.

Brigitte Bardot, Jack Sernas, and Rossana Podestà.

Queen Hecuba (Nora Swinburne), one of the first to welcome Helen's presence in Troy, is also wary of the gods. As she warns the Spartan queen against returning to Menelaus, a reference to the Fates is made, thus foreshadowing a grim future. Over time, many war-weary Trojans wish for Paris and Helen to be cast out of the city as a means of avoiding further bloodshed. She is compelled to confront the unruly folk, but Hecuba prevents such action:

HECUBA (to Helen): The high priest says that even the gods fight each other. Some for Athena and Greece, some for Troy and Aphrodite. How then could I blame you for this war?
HELEN: I could stop it.
HECUBA: There is no one who could.
HELEN: I could…if I return to the Greeks, to Menelaus.
HECUBA: Go back to someone you so despise?
HELEN: Oh, if it would bring an end to war and restore Paris to the love of the Trojans.
HECUBA: He'd never let you go.
HELEN: And could I ever leave him? You must help me to decide.

HECUBA: Would you defy the Fates? No mortal should attempt so much, Helen.

The Fates of Greek mythology, three incarnations of destiny, were believed to have controlled the lives of every mortal from birth to death. Hecuba's words essentially presage dire consequences. The Fates are indeed defied as Helen returns to Menelaus upon the narrative's conclusion. Coincidence or not, Hecuba's three sons (Polydorus, Hector, and Paris) ultimately perish as casualties of war. During the film's final battle, Ulysses displays an air of confidence as a Trojan defeat is imminent. He congratulates the bloodthirsty brother of Menelaus, boldly declaring, "Magnificent leadership, Agamemnon. Athena will reward you with all the glory." A short time later, however, Paris appears just as confident as he says to Helen, "The gods are with us." Yet, it eventually becomes clear that such is not the case, as the film's protagonist meets his unfortunate demise. Blaise Pascal, the French mathematician of the seventeenth century, once said, "We sail within a vast sphere, ever drifting in uncertainty, driven from end to end." In Wise's world of fiction, such rhetoric, perhaps, rings true.

"From my perspective, and I was only fifteen years old at the time, *Helen of Troy* was a huge production," Janette Scott said. "I believe the amount of money spent on such a production was greater than that of any other picture of the period. In order to get the film made, Warner Bros. was most likely using its frozen assets in Europe. I think that was probably a reason why, in the mid-1950s, there were a great many American films that suddenly started being made in European countries. Warner Bros. owned fifty-one percent of Associated British Picture Corporation, of which I was a contract player. And although I had to test for the part of Cassandra, I'm sure my employer pushed for me to be cast. This way, the production wouldn't be obligated to pay me a lot of money since I was already under contract.

"I tested at Elstree Studios in England. But the audition process was not that extensive or difficult since I had been working regularly in the industry.

As arrangements for the test were being made, and because *Helen of Troy* was an American production, the casting department thought I should have bigger boobs. I was then provided with a pair of falsies, which were totally ridiculous for me to wear under my so-called toga outfit. But when we got to Rome, one of the first things Robert Wise said was, 'Get rid of those falsies!' I therefore returned to my natural fifteen-year-old self. It was an interesting time in Rome because the city was in a golden age of being able to produce films beyond Vittorio De Sica's *Bicycle Thieves* and any of the other black-and-white pictures that reflected the poor life in Italy. Suddenly, the studios were making big, Eastman color films.

"Many problems occurred during the filming of *Helen of Troy*, but in those days, if you had 3,000 Spartans and 3,000 Trojans who were all called up for some kind of battle scene, problems occurred no matter what (unlike the modern era where a dozen people can be digitally reproduced to create thousands more). Back then, representatives of the communist trade union managed to integrate with the Trojan extras, whereas representatives of their opposition mixed with the Spartans. Problems were therefore commonplace. I believe the main problem, if I remember correctly, was that the entire cast, including Sir Cedric Hardwicke, could not understand why Rossana Podestà had been cast in the role of Helen. In addition, the publicity department, comprised of Americans, and the production unit, which consisted primarily of Italians, were both dumbfounded. Podestà was short and bordering on being dumpy. In fact, people of the wardrobe department would refer to her as 'The Dumpling.' It seemed like the camera always had to be placed low and pointing upwards in order to give her a bit of height, because she was short, not petite, but short. Podestà had a baby just prior to the beginning of production. I don't know how many pictures she had done before *Helen of Troy*, but it seemed to me that she didn't realize there had to be a certain amount of discipline and professionalism when showing up on the set to begin filming for the day. And many, many times, I would hear people in passing say, 'Oh, we're gonna have to change the schedule today because Rossana has stayed at home to play with the baby.' It was a very strange casting choice.

"Jack Sernas, on the other hand, was professional and charming in every way possible. He looked after himself and was constantly on the set doing exercises in the corner, making sure his legs were well-waxed and looking as beautiful as Paris was meant to look. It was Rossana that no one could understand. I believe her voice is dubbed for the final cut of the film. And that doesn't surprise me because she learned the lines just through the sound of them without really being aware of what she was saying. Rossana didn't even attempt to understand what she was saying. No effort was made on her part to make sure she understood the role, which is staggering for that time. *Helen of Troy* is quite historical, and despite the amount of money spent on such a production, it didn't seem to make any impression on Rossana at all. Little Brigitte Bardot, of course, was the publicity department's dream. Her husband, Roger Vadim, frequently accompanied her onto the set. He was really pushing her to a great extent, because in the years following *Helen of Troy*, but not because of *Helen of Troy*, Brigitte became one of Europe's biggest female stars.

The agony of war.

"At the time, I got the impression Mr. Wise wasn't very happy. I'm not sure if it had anything to do with the way the production was going, or maybe he wasn't happy because he was doing this specific film. I didn't know for sure. And being only fifteen, I wasn't able to get into any personal conversations with him in order to find out what was on his mind. My attitude towards him was nevertheless one of great respect. But he did keep his distance. A majority of the cast was British, brought over from England to Italy. From our perspective, Wise didn't really direct. He would place us and say things like, 'Let's try it.' We would then rehearse, and he'd eventually say, 'Okay, we're ready to shoot.' But I don't remember him ever getting involved with any of the performances. I suspect he wasn't that thrilled with doing these big productions. When you're a child actor, and because the 'grown-ups' are inclined to ignore you a little bit, you sit and watch and listen, and learn a heck of a lot without being totally involved. Overall, Robert Wise struck me as a quiet, dignified man who generally kept to himself while staying in control of such a huge production. He ended up with a workman-like film that should have had more of an impact than it did. It doesn't really stand up to the test of time."

Janette Scott as Cassandra.

Helen of Troy premiered on January 26, 1956, but later failed to earn any Academy Award nominations. Bausch & Lomb nevertheless won an Oscar in 1954 for its development of the CinemaScope lens. Not everybody, however, was sold on the new technology. Fritz Lang, a filmmaker whose name has become synonymous with German Expressionism, once said, "CinemaScope is only good for funerals and snakes." He naturally adhered to a different cinematic style, as is evidenced with his extraordinary noirish pictures. Not only was *Helen of Troy* the first CinemaScope production to be directed by

Wise, it was also the first of his films to begin with an overture. Such an introduction consisted of an orchestral piece that was usually accompanied by an elaborate visual background.

Overtures are present within a notable selection of Wise's films, such as *West Side Story* (1961) and *Star!* (1968). His long-standing tradition eventually came to an end upon the release of *Star Trek: The Motion Picture* (1979), which also marked the end of his professional collaboration with designer Maurice Zuberano. In regard to *Helen of Troy*, Zuberano, a skilled artist, created the film's many continuity sketches. He and Wise initially worked together, albeit in separate departments, during the production of *Citizen Kane* (1941). Through the years, the two became quite familiar with each other's styles, and with Wise in the director's chair, both men collaborated on a total of eight productions, including *Helen of Troy*. Wise's relationship with Zuberano, in short, was productive, remarkable, and essentially one of many he would come to enjoy over the course of his lengthy motion picture career.

21
TRIBUTE TO A BAD MAN

(PRODUCED 1955, RELEASED 1956)

> "One cannot be pessimistic about the West. This is the native home of hope. When it fully learns that cooperation, not rugged individualism, is the quality that most characterizes and preserves it, then it will have achieved itself and outlived its origins. Then it has a chance to create a society to match its scenery."
> - Wallace Stegner

In June of 1955, Robert Wise traveled to Colorado for the production of MGM's *Tribute to a Bad Man*. Similar to *Helen of Troy* (1956), it was to be a CinemaScope film. Wise relished the opportunity to work with Spencer Tracy, who had been cast as the lead. It was not long, however, before problems began to arise. Tracy developed a cyst on his cheek and immediately made plans to visit a doctor. Meanwhile, Wise pressed forward and filmed whatever he could in his lead's absence. Tracy eventually arrived on the set. The cyst had been removed and a bandage covered the surgical incisions. Upon encountering Wise, Tracy removed the gauze and asked, "Do you think this is going to be okay?" Tracy was overcome with emotion. Wise assured him that all was well and did not anticipate any future problems, but Tracy gradually began to complain about the altitude, often finding it difficult to breathe. Several days later, he informed Wise that he would be unable to continue with the production. MGM was notified and filming was delayed. The studio made several attempts to acquire Clark Gable for the vacated role, but to no avail. Some questioned whether Tracy was replaceable. To fill his shoes would be a daunting task. Yet, on August 15, 1955, production resumed with an optimal cast in place, and Wise was more or less in awe of Tracy's replacement: James Cagney.

James Cagney.

In 1875, Steve Miller (Don Dubbins), a young man from Pennsylvania, travels the West on horseback. He discovers Jeremy Rodock (Cagney), the proprietor of a large valley, to be engaged in a gunfight with horse thieves. Miller intervenes and the bandits flee, but Rodock is wounded. Miller comes to his aid. The two subsequently travel to Rodock's ranch. Upon arrival, Miller meets Jocasta "Jo" Constantine (Irene Papas), Rodock's significant other, and immediately becomes enamored with her beauty. Shortly thereafter, horses are stolen from the ranch. Rodock suspects L.A. Peterson (James Bell), his former partner. Meanwhile, McNulty (Stephen McNally), the ranch foreman, continuously makes advances towards Jo. Rodock becomes privy to such behavior and fires him. Additional horses are later stolen during a separate incident; Peterson, under pressure from fellow associates, is partly responsible. A gunfight ensues and he is killed. Rodock then captures a co-conspirator of Peterson's and hangs him without hesitation. Miller is aghast at the killing, thereby making it difficult for him to remain acquainted with Rodock. In addition, Miller struggles to control his feelings for Jo.

McNulty eventually joins forces with Rodock's adversaries. He steals Rodock's horses and cuts their hooves as a means of debranding them. McNulty is nevertheless caught prior to making a getaway. As retribution, he and his associates are forced to remove their shoes and march countless miles to a predetermined location. Before the journey can be completed, Rodock surprisingly decides to liberate the worn, suffering men. A frustrated Jo eventually departs the valley with Miller. She believes Rodock is unwilling to commit to their relationship. Miller, however, informs Jo that he has seen a change for the better in Rodock's otherwise gruff personality. Miller subsequently comes to the realization that his future does not lie with her. He returns Jo to Rodock, who then proposes marriage. She accepts without hesitation.

During the production of *Tribute to a Bad Man*, the film's working title was *Jeremy Rodock*. Such a title is fitting, as Cagney's character is arguably the most important, and complex, of the narrative, but also significant is the film's opening monologue. Immediately following the credits, the voice of Steve Miller is heard. He begins, "It was 1875 in the spring. I was on my way west from Laramie when I saw, for the first time, Mr. Jeremy Rodock's valley." As the words are spoken, Wise transitions to a noteworthy image, thus affording his audience a view of the majestic, green valley.

Miller continues, "If [the valley] had another name, I never found out. It wouldn't have mattered. It was always Mr. Jeremy Rodock's valley, just as the horses of the country were always known as Rodock horses, and when they hung a horse thief, they called it Mr. Rodock's justice." From the beginning, Wise emphasizes the importance of his protagonist. Yet, an additional proclamation reveals a deeper meaning of the narrative, as Miller ultimately declares, "I was a boy when I entered Mr. Rodock's valley. But when I left, I wasn't a boy anymore." *Tribute to a Bad Man* is not so much a tribute to the character of Jeremy Rodock as it is a testimony to his impact on the maturation of Steve Miller, as the latter is gradually afforded important life lessons in death, compassion, and love. However, Miller's knowledge is obtained not through his acceptance of Rodock's standards, but instead, by his refusal to follow such standards.

Mr. Jeremy Rodock's valley.

Seconds after Miller informs the audience via the opening monologue that he "picked up a few pointers on how men die quickly and how they keep from dying quickly," he happens upon a gunfight and chooses to intervene, and he is later chided for his actions. His decision is based primarily on empathy. As Miller arrives on the scene, he observes the conflict from a relatively safe distance. Two men on horseback continuously fire at a lone individual, who, crouching behind a dead horse for protection, is clearly at a disadvantage. The distance between both parties is approximately a few hundred feet, and the unknown assailants prepare to close in on their target. Miller then makes his presence known, resembling one who intends to open fire on the duo. Both men become aware of the newcomer and subsequently depart.

Shortly thereafter, Miller approaches and encounters Rodock, the disadvantaged individual. The latter is not only wounded, but he also appears to be perturbed at the unexpected intervention, stating, "You oughtn't to move in on a gunfight until you've figured out which side is which!" Nevertheless, the conflict was mismatched, and Miller took the initiative to aid Rodock prior to learning what instigated the gunfight. They become acquainted and, throughout the film, lessons in death and how it can be avoided, are presented. There is safety in numbers, and as *Tribute to a Bad Man* concludes, Miller departs the valley for the last time, having learned to survive a foreign environment under difficult circumstances. Others, however, are not as fortunate.

Miller's monologue touches upon "how to be cruel and how not to be cruel," thus foreshadowing his conflict with Rodock regarding the atrocities of "hanging fever." Without McNulty, however, Miller most likely would not have been afforded an important life lesson in compassion. His association with the provocative foreman, although brief, ultimately proves beneficial. Upon meeting each other for the first time, McNulty is quick to make reference to "hanging fever" and refers to it as a sickness. Rodock hangs those he deems guilty without presenting his case to a trial or jury. Factoring into his philosophy is the distance to the nearest courtroom, which is hundreds of miles from the valley. Nevertheless, McNulty frequently takes note of Rodock's demeanor and can determine when the so-called fever is rising. At one point, he remarks to Jo, "I don't know when [Rodock's] worse, when he's hanging [his enemies] or not hanging [his enemies]."

Shortly thereafter, McNulty's employment at the ranch is terminated and he is subsequently beaten by Rodock. Yet, despite the circumstances, McNulty and Miller part amicably. Later, when Rodock prepares to hang Hearn (Onslow Stevens), an associate of Peterson's, McNulty is not present. Miller, however, reflects back on his conversation with the ex-foreman and immediately begins to realize firsthand the horrors of the atrocious fever. He pleads with Rodock to abort the execution, but to no avail. Although neither see eye-to-eye, Miller is able to better understand the importance of human compassion in the aftermath of the merciless killing, and when McNulty re-enters the picture and is later forced to trek through the open range without his shoes, Rodock, too, becomes compassionate and ultimately sets him free. Miller and McNulty, however, share a mutual respect not only because of their views on hanging fever, but also because of their romantic interest in the same individual.

Irene Papas as Jocasta "Jo" Constantine. The role was originally offered to Grace Kelly, who passed on the opportunity to star in Robert Wise's film.

Jo, clearly on Miller's mind as he reflects upon the issue of "what love isn't and what it is," ultimately chooses a destiny that lies with Rodock, partly due to Miller's defiance; both men simply underestimate each other. Upon the film's conclusion, shortly after Miller and Jo depart the ranch, the former struggles to comprehend Rodock's change in personality. He says, "[Rodock's] a rough one to figure. You think you know him, and you don't." Jo listens intently. Miller appears perplexed as he speaks of Rodock's newfound compassion. The latter then approaches from the distance. Upon reaching Jo, he returns her jewelry and abruptly retreats to whence he came.

Rodock anticipates that Miller will be undeterred and continue his journey with Jo in tow, but such is not the case. Miller returns in the direction of the ranch. It is not his intention to oppose Rodock. Miller simply opts for harmony and finally understands the meaning of love. Rodock and Jo belong together. Despite their many quarrels, a mutual trust has developed and their love for each other has grown. Miller not only believes in their union, but he also understands that his future lies elsewhere. As he departs the valley for the last time, he states, "I never saw Mr. Rodock again, and I never saw

Jocasta again, but I carried them with me wherever I went, and I loved them both my whole life long."

"Robert Wise was never a loud yeller," stuntman Jack Young said in regard to the production of *Tribute to a Bad Man*. "We all met him upon arriving in Colorado. Regarding James Cagney, I loved the little man. He was very short. The crew usually wanted to place him on an apple box so he wouldn't appear to be so small. Apple boxes, which stood about eight inches off the ground, were really popular on movie sets back in those days. I worked several times with Robert Taylor, and he, too, sometimes had to stand on an apple box because of his height. He used to hate it, but the crew set up the box nonetheless. If the script ever called for Cagney's character to engage others in conversation, and if the storyboards indicated that he was to be the only performer featured in the shot, then he stood on an apple box. However, if the presented conversation happened to include more than one individual in the frame, Cagney would stand two or three feet beyond the others so that he didn't look as small. I've forgotten his exact height, but I'm guessing it was somewhere around five feet six inches tall.

Hanging fever.

"Following the filming of the fight scene between Cagney and Stephen McNally, most of it was cut out. I'm not sure why because it was a good, lengthy fight scene. I was Cagney's stunt double and Danny Sands doubled McNally. While we were choreographing the scene, Cagney stayed put and barely moved so he would know exactly what to do and where to be for his close-ups. I loved that!

"In addition to Cagney, I enjoyed spending time with other members of the cast. Irene Papas was such a sweetheart. Everybody fell in love with her. She was so soft-spoken that people always had to ask her to repeat her answers whenever she was asked any questions. And I know Mr. Wise kept telling her, 'Raise your voice. I need you to be a little louder.' Stephen McNally was a good man. Sometimes, he'd tell jokes, but they weren't that funny. I nevertheless enjoyed being around him. Don Dubbins was a nice boy. He was just getting started in the business. Robert Francis was supposed to play the role of Steve Miller, but tragically, he died in a plane crash about a week prior to filming. Therefore, Don Dubbins was hired rather quickly. I still can't believe what happened to Vic Morrow in 1982. What a terrible way for a man to die! He was decapitated by a helicopter rotor while performing in a scene from *Twilight Zone: The Movie*. In the aftermath of Morrow's accident, I refused to become a stunt coordinator because I didn't want to be responsible for somebody else's life.

Stephen McNally.

"Following the conclusion of my career as a stuntman, I made the transition from exerting myself in front of the camera to working productively behind the scenes, as I had become a casting and location manager. In 1979,

I worked on a film called *The Wild Wild West Revisited*. It was a spin-off of the original television series. Its director, Burt Kennedy, was a good friend of Cagney's. One day, I received a message on my walkie-talkie stating that Mr. Cagney was on his way to the set to have lunch with our director. For me, it was an opportunity to visit with a man I hadn't seen in years. I remember being on the set when a van approached, and I arranged for the vehicle to occupy a nearby parking space. The door then slid open, and there was James Cagney. He must have weighed about three hundred pounds! I couldn't believe how much weight he'd gained through the years. He was pretty crippled up, but what really impresses me is that Cagney remembered me after so many years. That was a highlight of my life.

"Going back to *Tribute to a Bad Man*, the cast was amiable and really respected the crew. Most of the directors and performers of the era appreciated the stuntmen, although we didn't receive screen credit in those days. If one views the Internet Movie Database page of a stuntman or other crew member, he or she is usually listed as 'uncredited' for a particular job of the 1940s or 1950s. I got started in March of 1947. Many don't realize that, in modern times, stunt people are not always with a production from beginning to end. One will go for certain things. The job might take three days, a week, two weeks, or whatever time is necessary to do a particular stunt or stunts, and then you move on. I was on the set of *Tribute to a Bad Man* for just about the entire production, because in those days a stunt man would also serve as a stand-in, or a lighting double, for the actor. Nowadays, stand-ins and stunt people are separate, but this happened rather early in the history of the film industry. In addition to being Cagney's stunt double, I was also his stand-in. For the most part, I reported to the first assistant director and the lighting cinematographer. I also worked for the stunt coordinator, Carl Pitti. He actually had a small part in the film. I worked with him on multiple occasions, both before and after the production of *Tribute to a Bad Man*. We belonged to the Stuntmen's Association and were like family.

"I've been banged up pretty bad throughout my career. On the set of *The Alamo*, the John Wayne picture, I broke my back and ended up with a punctured lung. These days, at eighty-nine years of age, I'm not in the greatest of conditions, but I wake up every morning, pinch myself, and if it hurts I just laugh like hell. One more day! I've had the most wonderful life a guy could ask for. I did what I wanted, when I wanted, and how I wanted. So many people live a life in a job or marriage they hate. What kind of a life is that? I was married four times and could never get it right. My last divorce was in 1982, and at that point, I decided I had learned a lesson. Marriage simply wasn't for me. Although I've got four kids from all of those marriages, I like being alone and I've lived as such for over thirty years.

Vic Morrow as Lars Peterson.

"Regarding Mr. Wise, he was fairly soft-spoken and always had a smile. I don't ever remember him being gruff or unhappy or anything like that. However, being a stuntman, I was off practicing when Wise was shooting scenes with the principals. Therefore, I wasn't around him as much as the others. I'm thinking Wise was in his early forties around the time of *Tribute to a Bad Man*. He always dressed nice. Sometimes, he even wore a suit when we were shooting interiors. The jacket and tie would usually be off before the day was out, but he occasionally appeared with a suit in the morning. The ranch house where a few of the scenes take place was built specifically for the film. I vividly remember how the production began for me. We flew into Grand Junction, Colorado. We were then taken to Ridgeway and lived in mobile homes. There wasn't much going on in the area at the time, but Wise really wanted to capture that beautiful background with the mountains and everything. The location was just gorgeous, and the weather was cold; we had some snow in the mountains. Somebody, I can't remember who it was, always used to refer to Robert Wise as Bobby Earl. I guess this person had known him for quite some time. Overall, I enjoyed meeting and being around Mr. Wise. He was pleasant, and his demeanor, in turn, caused the crew to be pleasant. In short, Wise was a good director who cracked a soft whip. Film directors usually have the whole movie in their heads before they start a production. It's just a matter of continuity and keeping up with it."

Tribute to a Bad Man premiered in New York on March 30, 1956. Two weeks later, it was released in theaters across the country. The film marked Wise's first and only collaboration with James Cagney, who seldom appeared in Westerns throughout his career. Instead, gangster roles were arguably Cagney's greatest forte. He nevertheless understood Wise's predicament as the cast and crew struggled during the film's early stages of production. On location in Colorado, the group became severely limited in regard to what could be accomplished, especially in the absence of an established protagonist. Yet, upon Cagney's replacement of Spencer Tracy, the production resumed without incident, and Wise essentially found himself in good company.

The cast and crew remained dedicated throughout the production. Robert Surtees, the film's director of photography, worked tirelessly to create vivid depictions of the Old West. A majority of *Tribute to a Bad Man* consists of exterior shots intended to illustrate a particular realism of the period. Furthermore, regarding the scene in which Hearn is hanged, Surtees requested that the crew delay until the weather was overcast so that an ominous setting could be established. Despite having to wait several days for the conditions to become ideal, Wise was nevertheless accommodating, and the end result proved beneficial, as the scene remains one of the most memorable of the picture. In short, the executives of MGM were pleased with Wise's achievement. Furthermore, they eagerly anticipated the theatrical release of *Somebody Up There Likes Me* (1956), another picture Wise directed for the studio. The film's production wrapped around the same time *Tribute to a Bad Man* premiered in New York. William Feather, the late author, once said, "One way to get the most out of life is to look upon it as an adventure," and Robert Wise, a man who often endured a fast-paced work schedule, especially during the prime of his career, steadfastly made the best of such an adventure.

Don Dubbins and Irene Papas both received praise for their performances in *Tribute to a Bad Man*, ultimately earning them long-term contracts with MGM.

22
SOMEBODY UP THERE LIKES ME

(PRODUCED AND RELEASED 1956)

> "Be a first-rate version of yourself, instead of a second-rate version of somebody else."
> - Judy Garland

Seven years following the theatrical release of *The Set-Up* (1949), Robert Wise set forth to direct another boxing drama. *Somebody Up There Likes Me*, an MGM production, depicts the real-life story of Rocky Graziano, the former middleweight boxing champion of the world. Ernest Lehman was hired by the studio to pen the film's script. He was immediately provided with Graziano's autobiography. Although it proved to be an invaluable resource, Lehman additionally took it upon himself to interview the ex-champion's friends and family in order for his script to be painstakingly accurate.

Somebody Up There Likes Me marked the second collaboration between Lehman and Wise. Without a doubt, both men excelled tremendously in their respective crafts. Wise, furthermore, had the utmost confidence in his writer. He was nevertheless concerned about landing the ideal lead for his picture. MGM sought James Dean for the role of Graziano, but the former's tragic death on September 30, 1955, altered the course of the film's production. Eventually, Wise and the studio decided to cast a young, up-and-coming actor on loan from Warner Bros. His name was Paul Newman, and not only was he perfect as Graziano, he subsequently turned in an Oscar-worthy performance.

Paul Newman.

Rocco "Rocky" Barbella (Newman) opts to live a life of crime with his cohorts. At times, he is caught and remanded to a Catholic protectory. Barbella, however, frequently escapes to resume his criminal career. He is eventually sent to a state reformatory, where he meets Frankie Peppo (Robert Loggia), a boxing enthusiast. In time, Barbella's behavior proves uncontrollable, regardless of where he is incarcerated. Following a stint at Rikers Island, he is drafted into the United States Army. Barbella loses his temper and strikes a superior officer. He flees to Stillman's Gym, a locale known to be frequented by Peppo. The latter, however, is serving time at Sing Sing. Barbella instead becomes acquainted with Irving Cohen (Everett Sloane), a boxing promoter, and introduces himself using the pseudonym of Graziano so as to avoid detection by the authorities. It is not long before Barbella showcases considerable talent in the ring, but he is eventually apprehended and court-martialed by the military. A dishonorable discharge and one-year prison sentence follow.

Upon his release, Barbella returns to boxing and adopts Graziano as his professional name. Success abounds, and he is classified as a "promising young middleweight." Graziano's life outside of the ring takes an interesting turn when his sister, Yolanda (Donna Jo Gribble), introduces him to her friend, Norma Unger (Pier Angeli). A romantic relationship develops and leads to marriage, and shortly thereafter, Norma gives birth to a baby girl. Meanwhile, Graziano's career flourishes. Peppo eventually resurfaces, and his associates intend to bet against Graziano in an upcoming fight, as the out-of-state odds are astounding. Peppo proposes an offer of $100 thousand. The money will go to Graziano on the condition that he purposely loses the bout. If he does not comply, his military discharge and incarceration will be made public, thereby damaging his reputation and overall image. Graziano therefore opts out of the fight and instead fakes a back injury; the District Attorney's office investigates. Graziano, however, refuses to name Peppo as an accomplice, ultimately violating a state regulation. As a result, his boxing license is subsequently revoked by the New York State Athletic Commission. The media eventually learns the details of Graziano's troubled past, and a period of decline ensues. Cohen later arranges for him to compete in the World Middleweight Title Fight in Chicago, granted by the Illinois Commission. Graziano faces Tony Zale (Court Shepard), a fighter who defeated him months earlier, and emerges victorious. Upon returning to New York, a victory parade is scheduled in Graziano's honor. He urges Norma to "drink it all in while it lasts."

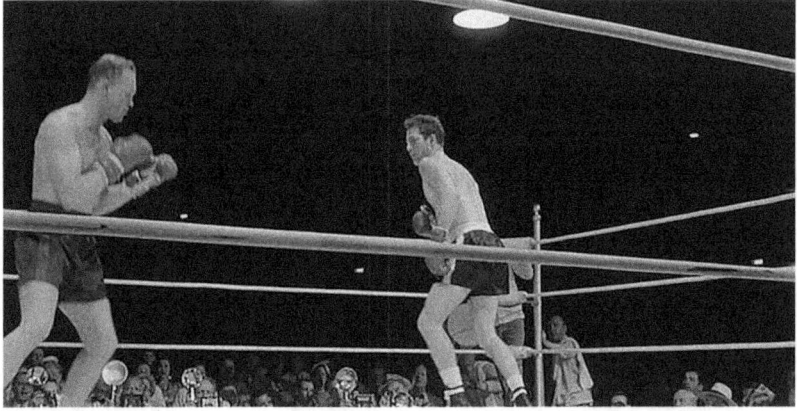

Rocky battles Tony Zale for the World Middleweight Title.

Wise does not waste any time introducing the character of Nick Barbella (Harold J. Stone), Graziano's father. Following the opening credits, the narrative begins in the family's crowded apartment, where a so-called boxing lesson transpires. Several of Nick's friends look on as the young Graziano, tears in his eyes, takes a beating at the hands of his father. To begin the following scene, Wise transitions to the exterior of a drugstore. Displayed in its window is an advertisement for razor blades. An inanimate Gene Tunney, the world heavyweight champion of the era, appears within a cardboard cutout. The advertisement states, "FOR FATHER'S DAY, GENE TUNNEY SAYS, 'GIVE HIM HAMMERHILL BLADES.' THEY'RE A KNOCKOUT!" In a fit of anger, the young Graziano, flooded with thoughts of his abusive father, breaks the window. His lone action marks the beginning a years-long crime spree.

Later in the narrative, Wise transports his audience to the same location outside of the drugstore, and again, displayed in the window is an advertisement for the blades. This time, however, the adult Graziano is featured instead of Tunney. Much has essentially transpired through the years. Standing at the drugstore's exterior, Graziano glances upward at the family's apartment. A single light emanates from one of its windows. Shortly thereafter, Graziano enters the apartment and encounters Nick. It is not long before the two begin to argue. Graziano then cites his father's inability to follow through with earlier aspirations of becoming a professional fighter:

GRAZIANO: That's all you can do is talk tough, but you ain't so tough. You wasn't even tough enough to take the decision from Ma when she told you to hang up the gloves and quit fightin'. And you been fightin' that one in your head ever since, haven't you? Yeah, and you still ain't won it. And you never will. Cause it's all over for you, no matter how much booze you take. But it ain't over for me. I got a wife. I got a kid. I got a home in Ocean Parkway. And I'm fightin' Tony Zale for the championship of the world! I ain't gonna be decisioned out of nothing, especially by you!

Upon a failed attempt to strike Graziano, Nick begins to sob. Years earlier, he told his young, weeping son that he hates crybabies. Nick, however, exhibits a disdain for sensitivity until his emotions are ultimately exposed. A turning point in the narrative is reached when Graziano assures his father that he will defeat Zale in the upcoming fight, boldly stating, "Don't worry about a thing!" Throughout the film, Graziano makes such a statement on more than one occasion, but it is usually made in an attempt to pacify the person to whom he is speaking, namely his anxious mother, Ida (Eileen Heckart). Yet, when Graziano speaks these words to his father, he does so with confidence. At the time of the rematch with Zale, Wise frequently transitions from the venue, Chicago Stadium, to the Barbella living room, and a proud Nick listens in anticipation of the fight's outcome. In addition to Graziano's childhood dwelling, Wise transitions to locations (i.e., a crowded bar, Graziano's Ocean Parkway home, and the candy store of Graziano's old neighborhood) inhabited or frequented by those who have had the most profound effect on the middleweight's life, more so, in fact, than Nick Barbella.

During the film's climactic fight, the action sometimes shifts from the venue to a crowded bar, where Sergeant John Hyland (Judson Pratt), Graziano's one-time mentor, carefully listens to play-by-play updates of the contest. Their relationship, which begins at Leavenworth Disciplinary Barracks under extraordinary circumstances, essentially thrives due to a mutual respect. One day in the prison yard, Heldon (Arch Johnson), an unruly inmate, attacks Graziano. A fistfight ensues and Graziano prevails in under a minute. Hyland, an administrator of the barracks, bears witness to the scuffle and arranges for a private meeting to take place between him and Graziano at the facility's boxing gymnasium. Interestingly enough, he introduces himself only as John Hyland. He does not make reference to his military rank or any other title. It immediately becomes clear that Hyland is intent on treating Graziano as his equal, not his inferior. He then speaks of Leavenworth's boxing squad, and Graziano is subsequently encouraged to join:

HYLAND: You got something inside of you that a lot of fighters don't have, never will have ... no matter how much I teach them: hate. I don't know why it's there. I only know that if anybody hits you, he better start ducking fast. Because that hate pours into that right hand of yours and makes it like a ... like a charge of dynamite. What a great big waste of a lot a hate. Your whole life you've let it get you into trouble. Why don't you start letting it do some good for ya?

Following his sentence at Leavenworth, Graziano's life undergoes significant change. He does everything in his power to avoid any kind of trouble with the law. Consequently, Graziano violates a state regulation upon reuniting with Peppo, but his actions are relatively blameless, as he attempts to avoid the exposure of past mistakes. Hyland, in essence, is responsible for Graziano's turnaround. "Make that hate of yours work for you inside the ring where it'll make a living for ya...instead of outside the ring where it'll just go on lousing up your life forever," Hyland says at the time of the aforementioned meeting. His advice is heeded, but another individual is ultimately responsible for finishing what the sergeant started.

Pier Angeli.

A frantic Norma, remaining in close proximity to the radio as she listens to the climactic rematch in the family's Ocean Parkway home, ensures Graziano's success in the ring, simply because she understands him much better than he does himself. Her occasional arguments with Cohen essentially serve as a precursor to such success. When Graziano first learns of the Chicago bout, he voices his disapproval, asking, "Why have I gotta fight in a foreign city where I ain't got no friends? They don't want me to win there. I gotta tell you that?" Without another word, he exits the scene, leaving Cohen dumbfounded. Norma, however, understands that the only way Graziano can be successful is if he goes to Chicago and follows through with such a commitment. Shortly thereafter, the three depart New York and begin preparations for the upcoming fight, but Graziano remains agitated at everyone and everything.

Tempers flare one evening in a Chicago hotel room, as Norma makes it painstakingly clear to Cohen that her husband will need to live with his past and not allow for it to hinder any future success. "It's time you and I stop looking the other way every time he gets mad at the world for the trouble he gets into," she tells Cohen, but the argument continues:

COHEN: Please, Norma, I thought you were gonna help us. I thought you wanted Rocky to win the fight.
NORMA: All right. But what about all the fights after that one? What about the years that come after he has to give up fighting?
COHEN: But Norma....
NORMA: I'm his wife, not his manager. I'm gonna be living with him long after you stopped worrying about his weight and his footwork and whether or not he's getting enough sleep!
The sound of a slamming door is immediately heard, as Rocky flees Chicago for New York. Yet, the impromptu jaunt ultimately proves beneficial, partly due to the place and person he visits first upon his arrival.

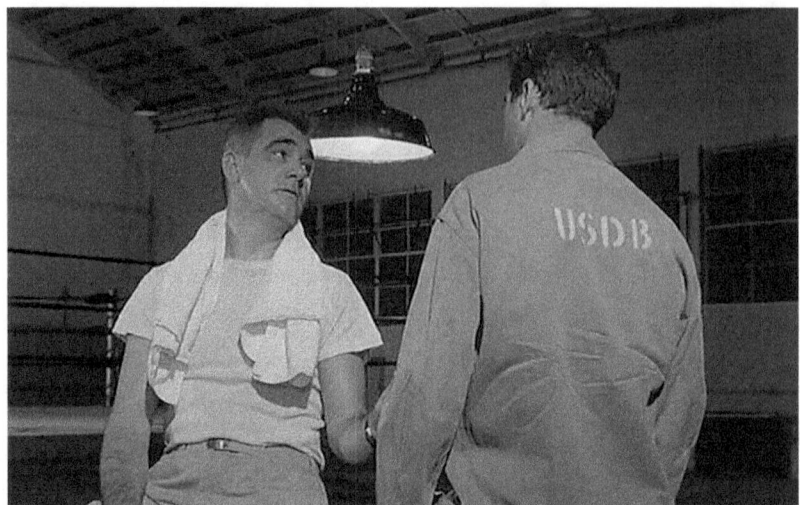

"I don't think you'd ever show any real style like some of my boys, but you'd probably lick 'em all. You'd lick 'em all because you've got something inside of you that a lot of fighters don't have...never will have...no matter how much I teach them. Hate."

Benny (Joseph Buloff), a positive influence on the troubled middleweight and affable proprietor of the candy store in Graziano's old neighborhood, eagerly tunes in to the climactic bout along with the fellow patrons of his establishment. At the time of the aforementioned jaunt to New York, a reminiscence at the store of those long gone ultimately leads to a lesson regarding the importance of responsibility. Benny updates Graziano as to the fate of his former cohorts:

BENNY: So many of the old 10th Street gang are gone. Fidel killed in a holdup, Sammy doing thirty years, and Shorty the Greek broke his spine driving a getaway car.

Benny continues his update of the gang, but Graziano is unwilling to listen.

BENNY: The whole world is not so different from my candy store. Someone comes in, sits down at the fountain, asks for a soda. I give him a soda. He drinks the soda. I give him a check. He's got to pay for it. It's the same out there. He who wants a soda must be willing to pay the check. You do something wrong, Rocky, you got to pay the check. It's a very simple truth, yet some men find it difficult to understand.

Upon exiting the store, Graziano encounters Romolo (Sal Mineo), a childhood friend and sole remaining member of the 10th Street gang. Romolo speaks of opening a flower stand as a front for an illegal bookmaking operation. A surprised Graziano grabs him by the collar and says, "I don't wanna lose you. Can't you understand that? You're gonna get killed if you don't wise up and turn a leaf you pathetic little jerk," but Romolo concludes that neither of them have any kind of chance for a successful life.

During the following scene, as Graziano strolls through the old neighborhood by himself, he observes a pair of juveniles escorted by two policemen into the local precinct. He also discovers a homeless man to be sleeping on a sidewalk. Graziano is essentially reminded of his past, in addition to what might become of the future. Shortly thereafter, he arrives at the drugstore's exterior and faces the cardboard cutout of himself. In time, the significant exchange between Graziano and his father transpires, and Benny's words suddenly ring true, as people must be held accountable for the life decisions they make. Graziano ultimately returns to Chicago, but not before visiting the candy store to obtain a pack of maple walnut ice cream for Norma, and it is a foregone conclusion that, during such an encounter with Benny, Graziano made sure to pay the check.

"Steve McQueen, at the time my soon-to-be-husband, was offered a small part in *Somebody Up There Likes Me*," Neile Adams said. "Pier Angeli and Paul Newman had their own limousines to take them to and from the set. One day, the crew was shooting a scene very early in the morning and Steve was cold. Pier Angeli's limo happened to be unoccupied because she was performing in the scene. Steve jumped in the car, picked up a newspaper, and began to read it. The car door suddenly opened and Vic Damone, the famous singer and husband of Pier Angeli, entered the vehicle. He said, 'You know, this is my wife's car and you can't stay here.' Steve casually put down the newspaper and replied, 'No shit?' Then, without another word, he picked up the paper and resumed reading with no intention of leaving the limo. Finally, when Pier Angeli returned, Steve left. But it sure took him awhile to do so, and Steve and Vic Damone never spoke to one another again.

Angela Cartwright and Pier Angeli. Cartwright would later appear in *The Sound of Music* (1965) as Brigitta, one of the seven von Trapp children.

"The competition between Steve and Paul began during the production of *Somebody Up There Likes Me*. Jimmy Dean was supposed to play the lead but passed away. The part was eventually given to Paul, probably because of his connection to the Actors Studio. I don't believe anybody else auditioned for that role. Steve was rather put out about it because he really wanted to try for the part of Rocky Graziano. Instead, he was offered the smaller role of Fidel. But Steve and Paul remained good friends. Steve would sometimes tell me, 'I'm gonna catch up with that dude someday.' A lot of it had to do with Paul being represented as a rebel type before Steve, who would occasionally say, 'I was out stealing hubcaps while he was still in college for God's sake!'"

"I consider Robert Wise to be one of the best directors in the history of our industry. It was a privilege to work with him. *Somebody Up There Likes Me* was not only my first film, but also my first job," said Michael Dante, who appears early in the narrative as Graziano's childhood friend, Shorty the

Greek. "I fondly wrote about the experience in my autobiography, *Michael Dante: From Hollywood to Michael Dante Way*. In 1956, I was under contract to MGM. The film was shot on location in New York, and we stayed at the Warwick Hotel. I lived in Stamford, Connecticut, which is literally fifty minutes from Times Square. My friends and family were able to visit the New York locations where we worked.

Robert Loggia as Frankie Peppo.

"*Somebody Up There Likes Me* happened to be Steve McQueen's first picture as well. Regarding our introduction to one another, I remember being at the hotel. It was raining really hard that day. I was standing under the canopy of the hotel entrance and couldn't even see across the street. A limousine was on its way to collect me and a few others who were going to the set. As I was waiting, a motorcycle pulls up and the rider is completely drenched from head to foot. He didn't have one bit of rain gear. He looked at me and said, 'Hey, man! Do you know where the *Somebody Up There Likes Me* company is working?' And I replied, 'Yeah. As a matter of fact, if you wait about five minutes, a limousine will come around and you can ride with us to the location. There should be a place for your bike in the hotel's parking lot.' He then said, 'No, man. I'm gonna ride the bike.' It was pouring and he was so wet! He was wearing a little cap, and he had a jacket, but it was not a rain jacket.

"The limousine arrived and off me and the others went to the set. During the trip, I kept looking back to see if Steve was close by and following us, and he was. He followed us right to the location. I arrived on the set first and was as dry as a bone. I went inside and there were two towels in the dressing room. It wasn't like the lavish dressing rooms of modern times. This was just a place where one could change his or her wardrobe. There was space for about two chairs and that was it. I had been on the set for about five minutes when, in from the rain, Steve arrived. He said, 'Hey, man. I'm Steve McQueen.' And I replied, 'Hi, Steve. My name is Michael Dante.' I then offered my towels. He didn't have a dry mark on his wardrobe; a lot of the water had fallen to the floor. On this particular day, shooting was cancelled. We got rained out.

"The next day featured beautiful weather. The location was on the east side of New York. Our introduction to Bob Wise was a privilege. We were all so respectful of his talent. Paul Newman, Sal Mineo, Steve McQueen, and I were the four actors performing in the day's sequence. It was the youth sequence, when Rocky was young and in trouble a great deal. Our characters were stealing radios from apartment buildings, lifting furs from the backs of trucks, striping tires from automobiles, and taking wardrobe from the garment center. One particular shot was photographed with a Mitchell Camera, an apparatus that was very popular in those days. It was set up on a dolly. A 2' x 6' plank was used to support the equipment. The camera was secured on the dolly, but there was about a three or four foot hangover. I'm not sure why.

"It then came time to shoot the scene where Paul steps in front of the approaching fur truck. There were about 200 people watching the action from behind a roped-off area of the set. The truck traveled down the street to a particular mark just before the camera, and Paul steps into the street to stop the truck, which was not going very fast at that point. The driver then sticks his head out of the window and says, 'What are you trying to do, get killed?' And Paul, in the vernacular of Rocky Graziano, replies, 'No, I just wanted to see whether your brakes worked.' Anyways, the camera crew lined up the shot. Sal Mineo was the closest to the truck; Steve and I were positioned near a big brick wall, about twenty yards away from the vehicle. Our backs were to the truck. We were trying to be obscure and not make it look like we were ready to start stealing furs. There were so many pigeons, about a couple hundred of them, in the area. Steve was fascinated with those pigeons in regard to their ability to fly, where they made their homes with their mates, and so forth. It was an unbelievable scene with that kind of setting. Only a sidewalk separated us from the brick wall. The background was all brick and pigeons. Then, Bob said, 'Okay, let's do a rehearsal of this scene.' He had an actor, not a stuntman, doing the driving. The actor drove the truck, which had one of those stick shifts that you can hear all the way in Pittsburgh. He promenaded down the street and hit his mark. Paul jumped in front of the vehicle. Dialogue was exchanged, and Bob eventually said, 'Okay, let's go a little faster and we'll go for a take.' Steve's back was to the truck, and he was really interested in paying attention to those pigeons. Sal was fine. He was going to be the first one on the truck. We'd do our heist. And then I was going to be the last one off of that truck. I kept thinking about what was going to happen as it picked up speed. I faced the challenge of jumping off without falling on my face.

"Bob called 'Action!' and then the truck started its approach. You could hear it from downtown. Suddenly, the master cylinder started making this booming sound, and the driver found himself in a situation where he couldn't stop it from doing so. He headed directly towards the camera and Paul. Fortunately, Paul was barely able to get out of the way. But that extended plank, which should have been reduced in length, was out in the path of the oncoming vehicle. When the driver turned away from the camera, he hit the plank, and the camera operator shot up in the air towards the skies. I'm amazed that he wasn't killed. It was unbelievable. When the truck driver saw the camera operator go up into the sky, he mistakenly assumed that he hit all of the crew members who happened to be standing behind the camera, but such was not the case. All he saw was a body go up. The driver then turned, and the truck was suddenly heading towards Steve and me. I immediately pushed Steve out of the way, unsure if he was going to be injured in the process. The truck then hit one of those lampposts that looked like a duck and finally came to a stop. The driver was in shock. I ran to the vehicle and was the first one there. The driver kept saying, 'I killed him! I killed him!' I shook the driver to get his attention, but he was in total shock.

"People from the first aid department quickly arrived on the scene, and Bob Wise, being the director that he was, in addition to the man that he was, said, 'We're done for the day! That's it! I want another truck, and I don't want another driver. I want the same driver, and when he's ready, we'll do the scene. We'll do it again. I don't want anybody to replace the actor.' It was a very admirable gesture. Of course, the actor was so appreciative when he later learned that he wouldn't be fired from the job. He was sent to the hospital and had been sedated in order to stay calm. Everybody turned out to be okay, even the fellow that was operating the camera, but at the time, it looked like a rocket was going into the air; miraculously, when he made it down, there weren't any injuries to speak of. He came right back to work the next day and the scene was filmed several days later when the actor was ready and had become settled. Mr. Wise arranged to get another truck that was operable. He was a class act. Everybody thought his handling of the entire incident was great, especially since he took the time to wait for the actor to become available. Some directors would have sought a replacement and kept shooting, but Wise gave this guy enough time to regain his confidence. I remember talking with Paul, Sal, and Steve the day after the accident. We all concurred that Bob's actions were very noble.

"There's no question in my mind that Paul Newman's performance in *Somebody Up There Likes Me* is his most creative. Why? Because it was such a departure from his true self. He was about as ethnic as a glass of milk. With those blue eyes and handsome looks, he did not look a thing like Rocky Graziano, but Paul was brilliant in such a performance. I learned a thing or two about boxing while I was going to school, and I can confidently say that Paul had all of the moves that Rocky had. He was so believable in the role. As an actor admiring another actor's work, and for Paul to be so far from his own self, I can say it was absolutely fantastic.

"Rocky Graziano sometimes appeared on the set. He had a great sense of humor. Many years later, I ran into him in Beverly Hills. After we exchanged greetings, I asked him a question that had been on my mind for some time. 'Whatever happened to the real-life Shorty the Greek?' Rocky then spoke of a terrible tragedy that had occurred. 'Shorty was riding in the back of a truck,' he said, 'And the truck got into an accident and he was decapitated.' Since I portrayed Shorty the Greek in the movie, I often wondered what had become of him. It was terrible to receive that kind of news.

"Everybody who is young is promising. The world should sue the young for breach of promise."

As Rocky fights, those of the neighborhood remain indoors with their ears glued to their radios in eager anticipation of the match's outcome.

"Much later after the production of *Somebody Up There Likes Me*, I met with Robert Wise as he was preparing to direct another picture. A casting agent arranged for the meeting to take place, but Wise told me I looked a little too good for a part in his upcoming film. He was looking for somebody a little older and more broken down. I always thought of Wise as being a little on the shy side when it came to social interactions. Of course, there's nothing shy about the films he made. Wise certainly got the message across regarding his work as a director. He was not vociferous. During any conversation, he was not forceful or aggressive. He was such a gentleman, sensitive and soft-spoken conversationally. Before Wise and I parted ways on that specific day, we reminisced about *Somebody Up There Likes Me*, and we also commented about how the years go by so fast. In short, Wise was not just a great director, he was a wonderful man."

"Sometimes, I think I never should've left the lingerie business. I was the happiest man in Ladies Underwear."

Somebody Up There Likes Me premiered in San Francisco on July 3, 1956. Two days later, it debuted in New York to a sold-out crowd. Wise's film eventually garnered three Oscar nominations, and on March 27, 1957, at the 29th Academy Awards, *Somebody Up There Likes Me* won the Oscar for Best Art Direction and Best Cinematography, both of the "Black and White" category.[34] It was nominated for Best Film Editing but ultimately lost to *Around the World in 80 Days* (1956). Many, however, were surprised that Paul Newman was snubbed by the Academy, as not even a nomination was earned for his memorable performance.

Midway through the film, Graziano argues with Norma as he declares, "It's for the birds!" He does not mince words, especially when the topic is romance. Through the scene, Wise pays homage to an earlier film, *Something for the Birds* (1952). Yet, such a scenario is also significant because it marks a turning point of the narrative. Graziano eventually comes to realize the importance of love and companionship. The film's tagline appropriately declares, "A Girl Can Lift A Fellow To The Skies!" Newman shined in his role partly due to the on-screen chemistry he shared with Pier Angeli, and although he went on to have a stellar career, she did not.

Sadly, in 1971, Angeli was found dead at the young age of thirty-nine from a barbiturate overdose. Mere speculation indicated she had taken her own life, but some argued that, despite two failed marriages, exciting prospects were beginning to appear on the horizon. Angeli had recently been cast in Francis Ford Coppola's *The Godfather* (1972) and was said to be thrilled about the upcoming opportunity. The world, however, will probably never learn the ultimate reason behind her demise. In addition to Angeli, Sal Mineo's life ended tragically when, in 1976, he was murdered outside his West Hollywood home during an apparent robbery attempt. He was thirty-seven. Regarding Wise, he was fortunate to have known and directed both Angeli and Mineo during those brief two months in 1956, as their time together, although short-lived, essentially became an experience that was one for the ages.

---

34 The Oscar for Best Art Direction was awarded to Cedric Gibbons and Malcolm F. Brown (art direction), as well as Edwin B. Willis and F. Keogh Gleason (set decoration). The Oscar for Best Cinematography was awarded to Joseph Ruttenberg.

Michael Dante as Shorty the Greek.

Sal Mineo.

23
THIS COULD BE THE NIGHT

(PRODUCED 1956, RELEASED 1957)

> "If you get, give. If you learn, teach."
> - Maya Angelou

Harper's Magazine, in publication since the mid-nineteenth century, was especially popular during the 1950s, a time when the American economy and culture were booming. Featured on a monthly basis in the magazine were fact, fiction, and opinion, all presented by writers of varying backgrounds. Cordelia Baird Gross, a relatively unknown author, penned a short story for *Harper's* entitled *Protection for a Tough Racket*. It was featured in the December, 1954 issue and attracted the attention of more than one studio. MGM ultimately proved to be the most interested, acquiring the motion picture rights within a year of the issue's publication.

Isobel Lennart, a one-time mail room employee of MGM, wrote a script based on *Protection for a Tough Racket*. She also adapted ideas from *It's Hard to Find Mecca in Flushing*, another of Gross's short stories. Lennart's finished script was entitled *This Could Be the Night*. Robert Wise, on the heels of *Somebody Up There Likes Me* (1956), accepted MGM's offer to direct the picture. The studio sought an ensemble cast. In addition, Ray Anthony, the well-liked bandleader and songwriter, agreed to appear in the film with his orchestra and also recorded the picture's soundtrack. Prior to its theatrical release, the music of *This Could Be the Night* was promoted as "THE KIND YOU HEAR THROUGH YOUR FEET."

Anne Leeds (Jean Simmons), a New York school teacher, desires supplemental income and is hired as a part-time secretary for The Tonic, a popular, yet infamous, night club. The establishment is rumored to have earlier harbored bootleggers during the Prohibition era. It is not long before Anne is fired by co-owner Tony Armotti (Anthony Franciosa) over what she considers to be a trivial matter, but Rocco (Paul Douglas), the other owner, takes exception to the decision and demands she be rehired. Armotti therefore goes to Anne's classroom to make amends. She agrees to return but continues to believe he is an unfair judge of her character. Rocco blames himself. Years earlier, he took Armotti under his wing. In the aftermath of a failed marriage, Rocco became a cynic and firmly believes Armotti followed suit.

Anne learns that the staff and clientele of The Tonic have classified her as a greenhorn, one who lacks experience and sophistication. She believes Armotti to be responsible and confronts him at his place of residence, a private apartment above the club. Anne explains that her reason for moving to New York from Massachusetts was to meet new people and make new friends. Armotti, however, will not allow it to happen at his club. Anne chides his narrow-mindedness, and in the heat of their argument, they kiss. Anne confesses her love for Armotti, who insists the feeling is not mutual. Rocco later becomes privy to the incident and strikes his fellow business partner in anger. He simply does not wish for Anne to be hurt in any way. She eventually quits, and several of the club's employees become downhearted upon hearing the news. Anne finds employment with a competing night club but is unaware that the establishment serves as a front for bookmakers. Armotti pays her a visit just as police raid the premises. He helps Anne to escape and thus avoid incrimination. Much to the delight of those at The Tonic, Armotti rehires her for the second time. He and Rocco therefore anticipate better days on the horizon.

"A leopard never changes his stripes."

As *This Could Be the Night* begins, Wise presents viewers with a nighttime image of the New York City skyline. The opening credits conclude shortly thereafter, and courtesy of a cinematic time-lapse technique, night becomes day. Such a presentation is indicative of The Tonic's hustle and bustle, as much transpires within the club's confines from sunset to sunrise, and upon Anne's introduction to the establishment, she becomes acquainted with many. One such individual is Stowe Devlin (Tom Helmore), an attorney who, much to the chagrin of Leon (J. Carrol Naish), The Tonic's head chef, prefers to cook his own meals. Devlin frequently finds solace dining in the club's office. Upon meeting him for the first time, Anne discovers they are both from Massachusetts. She takes comfort in knowing he "speaks [her] language." Devlin's timely appearances in The Tonic's office not only correlate with Anne's acclimation to the establishment, but also with that to Armotti. In addition, such episodes foreshadow her ill-fated employment with the competing night club.

With each trip that Devlin makes to the office, Anne is revealed to have become more accustomed to The Tonic. A difference in her confidence level is evident when comparing his first visit with that of the second, and upon his third appearance, it is clear she has completely emerged from her shell. Shortly after Anne and Devlin become acquainted, she attempts to ask him some questions about The Tonic, but he refuses to address any inquiries, declaring, "If you're in a foreign country, you ought to learn the language from the natives...not another tourist." During their second meeting, she appears upset, admitting he was "unpleasant but right" to avoid giving her "the lowdown on everyone." The phone then rings. Anne answers it and places the call on hold. Devlin attempts to offer some guidance, but with an air of confidence, she essentially makes it clear to him that his help is unnecessary. Anne proceeds into the lounge. Through trial and error, she comes to understand the club's preferred method of delivering phone messages. An impressed Armotti eventually remarks, "You learn fast!"

At the time of Devlin's third visit to the office, Anne has become fully acclimated to The Tonic. He is impressed with how far she has come and thus expresses an interest in taking her to "a movie and an early supper." Yet, before she can commit to a decision, Hussein Mohammed (Rafael Campos), a bus boy, enters with news of his upcoming algebra exam. Because Anne is a teacher, he seeks her help. Devlin eventually departs the office. His actions, however, are not attributed to Hussein's arrival, but instead, to the strange behavior of another.

Joan Blondell, Jean Simmons, and Anthony Franciosa.

Armotti's demeanor towards Anne fluctuates primarily due to Devlin's appearances in the office. Armotti is not only jealous of the rapport she develops with others, but he also becomes perturbed with the so-called intrusiveness of Devlin, who, in actuality, is his close friend. Early in the film, Armotti takes pride in a recent liaison with an unnamed female. He appears to spite Anne while whispering the tryst's details to Devlin. Armotti's respect and admiration for Devlin at such a point of the narrative is obvious. In time, Anne establishes a strong rapport with the club's employees and patrons. As Armotti becomes aware of such rapport, his relationship with Devlin undergoes a noticeable change. Armotti later speaks his mind and chooses to be blunt while expressing his dissatisfaction:

ARMOTTI: There's a big room outside with lots of tables.

DEVLIN: And lots of smoke.

ARMOTTI: If you're so delicate, go find yourself another hash house! Or, do you have to be thrown out of here?

DEVLIN: I don't know what's come into your life lately, but what it's doing to your disposition is a crime.

ARMOTTI: Well, it's my life, my club, and my disposition!

As Devlin prepares to leave the office, he pauses to address Anne.

DEVLIN: How about tomorrow?

ANNE: Ah, I'll let you know.

Devlin departs. Shortly thereafter, Armotti presses the issue.

ARMOTTI: I don't want him eating in here.

ANNE: Well, I can't very well tell him not to. He's one of our best customers.

ARMOTTI: And I'd like to point out that there's a house rule: the help don't date the customers.

ANNE: The employers don't date the help. That's the rule.

ARMOTTI: Do you know anything about the guy?

ANNE: I know he's one of your best friends.

ARMOTTI: Well, if you had any sense that should be enough!

In what is undoubtedly a pivotal moment of the film, Armotti ceases to be the insensitive man Wise has portrayed him to be. Instead, a sense of empathy is apparent. Armotti leaves the office, and an intrigued Anne chooses to follow him to his apartment. Her actions are an indirect result of the recent exchange. Had Devlin not been present in the office, Anne's pursuit of Armotti would not have transpired. Under the circumstances, the latter gradually becomes protective of her, especially at a time of great need.

Neile Adams as Patsy St. Clair. Ray Anthony appears in the background with his orchestra.

Coincidentally, the subject of Waxie London (Murvyn Vye), Rocco's troublesome associate, is often raised in Devlin's presence, thus foreshadowing Anne's ill-fated employment with London's night club. Untimely telephone calls serve as omens of troubling times, thus leading to a period of unrest only Armotti can resolve. Seconds after Anne and Devlin begin their first encounter, the phone rings. She scrambles to answer it:

ANNE: Hello? Um. . . .
It quickly becomes clear that she has picked up the wrong receiver. Upon locating the correct phone, she attempts to compose herself prior to speaking.

ANNE: Mr. Rocco's office. Uh, no he isn't. May I take a message? Who did you say? Yes. Waxie's ten is up tomorrow.

As Devlin hears London's name, it piques his interest. Anne continues her telephone conversation.

ANNE: And what does Mr. Rocco want to do about it? I-i-is that what you said?

DEVLIN: Waxie London ... been in Sing Sing ten years ... gets out tomorrow. Does Rocco want to throw him a party for Auld Lang Syne? Got it?

Anne is satisfied with Devlin's explanation and hangs up the phone. Later, as Devlin appears in the office for the fourth and final time of the film, he prepares to dine. Anne, however, is nowhere in sight. At such a point of the narrative, she has recently resigned her position as secretary of The Tonic. Devlin's appearance remains significant, because Rocco, present in the office, then receives a call from London. Anne is the topic of their telephone conversation. London wishes to hire her as a secretary for his newly-established night club. Rocco sees no harm in providing Anne with a glowing reference. Armotti, also present, overhears the exchange. He senses trouble and immediately departs for London's club. A crisis is ultimately averted. Without Armotti, Anne's future would have been one of uncertainty. Instead, she returns to The Tonic, and once again, all is right with the world.

"One thing that really surprised me was the way Bob Wise worked with his cast," Neile Adams said in regard to her appearance as Patsy St. Clair, a performer of The Tonic. "I didn't have a very big role in *This Could Be the Night*. Therefore, Bob didn't direct me, but he did visit with his supporting cast from time to time. Jack Baker did the choreography. During the day, Bob would check in with me as many times as he could, sometimes while I was doing my dance rehearsals. Regarding his directing style, he liked his storyboards and always had them in close proximity. If Bob felt his actors were on track with their performances, he didn't direct them or delve into the specifics of their characters. His style was similar to that of George Abbott, who directed me in the Broadway production of *The Pajama Game*. Mr. Abbott's directions went something like, 'Okay! You start walking away from Point A when you hear a specific word. Then, by the time the next line is recited, you should be stationed at Point B in order to go around the bench and so on and so forth.' Since Bob didn't speak with me about my character, I came up with the ideas myself. But I would imagine he had a different approach with Jean Simmons, Paul Douglas, and Tony Franciosa, who were the actual stars of the film. I played the part of a stripper who enjoyed cooking, so I suppose there wasn't much for Bob to say to me concerning my character.

Paul Douglas.

"In regard to other members of the cast, Jean Simmons was great. I didn't have that much interaction with her primarily because we couldn't rehearse together. A few weeks prior to the start of production, she gave birth to a baby girl. Her stand-in rehearsed with me instead. When it came time for Jean and me to do our scenes, I discovered she was very introspective and didn't talk that much. The one who talked a lot was Joan Blondell. I loved her. It's funny that she played my mother; she and I looked nothing alike. But Joan told me all kinds of stories about the old days. By the time I met her on Bob Wise's set, she had been around for a long time. She appeared in many musicals with Dick Powell and the two were married for several years. I loved hearing all about that! I wasn't crazy about Tony Franciosa, so I stayed away from him. In fact, nobody was crazy about him. I'm sure Jean got along well with him. But he was probably very careful around her since she was *the* star of the picture.

"Steve McQueen, my soon-to-be husband, would sometimes spend time with me on the set. He had recently worked with Paul Newman during the production of *Somebody Up There Likes Me*. Paul, who was getting ready to do another film for Bob Wise, used to visit during my rehearsals. Steve and I were actually married while I was working on *This Could Be the Night*. He called me from back east one day and said, 'I'm coming out [to Los Angeles] to make an honest woman out of you.' I didn't know what he meant, so I consulted Julie Wilson, a fellow castmate. She knew Steve from a production they did together in New York. 'When he says he's coming to California to make an honest woman out of you,' Julie said, 'he means that the two of you are getting married, you idiot!' Days later, on a Friday afternoon, Bob Wise excused me from the set, and Steve and I got married that night. The date was November 2, 1956."

Tom Helmore as Stowe Devlin.

Production of *This Could Be the Night* wrapped in December of 1956. The film's nationwide release became slated for May 17th of the following year, and MGM sought to market its upcoming picture with a clever advertisement. The official trailer begins with a bold declaration, stating, "THE BRIGHTEST LIGHTS ON EARTH. ONE MAN KNOWS WHAT MAKES THEM SHINE -" Earl Wilson, a Broadway gossip columnist, is then introduced and wastes little time presenting "another Wilson" to viewers, as the encouraging Julie Wilson aims to foster an interest in Wise's film.[35] Her performance as Ivy Corlane, a featured singer of The Tonic, is memorable. In the trailer, she enters the establishment's kitchen and declares, "Boys, men, and chefs ... this could be the night!"[36]

The remainder of the cast is presented through a series of clips, and special attention is granted to Jean Simmons as she is described as "the real rave" of the film. Wise, among many, was in awe of her extraordinary aptitude for performing. Interestingly enough, as the post-production phase of *This Could Be the Night* transpired, he was afforded the privilege of directing Simmons in yet another picture for MGM, and it essentially became an undertaking that took them far beyond the confines of the studio.

---

35 Earl Wilson and Julie Wilson were not related to one another.
36 A slight variation exists between the trailer and film regarding the recitation of Julie Wilson's notable line. In the film itself, she states, "Friends and neighbors, the time is right! This could be the night!"

Chuck Berry, who rose to prominence in the 1950s with hits such as "Johnny B. Goode" and "Roll Over Beethoven", makes a brief cameo as a guitarist at Waxie London's club.

24
UNTIL THEY SAIL

(PRODUCED AND RELEASED 1957)

"War must be, while we defend our lives against a destroyer who would devour all; but I do not love the bright sword for its sharpness, nor the arrow for its swiftness, nor the warrior for his glory. I love only that which they defend."
- J.R.R. Tolkien, *The Two Towers*

Robert Wise engaged in extensive research in order to prepare for his next film. *Until They Sail*, a drama regarding the lives of four sisters in New Zealand during World War II, essentially addresses the hardships of separation from loved ones. The script, written by Robert Anderson, was adapted from James A. Michener's short story of the same name. Prior to production, Wise ventured "down under" to interview a group of women whose husbands, years earlier, departed New Zealand to fight in the war. He naturally sought the most accurate of depictions.

Earlier, Wise and producer Mark Robson, using their own money, purchased the rights to Michener's story by means of Aspen Pictures, their production company; the two anticipated a major success. Wise and Robson, however, faced several obstacles while attempting to assemble the ideal cast and could not get their project off the ground. As a result, the rights to "Until They Sail" were regretfully sold to Hecht-Hill-Lancaster, an up-and-coming production company.³⁷ MGM nevertheless developed an avid interest in Michener's work and eventually acquired the coveted literary property for the right price. At the time, Wise was under contract to the studio. When MGM ultimately presented him with the opportunity to direct an adaptation of Michener's story, he gladly accepted.

Jean Simmons, Joan Fontaine, and Sandra Dee.

In Christchurch, New Zealand, Barbara Leslie Forbes (Jean Simmons) lives with her three sisters, Anne (Joan Fontaine), Delia (Piper Laurie), and Evelyn (Sandra Dee). Barbara experiences a sense of loneliness upon the departure of her husband. Delia becomes engaged to Phil "Shiner" Friskett (Wally Cassell), an obnoxious local, and they are married shortly thereafter. The war intensifies, and Shiner is called to active duty overseas; Delia later goes to Wellington in search of male companionship. Time passes, and the ships of American servicemen dock in Christchurch. The sisters become acquainted with Richard Bates (Charles Drake), a well-mannered captain of the United States Marine Corps. Barbara eventually travels to Wellington and discovers Delia to be in a relationship with Andy (Adam Kennedy), an American lieutenant. Delia longs for a better life and speaks of divorcing

37 Robert Wise would later become affiliated with Hecht-Hill-Lancaster during the production of *Run Silent Run Deep* (1958).

Shiner upon his return from the war. Andy introduces Barbara to Captain Jack Harding (Paul Newman), another American who is recently divorced and homesick. She later returns to Christchurch searching for meaning in her own marriage. Anne becomes annoyed with the liberties taken by some of the servicemen in town, leading Bates to issue a personal apology on behalf of the corps. Despite Anne's skepticism of Americans, she becomes attracted to him. Word arrives that Barbara's husband, Mark, has been killed in action. In time, Anne and Bates plan to marry. She becomes pregnant. Bates's unit sets sail a short time later. Meanwhile, Harding, who has been promoted to the rank of major, arrives in Christchurch and reacquaints himself with Barbara. Tragically, Bates becomes a casualty of war upon losing his life in the Battle of Tarawa. Harding and Barbara spend many of the passing days together. He appreciates her companionship, but also the bottle, as a remedy for loneliness. Months pass, and Anne's baby is born. Harding receives orders to ship out to sea. Upon his departure, he and Barbara kiss passionately. Later, Evelyn's beau, Tommy (John Wilder), returns from the war. They ultimately depart for Auckland to be married. Anne and her infant son fly to Oklahoma, where they are to live with Bates's family. Delia arrives in Christchurch in anticipation of Shiner's return from overseas duty. Yet, when he learns of her intention to divorce him, tragedy ensues. Shiner murders Delia in cold blood and is tried in a court of law. Harding is called to the stand and offers testimony regarding Delia's promiscuity. Despite Barbara's frustration with such testimony, she more or less forgives him as they anticipate a new life together.

In promoting Wise's film, a theatrical trailer emphasizes the importance of the narrative's primary characters, as an unseen narrator declares, "*Until They Sail* is the frank and intimate story of four sisters, and how each of them found love in their own way. Delia gave too freely of her love. And Anne - Iceberg Annie they called her - Anne was too proper to get involved and too human not to. To Evelyn, flirting was a teenager's prerogative; and Barbara thought she knew all about love. *Until They Sail* has thrilling moments of strong adult drama, but none more vivid than the return of the husband Delia tried to forget."

The city of Christchurch. New Zealand's government and military were very cooperative during the production of *Until They Sail*.

Indeed, much transpires throughout the picture's duration. In the beginning, the sisters speak of their only brother, Kit, who has sailed away to fight in the war. He is never seen by the audience, as his demise transpires a short time following his departure. Yet, with news of Kit's death comes the announcement of Delia's engagement to Shiner, thus foreshadowing the trouble that is to follow. Wise sets the ensuing wedding, in short a dreary ceremony, against the backdrop of a raging storm. As the film continues, Wise's inclusion of distinct story elements (i.e., cigarettes, a war map, and periodic radio broadcasts), ultimately offers a better understanding not only of the film's characters, but also of their day-to-day lives.

Cigarettes, prominently featured in *Until They Sail*, come to be associated with a selection of the film's characters as the narrative progresses from one scene to the next. The tobacco motif particularly establishes a sharp contrast between Bates and Shiner. Following Barbara's return from Wellington, where she had earlier referred to Harding's cigarettes as "legal tender of the occupying army," Anne extends a dinner invitation to Bates. Upon the meal's conclusion, everybody adjourns to the home's living room; Barbara pours a cup of coffee for Bates. Evelyn, meanwhile, seeks an accompaniment for the coffee:

EVELYN: Shiner left some cigars.
ANNE: Oh, darling. It's been so long. They'd dry out.
BATES: Oh, that's alright. I've got cigarettes.

Paul Newman as Captain Jack Harding. *Until They Sail* marked Newman's second and final collaboration with Robert Wise, who was partly responsible for jump starting the young actor's career.

Anne's words conjure memories of a previous scene. As Delia and Shiner become acclimated to married life, all is not well. "I've got a feeling the army's blowing down my neck, so I'm looking into the air force. That's the soft life," he says with an air of confidence. Delia and her sisters surround Shiner, who basks in the sun while lying on a hammock. The cigar on which he puffs suddenly goes dry. Upon relighting it, Delia tosses the match in disgust. In her sudden rush to get married, she has chosen the imperfect mate, and the dried-up, worthless cigars that Shiner smokes essentially become symbolic of his character. Bates, a true gentleman, prefers a much different brand of tobacco. At the time of the aforementioned exchange in the home's living room, he rejects Shiner's cigars in favor of his own cigarettes. Bates is eventually deployed to Tarawa. Harding arrives in Christchurch shortly thereafter, and upon his reunion with Barbara, he again offers her a cigarette. "Why do American lighters always work?" she asks. Later, Harding presents Barbara with such a lighter, and it is offered as a special gift during the most festive of holidays.

As the yuletide season is celebrated at the sisters' home, the shadow of a Christmas tree is projected against a war map, an adornment of particular significance to the narrative, but it gradually comes to be a representation of hardship and grief. Early in the film, Barbara and Anne hang the map on a living room wall in eager anticipation of enhancing it with special pins:

BARBARA: Well, now, one pin for Kit and one for Mark.

The pins, each containing a flag, designate the approximate location of the sisters' loved ones. Delia chooses a red one for Kit simply because it is "a happy color." The flag is placed along the coast of New Zealand as his ship sets sail for Wellington. "There you are, Kit! Have a fine time ... a fine time," Delia says. Barbara decides on a white flag for Mark. Anne then inserts a flag for the sisters' deceased father. She later decides on a green one for Bates, as it matches the color of his uniform. Following his deployment, Anne is unsure of his unit's location and ponders where on the map to move his pin. At the same time, Barbara removes Mark's flag in anticipation of repositioning it to a different area, but as she does so, the doorbell is heard, and news of his demise is delivered shortly thereafter. In time, it becomes evident that those represented with pins on the map do not return alive.

Upon the film's conclusion, as Barbara learns of Delia's murder, she immediately faints, and Wise projects Barbara's falling shadow against the dreaded map. Hence, an object originally perceived as a special memento essentially becomes a symbol of death and mourning. Later, as Barbara receives a news update regarding Shiner's trial, she suddenly removes the map in a rage and immediately thrusts it into the fireplace. It burns rapidly, and the words "WAR MAP" are visible for mere seconds before disappearing forever. Yet, although the update is upsetting to Barbara, the source of such an update bears much significance to the overall narrative.

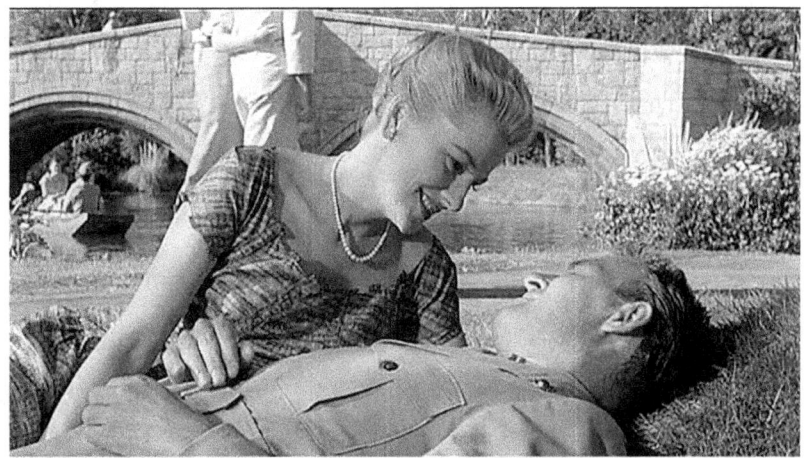

"We'll make each moment so tender, until they sail."

Directly below the map's former location stands a radio, which, throughout the film, provides periodic broadcasts that affect the sisters' day-to-day lives. The timing of every other report, in essence, signifies a major turning point in Anne's life. Early in the narrative, she crosses out a number of the map's South Pacific landmarks as a British newsman declares, "It was officially announced that the American fortress of Corregidor at the entrance of Manila Bay surrendered today. It was the second day of the final Japanese assault started on Tuesday." Anne's frustration is evident. "Where's Dad with his ship? Where's Mark with the New Zealand division? Where's Kit?" she asks, but Evelyn then announces the arrival of American servicemen in Christchurch. Anne and Bates eventually lay eyes on one another for the first time. Two reports later, the newsman informs all listeners that "the marine landing on Tarawa may perhaps be the costliest operation to date in the Pacific war." At such a point of the film, Anne and Bates have become engaged to be married. She places his flag on Tarawa and abruptly turns off the radio.

Anne then informs Barbara of her pregnancy. The audience learns of Bates's tragic demise shortly thereafter. Upon the narrative's conclusion, and again, two reports later, the war nears its end as news of Hiroshima's destruction is delivered. During the broadcast, a courier arrives in search of Anne. He presents her with 500 pounds and a cable. Bates's mother, through her note, beckons Anne, a "beloved daughter," to come to Oklahoma with the child. In succession, the film's primary characters exit the picture, never to be seen throughout the film's remainder, and Barbara, the last of the sisters to remain in Christchurch, ultimately departs for Wellington to begin the next chapter of her life.

Piper Laurie.

"Working with Robert Wise was magnificent. It was such a joy and everything was done so well," Ralph Votrian said in regard to his performance as Max Murphy, the American soldier who courts Evelyn while Tommy is overseas. "I did small roles for other big movies. Most of the things I did for live television were big roles. The radio stuff ... big roles. But of all the big movies I did, *Until They Sail* was the true joy. In 1956, I performed in a film called *Tea and Sympathy* after seeing the play on which it was based. I got hired and worked on that picture for a couple of months. My role was that of a student in a fraternity house who kept picking on the poor little sissy boy who was about 6'0". The rest of us were about 5'6". I had the opportunity to work with some of the top actors in the industry, but things got even better with *Until They Sail.*

"Robert Wise was so skilled at what he did. I had a dance scene with Sandra Dee. Wise made sure that I was afforded a week of rehearsals with her and a choreographer. He was very pleasant and kind, and such qualities are evident from his work. At the time of production, Sandra Dee was very young, around fifteen years of age. She was a sweetheart and easy to work with. We danced up a storm and had a great time. Years later, she appeared in a play in Beverly Hills. I was there and stopped to chat with her. She had become a prominent person around town. We hadn't seen each other for many years. Then, in 2005, she died awfully young at the age of sixty-two.

"War makes strange bedfellows."

"There was nothing negative about being on Robert Wise's set. It was a joy of my life everyday I showed up. I was in my late twenties, and I had been acting since I was in the seventh grade. In my first scene with Sandra Dee, I'm flirting with her. What a thrill that was, and it worked out really well! She was a great performer and a very talented dancer. Then, I got to do a scene with Jean Simmons, in which my character insults hers. Again, when I reflect back on the times of my film career, when I would have a little glimpse of a scene here and a little glimpse of a scene there, I can easily conclude that *Until They Sail* is the most outstanding of my experiences due to the picture's solid writing and great directing. It really gave me a shot at doing something substantial."

Upon its theatrical release, *Until They Sail* was advertised as a film in which "loneliness and sex are universal themes . . . take a country of women without men . . . bring in the marines . . . and there must be an explosion!" Wise's picture, however, does not begin with such an explosion. Instead, the serene, musical notes of the titular song, performed by an up-and-coming Eydie Gormé, gradually set the stage for what is to follow. A casualty of the narrative, one of many, is that of Mark, Barbara's spouse. Immediately prior to receiving such tragic news, she and Anne examine the war map and become fixated on North Africa, specifically the Libyan port of Tobruk. The landmark is a reference to the setting of *The Desert Rats* (1953), a film directed by Wise years earlier. Yet, perhaps more interesting regarding Wise's world of fiction is the name displayed on the marquee of a Christchurch movie theater, visible during the opening minutes of *Until They Sail*. As the sisters take in a festive parade, *Mutiny on the Bounty* (1935), another MGM picture, is advertised in the background, and especially significant is the film's star, whose name also appears on the marquee, because it was he who would ultimately be cast as the lead in Wise's next production.

Sandra Dee and Ralph Votrian.

The parade concludes.

25
RUN SILENT RUN DEEP

(PRODUCED 1957, RELEASED 1958)

"We shall never forget that it was our submarines that held the lines against the enemy while our fleets replaced losses and repaired wounds."
- Chester W. Nimitz

In 1945, Harold Hecht, a New York-based talent agent, attended the Broadway production of *A Sound of Hunting*, a World War II stage drama. The play was short-lived, closing after a mere three weeks of performances, but Hecht, who happened to be in the right place at the right time, attended the show on a memorable evening. A featured performer by the name of Burt Lancaster excelled in his portrayal of Joseph Mooney, a troubled American soldier. Hecht was undeniably impressed and soon had himself a new client. Within a year, Lancaster was in Hollywood working on *The Killers* (1946), his first feature.

Hecht eventually made the decision to try his hand at producing. Shortly thereafter, Lancaster followed suit but also remained committed to acting. Together, the two produced a number of films over the course of several years. James Hill, a writer, joined the duo during the mid-1950s, which led to the formation of Hecht-Hill-Lancaster Productions. In 1957, they began preparations for a film reminiscent of earlier times. Similar to *A Sound of Hunting*, *Run Silent Run Deep* is a World War II drama. Unlike the former, however, the latter does not take place on dry land.[38] Instead, *Run Silent Run Deep* is set primarily on a submarine in the Pacific Ocean. Hecht-Hill-Lancaster anticipated an elaborate production. Fortunately, the personnel of Submarine Flotilla One, a maritime command center in San Diego, offered their full support of such a production. In addition, the United States Navy and Department of Defense were very cooperative, and by the time filming commenced on September 16, 1957, several notables of the industry, including Clark Gable and Robert Wise, committed themselves to the project.

Clark Gable.

In 1942, a U.S. Navy submarine under the command of P.J. "Rich" Richardson (Gable) is destroyed by enemy forces off the coast of Japan. A year later, after being relegated to desk duty within the confines of a Pearl Harbor office, he continuously reflects upon the battle's outcome. The *USS Nerka*, a submarine whose commander has fallen ill, arrives at the harbor for a brief layover. Lieutenant Jim Bledsoe (Lancaster), the boat's executive officer,

---

38 *A Sound of Hunting* is set in Cassino, Italy. It concerns a group of eight American soldiers who prepare to return home to the states when a member of their unit goes missing. Together, the remaining troops unite to find their fellow brother-in-arms.

prepares to take over as the new commander of the vessel. Four American submarines, however, have been lost in Japanese waters over the past year. Superior officers of the navy board therefore decide to replace Bledsoe with Richardson, who knows the area better than any other commander. Following the departure of the *Nerka*, several drills are conducted. Many believe Richardson will take the submarine to the Bungo Straits, a notorious graveyard for sunken vessels. Shortly thereafter, he reveals his intention to travel near, not to, the area.

The *Nerka's* initial encounter with Japanese forces results in a victory. Yet, despite having orders to avoid the Bungo Straits, Richardson eventually directs the submarine to the so-called graveyard. He seeks revenge for his lost vessel. Despite Bledsoe's protests, Richardson claims he is not disobeying orders, as his decision is being made "due to conditions of special advantage." As the *Nerka* prepares to attack a Japanese fleet, a group of enemy planes is discovered. The submarine submerges. The depth charges of a Japanese destroyer, however, cause partial damage to the *Nerka*, killing three of its crew. Furthermore, Richardson suffers a concussion. The *Nerka* retreats to a safe position, but despite Richardson's condition, he is determined to revisit the straits. Bledsoe chides him for disobeying orders and assumes command, demanding a return to Pearl Harbor. Nevertheless, when a Tokyo radio station mistakenly issues a false report of the *Nerka's* destruction, Bledsoe uses it to his advantage.

Richardson's condition worsens and he is confined to a sickbed. Upon arrival at the straits, the *Nerka* engages a Japanese fleet in battle. An American victory appears imminent until the discovery of an enemy submarine, responsible for the earlier destruction of the four American vessels. A disoriented Richardson emerges from his quarters and helps guide Bledsoe in battle. The *Nerka* destroys the Japanese submarine with a pair of torpedoes. Later, the Americans celebrate their victory. Richardson, however, succumbs to his injuries and dies. He is buried at sea as Bledsoe delivers the eulogy.

Burt Lancaster and Joe Maross.

Run Silent Run Deep was adapted from the 1955 novel of the same name, written by Edward Latimer Beach Jr., a respected submarine commander of the U.S. Navy whose father, also a naval officer, served in three wars. The film's script was penned by John Gay and differs significantly from its source. For example, Beach's novel takes place partially on the East Coast and is initially set during the time of the attack on Pearl Harbor. Furthermore, it introduces the character of Laura Elwood, Bledsoe's girlfriend. Although Wise's film features a different narrative, Bledsoe nevertheless remains important. Upon Bledsoe's introduction to the audience, it becomes clear he is highly respected by his fellow shipmates. Richardson eventually assumes command of the *Nerka*, and as the film progresses, a lack of professionalism amongst a selection of the *Nerka's* original crew becomes apparent. Yet, the shortcomings of those loyal to Bledsoe, whether such limitations appear in the form of ignorance, bigotry, or insubordination, ultimately work to his advantage.

Petty Officer 1st Class Russo (Nick Cravat), somewhat ignorant of the vessel's rules and regulations, dumps garbage into the sea at the most inopportune of moments, inadvertently leading to a breakthrough in Bledsoe's troubled relationship with Richardson. Issues of miscommunication subsequently result in a tense, but necessary, argument. Initially, a routine drill transpires as the *Nerka* begins to dive. Russo is topside, disposing of the submarine's refuse, when an alarm sounds, thus marking the beginning of the exercise. He scrambles from his position and barely manages to alert those inside the *Nerka* of his predicament just prior to the vessel becoming completely submerged. A disaster is avoided, but in the aftermath, Richardson, atop the submarine with a select few, demands answers:

RICHARDSON: Who gave you permission to dump the garbage?
RUSSO: Mr. Cartwright, sir.
Cartwright (Brad Dexter), a commissioned officer of the vessel, is present and attempts to offer an explanation.
CARTWRIGHT: I thought he'd already asked the O.D., sir.
Petty Officer 1st Class Ruby (Don Rickles), also present, appears confused by Cartwright's response and interjects.
RUBY: I was on the bridge with Mr. Beckman and I didn't hear. . . .
Richardson interrupts Ruby, abruptly ordering him and Russo into the vessel. He then confronts Cartwright:
RICHARDSON: The captain gives permission to dump the trash and only the captain. Instead of losing time on this drill, we almost lose a man!
Later, in Richardson's quarters, he confronts Bledsoe in search of an explanation regarding the crew:
RICHARDSON: Is this the kind of cooperation you usually get?
BLEDSOE: No, sir.
RICHARDSON: You know a man could've been killed today. The responsibility is yours, Mr. Bledsoe. You're in charge of the drills.
BLEDSOE: I have no excuses, sir. But under the circumstances, the crew did their best.
The two begin to argue. Earlier, the *Nerka* was afforded the opportunity to attack and destroy a Japanese submarine, but Richardson opted against it. The crew was dismayed, especially because they had partaken in several

drills leading up to the encounter. At the time of the argument, Bledsoe decides to question the purpose of such drills:

BLEDSOE: It's one thing to drill a crew for fighting. But when you duck a Jap sub, they wonder why they should break their backs on drills when the captain has no stomach for attacking. What does he want ... obedience, efficiency, or the best drilled cowards in the navy?

RICHARDSON: Mr. Bledsoe, tell them I'm doubling the drills starting tomorrow.

BLEDSOE: Yes, sir.

Bledsoe prepares to depart but then delays.

BLEDSOE: You might as well know, sir, I don't believe it.

RICHARDSON: Believe what?

BLEDSOE: That you ran away from that sub from cowardice.

Bledsoe, in essence, does not share the opinion of others. Hence, a turning point in his relationship with Richardson transpires. Although Bledsoe takes exception to the superfluous drills, he is aware that the captain's peculiar tactical decisions, declared by some to be acts of cowardice, are not made on a whim. Only the finest of the U.S. Navy desire a will to persevere. Such qualities of perseverance and tenacity, however, do not apply to every crew member aboard the *Nerka*.

Cartwright is a man of several weaknesses, but of such weaknesses, his bigotry ultimately works to Bledsoe's advantage, enabling the latter to finish what Richardson started. Cartwright's feud with Yeoman 1st Class Mueller (Jack Warden), an officer of German heritage, is central to a fortuitous sequence of events and leads to the most unexpected of resolutions. Their conflict essentially begins during a coffee break. Cartwright jokes with his circle of confidants, sarcastically dubbing Richardson "the drill master." Mueller arrives on the scene to deliver a watch list. Cartwright seizes the opportunity to question the yeoman's relationship with the captain. Mueller does not take the bait, thus avoiding an altercation. Cartwright becomes angry and antagonistically refers to Mueller as "Kraut," a derogatory term for Germans.

Shortly thereafter, the *Nerka* destroys a Momo-class destroyer in battle, and Mueller, opting to approach Cartwright's insult with a sense of humor, signs his name "Kraut Mueller" when composing a memorandum of the victory. The note is eventually discarded.

Later, following the ill-fated engagement during which Richardson is injured, a special announcement is transmitted across the airwaves. Tokyo Rose, a female broadcaster of Japanese propaganda, declares the sailors of the *Nerka* to be dead. She refers to individual crew members by name, specifically making reference to "Kraut Mueller." Bledsoe overhears the announcement and concludes the Japanese were able to detect the *Nerka* through the submarine's refuse. He immediately becomes aware of the tactical advantage. Enemy forces, naturally, will not suspect an attack from a vessel they believe no longer exists. Bledsoe sets forth to fulfill Richardson's objective. He guides the *Nerka* into battle and is ultimately victorious, thus commanding praise from his men. Such praise is also evident upon the film's beginning. As Bledsoe is first introduced to the audience, he is presented with a special jacket as a token of the men's appreciation. It is embroidered with the word "CAPTAIN." The gift bearer, in particular, appears proud, but looks can sometimes be deceiving.

The *Nerka* slowly rises to the surface.

Kohler (Joe Maross), the Chief of the Boat, assumes a relatively insubordinate attitude towards Bledsoe in the days following the *Nerka's* departure from Pearl Harbor, thus prompting Bledsoe to confront Richardson regarding the Bungo Straits, and consequently expose a harsh truth. The change in demeanor accompanies the change of command. Kohler initially praises Bledsoe, as he deems him to be the next captain of the *Nerka*. When Richardson assumes command, however, the tide begins to turn. Following a series of drills, Bledsoe confers with some of the men. He makes it clear to those present that they are under orders to avoid the Bungo Straits. Bledsoe then goes "down below" to begin a thirty-minute break, only to find Kohler waiting for him.

The Chief of the Boat, who has been eavesdropping on the conversation, confronts Bledsoe. "Now that you've explained the orders, how do you explain the purpose of these drills," Kohler asks. Although his question goes unanswered, he nevertheless foresees trouble on the horizon. Kohler suspects Richardson will take the *Nerka* to the Bungo Straits. In time, the aforementioned verbal exchange between Cartwright and Mueller, to which Bledsoe bears witness, transpires. Shortly thereafter, the area is cleared. Bledsoe, however, remains behind. Kohler, who is revealed to have eavesdropped on yet another exchange, arrives on the scene with a self-satisfied smirk on his face. His theory, that Richardson's mere presence will cause nothing but unrest aboard the *Nerka*, gains credibility. Without hesitation, Bledsoe simply tells Kohler to "shut up." Kohler leaves, albeit reluctantly. The *Nerka* eventually confronts and defeats a Momo-class destroyer, and later, Kohler approaches Bledsoe to speak his mind:

BLEDSOE: Not now, Kohler!
KOHLER: Don't shut me up again, Lieutenant. I've seen all kinds of captains. We've seen 'em together. But I never saw one run away from a Jap sub before, then take on a destroyer with a shot I didn't even know was in the book. There has to be a reason!

Bledsoe becomes persuaded to challenge Richardson, who subsequently confirms that the *Nerka* is indeed headed for the Bungo Straits. It has been a destination of the captain's since long ago. Bledsoe becomes enlightened, and Kohler, although a persistent nuisance, proves resourceful in a time of peril.

"The first week of filming took place on location in San Diego," said Eddie Foy III, who appears in the film as Petty Officer 1st Class Larto. "I did not travel there, but I remember that Mary LaRoche, Clark Gable, and Jack Warden did. The set of the submarine in Los Angeles was fascinating. Most of us hadn't worked on anything like that before. Half of the set consisted of the sub. It was broken up into different areas where Robert Wise would shoot various scenes. Being on that set was like being in a submarine. Two submariners were employed as consultants and remarked how well the set had been designed. Everything was to scale. The film takes place during the 1940s, so the sub wasn't as big as modern submarines. Nevertheless, we were all very impressed.

Jack Warden.

"The cast was not required to undergo any military training in order to prep for the film. If we didn't know what we were doing, we would obviously ask Mr. Wise. If some kind of technical issue arose during filming, the two submariners handled it. They also appeared in the picture. When most of us began work during the second week of filming, we reported to Goldwyn

Studios and didn't see Gable until the afternoon of either the first or second day of that week. And he traditionally didn't come out of his dressing room until eight o'clock in the morning. I'm surmising this was a stipulation in his contract. Gable would usually depart the set at five o'clock in the afternoon. Most days, during lunchtime, he wouldn't eat with the cast and crew. I'm not sure where he went to eat his lunch, but he didn't do so on the set.

"One day, Robert wanted to film a scene between Gable and myself. He figured that I would be comfortable with such a scenario considering my family history. Gable had known much about the Foys and their work within the studio system. I had never met him until the day he and I did that scene together. The first thing I noticed upon seeing Gable for the first time was that his hands shook. I think he may have been nervous. We started at eight o'clock on that particular morning. During the first take, I blew a line. Robert calmly said, 'Let's do it again.' By quarter of eleven, Gable and I still hadn't gotten those three lines out of our mouths. I would blow it, and then he would blow it. One time, I said the line perfectly and was proud of my performance, but then Gable blew it. We looked like idiots standing there. And then, Robert suddenly noticed something and said, 'Give me one more.' And we both hit it perfectly! I remember the experience like it was yesterday. 'Okay,' Robert said, 'after lunch, we'll probably do some coverage and so forth. If there are any problems, we'll pick it up.' But as it turns out, everything was fine. Around four o'clock, they shot Gable and got a close-up. I sat off camera and read my lines.

"At five o'clock, I was preparing for my close-up. The script girl was reading Gable's lines to me. He then emerged from his dressing room and approached Robert, asking, 'What are you doing?' Robert replied, 'I'm doing Eddie's close-up from this morning's shot. You go ahead and go home and I'll see you tomorrow morning.' And Gable said, 'Let me do my off-camera lines. You've already got enough on your mind as it is, Bob.' Then, we got it right away, and Gable bid us farewell. He wore a little pork pie hat and walked out while everybody was standing there with their mouths open. And every time we had to do pick-ups or anything like that past five o'clock, Gable was there, and he was in the picture, and he was a total pro. I don't remember Burt Lancaster staying past his scheduled time to complete any scenes, but I didn't have much interaction with him on the picture at all. Every time he appeared with the crew, there were always a lot of people around. But to see the way Wise and Gable worked together was just magnificent. Robert's whole style of direction was very soft. It was very easy. He was a gentleman at work. I don't remember if he frequently wore a tie, but I think I saw him wear a tie to work one day. Everybody was at ease because the lead didn't scream and yell at the director. Wise was a gentleman; and Gable was the king! There were no ifs, ands, or buts about it.

Don Rickles, in addition to Joe Maross (right), made his feature film debut with *Run Silent Run Deep*.

"At the time of production, members of the cast were all very close with one another. Jack Warden and I remained dear friends up until the day he passed away. The only person who didn't really mix well with us was Lancaster, because he was one of the producers. But the rest of the guys, the crew, and even Gable, we enjoyed it. Don Rickles had never done a picture before. He and I knew each other prior to the production of *Run Silent Run Deep*; I would go to see his stand-up comedy routine. And Don, a lot of people don't know, is a boxing fan. I myself am a passionate fan of the sport. There was never a fight in the country that I didn't know about - I always knew the results. A lot of guys on the set would usually ask, 'Who won the fight last night?' Don and I remained friends after the picture. When I left Los Angeles to become an entertainment director in Las Vegas, the first guy I hired for a period of over six years was Don. Of all the guys on that set, he and I were probably the closest. Warden was a close second. It was a great time. And that atmosphere was set by Robert Wise. He had a unique way of talking to actors in order to make sure they were comfortable with what they were doing.

"Since I eventually became a casting director, I knew most of the kids who appeared in *The Sound of Music*. I also knew most of the guys from *West Side Story*, because a lot of us had worked together in New York and on the road with *Damn Yankees*. The kids from *The Sound of Music* all thought Mr. Wise was the best. He had a unique way of keeping those kids together as a family. Mr. Wise was the one director I worked with who had a special way of keeping an actor relaxed. If he called you into his office asking for changes in your performance, and if you were unsure of how to execute such changes, he was on top of it. You would never worry that something was going to go wrong. Actors see a casting director, director, or producer during a meeting and sometimes think they're going to be fired because they're not doing a good job. But that never happened with Mr. Wise.

"Robert Wise had an incredible eye for detail. In his resume, there are two pictures that are two of the great classics we have in film. One is called *The Set-Up* with Robert Ryan. And the other, *Somebody Up There Likes Me*, is about a friend of mine, Rocky Graziano. I was raised around him. The idea of a four-round fighter, a man fighting only for a few bucks to buy a steak after the fight, is brilliant. One day on the set of *Run Silent Run Deep*, Mr. Wise asked me about my interest in boxing. We talked all about *The Set-Up* and *Somebody Up There Likes Me*. We talked about the craziness that went on with Graziano, because he was a mad man. But he was wonderfully mad. Both of those films are just amazing. Mr. Wise shot *The Set-Up* at Hollywood Legion Stadium and captured every nook and corner of that building.

And that's exactly what he showed in the final cut of the film. Look who he started out with…Orson Welles, one of the best characters in the business. I was a casting director for forty-two years. I think I've worked with practically everybody, even Mr. Otto Preminger, and of all those people, I've never forgotten Robert Wise.

Composer Franz Waxman.

"To this day, when people ask me about the people I've worked with, I always mention Robert Wise. The qualities I remember most are his gentleness and kindness. One day while working with Otto Preminger, I heard him say, 'The secret to making a great film is having a great cast.' Mr. Wise sometimes worked with performers who were not up to standards, but he remained gentle and told them what he wanted. He did not get up and do it for them. He wanted people to bring their own textures to the roles. He wanted people to bring their own being to the roles.

"Regarding *West Side Story*, Mr. Wise had some of the best young dancers from New York. When I first heard he was going to direct that film, I said to myself, 'Gosh! He's never done a musical!' But I have come to realize that it's one of the classic motion pictures of its style, and there are very few films like it. The same thing goes for some of the other films Mr. Wise directed. His integrity to the script, to the actor, and to himself, as a director, was quite noticeable. There was no compromise with him. As an actor, you gave him your best performance. I hope, and I really mean this, that one day, I get to see Robert Wise again. Because the motion picture industry misses him terribly. Speaking of Mr. Wise brings tears to my eyes. That's simply the way I feel. There's nobody who could ever stand up to what he did."

Twenty years prior to reuniting on the set of *Run Silent Run Deep*, Burt Lancaster and Nick Cravat performed together in various circus acts.

Run Silent Run Deep debuted in New York on March 27, 1958. In addition, an underwater submarine premiere of the film transpired aboard the *USS Perch* near Terminal Island (Los Angeles). The vessel, like the *Nerka*, was named after a fish. Perch is the common name for freshwater game fish, whereas nerka refers to sockeye salmon. Such a naming convention was rather typical during the mid-twentieth century. Regarding the historical *Nerka*, it unfortunately did not become part of an official fleet, as its construction contract was cancelled approximately one year prior to the end of World War II.

Too close for comfort.

Wise strived to make his film as authentic as possible, despite occasionally being met with resistance. James Hill and Burt Lancaster were reported to have edited the film following the submission of the director's cut. The script itself underwent substantial rewrites during production. Yet, despite multiple disagreements over the structure of the film, the final cut of *Run Silent Run Deep* proved to be remarkably entertaining. As a director, Wise established a powerful onscreen connection between his two leads. The scene during which the characters of Richardson and Bledsoe meet for the first time is memorable. "I wanted a boat. The board gave it to me," an arrogant commander says to his new executive officer. The exchange foreshadows a similar scenario of Wise's *Star Trek: The Motion Picture* (1979), as Admiral Kirk unexpectedly assumes command of the *USS Enterprise* from a frustrated Captain Decker.

In regard to the antagonists of *Run Silent Run Deep*, Wise's portrayal is unique. Not once does he provide Japanese translations, as the intense mindset of the enemy, occasionally evident in the form of nonverbal cues, is sufficient for audience interpretation. Albert Einstein once said, "Logic will get you from A to B. Imagination will take you everywhere." Naturally, Wise expected a sense of such imagination within theatergoers. He would not have had it any other way.

26
I WANT TO LIVE!

(PRODUCED AND RELEASED 1958)

"Learn from the mistakes of others. You can't live long enough to make them all yourself."
- Eleanor Roosevelt

Edward S. Montgomery, a longtime journalist for the *San Francisco Examiner*, was awarded the Pulitzer Prize only a few years into his employment with the newspaper, as his tenacious coverage of the dangers of tax fraud was applauded by critics and readers alike. The award signified a momentous achievement in Montgomery's storied career, but the pinnacle of such a career was yet to come. Enter Barbara Graham, a convicted murderer set to die in San Quentin's gas chamber. Montgomery's in-depth reportage of the ordeal, transpiring primarily from 1953 to 1955, afforded him the opportunity to interview her up close and personal.

At the time, only two women had been executed in the state of California, and for what it was worth, Montgomery sought to set the record straight. Walter Wanger, a Hollywood producer, became intrigued with the case against Barbara Graham, partly due to his own incarceration years earlier. In a jealous rage, he blatantly shot and wounded his agent following a dispute over his wife, actress Joan Bennett. However, Wanger ultimately served a brief, four-month sentence due to his attorney's use of a "temporary insanity" defense. Later, in 1957, Wanger met with Montgomery and developed the idea for an upcoming film. Screenwriters Nelson Gidding and Don Mankiewicz were hired and given access to several resources, including the letters Barbara Graham wrote to Montgomery during her time in prison. Upon the script's completion, Robert Wise became slated to direct Wanger's film, aptly titled *I Want to Live!*

"I'm the little ball bouncing around a roulette wheel, everyone betting me to land where it's gonna do them the most good."

Barbara "Bonnie" Wood (Susan Hayward), a prostitute, provides a false alibi for two friends accused of robbing a delicatessen. Unable to deceive the authorities, she is subsequently convicted of perjury and sentenced to one year in jail. Upon her release, Barbara is warned not to violate her probation. However, she abruptly leaves town and becomes involved in the criminal activities of Emmett Perkins (Philip Coolidge), a master swindler, and his partner, Jack Santo (Lou Krugman). In an attempt to withdraw from her life of crime, Barbara eventually marries Henry "Hank" Graham (Wesley Lau), a bartender with whom she has become friendly. Bobby, their son, is born shortly thereafter. Financial difficulties abound, and Graham battles drug addiction. He disappears, abandoning Barbara and Bobby; mother and son therefore seek refuge with Perkins. The latter's associate, Bruce King (James Philbrook), prepares to depart for Mexico and offers to take Barbara and the child with him. She coldly snubs King's offer. Barbara eventually sends Bobby to live with Graham's mother. Meanwhile, King is apprehended while trying to cross the border. An ensuing police raid culminates in Barbara's arrest. Perkins and Santo are also taken into custody. Barbara is questioned in regard to the beating death of Mabel Monahan, a crippled Burbank widow. Barbara proclaims her innocence, but King, perhaps feeling rejected, declares to authorities that she is the killer. His testimony ultimately enables him to go free.

Later, Barbara is convicted and sentenced to die in San Quentin's gas chamber. An appeal is filed, but to no avail. Montgomery (Simon Oakland) attempts to get an exclusive statement from Perkins in the hopes of clearing Barbara's name, deducing that if she is the last of the three to be executed, her accomplices will "break down" and confess to the murder before it is too late. Yet, such efforts prove unsuccessful, as Barbara is the first to be gassed. Following the execution, Montgomery receives a letter addressed to him in her handwriting. It states, "There isn't much I can say with words. They always fail me when most needed. But please know that with all my heart, I appreciate everything you've done for me."

Gavin MacLeod.

Philip Coolidge as Emmett Perkins.

As *I Want to Live!* was being produced, the film's working title was *The Barbara Graham Story*. Many outside the greater Los Angeles area, however, were unfamiliar with both Barbara Graham and the Monahan murder. It was therefore decided that a title change was for the better. Yet, upon the premiere of *I Want to Live!*, theatergoers nationwide were quick to cite its inaccuracies, essentially taking exception to Wanger and Wise's retelling of the ordeal's events. Montgomery, too, endured his share of criticism. Some questioned the presence of a San Francisco journalist at a Los Angeles trial, especially those who considered the Monahan killing to be a local affair, but Montgomery was not directly involved in the reportage of the trial's details. Instead, he is believed to have rewritten another journalist's account. Nevertheless, unlike his fellow colleagues, Montgomery was successful in establishing a solid rapport with Barbara Graham and maintained close contact during her final days in San Quentin.

Wise himself visited the maximum-security prison prior to the film's production. He also attended an execution, believing such an experience would improve his overall direction of the picture. Despite the aforementioned criticism, *I Want to Live!* was generally well-received by critics and audiences alike. The film was interpreted by some as a condemnation of the death penalty, but a deeper meaning lies elsewhere within the portrayal of Barbara Graham's trying ordeal. The omission of a real-life figure, as well as the inclusion of one fictitious, suggests a presumption of innocence. Furthermore, Wise's depiction of Barbara Graham as a victim of entrapment ultimately garners sympathy from audiences.

Baxter Shorter, a real-life criminal and master safecracker, was an accomplice to Mabel Monahan's murder, and no actor portrays him in *I Want to Live!*. His testimony to police ultimately benefited the prosecution's case against Barbara Graham. Shorter's absence therefore strengthens the narrative in her favor. According to the film, the Monahan murder mob consists of Barbara Graham, Emmett Perkins, Jack Santo, and Bruce King.[39] Yet, Shorter was just as involved as the others. The homicide essentially stemmed from a robbery attempt gone wrong. In the aftermath, Shorter declared that he and an abettor, Billy Upshaw, had earlier cased Monahan's residence because they believed a safe containing approximately $100 thousand was located in the home. When the time came for the heist, Shorter asserted that a lady known only as Mary helped the group gain access to the house. The police eventually asked him for a description of the woman, and it fit that of Barbara Graham.[40] Additionally, Bruce King, or John True, offered testimony placing her at the scene of the crime, suggesting she was in possession of the gun supposedly used to beat Monahan to death. Earlier, when questioned by the police, Shorter confirmed such testimony.[41] His inclusion in *I Want to Live!*, had it occurred, most likely would have complicated matters. Perhaps, as a means of evoking public sympathy, screenwriters Nelson Gidding and Don Mankiewicz instead crafted a fictitious character.

39 In reality, Bruce King's name was John True.
40 Baxter Shorter was later kidnapped, never to be seen again. His wife bore witness to the abduction and identified Emmett Perkins and Jack Santo as the kidnappers. Yet, at the time of the trial, Shorter's disappearance was not particularly relevant to the case against Barbara Graham.
41 Although Shorter confirmed True's testimony that Barbara Graham was in possession of the gun used to beat Monahan to death, an alternate theory suggests Perkins, in actuality, was the one to have hit Monahan with the gun and also tie a pillow case around her head. Furthermore, the autopsy report revealed that death was due to strangulation and not blunt force trauma.

Carl G. G. Palmberg (Theodore Bikel), a psychologist who appears in the film at the California Institution for Women at Corona, proclaims Barbara's innocence. He essentially cites distinguishing traits of her character. Palmberg's administration of the Rorschach test leads to significant findings. Upon preparing to depart the institution, he discusses such findings with Al Matthews (Joe DeSantis), an attorney of Barbara's, as well as Montgomery:

PALMBERG: I'm convinced she couldn't have done it. She has a positive aversion to violence, physical violence, not emotional.

His words ring true. Throughout the course of the film, Barbara does not commit a violent act. Instead, the opposite is depicted, as she is physically assaulted by Hank Graham and Jack Santo on two separate occasions. At the time of his discussion with Matthews and Montgomery, Palmberg also questions the validity of Bruce King's testimony:

PALMBERG: She's left-handed.

MONTGOMERY: I never noticed that.

PALMBERG: No, I didn't see it mentioned in any of your articles. Bruce King testified that she did it with the gun in her right hand.

Although Palmberg's assertion is bold, his character is fictitious. Furthermore, following the theatrical release of *I Want to Live!*, multiple sources disputed the suggestion that Barbara Graham was left-handed. *The Los Angeles Times* published a facsimile of a police report disclosing that she was right-handed. Nevertheless, the character of Palmberg evokes sympathy from audiences. He offers Barbara a glimmer of hope. The United States Supreme Court eventually grants her a stay of execution, but news of Palmberg's death is delivered shortly thereafter, and along with it, the denial of Barbara's petition. Her fate, however, was very likely sealed during an earlier scene of the film.

Ben Miranda (Peter Breck), an undercover police officer, tricks Barbara into admitting she was at the Monahan home at the time of the murder, and through Wise's depiction of the sequence, such tactics appear unfair.

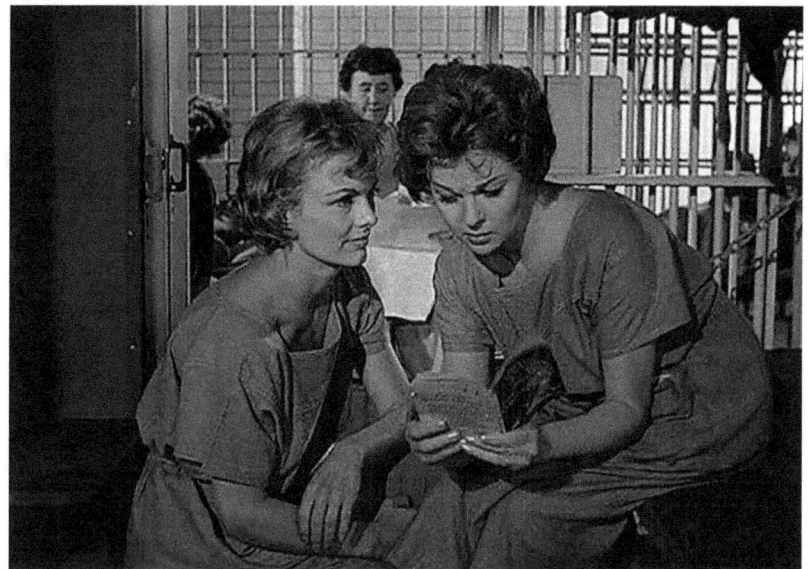

The script's suggestion of a romantic relationship between "Rita" and Barbara was strongly protested by the Production Code Administration (PCA) and eventually dropped altogether.

It essentially becomes an entrapment of the cruelest kind. In jail, as Barbara awaits the trial's outcome, she is approached by Rita (Marion Marshall), a fellow inmate. The scene of the crime becomes the topic of their discussion. Barbara has an uncorroborated alibi but insists she was absent from the Monahan home:

RITA: You really weren't there?
BARBARA: That's right, Your Honor.
RITA: Then, you've only got one problem, sweetie. You weren't with anybody some other place.
BARBARA: I was with my husband ... he skipped, and my son, age one.
RITA: I've got a friend. His name's Ben. He could use money.

A meeting between Miranda and Barbara is subsequently arranged. During their exchange, the two concoct a phony story. Yet, prior to his departure, Miranda demands to know Barbara's true whereabouts on the night of the murder:

MIRANDA: Where were you that night, really? Look, I've gotta know. If someone saw you where you really were and they show up at that trial where does that leave me?

BARBARA: Nobody saw me.

MIRANDA: How can you be sure? You're not even sure where you were.

BARBARA: I'm sure, but I can't prove it. If I could, I wouldn't need you, would I?

MIRANDA: Ah, suit yourself. Much as I'd like to save that gorgeous hide of yours, I just can't take that kind of a chance. We better forget the whole thing.

Miranda makes as if he is preparing to leave, but such behavior is merely part of his scheme to entrap Barbara. She takes the bait.

BARBARA: Come back!

MIRANDA: Yeah? You got something you wanna say?

BARBARA: You've really got the hammerlocks on me. What do you want?

MIRANDA: You were there, weren't you?

BARBARA: Is that all you'll believe?

MIRANDA: It would be an easy thing to believe, and I wouldn't have to worry.

BARBARA: I'll double your money.

MIRANDA: Oh, baby!

Again, Miranda feigns disinterest. He rises from his chair.

BARBARA: Ben!

Miranda returns to his original position.

BARBARA (nodding): Have it your way.

MIRANDA: You were with them, with Perkins and Santo? Because if you were, it's okay. It'll be my story against Bruce King's. You were with them, uh?

BARBARA: Alright, alright, alright . . . I was with 'em!

On that note, Barbara's fate is virtually sealed. Later, in court, Miranda takes the stand to testify on behalf of the prosecution. In retrospect, Barbara's exchange with Miranda is ambiguous. To audiences, her innocence appears uncertain. Yet, through Wise's portrayal of the scene, Barbara's ultimate declaration to Miranda is not to be interpreted as a voluntary confession, but instead, one that is forced and perhaps fabricated out of desperation.

Simon Oakland's portrayal of Edward S. Montgomery marked the first of three collaborations with Robert Wise. He would later appear in *West Side Story* (1961) and *The Sand Pebbles* (1966).

In March of 1960, over a year after the theatrical release of *I Want to Live!*, an article in *The Los Angeles Times* revealed that Barbara Graham purportedly confessed her participation in Mabel Monahan's murder to Harley Teets, the warden of San Quentin. A priest at the prison is also believed to have extracted a confession immediately prior to the execution, but the true extent of Barbara Graham's involvement may never be known. Emmett Perkins and Jack Santo were put to death in the gas chamber on the same day as her. Hence, the date of June 3, 1955, marked California's first triple execution.

In regard to Wanger and Wise's film, a *Daily Variety* review declared, "In portraying Barbara Graham as innocent, *I Want to Live!* is perhaps the most damning indictment of capital punishment ever presented in any entertainment medium." It ultimately earned a total of six Academy Award nominations; Wise himself was nominated for Best Director. Yet, on April 6, 1959, Susan Hayward emerged as the film's lone victor, winning the Oscar for Best Actress. Earlier, Wanger did everything in his power to coax her into playing the lead, and such diligence proved beneficial.

Regarding the role of director, however, Wise was not the first choice. Wanger initially sought Edward Dmytryk, who had spent a year in prison as a member of the Hollywood Ten.[42] He figured the Dmytryk's previous history of incarceration would help to better set the mood of the picture. Nevertheless, Wise turned out to be the ideal choice. Ironically, a pair of his earlier films foreshadow *I Want to Live!*, specifically its title. During an opening scene of *Two Flags West* (1950), Joseph Cotten, performing as Colonel Clay Tucker of the Confederacy, begins a speech to his men with the words, "Say I want to live," and Valentina Cortesa, starring in *The House on Telegraph Hill* (1951) as a concentration camp survivor destined for America, declares in narration, "How the will to live survives in a place like Belsen, I do not know. But I wanted to live!"

Susan Hayward, like Joseph Cotten and Valentina Cortesa before her, shined in her portrayal of one who values the essential qualities of life. Nevertheless, of the three roles, Hayward's was the most challenging, and audiences took notice. During an early scene of *I Want to Live!*, shortly after Barbara is taken into custody, Montgomery speaks with a colleague via telephone, remarking, "Graham's the one who'll sell papers." The irony is palpable. Because Susan Hayward, like the character she portrayed, ultimately sold Wanger and Wise's film to the general public through such extraordinary star power.

---

42 The Hollywood Ten consisted of screenwriters and directors who were questioned by Congress regarding their alleged involvement with the Communist Party. Following their refusal to answer such questions, they were cited for contempt and blacklisted in 1947.

During the incarceration of the real-life Barbara Graham, she underwent a religious transformation and returned to her Catholic roots. Note the cross above Susan Hayward.

Robert Wise's direction of Susan Hayward is comparable to that of Barbara Stanwyck (right, from *Executive Suite* [1954]). The sudden ringing of a telephone, similar to that of a clock tower bell, triggers the fieriest of emotions.

Producer Walter Wanger.

27
ODDS AGAINST TOMORROW

(PRODUCED AND RELEASED 1959)

> "I think one of the major things a director has to do is to know his subject matter, the subject matter of his script, know the truth and the reality of it. That's very important."
> - Robert Wise

Robert Wise traveled to New York to direct his next motion picture. Such a locale was one he would come to visit on several occasions throughout his career. Nelson Gidding, a credited screenwriter of *I Want to Live!* (1958), was hired to craft an adaptation of William P. McGivern's novel, *Odds Against Tomorrow*. Yet, Gidding was not without help. Although it was virtually unknown at the time, Abraham Polonsky, blacklisted for refusing to testify before the House Un-American Activities Committee (HUAC) in 1951, contributed greatly to such an endeavor. Discreetness, however, was of the utmost importance. Franz Kafka, the European novelist, once said, "A non-writing writer is a monster courting insanity." Polonsky, in essence, was not going to let the government prevent him from pursuing his life's passion.

Hence, he and Gidding worked tirelessly to finish their script. HarBel Productions, Inc., the company responsible for producing *Odds Against Tomorrow*, was founded by and named after Harry Belafonte, the popular singer. He was cast as a lead in the picture along with Robert Ryan and Ed Begley, and on February 24, 1959, Wise and company got underway at Gold Medal Studios in the Bronx.

Harry Belafonte.

Dave Burke (Begley), an ex-police officer, summons Earle Slater (Ryan), an ex-con, to his apartment and suggests the two collaborate to execute a $50 thousand bank heist. As Slater departs, Johnny Ingram (Belafonte), an associate of Burke's, arrives on the scene. Ingram is presented with the same proposal. It entices him, especially since he owes Bacco (Will Kuluva), a local bookmaker and mobster, over $7 thousand. Burke and Slater depart New York City for Melton, the location of the targeted depository. Upon arrival, they reconnoiter the bank's security. Slater's racist views emerge, as he has no desire to work with Ingram, who is Black. Burke and Slater return to New York City a short time later.

Meanwhile, Bacco presents an ultimatum. If he does not receive the money owed to him in a day's time, Ingram will be killed. The latter's ex-wife, Ruth (Kim Hamilton), and child, Eadie (Lois Thorne), are also targeted. Burke, however, pays Bacco in full. He does so as a means of recruiting Ingram to participate in the heist. Slater, on the other hand, becomes committed to Burke's scheme primarily due to the recent marital woes he has endured. The three men travel separately to Melton in preparation for the robbery. Time passes, as day slowly becomes night. Shortly after six o'clock in the evening, the heist begins as the guard of the bank's side door is subdued. The money is collected, but Ingram and Slater begin to argue over who will drive the getaway car. In an attempt to retrieve the vehicle, Burke hurriedly exits the bank, thus arousing the suspicion of the local authorities. Shortly after the building's alarm is triggered, he is shot multiple times by a police officer. Ingram and Slater find themselves stranded, as the keys to the car are in Burke's possession. The police converge upon the bank. A wounded Burke, finding no means of escape, fatally shoots himself. Tensions between Ingram and Slater come to a head, leading both men to begin fighting amongst themselves. Upon fleeing the bank, a foot chase ensues, as Ingram pursues Slater like a predator its prey. The two eventually encounter each other atop an oil tank complex. Shots are fired, thereby rupturing the tanks. As a result, Ingram and Slater are instantly killed by the ensuing, massive explosion.

Robert Ryan.

Upon the film's beginning, as Ingram arrives at the Hotel Juno, Burke's place of residence, his flashy car attracts the attention of the local children, who eagerly approach the vehicle to get a better look. Ingram then asks, "Who'd like to make themselves a fortune?" He reaches into his pocket and provides each child with a coin on the condition they stay off the car. Such an exchange is ironic considering Burke then poses the same question to Ingram and Slater. The opening minutes of *Odds Against Tomorrow* are indeed noteworthy. Prior to entering the hotel, Ingram crosses paths with the exiting Slater. The two barely notice one another, and forty-five minutes of the film transpire before a formal introduction between the two is made. Yet, their differences become clear from the get-go.

When Slater first enters the Hotel Juno, he is rude to the clerk (Ed Preble) and coldly snubs the elevator operator (Mel Stewart). Practically the opposite is displayed upon Ingram's entrance into the building. Furthermore, Ingram drinks his whiskey straight, whereas Slater prefers it with water, but despite such differences, both men, as well as Burke, are virtually alone in the world and find it difficult to make a true connection with others. As they venture to Melton in preparation for the robbery, Wise presents three separate, unique moments of solitude. The sequence begins with Ingram, continues with Slater, and concludes with Burke.

As the journey commences and Ingram travels to Melton by bus, he appears withdrawn, choosing to avoid communication with the other passengers, some Black, some White, instead remaining transfixed on the surrounding countryside. Naturally, his demeanor is fitting considering his apprehension of the upcoming heist, but the scene, reminiscent of an earlier moment at his ex-wife's apartment, offers a candid reflection of his frustration with society. The day before the heist, Ingram arrives at Ruth's place in semi-eager anticipation of a Central Park outing with Eadie. Unbeknownst to him, a meeting of the parent-teacher association (PTA) transpires at the apartment. Ingram appears surprised as he stares at the attendees, some Black, some White.

An uncomfortable silence is subsequently broken as Ruth introduces Ingram to the committee members. They are cordial and offer nothing but warm greetings, but he remains uneasy and gradually makes his way towards the apartment's exit. Ingram later expresses frustration regarding Ruth and her "White brothers" as he declares, "Why don't you wise up, Ruth? It's their world and we're just living in it!" Her primary concern, however, is Eadie. Ruth simply desires a safe environment for her daughter, very much aware that Ingram will not be able to provide such a setting with "a deck of cards and a racing form." In short, he is susceptible to criticism from those who know him all too well. Such criticism, nevertheless, is not always adverse.

At the time of the Central Park outing, Ingram discovers Bacco's henchmen to be watching his every move. He discreetly departs a merry-go-round to confront them. Eadie, unaware of the circumstances behind her father's abrupt departure, teases him for being "too old" to ride on the carousel. Later, in a completely separate incident, Slater is chastised by his wife, Lorry (Shelley Winters), for being "old." Interestingly enough, both occurrences trigger the men's commitment to Burke's scheme. Yet, between Slater and Ingram, one's frustration with society is more severe than that of the other.

"A man always dreams about what he wants, or what he's afraid of."

Ed Begley as Dave Burke.

Slater, a narrow-minded bigot, travels to Melton by car, spending the first leg of his journey alone with nothing but his thoughts and "a hopped-up motor with dual carburetion." As he pushes the limit while driving along a desolate country road, reaching a speed of approximately 110 miles per hour in the process, a reflection of his true persona is revealed. Such actions are reminiscent of Slater's earlier encounter with Helen (Gloria Grahame), a flirtatious neighbor. In the scene, the situation becomes tense as she delves into his criminal past, daringly testing the boundaries with her line of questioning:

HELEN: How did it feel when you killed that man?

Although Slater is at first taken aback, he inevitably admits the experience was scary, yet enjoyable. Furthermore, such words essentially define his wild escapade en route to Melton. Similar to the manner in which Slater drives the car, he pushes the envelope with Helen. Sensing she is vulnerable, he compares her to his victim of years past. "[The man] dared me . . . like you are now," Slater declares. As a consequence, their tryst begins. Shortly thereafter, an unsuspecting Lorry seeks to reconcile with Slater. "I'm gettin' too old to take things slow," he tells her. Slater ultimately believes himself to be at a point of no return. He says, "If I don't make it now, I never will. I mean with you, too. It's now or never." However, as Slater journeys to Melton, a lack of appreciation for Lorry is evident. She nevertheless continues loving him. Alas, the individual who awaits Slater's arrival en route to Melton is not as fortunate. The life of such an individual, in short, is completely devoid of romance.

Burke, a single man whose only true companion is Yuley, a neglected German shepherd, poses as a hunter alongside a semi-desolate country road, waiting alone as a group of huntsmen, accompanied by their loyal gun dogs and retrievers, actively pursue game in an open field. Regardless of the circumstances, Burke is continually portrayed as an outsider. Within the film's opening minutes, as he welcomes Slater to his apartment, he reflects upon his time as a police officer, declaring, "I was on the force thirty years. I had my own squad, and I knew everybody. Everybody was my friend until they needed a patsy." Sadly, it becomes evident that many took advantage of Burke, and, despite the amount of time invested, he perhaps never belonged on the force in the first place. On the brink of the robbery, as he loiters outside a Melton restaurant, a pair of exiting hunters notices his attire and engages him in brief conversation:

HUNTER #1: Get anything?
BURKE: Not a shot.
HUNTER #2: We jumped a couple of rabbits.
BURKE: Good.

The conversation concludes as quickly as it begins. Burke cannot relate to the pair primarily because he is not a hunter. Instead, his mind is focused on the impeding robbery. As the heist eventually transpires, Burke exits the bank in order to retrieve the getaway vehicle. A nearby policeman takes notice. "Hold it, Mister. You there, the hunter," he calls. Burke then turns to face the officer, who mistakes him for somebody he is not. Little does the policeman know that the so-called hunter is, in fact, an ex-cop. As Burke advances towards the squad car, he cannot help but reminisce of a lost past. Earlier, upon his arrival in Melton, he stood in front of a statue and took note of its engraving, which states, "Whatsoever thy hand findeth to do, do it with thy might." The words mark the beginning of a Bible verse from the Book of Ecclesiastes of the Old Testament, but the remainder of the verse, omitted from the statue and film, ironically proclaims, "For there is no work, nor device, nor knowledge, nor wisdom, in the grave, whither thou goest."

Reconnoitering the bank's security.

Odds Against Tomorrow premiered in New York on October 15, 1959. Over thirty years later, in the mid-1990s, the Writers Guild of America finally acknowledged Abraham Polonsky as a true screenwriter of the picture, thus restoring his name to the official credits. In addition to Polonsky, several notables were involved with the production of Wise's film. Cicely Tyson, in one of her first ever screen roles, appears as the bartender of the club where Ingram, a talented singer and musician, performs. In addition to her Oscar and Golden Globe nominations for Best Actress in 1973, she became a three-time winner of the Emmy Award in 1994.[43] Regarding Tyson's brief appearance in *Odds Against Tomorrow*, it is somewhat ironic. Her character works at a jazz club. Tyson would later marry Miles Davis, the great trumpeter and composer.

Along with Tyson, several up-and-coming performers are featured in Wise's film. During a memorable exchange at a Manhattan bar, Slater is confronted by a young, arrogant soldier. The confrontation, of course, ends disastrously for the latter. Wayne Rogers, perhaps most famous for his portrayal of Trapper John on the television sitcom *M*A*S*H* (1972), appears as the soldier. The narrative, in short, contains many unforgettable scenes, but Wise's depiction of the film's beginning and end is especially noteworthy due to the similarities between the two.

Immediately following the opening credits, the audience is presented with a vivid setting. The wind blows hard in New York City; a puddle, nestled along a deserted sidewalk, contains a series of ripples, thus signifying the turbulence that is to follow. *Odds Against Tomorrow*, dominated by issues of racial discrimination, transpires over the course of approximately ninety minutes, and upon the film's conclusion, as the credits begin to roll, Wise presents a similar puddle in Melton. Again, many ripples are present. Alas, the aforementioned issues remain unresolved, and such issues lead to the protagonists' demise.

Earlier, as the robbery attempt begins, Ingram, disguised as a waiter from a nearby restaurant, repeatedly knocks on the side door of Melton's First National Bank. Those inside come to rely on the delivery of their dinner at a particular time of the evening. Initially, Ingram's knocking is met with silence. As the three men become concerned, so, too, does the audience. Their crime is despicable. Yet, due to Wise's portrayal of the events, we find ourselves rooting for the trio, and they almost pull off the caper, but Slater's hatred of

---

43 Cicely Tyson's Oscar and Golden Globe nominations were the result of her performance in Sounder (1972). She earned two Emmy Awards in 1974, one for Outstanding Lead Actress in The Autobiography of Miss Jane Pittman (1973), and the other for Actress of the Year. In 1994, Tyson received a third Emmy Award for her performance in Oldest Living Confederate Widow Tells All (1994). It was of the Outstanding Supporting Actress category.

Ingram, based on bigotry, delays their departure, and the whole scheme goes south.

With a title of *Odds Against Tomorrow*, it is almost certain the heist will fail, as the word "against" suggests a negative connotation. Naturally, had Wise's film been titled *Odds in Favor of Tomorrow*, a much different narrative would have been presented to audiences. An ironic exchange transpires upon the trio's arrival in Melton. Ingram bears witness to an auto accident and is questioned by a nearby policeman. Such an exchange is cause for concern, as it could very well affect the impending robbery attempt. Shortly after the exchange, as the three are alone together, Burke says, "Listen to me, Johnny. That cop wouldn't recognize you in a hundred years. We have to take some chances. You're a gambling man. Gamble," and Ingram, aware of the irony, casually retorts, "Depends on the odds."

A chance encounter en route to Melton.

The Fifties

Robert Ryan and Shelley Winters.

Robert Wise and his crew on location.

PART III
PRIMETIME!

28
WEST SIDE STORY

(PRODUCED 1960-1961, RELEASED 1961)

> "Dance is like life. It exists as you are flitting through it, and when it's over, it's done."
> - Jerome Robbins

During the late 1500s, the great William Shakespeare penned *Romeo and Juliet*, his famous tragedy about two young lovers from feuding families, and, although it was unknown at the time, the play would go on to inspire multitudes of adaptations. Centuries later, in 1947, Broadway producer Jerome Robbins conceived a modernized American version of *Romeo and Juliet* set against the backdrop of World War II. He appreciated Shakespeare's use of conflict between the Montagues and the Capulets, the aforementioned families, and envisioned a similar, fictitious scenario concerning a Jewish family's feud with an anti-Semitic clan. Robbins approached playwright Arthur Laurents with his idea for a contemporary musical adaptation to be composed by Leonard Bernstein.

Initially, the proposal was warmly received, but differences of opinion abounded, and the project was shelved for several years. In due course, others became involved. Lyricist Stephen Sondheim, considered by some to be the final piece of the puzzle, joined the venture. Laurents ultimately made revisions to the narrative and its characters. Furthermore, he and Bernstein opted to add a gang theme to the story, and on September 26, 1957, *West Side Story* opened on Broadway at the Winter Garden Theater.

In addition to spawning a national tour and two-year run in London, *West Side Story* attracted the attention of many Hollywood dignitaries, including that of Robert Wise. It was not long before he agreed to produce and direct a motion picture adaptation. Harold Mirisch, a film executive and co-founder of The Mirisch Company, approached Wise with an unusual proposition. Robbins had originally been hired as the film's choreographer but desired more involvement with the upcoming production. Mirisch therefore considered offering Wise a position as co-director. At the time, it was unheard of for a film to be directed by two individuals. Wise initially refused Mirisch's proposition and decided that Robbins should be the sole director. Wise nevertheless remained committed to serving as a producer of the film. In time, however, he reconsidered, figuring it was in his best interest to co-direct with Robbins. Yet, midway through the production, The Mirisch Company abruptly dismissed Robbins. Such a dismissal supposedly transpired due to concerns over the film's budget, and Wise, among many, was taken aback at the sudden departure of an invaluable colleague.

In a New York City of the mid-twentieth century, rival street gangs fight for control of the city's Upper West Side. The Jets, comprised of Caucasians, and the Sharks, comprised of Puerto Ricans, are constantly at odds with one another. Schrank (Simon Oakland), a police lieutenant, and his associate, Officer Krupke (William Bramley), frequently attempt to restore justice amidst the chaos. Riff (Russ Tamblyn), leader of the Jets, vows to put an end to the Sharks in an upcoming "all-out fight." He seeks the help of Tony (Richard Beymer), an original founder of the Jets who has since quit the gang to pursue steady employment. A dance is held at a local gymnasium; both gangs, including Tony, attend. The venue is designated as neutral territory. Tony takes notice of Maria (Natalie Wood), a Puerto Rican woman, and instantly becomes enamored with her. She develops mutual feelings as they dance together, but Bernardo (George Chakiris), Maria's brother and leader of the Sharks, intervenes. He abruptly sends her home. Riff approaches Bernardo and calls for a council of war. Later, the Jets and the Sharks meet at the neighborhood candy store to determine where and how their ultimate rumble will transpire. Maria learns of the forthcoming battle from Anita (Rita Moreno), Bernardo's girlfriend. Maria pleads with Tony to intervene, but his attempts prove futile, as Bernardo stabs and kills Riff shortly after the battle begins. Tony becomes enraged. He obtains Riff's knife and swiftly dispatches Bernardo. Maria is devastated upon receiving the news but, fearing abandonment, does not wish for Tony to surrender to the police. He becomes a prime target of the Sharks.

Jerome Robbins.

Chino (Jose De Vega), Bernardo's preferred suitor for Maria's hand, intends to find and kill Tony. Anita attempts to warn the Jets, but they forcefully accost her until Doc (Ned Glass), the candy store owner, comes to her rescue. In the aftermath, she angrily, and falsely, declares that Chino has killed Maria. Tony eventually receives the erroneous report. He takes to the streets in search of Chino. Unexpectedly, Tony encounters Maria. The two rush towards each other and prepare to embrace, but Chino emerges from the shadows and shoots Tony, who subsequently dies in Maria's arms. In addition to Schrank and Krupke, the Jets and Sharks arrive on the scene. Maria chides those who are driven to kill because of hate. Chino is taken into custody.

Upon the theatrical release of *West Side Story* on October 18, 1961, many were quick to cite the differences between the stage and film versions. In the original Broadway production, the intermission transpires immediately following the rumble, an event during which the two important characters of Riff and Bernardo are killed, leaving a void no one can fill. Earlier, Riff rallies the Jets during his rendition of "Cool", an inspiring song of self-control and composure. The film, however, presents a different scenario.

Approximately fifteen minutes into the second act, the rumble occurs, and along with it, the death of Riff. Shortly thereafter, Ice (Tucker Smith), a character created specifically for the film, becomes the new leader of the Jets. Through his performance of "Cool", the gang reunites to confront whatever obstacles lay ahead. Yet, Ice is not Riff, and at such a point of the narrative, the mood has changed. The deaths of Riff and Bernardo mark a pivotal moment of the film, thus signifying the beginning of the end. Following the rumble, Tony and Maria quarrel over her brother's demise. The ensuing rendition of "Somewhere", a duet of love and survival, nevertheless establishes their undying commitment to each other. Yet, as the song concludes, so, too, does a special period that began almost two hours earlier upon the film's overture. The conclusion of "Somewhere" essentially separates one half of the picture from the other, as both are different regarding content and style. During a particular scene of the first specified period, for example, Anita and

Bernardo discuss the impending meeting of the war council. It is important to him, but she believes his priorities are not in order. In addition, Anita makes it clear that if Bernardo would rather attend the meeting than spend time with her, she will not wait for him following its outcome. A difference of opinion regarding the United States and Puerto Rico subsequently abounds:

ANITA: I'm an American girl now. I don't wait.
BERNARDO: Ah, back home, women know their place.
ANITA: Back home, little boys don't have war councils.
BERNARDO: Ah, but they do here. You want me to be an American, don't you?

Through the direction of both Robbins and Wise, an aura of American patriotism is established during the first, aforementioned period of the film, and such patriotism is ultimately reflected within Doc's candy store, the "America" sequence, and Maria's bedroom.

From the street, if one peers into Doc's candy store, an American flag becomes visible, thus representing the patriotic devotion of the establishment's affable owner. At the time of the war council meeting, the bigoted Lieutenant Schrank proclaims his preconceived notions of nationalism, inadvertently uniting the rival gangs for a brief period. He asks, "So what if [the Puerto Ricans] do turn this whole town into a stinkin' pigsty?" Bernardo leaps from his seat as he prepares to strike Schrank, but Riff and Ice, of all people, restrain the Shark leader from doing something he will surely regret. Schrank demands for Bernardo and his gang to vacate the premises. "It's a free country and I ain't got the right," Schrank says. "But I got a badge. What do you got? Things are tough all over. Beat it!" As the Sharks leave, they whistle "My Country Tis of Thee". Patriotism, in essence, is clearly in the air. Furthermore, Riff is positioned near a special adornment of Doc's store. Hanging on the wall is an oil painting. It is a replica of John Trumbull's *Declaration of Independence*, thus representing the origin of the United States. Following the departure of the Sharks, Schrank seizes the opportunity to interrogate the Jets regarding the upcoming fight:

SCHRANK: Okay, fellas. Where's the rumble gonna be?

His question is met with silence. Alas, the bigotry continues.

SCHRANK: Come on! I know regular Americans don't rub with the gold teeth unless something's gonna. . . .

Tony interjects, but any comments he attempts to make are silenced by Schrank. Despite further inquiries, the lieutenant is unable to learn the location of the rumble. The Jets eventually depart, leaving Schrank alone with Doc and Tony. Schrank's frustration is evident.

SCHRANK (to Doc): You try keeping hoodlums in line and see what it does to you!

"It wouldn't give me a mouth like his," Doc says to Tony immediately following Schrank's exit from the store. A verse from "My Country Tis of Thee" declares, "Let all that breathe partake," and Doc is a firm believer in such rhetoric. Furthermore, the Sharks take pride in their rendition of the tune. Their behavior is reminiscent of an earlier scene, and the irony is uncanny particularly because "My Country Tis of Thee" is commonly known by another name.

"America", a well-known song of *West Side Story*, is performed by the Sharks and "Their Girls" during a memorable sequence in which patriotic sentiment is paramount from one "island" to the next. A certain degree of independence is exhibited amongst the group. Anita begins, singing, "*Puerto Rico, my heart's devotion, let it sink back in the ocean!*" Shortly thereafter, she confesses, "*I like the island Manhattan!*" Bernardo, however, earlier reminds her that "Puerto Rico is in America now." Not only did the tropical island become a United States territory in 1898, it also became independent from the Spanish Empire. Anita and Bernardo clearly have differing points of view. Furthermore, the two argue over Maria and her desire to become an independent woman in America. During a particular scene, Bernardo reminds his sister that he left Puerto Rico long before her. "Someday, when you're an old married woman with five children, then you can tell me what to do. But right now, it is the other way around," he explains. Shortly thereafter, in Maria's absence, Anita and Bernardo discuss the issue further:

ANITA: You know, she has a mother . . . also a father.
BERNARDO: They do not know this country any better than she does.

The youths of *West Side Story*, regardless of gang affiliation, are generally independent from parental guidance. In the case of Maria and Bernardo, their parents are not directly presented to the audience at any point of the film. Their father's voice becomes audible at times. Furthermore, as news of Bernardo's death is delivered, a brief image of somebody suggested to be his mother, standing at the bottom of a stairway, becomes visible. Both parents, however, remain virtually unseen throughout the narrative. The "America" sequence, in short, inspires independence. Yet, it also awakens a sense of hope and happiness within its performers. In the heat of the moment, Anita declares, "*Life can be bright in America*," and Bernardo essentially basks in the revelry. Maria, however, is notably absent, instead remaining behind at a most special locale.

John Trumbull's *Declaration of Independence*.

Maria's bedroom periodically features an illuminating array of red, white, and blue colors, symbolizing not only the layout of the American flag, but also an ongoing quest for personal independence. Such an array essentially becomes visible in areas she frequents the most. In the rumble's aftermath, Tony goes to Maria's place. As he enters through her bedroom window, patriotic colors are reflected upon his figure. The entrance to the room features a design of double doors, each containing stained glass windows of several colors. Yet, only those of the red, white, and blue shades illuminate the area at the most significant of times, especially during the ensuing "Somewhere" sequence as Tony and Maria come to realize, "*There's a place for us.*" To them, such affection could only transpire in America. Interestingly enough, the boutique of Madam Lucia (Penny Santon), Maria's employer, features a similar array of colors. It is the setting of Maria's earlier conversation with Anita and Bernardo regarding the upcoming dance. Maria exhibits a most fashionable outfit, and her white dress is almost complete with its accompanying red sash:

MARIA: It is most important that I have a wonderful time at the dancing tonight.
BERNARDO: It is?
MARIA: Because tonight is the real beginning of my life as a young lady of America.

Without another word, Maria begins to spin gracefully. As the transition to the gymnasium begins, her figure becomes illuminated with the red and white colors that match her attire. Seconds later, traces of blue become visible, and of the three colors to adorn the American flag, blue signifies perseverance. Maria, in essence, is determined to be successful "as a young lady of America." Regarding the boutique, dresses of several shades are featured throughout its interior, but the camera's emphasis is primarily on those of the red, white, and blue colors. Later, following the intermission, the girls of the boutique present a memorable rendition of "I Feel Pretty". At one point, Maria emerges from behind a row of hanging dresses, and during such a moment of the film, she flaunts a felicitous crown as her cohorts appropriately chant, "America, Miss America!"

"Jerry Robbins cast me as Riff in the London production of *West Side Story*," George Chakiris said. "I performed in this capacity for a year and a half. When screen testing for the film began, those in the London cast were included. For my test, I performed one scene as Riff and the other as Bernardo. About five of us were tested on a particular day. We did these tests in black-and-white. Ken LeRoy, the original Bernardo, also tested for the role of the Shark leader. A number of different people were basically tested for a number of different roles. But once I had tested for the role of Bernardo, it was decided, I think by Jerry, that I should test again. I remember being in London at the theater's stage door just prior to showtime when I received his phone call. He said, 'We liked your test and we'd like you to test again in color. Would it be possible for you to take a week's leave of absence from the show?' Of course, I was immediately granted permission.

"I flew to Los Angeles and tested as Bernardo. Jerry directed the test, which was done with a girl who, at the time, was a really hot contender for the role of Anita. Her name is BarBara Luna. It was during that trip to the West Coast that I met Bob Wise for the first time. I eventually flew back to London to rejoin the show as Riff. Time passed, but there was no news from Los Angeles. I figured I didn't get the role and that was that. Weeks later, however, I received a telegram stating that I had been cast as Bernardo.

"Performing in the film always felt challenging, but working for Jerry was exciting. He was such a perfectionist with himself, and that extended to everybody else. The working atmosphere of *West Side Story* was extraordinary. Everybody loved what they were doing so much. One scene called for a filmed close-up of me against a red brick wall. And as the camera rolled, I could sense that Jerry wanted more out of my performance. Another challenging aspect of the production was filming the war council scene at the drug store. The reason it felt this way, was because that was the first thing we shot after

Jerry Robbins was gone. His departure was, of course, a big shock to all of us. Jerry's presence was always with me no matter what we were doing.

"During the filming of the war council scene, I realized that Bob's way of working with actors was quite different. In between takes, I often thought about the quality of my performance and how I could perhaps make it better. However, every song, musical sequence, and scene was rehearsed way before we started shooting. It was as if we were rehearsing for the theater and everybody knew what they were supposed to do. Bob was patient. If a particular scene wasn't working for him, he would just keep at it until it was right. There's a scene where Susan Oakes, who appeared as Anybodys, goes to Richard Beymer, or Tony, and tries to get him out of the playground because the police are coming. From my recollection, she had to do that in about sixteen takes. Susan became confused because she wasn't sure why she had to keep doing it over and over again. But I think Bob was such an incredible filmmaker.

"Too many people have said Richard Beymer was miscast and I disagree. He had a very tough time. His first day of filming happened to be the day after Jerry left, so he never had the benefit of Jerry's direction. I loved Natalie Wood, but she didn't speak to Richard. Such circumstances only made things more challenging for him. Richard spent time with Sandy Meisner, the great acting teacher, and sometimes telephoned others for guidance. I think Bob's overall direction of Richard and Natalie is beautiful. Sometimes, prior to shooting, he would say things like, 'Let's put a little salt and pepper into this take. Let's keep it alive.' But I believe Richard Beymer gets the short end of the stick too often and people don't understand why. He was such a young guy at the time and didn't receive as much guidance as the others.

"We all sensed that we were working on something of an enormous, wonderful quality. Although we were not without our share of obstacles, performing in the film wasn't always a challenge because we often reflected back on the many rehearsals we did prior to shooting, and I also remember working in the theater with Jerry. The heart and soul of *West Side Story*, so to speak, came from him. When we were filming the prologue in New York, I remember Jerry was out on the street with us and Bob was further back, sort of like a father figure. It made sense. Bob was the experienced filmmaker, so my guess is that he looked at things from a distance to make sure everything was correct. But as I recall, it was Jerry who was often face-to-face with us, and I'm sure he and Bob discussed everything together. They both had an agreement as to how the picture would work for audiences.

Natalie Wood.

"The production of *West Side Story* was altogether a beautiful experience for me. We were all so lucky to be there. My favorite sequence is the 'America' number. We had so much fun, and Bob was fantastic. He let us play and sometimes allowed for us to ruin takes. I remember one time, at the end of a long day of filming, Jerry said we all had really good spirit considering the way we were working and the way we felt. I do not have any bad memories of the production. Regarding Natalie and her refusal to speak with Richard, that was something I never observed. But I definitely heard about it. Natalie was so darling to me; I loved her. I believe everybody loved Natalie. Jerry, I think, was *in* love with Natalie. She was only twenty-three at the time. But she was an experienced performer and had been in movies since she was a kid. I have two very short scenes with her. In retrospect, I enjoyed watching her perform even when I wasn't involved. Natalie was so smart, so intelligent. I had to remind myself that she was only twenty-three. It was impossible not to like her. Maybe her avoidance of Richard was not a good thing, but nothing like that ever happened to me. I can only speak to that working relationship from the outside. I don't know what her reasons were.

"The first day Natalie came onto the set, the rest of us were rehearsing on the second floor and had a view of the street below. We were rehearsing the 'America' number and Natalie was walking up the street, probably to rehearse. So, the first time I saw her, it was from a bit of a distance. She was dressed very casually and was ready for work. Natalie never wore any makeup. She was so beautiful and didn't need it. When she first came on board, we all thought, 'Wow! There's a movie star here!' It's not through anything she did. It was just the perception of the people around her. I'm sure that whenever Elizabeth Taylor walked onto a set, people definitely took notice. Like Natalie, the history of who she was preceded her. There was a beautiful sweetness about Natalie that I really liked. I got to be friendly with her a bit; there were some times when I went to her home. So, my experience with Natalie professionally and privately was always great. I remember being in Paris one evening having dinner with some friends when we heard the news of her death. It was just so hard for me to believe. I remember thinking, somebody needs to turn back the clock. This is wrong. This should not have happened. It was just awful.

"I think *West Side Story* was a great experience for The Mirisch Company and Walter Mirisch, the film's executive producer; I know it was also a great experience for Robert Wise. Among the movies that he made, I think people remember him more for *West Side Story* than anything else he ever did. The same might even apply to the careers of Jerry Robbins and Leonard Bernstein. The film was such an enormous success and continues to have a life.

"Robert Wise was a young guy around the time he edited *Citizen Kane*. His style not only as an editor, but also as a director was extraordinary. Whenever I attend a screening of *West Side Story* for one reason or another, I see something new on the screen every single time. Bob's editing is just fantastic. Although the credited editor of *West Side Story* is Thomas Stanford, I'm thinking Bob must have had some kind of an influence on him.

George Chakiris earned an Oscar for Best Supporting Actor.

"Bob directed some great films throughout his career. *I Want to Live!* with Susan Hayward was just incredible. As far as I was concerned, Bob was one of the nicest people on the planet. Back in 1998, the American Film Institute paid tribute to him; lunch was served and everybody was there.

People were asked to get up and speak, and everybody basically had that one special thing to say about Bob. They expressed how much they loved him, what a gentleman he was, and how great it was to work with him. And of course, all of it is true. Bob didn't try to put a style or a stamp on the movies that he directed. He just made each movie the way it simply needed to be made. With some directors, you can recognize their style. With Bob, his style, if that word applies, was just to do that particular film the way it should be made. And he was always right. I thought the world of him. Following *West Side Story*, Bob directed *Two for the Seesaw* with Shirley MacLaine and Robert Mitchum, and I often thought how I'd like to be a fly on the wall and watch the production of that film, just to see such talented people at work!"

The 34th Academy Awards took place in Santa Monica, California, on April 9, 1962. The evening was indeed special, as *West Side Story* ultimately earned a total of ten Oscars. Additionally, for the first time in motion picture history, the award for Best Director was shared by two people. Wise was grateful, and Robbins, despite his abrupt dismissal from the production, had good reason to be proud of the film. *West Side Story* was nominated an astounding eleven times, but Ernest Lehman, whose script made him a contender for the Best Adapted Screenplay award, was unable to accomplish the same feat as his colleagues. Incidentally, he lost to Abby Mann, the screenwriter of *Judgment at Nuremberg* (1961). Such a film earned the same number of nominations as *West Side Story* but capitalized with only two Oscars. Regarding Lehman, he was not without his share of challenges while crafting his adaptation. The scene during which Riff struggles to recruit Tony for the war council is especially noteworthy:

RIFF: Tony, you're not even listenin'.
TONY: I read you loud and clear, Riff.
RIFF: Then, why don't you say somethin'?
TONY: Cause I don't wanna hurt your feelings. You're my buddy, my pal, my best friend!

RIFF: Womb to Tomb?
TONY (approaches Riff): Birth to Earth!

Instead of "Birth to Earth," the phrase "From sperm to worm" is featured in the stage production. Lehman, however, was compelled to satisfy the censors and ultimately made revisions to the original dialogue.

West Side Story features an array of extraordinary characters. The background history of such characters, too, is colorful. Around the time of the aforementioned exchange, the audience becomes privy to the fact that Riff has lived with Tony's family for over four years. Later, as the Jet leader sings "Gee Officer Krupke!", we are afforded the opportunity to learn more of Riff's background and social upbringing, but the exchange between him and Tony is especially important because it leads to the latter's rendition of "Something's Coming", thus foreshadowing a chance encounter with Maria.

Natalie Wood, the star of *West Side Story*, does not make her first appearance until approximately thirty minutes into the film. Yet, upon her introduction to the audience, an entertaining narrative simply becomes captivating. At the dance, Tony finds his soul mate. His rendition of "Maria" follows shortly thereafter, and a smitten Tony speaks his true love's name almost twenty times throughout the song's short duration. Later, he goes to Maria's apartment. As the brief journey concludes and the lovers reunite, "Tonight", arguably the production's most popular number, is presented to the audience. The music of Leonard Bernstein and lyrics of Stephen Sondheim, in addition to the contributions of many others, enable the film to transpire at the smoothest of paces. William Shakespeare once wrote, "If music be the food of love, play on." It is therefore fitting that, even in death, the distinguished playwright inspired the creation of what many consider to be the greatest musical of all time.

29
TWO FOR THE SEESAW

(PRODUCED AND RELEASED 1962)

> "The most painful thing is losing yourself in the process of loving someone too much, and forgetting that you are special too."
> - Ernest Hemingway

In 1962, Robert Wise reunited with Robert Mitchum for the production of a most extraordinary picture. The two had previously worked together during the filming of *Blood on the Moon* (1948), but instead of the Old West, *Two for the Seesaw* takes place in a mid-twentieth century Manhattan. Wise sought a genuine look for his film and therefore planned to shoot on location. The script, written by Isobel Lennart, was adapted from William Gibson's stage play of the same name. The impending production of *Two for the Seesaw* became especially noteworthy because it marked Wise's introduction to a talented young actress.

Shirley MacLaine had earlier captured the nation's attention with her stellar performances in Alfred Hitchcock's *The Trouble with Harry* (1955) and Billy Wilder's *The Apartment* (1960). Wise sought quality acting from his leads but also expected them to be mindful of industry regulations. At one point during the filming of a scene in which MacLaine and Mitchum's characters kiss, Wise used a stopwatch to measure the brief period of passion. MacLaine was surprised, but Wise was simply being wary of the Hays Code. A prolonged kiss would have meant trouble with the censors. MacLaine, in time, became acclimated to Wise's methods, and going forward, she knew what was expected of her and essentially set forth to excel.

Jerry Ryan (Mitchum), a lawyer from Nebraska, endures loneliness upon moving to the New York, but Oscar (Eddie Firestone), an old friend from back home who also lives in the big city, hosts a party. Ryan reluctantly attends and encounters Gittel "Mosca" Moscawitz (MacLaine), a dancer. He later asks her to dinner and ultimately discovers that, like him, she is the victim of a failed marriage. Following the meal, they go to Gittel's apartment. A discussion of personal beliefs and expectations ensues, and Ryan kisses her shortly thereafter. Gittel invites him to stay the night but he abruptly leaves. The following day, Ryan phones her and speaks of his wife, Tess, whose family owns a law firm. He was accepted into the business but believes such acceptance was simply a "handout" from Lucius, his father-in-law. Ryan makes it clear to Gittel that he is not a needy person. He is eventually hired to do briefs for Frank Taubman (Edmon Ryan), a prominent New York attorney. With his new source of income, Ryan intends to rent a loft and then convert it into a dance studio for Gittel. Their romance blooms.

One evening, Tess phones Ryan and confesses that she cannot forget about him. Gittel is present during the exchange. Afterwards, she struggles to control her emotions. Ryan and Gittel then come to the realization that they are both uneasy about their newly established relationship. Sophie (Elisabeth Fraser), Oscar's wife, later phones Gittel and questions her about the future, demanding to know if Ryan has discussed the prospect of marriage. An angry Gittel abruptly ends the conversation. She then decides to phone Ryan at his office but learns he is on another call to Nebraska. Gittel deduces he is speaking with Tess, and jealousy ensues. Ryan later visits Oscar, who hosts another party, and expects to find Gittel. Ryan, however, is intercepted by a curt Sophie. She informs him that Gittel left the party with another man. To add to Ryan's woes, he continuously debates whether studying for and passing the state's bar exam, which will enable him to become a practicing attorney in New York, is in his best interests. Gittel encourages him to do so, but he is more concerned about her rendezvous with Jake, an ex-flame. In turn, she is insecure of Tess. A confused Ryan considers returning to Nebraska, where he is a member of the bar.

That evening, Gittel begins hemorrhaging. Ryan accompanies her to the hospital in an ambulance. Gittel eventually returns home and becomes bedridden for a short while, and Ryan looks after her. In time, he returns to work. Upon Ryan's arrival at the office, Tess phones him and declares that their divorce has been finalized. He does not share the news with Gittel. Ryan, meanwhile, passes the bar exam and prepares to move into her apartment. Gittel does not become aware of the divorce until two weeks after its finalization. Ryan admits he was reluctant to immediately disclose such information due to being shaken up more than expected. He explains to Gittel that the bonds of matrimony cannot be held for naught. Hence, a sullen Ryan ultimately returns to Nebraska.

Shirley MacLaine.

Upon the film's beginning, Wise presents an image of the expansive New York City landscape, and in the middle ground is the Brooklyn Bridge. Within seconds, Wise transitions to the character of Jerry Ryan, who casually glances towards the East River from a railing of the bridge. Thus begins his long walk into Manhattan, and the opening credits commence shortly thereafter. From the get-go, Wise makes it clear that something is not right with Ryan. The Midwest native essentially struggles to become acclimated to his new surroundings, as he is unsure of how to begin the next chapter of his life. Upon meeting Gittel, Ryan expresses his concerns:

RYAN: I've been trying to make up my mind for a month.
GITTEL: What, to ask me to dinner?
RYAN: No, to . . . uh . . . get unstuck from a piece of fly paper. You know, after you've broken your leg in five different places, you hesitate to make that first step.

In time, however, Ryan obtains employment with Taubman's firm, and the latter eventually proposes the offer of a full-time position. Ryan's initial reaction is to negotiate his salary. Taubman therefore deems it best to continue their discussion at the upscale bar of the St. Regis Hotel:

RYAN: I think it's only fair to warn you. After a couple of drinks, my price goes up.
TAUBMAN: That's funny. Mine goes down.

Considering the film's title, one way of analyzing the exchange between Ryan and Taubman is by an analogy with a seesaw, as the two could potentially haggle for hours on end. Of course, their relationship is not central to the narrative. The stage belongs to Gittel and Ryan, and they are both apprehensive with regard to beginning a new life together. At one point, Ryan demands that Gittel meet him halfway. Yet, one half of the proverbial seesaw is not always in conjunction with the other. Such an apparatus is clearly symbolic of their relationship. The narrative, however, also presents a seesaw metaphor for the Ryan of New York and that of Nebraska. Furthermore, part of him is devoted to Gittel, whereas the other half remains committed to Tess, albeit reluctantly.

Ryan, upon finding employment in the big city, classifies himself and Gittel as "two halves of an apple," but an urban setting such as New York does not exactly conjure up any similarities between the bickering couple, only the obvious differences. Their relationship is triggered by a particular chemistry, thus reflecting a contemporary theory of the era. In the 1950s, a few years prior to the release of Wise's film, an "opposites attract" concept was presented by sociologist Robert F. Winch, who argued that people with differing personalities and needs are essentially attracted to one another. Although his theory was not met without controversy, it is relatively applicable to *Two for the Seesaw*.

At the Cantonese restaurant where Gittel and Ryan enjoy their first meal together, she asks, "What's it like in Nebraska? I've never been out of New York myself. From the Bronx to Manhattan to Brooklyn, this is your life, Gittel Mosca." The opposite, however, is clearly evident regarding Ryan, as he has spent very little time in the big city. Considering New York is affectionately referred to by many as The Big Apple, it is ironic that Ryan uses the phrase "two halves of an apple," because the city is simply not for him. He has not, nor will he ever, become acclimated to his new setting.

At one point, Ryan declares, "Half of me hasn't even been in this town," thus admitting the other half of his psyche remains in Nebraska. A fear of commitment is apparent. Ryan essentially struggles to make a decision pertaining to the New York bar exam. "I'm scared. I don't know how good I am away from Lucius," he says. Ryan is preoccupied with his divorce partly due to the impending separation from his father-in-law. The achievement of independence becomes a challenge.

Oscar, a fellow Nebraska native, has made the successful transition to New York. As his character is first introduced to the audience, he remarks, "I tell ya, Jerry. I get frightened when I think what could have happened to my talent if I'd stayed in Nebraska. New York saved my life. I'm painting with my guts now, boy!" Unlike Oscar, Ryan's acclimation to the big city does not come easy. Yet, between the two, Ryan has more on his plate. In the immediate aftermath of Gittel's hemorrhage, the New York bar exam becomes secondary to issues of greater importance. She and Ryan work to make things right in their relationship. Gittel, too, admits to being scared. As she recovers from the hemorrhage, it becomes common for her to see Ryan's belongings, such as his neckties, scattered throughout her apartment. Gittel figures such belongings will return to his place once her condition improves, but she does not want him to go and therefore remains in bed, "planted like a potato." Her health, however, is but one of several issues.

Gittel, upon learning Ryan remains partially committed to Tess despite the finalization of his divorce, asks, "How am I gonna give her competition? Have a hemorrhage twice a year? Trap ya that way? I got half of ya by being a wreck on your hands. Is that how we're gonna go on?" An abrupt change in the weather essentially signifies the beginning of the end. Late in the narrative, Tess informs Ryan that they are officially divorced. She then asks, "How does it feel to be free?"

During the following scene, as Ryan packs his belongings in preparation of moving into Gittel's apartment, the weather is rainy for the first time of the film. Ryan has passed the New York bar exam. He is free of Tess. All should be well, but such is not the case. As the rain pounds against the windows, Gittel senses that something is "out of whack" and makes a sudden declaration:

GITTEL: Jerry, why don't we just sort of quit horsing around and get married, huh? I mean after the divorce comes through, naturally. I got a lot of plans for us, Jerry. I won't be just a ball and chain. You know the first thing I'm gonna do . . . take up shorthand.
RYAN: Oh, shorthand's the one thing that romances lack from the very beginning.

GITTEL: So, then when you open your own office, there I am ... a shorthand secretary. You'll save a lot of dough on me.

Yet, the conversation takes an unexpected turn when Gittel learns Ryan's divorce was finalized two weeks earlier. An argument ensues, causing her to come to a painful realization:

GITTEL: You do all the giving. Because what I have to give, you don't want. And what I want, you can't give. Doesn't matter if I learn shorthand, or uh ... if I learn how to play a bugle standing on my head. You don't love me, *you don't love me*. And time isn't gonna make one lousy bit of difference. Ah, listen, Jerry. I'm the one in a trap.

Gittel figures that if Ryan moves into her apartment, she will ultimately persuade him to marry her. Hence, a sense of entrapment is mutual. Gittel and Ryan, a pair of opposites, therefore go their separate ways, thus validating the film's tagline, which appropriately states, "It just didn't figure that they would ... that they could ... that they did!"

Robert Wise confers with Shirley MacLaine and Robert Mitchum.

Two for the Seesaw premiered in New York on November 21, 1962. It fared well with theatergoers, especially those who knew of William Gibson's play and its subject matter. Several of Wise's earlier films, including *Three Secrets* (1950) and *Odds Against Tomorrow* (1959), candidly address the nature of divorce, and he would later revisit such an issue with the production of *Star!* (1968). Yet, in Wise's canon, themes of separation and divorce culminate in *Two for the Seesaw*. Critics, in short, praised Isobel Lennart's adaptation regarding her treatment of such a subject, but Robert Mitchum and Shirley MacLaine stole the show.

Following dinner at the Cantonese restaurant, Gittel invites Ryan up to her apartment, and it is not long before he tells her, "I may be too old for you." Mitchum, in reality, was seventeen years MacLaine's senior. Therefore, it is somewhat fitting when the character of Ryan, in speaking the film's final words to Gittel, reciprocates, "I love you, too, infant." The camera pulls back to reveal the most unique of sets, presented in the form of a stage. Gittel's apartment encompasses the left half of the set, whereas Ryan's encompasses the right. A solid wall separates the two locations, and although the concluding image resembles a split screen, it is, in actuality, the presentation of a single set.

On occasion throughout the film, Gittel and Ryan converse via telephone, and a clever use of the set is made in order to present their conversations similar to the way such conversations are depicted on the stage. Both performers, each in their respective settings, become simultaneously visible to the audience. Such an image enlivens the adaptation and, in the case of the final scene, makes for a memorable conclusion. As Ryan prepares to depart the big city, and as the camera captures the entire set (or stage), the words "THE END" are displayed on his side of the screen. Such words not only confirm the end of *Two for the Seesaw*, but that of Ryan's short-lived existence in New York.

30
THE HAUNTING

(PRODUCED AND RELEASED 1963)

> "The oldest and strongest emotion of mankind is fear, and the oldest and strongest kind of fear is fear of the unknown."
> - H.P. Lovecraft

When *Odds Against Tomorrow* (1959) premiered in New York, Robert Wise and screenwriter Nelson Gidding were quite pleased with such an accomplishment. Yet, on the heels of success, the two considered how to respond with an equally successful picture. Four days later, a review of Shirley Jackson's novel, *The Haunting of Hill House*, was published in *Time* magazine. Wise eventually took notice. While reading the novel in his Los Angeles office, he became engrossed in a particular "hair-raising" sequence. Gidding, who had been in an adjacent office brainstorming ideas for a new picture, suddenly burst into the room. A startled Wise jumped three feet out of his chair. Mindful of the profound effect Jackson's novel most assuredly had on its readers, Wise instantly recognized its potential for a motion picture adaptation. Shortly thereafter, the rights were acquired. Then, in the early 1960s, Wise and Gidding met with Jackson to discuss the overall narrative. They particularly questioned if she had ever considered a title other than *The*

Haunting of Hill House. Jackson admitted that the only other name she found to be appealing was *The Haunting*. Wise and Gidding, appreciative of her feedback, henceforth proceeded with their adaptation.

Ettington Park, located in Warwickshire, England, served as the exterior of Hill House.

In a remote part of New England, Dr. John Markway (Richard Johnson), a university professor, leases Hill House, an age-old mansion reputed to be haunted, in order to conduct a weeks-long investigation of the supernatural. He recruits "carefully selected" assistants; Eleanor Lance (Julie Harris), an overtaxed woman in need of a vacation, and Theodora "Theo" (Claire Bloom), a wondrous psychic, arrive at the premises and become acquainted with Markway. Luke Sanderson (Russ Tamblyn), the nephew of the mansion's owner, joins the team of researchers. He expects to one day inherit Hill House.

It is not long before Eleanor begins to experience strange phenomena. She often feels as if the house is somehow watching, or targeting, her. As a precaution, Markway suggests that Theo move into Eleanor's bedroom. He later discovers the nursery to be the heart of Hill House. It is the room in which Abigail Crain, the home's original inheritor, spent a significant amount of her time. Furthermore, when Abigail died, she was in the nursery. Eleanor questions whether or not "the haunting" is simply part of her imagination. Grace (Lois Maxwell), Markway's wife, arrives at Hill House and demands to "join the ghost hunt." Looking for a thrill, she intends to room in the nursery. In time, Grace disappears.

Eleanor, meanwhile, becomes entranced by the house's library. It contains a spiral staircase, which she climbs. Shortly after Eleanor reaches the top, Grace suddenly appears from above an open trap door of the ceiling. The door then slams shut. Markway later questions whether the sighting was genuine or not and makes preparations for Eleanor to leave Hill House permanently. As she departs in her vehicle, Grace is seen running rampant amongst the trees which line the mansion's driveway. Eleanor loses control of the car and crashes; she is killed instantly. Grace emerges from the woods and proclaims her innocence, asserting that it was never her intention to scare Eleanor. Grace believes the house is responsible for her earlier disappearance, as it deliberately caused her to become lost. Theo declares that, in addition to the supernatural, Hill House "now" belongs to Eleanor.

Julie Harris as Eleanor Lance.

In the beginning of Shirley Jackson's novel, a somewhat apprehensive Eleanor embarks on the final leg of her journey to Hill House. Against Markway's instructions, Eleanor makes a brief stop in Hillsdale, a village located a mere few miles from her destination.[44] "Do you like it here," she asks an employee of the local coffee shop, who is a shy, withdrawn girl. Eleanor struggles to engage her in conversation, simultaneously making a mental note to avoid any mention of Hill House, as Markway has warned that the people of Hillsdale "are rude to strangers and openly hostile to anyone inquiring about Hill House." Eleanor nevertheless remains cordial. She speaks of the town's mysterious appeal to "city people" and then alludes to a desire to one day build a house up in the hills. Privacy, in essence, is a relative luxury.

Upon taking the final sips of her coffee, Eleanor prepares to leave. "Good luck to you. I hope you find your house," the girl suddenly calls out to her. Eleanor's excursion into Hillsdale is absent from Wise's picture. Yet, such an excursion remains significant because it essentially foreshadows what is to come. Jackson's novel proceeds to draw a parallel between the peculiar phenomena of Hill House and the psyches of those who occupy it, and it subsequently becomes clear to the reader that Eleanor is the most affected of the story's characters, as she gradually becomes possessed by the house. Wise remains true to Jackson's original story, but his retelling of the narrative presents a plight escalated to higher levels, as the haunting of Eleanor takes on a new significance. Hugh Crain, the architect of Hill House, remains important. Yet, the circumstances behind his wife's death, in addition to the circumstances surrounding the death of his daughter's caregiver, are different. Furthermore, with Grace Markway's unexpected arrival at the house, the narrative becomes darker.

In Wise's picture, the demise of Hugh Crain's spouse is closely connected with that of Eleanor, whereas an association between both deaths is virtually nonexistent in Jackson's novel. A certain tree nestled upon the entrance to Hill House is of particular significance. As the film begins, a chilling narra-

---

44 The original name of Markway's character, as presented in the novel, is Dr. John Montague.

tion declares, "Hugh Crain's young wife died seconds before she was to set eyes on the house. She was killed when, for no apparent reason, the horses bolted, crashing her carriage against a big tree." As the film concludes approximately two hours later, Eleanor meets her demise in an eerily similar manner. However, according to Jackson, the death of Crain's wife transpires "when the carriage bringing her [to the house] overturned in the driveway, and the lady was brought – ah, *lifeless*, I believe is the phrase they use – into the home her husband had built for her." The tree is left unmentioned but instead factors into the fate of another. Early in the story, Jackson writes, "The last person who tried to leave Hill House in darkness – it was eighteen years ago, I grant you – was killed at the turn in the driveway, where his horse bolted and crushed him against the big tree." The unnamed individual goes without mention for the remainder of the novel. An emphasis on Hugh Crain, however, persists. The sudden, unexpected death of his wife leaves him "a sad and bitter man." In addition, he is "left with two small daughters to bring up."

"Welcome to Hill House. I'm Dr. Markway."

Only one daughter, Abigail (Janet Mansell), is born to the Hugh Crain of the film, and following the passage of time, the circumstances behind her caregiver's demise are different from those in the novel. Such a demise and its connection to the death of Eleanor's mother establishes the difference. Wise's film presents a parallel between two distinct pairs. The elderly Abigail (Amy Dalby), a bedridden invalid, dies while attempting to call for help by knocking on the wall with her cane. Her caregiver (Rosemary Dorken), positioned on the nearby veranda, fools around with a local farmhand and therefore becomes oblivious to the cries of her dying employer. Thus, the evil reputation of Hill House begins. The caregiver is consequently driven to suicide.

Later, Eleanor reflects upon the death of her own mother while speaking with Markway, stating, "The night my mother died, she knocked on the wall, and I didn't come." Upon the film's conclusion, as Eleanor is killed, the audience is led to believe that, similar to Abigail's caregiver, she was driven to madness by the unseen forces of Hill House. Hence, a parallel is established, as the relationship between the caregiver and Abigail is similar to that between Eleanor and her mother. Both the caregiver and Eleanor were neglectful of certain responsibilities. Hence, their fate was undoubtedly sealed courtesy of Hill House. A much different scenario is presented in Jackson's novel. Hugh Crain's youngest daughter, in later life, quarrels with her deceased sister's caregiver over the right to ownership of the house.[45] The caregiver becomes subjected to threats and is "forced to apply for police protection to prevent her enemy from attacking her with a broom." Like her counterpart in the film, she, too, commits suicide. In the novel, however, the circumstances behind such a suicide are different. The villagers, in support of Crain's daughter, believe the caregiver to be scheming and conniving. "Gossip is always a bad enemy," Jackson writes, and the caregiver, a "poor creature," succumbs to the pressure. The unseen, evil forces of Hill House, in essence, do not factor into her suicide. Furthermore, such an incident is not in any way

---

45 In the novel, the first of Hugh Crain's daughters precedes the second in death and is therefore deceased at the time of the quarrel.

connected to the fate of Eleanor or that of her mother. Regarding the Eleanor of the novel, she makes reference to the night her mother died, declaring, "She knocked on the wall and called me and called me and I never woke up. I ought to have brought her the medicine; I always did before. But this time she called me and I never woke up." The eldest of Hugh Crain's daughters, too, was neglected by her caregiver and died as a result, but again, her demise, like that of the caregiver, is not connected with the deaths of Eleanor or Eleanor's mother. Wise's film presents a different scenario. Regarding the fate of Eleanor's mother, it remains significant, but considerable attention is particularly granted to another character of Wise's narrative.

Claire Bloom.

Specific only to the film, Grace Markway's appearance at Hill House is unexpected, thus leading to horrific consequences for the frequently tormented Eleanor. Despite being married to the doctor, she is presented as a rival for his affections. Over time, Eleanor becomes frustrated with Grace's presence. She has come to spend many passing days with Markway. Grace, however, does not see her husband as often as she would like due to his fascination with the supernatural, and upon her sudden arrival at Hill House, a replacement of sorts transpires. Eleanor, believing Grace has essentially moved in on her territory, becomes more withdrawn from the house's occupants. It is therefore only a matter of time before the haunting ensues in full force. Sudden, random appearances of Grace virtually seal Eleanor's fate. Shortly thereafter, Wise's picture concludes.

In the novel, however, Jackson does not necessarily disclose the circumstances of Eleanor's death. Much is instead left to the imagination of the reader. Regarding Grace's inclusion in the novel, her appearance at Hill House is not out of the ordinary, as an invitation has been extended. Furthermore, she is joined by Arthur, a friend. Together, they conduct rudimentary experiments of the supernatural with their Ouija Board and Planchette. In short, Grace does not pose a threat, common or direct, to the Eleanor of the novel. Instead, the latter develops passionate feelings for Theo, not Markway. Yet, at the time of the ensuing adaptation, film censors provided the cast and crew with clear directions. Julie Harris and Claire Bloom were instructed not to touch one another on camera in sensual or provocative ways. Decades later, a remake of the same name was released in theaters, and by then, Hollywood developed a stance that was generally more lax.

"You're a college prof... a man with a PhD. You can't really believe there's such a thing as a haunted house."

In 1990, Ted Turner, the well-known media mogul, pressed forward with an agenda he considered to be noble. Select motion pictures of the black-and-white format were to be colorized as a means of making such pictures more appealing to the general public. Turner then intended to broadcast the films on his cable networks for millions to enjoy, but the initiative was not met without controversy. When Wise learned *The Haunting* was on Turner's list, he made specific reference to his contract, which stated that the 1963 classic could only be presented in its original, black-and-white format. It was clearly among Wise's most cherished pictures. He enjoyed shooting particular films, including *The Set-Up* (1949), in black-and-white. In specific regard to *The Haunting*, such a format set the most special of tones for his narrative.

Upon the arrival of Markway's guests, the good doctor assuredly remarks that "ghosts are a visible thing." Wise's picture, however, is completely devoid of apparitions. Later in the film, Luke Sanderson comments, "I haven't seen a damned thing." It was Wise's desire to instill in his audience a fear of the unknown. He directed *The Haunting* as a tribute to Val Lewton, an early mentor whose name remains synonymous with the horror genre. Tragically, Lewton did not live to see the film. Furthermore, Shirley Jackson died two years after the film's release at the young age of forty-eight. Throughout her career, she frequently refused interviews, steadfastly believing that her work spoke for itself, and over the course of several decades, such a presumption has proved, rather continuously, to be undeniably correct.

The nursery of Hill House.

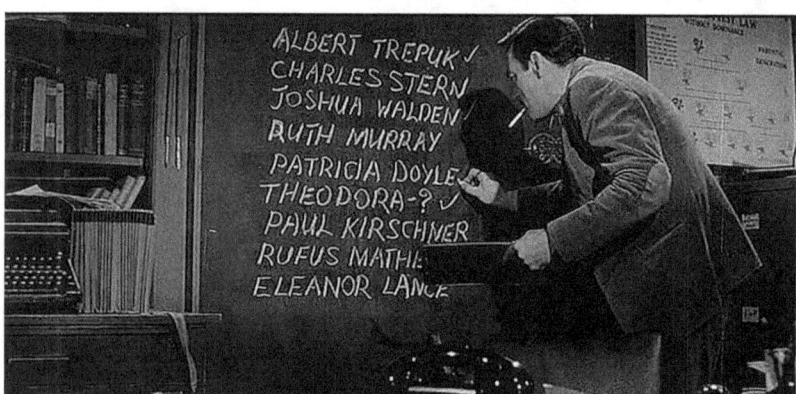

As Markway reviews a chalkboard containing a list of potential assistants, the name of Patricia Doyle, Robert Wise's first wife, is prominently featured.

31
THE SOUND OF MUSIC

(PRODUCED 1964, RELEASED 1965)

"If I were not a physicist, I would probably be a musician. I often think in music. I live my daydreams in music. I see my life in terms of music."
- Albert Einstein

The Trapp Family (1956), a film based on the memoirs of Maria von Trapp, concerns the story of a nun enlisted to care for the children of a widowed naval officer. Her real-life experiences not only attracted the attention of those in the motion picture industry, but those in the theatre as well. Richard Rodgers and Oscar Hammerstein II, the well-known Broadway producers, especially took notice.

The Trapp Family in America (1958), a sequel, was then produced and became an instant crowd pleaser. Rodgers and Hammerstein eventually began to exchange ideas for a new musical, working diligently so that fantasy could become reality, and on November 16, 1959, *The Sound of Music* premiered at the Lunt-Fontanne Theatre in New York. The show was an immediate success. A few years later, Darryl and Richard Zanuck, the father-son executive duo of Twentieth Century Fox, became determined to replicate the musical's success with a big screen adaptation. They approached Robert Wise to inquire about his interest in directing such an adaptation, but he claimed the story was a little too sentimental for his taste. Furthermore, Wise was fully committed to *The Sand Pebbles* (1966), a film in the early stages of pre-production.

The Zanucks, meanwhile, appealed to Stanley Donen and Gene Kelly, co-directors of *Singin' in the Rain* (1952), but to no avail. William Wyler was then approached, and he subsequently accepted the assignment. In addition, Ernest Lehman was hired to write the script. Both men flew to Austria in order to better prepare themselves for the production of their upcoming film. In time, however, Wyler lost motivation and requested that the Zanucks release him from his contract. Lehman nevertheless chose to remain with the production, and his countenance ultimately led to a reunion of sorts. Because Wise, Lehman's collaborator during the productions of *Executive Suite* (1954) and *West Side Story* (1961), had a change of heart, as *The Sand Pebbles* had become delayed. Wise therefore replaced Wyler as the director of *The Sound of Music* and sought to make the best of the situation.[46]

Richard Rodgers and Oscar Hammerstein II.

---

46 Robert Wise was also a credited producer of *The Sound of Music*. He formed Robert Wise Productions in part to balance his dual responsibility. His company later became affiliated with the productions of *The Sand Pebbles* (1966) and *Star!* (1968).

In Salzburg, Austria, during the "last Golden Days" of the 1930s, the Nazis loom on the horizon. Maria (Julie Andrews), the nun of a local abbey, is sent to the manor of Georg von Trapp (Christopher Plummer), a retired captain of the Imperial Navy, to serve as the governess of his seven children. Liesl (Charmian Carr), the eldest child, is in a secret relationship with Rolfe (Daniel Truhitte), a messenger and Nazi sympathizer. He expresses frustration with von Trapp, who has not accepted the Third Reich's rise to power. In time, Maria and the children grow close. She hopes for the widowed von Trapp to one day remarry, believing that the absence of a mother figure is detrimental to a productive childhood.

Baroness Schraeder (Eleanor Parker), a potential bride, and Max Detweiler (Richard Haydn), a family friend, arrive at the manor. Through Maria, the von Trapp children become exposed to the joys of singing, and their talents are showcased for the newcomers. An impressed Detweiler longs for the children to perform in his local folk festival. Maria eventually develops feelings for von Trapp. Unable to fully comprehend the meaning behind her emotions, she abruptly returns to the abbey, partly because the baroness has persuaded her to do so. Maria is greatly missed by the children. Meanwhile, Mother Abbess (Peggy Wood), head of the convent, explains to Maria that the "abbey is not to be used as an escape." Much to the delight of the children, Maria later returns to the manor, but her intention is to remain only until a new governess is found.

The baroness departs for Vienna upon realizing von Trapp is not right for her. The captain harbors mutual feelings. He soon confesses to Maria that she is the true object of his affections. Shortly thereafter, the two are married. Meanwhile, Herr Zeller (Ben Wright), an associate of von Trapp's, becomes the leader of a regional branch of the Nazi party. He expects the captain to join the new order, but the entire von Trapp family, including Maria, plans an escape to Switzerland. Zeller watches their every move. The family performs at Detweiler's festival and then seizes the opportunity to flee for the abbey. Upon their arrival, Nazis raid the premises. Rolfe, who has become an operative of the Third Reich, attempts to subdue von Trapp but ultimately lacks the courage to do so. With the convent's help, the family successfully escapes and crosses the border, climbing over a vast mountain range in order to accomplish such a feat.

The budding relationship between von Trapp and Maria is perhaps the most important aspect of the narrative. Initially, both are apprehensive of one another, and the two endure a rocky start to their relationship. Von Trapp, however, eventually admits his love for Maria, as does she for him. It is a joyous moment of the film. Naturally, Maria's relations with the other characters of the film are also important. Her respect for Mother Abbess is particularly noteworthy. As *The Sound of Music* begins, Maria is revealed to be singing atop a mountain. The scene is arguably the most famous of the film and has become easily identifiable by cinema enthusiasts across the globe. Shortly thereafter, Wise transitions to the abbey, where Maria explains the mountain's significance to Mother Abbess:

MARIA: That's my mountain. I was brought up on it. It was the mountain that led me to you.
MOTHER ABBESS: Oh?
MARIA: When I was a child, I would come down the mountain and climb a tree and look over into your garden.

Maria's connection with the mountain is clearly reflected in her singing, as *"the hills are alive with the sound of music."* However, it is not long before one realizes that her admittance into the abbey is premature. Midway through the film, Maria seeks refuge at the convent in an attempt to distance herself from the von Trapp manor, but the Reverend Mother, through her rendition of "Climb Ev'ry Mountain", suggests a different path for the film's heroine. Maria, in essence, must depart the abbey in order to confront that which troubles her. Interestingly enough, "Climb Ev'ry Mountain" provides an example of the differences between Wise's film and the original stage production. In regard to the latter, "Climb Ev'ry Mountain" concludes the first act. In the film, however, such a rendition does not transpire until the narrative's second act. Regarding the first act of Wise's picture, it features a selection of memorable numbers, but as a means of accentuating Maria's utmost significance to the story, particular attention is granted to the second-act reprises of such numbers, specifically "Sixteen Going on Seventeen", "My Favorite Things", and "So Long, Farewell".

The initial rendition of "Sixteen Going on Seventeen" evolves around an exchange between Rolfe and Liesl, but a reprise of the song later in the film essentially confirms Maria's profound influence on the eldest of the von Trapp children. In comparing both versions, two separate levels of respect become evident. Prior to and during the first rendition, Rolfe refers to Liesl as "Baby" despite her protests.[47] He insists that she needs someone older and wiser telling her what to do. Liesl is thus compelled to admit she is naïve and will grow to depend on Rolfe.

In time, however, Rolfe becomes affected by the Anschluss, Germany's annexation of Austria, and falls out of love with her, claiming to be "occupied with more important matters." Moments later, Liesl takes pride in referring to Maria as "Mother," and the reprise of "Sixteen Going on Seventeen" begins shortly thereafter. It provides Maria with an opportunity to educate Liesl regarding life's lessons as she gallantly sings, "*Gone are your old ideas of life. The old ideas grow dim.*" Nature must take its course. Liesl deems it best to wait a year before taking her relationship with Rolfe to the next level. If he is to be the one for her, only time will tell. In retrospect, their happiest moments of the film transpire during the first act, especially as they seek refuge inside von Trapp's glass gazebo. Such an event, as it happens, is precipitated by a specific, yet random, force of nature.

A heavy thunderstorm later sends the terrified von Trapp children to Maria's bedroom, where she performs "My Favorite Things". It is a song that inspires hope, especially during the second act as a reprise of the number

---

47 Robert Wise's film, *This Could Be the Night* (1957), presents a similar scenario between two of its main characters. Tony Armotti refers to Anne Leeds as "Baby," a nickname the latter deems condescending.

invigorates Maria's valiant return to the manor. Through the song, she fulfills a bold objective. At the time of the first rendition, the children become comfortable with Maria and even share some of their favorite things with her. But the verse which states, "*When the dog bites, when the bee stings, when I'm feeling sad,*" is essentially symbolic of the immediate future. As Maria attempts to repeat such a verse, von Trapp makes a surprise appearance in the bedroom, thus interrupting her in the midst of the joyous tune. The children abruptly return to their rooms, and as Maria finds herself alone with the captain, he reiterates that "the first rule [of the] house is discipline." She then requests recreational clothes for the children, but von Trapp immediately denies such a request. He leaves. Upon discovering the material of the window's drapes to be suitable for clothing, Maria finishes the tune, resuming with the aforementioned verse.

Maria is proud of her idea, but it is not until the reprise of "My Favorite Things" that an important objective becomes fulfilled. In her absence, the children suffer. They have attempted to contact Maria through the abbey, but to no avail. Later, Brigitta (Angela Cartwright), the third eldest female of the von Trapp children, joins Liesl in the reprise as they sing, "*Raindrops on roses and whiskers on kittens.*" The others eventually contribute their voices to the effort, but then Gretl (Kym Karath), the youngest von Trapp of them all, asks, "Why don't I feel better?"

The singing nevertheless continues, and suddenly, Maria's voice becomes audible in the distance. Together, she and the children blissfully conclude a tune they began during the film's first act. The reprise of "My Favorite Things", much overdue, is a turning point of the narrative, because with Maria's return to the manor, she has at last earned the children's utmost respect, and through her, they become better prepared to deal with the intricacies of daily life.

The children's first-act rendition of "So Long, Farewell" reflects their acquired code of social etiquette as they formally bid those present goodnight, but it is the song's reprise upon the conclusion of the film that confirms Maria to be a stabilizing force of the von Trapp family. The contribution of Maria's vocals, or lack thereof, essentially outlines the difference between the two performances. At the time of the initial rendition, von Trapp hosts a lavish party at the manor, and as the children perform for the many guests, Maria excludes herself from the merriment. She simply looks on with admiration. Wise limits Maria's appearances during the scene, as he intends for his audience to be focused primarily on the children. Their performance is nothing short of exceptional.

Screenwriter Ernest Lehman. *The Sound of Music* marked his third and final collaboration with Robert Wise, whom, coincidentally, he preceded in death by a mere two months.

Upon the film's conclusion at Detweiler's festival, Maria becomes personally involved with the reprise of "So Long, Farewell" from beginning to end. She earlier exhibited a feeling of self-assurance during her memorable performance of "I Have Confidence", and at the time of the climactic festival, a pivotal moment of the film transpires.[48] The children are very much aware

---

48 The real-life Maria von Trapp is featured in a cameo role during the "I Have Confidence" sequence.

that an escape from Austria is imminent. Because of Maria, they become instilled with confidence. She has made significant transitions throughout her life, especially during her passage from the abbey to the von Trapp household, and the children, in essence, are on the brink of making the most important transition of their lives. Based on Maria's past experiences, she becomes the guiding force behind such a transition. She commands respect not only from the festival's attendees, but also from her newfound family as the reprise of "So Long, Farewell" comes to an end. The von Trapps consequently bid "*good-bye*" to Austria as they traverse the majestic mountains, and Wise concludes his picture at the very location it began.

"The audition process was extensive," Heather Menzies-Urich said in regard to her performance as Louisa, the second eldest of the von Trapp children. "It was week after week after week of going back to Twentieth Century Fox and then finally having the opportunity to do a screen test. It took place on a Friday. Following the test, I heard the words, 'We'll let you know on Monday.' The fun thing for me was that there were all of these kids in attendance, performers I had seen on television who inspired me to become an actress. Jon Provost, Kurt Russell, and several others were there in the school room waiting to audition. I thought to myself, 'Wow! This must be something really special!'

"And then on Monday, I received the news. My mother actually took the call while I was at school. I thought she would have notified me either way. As school let out for the day, I was sure I hadn't gotten the part because I didn't hear from my mother. When I finally got home, she was in the bathroom taking a shower. I knocked on the door and asked, 'Mom, did I get it?' She replied, 'Heather, your sister has an audition. We need to get her ready.' I then repeated, 'Mom, did I get it?' And she suddenly replied, 'Yes! You did! Now, will you go to your sister?' And that's how I found out that I had been cast as Louisa von Trapp in *The Sound of Music*. In hindsight, I was standing there in this dark hallway with my head against the bathroom door when I heard my mother's reply, and my life changed.

"When I appeared on *The Ed Sullivan Show* in 1965 with my fellow cast mates, it was amazing for me because The Beatles had just performed there. That's all I cared about. I remember touching the doorknob thinking Paul McCartney had touched that very doorknob! He looked in the same mirror in which I was looking! That's what it was all about for me. But it was fun to be there and recreate the 'So Long, Farewell' sequence that we had already done for the film. That's my favorite song because my father had come to pick me up from work the day that particular sequence was shot. I remember seeing him out of the corner of my eye standing right next to the camera. Robert Wise was on one side of the camera. And my father was on its other side. He had this look on his face, which I interpreted to mean, 'My God! This is amazing! My little girl is putting on quite a performance!' It was a look of pride. You can see it reflected in the expression of my eyes in the final cut of the film. I'll never forget that brief moment when I saw my father and became so excited that he was watching me. Word had spread throughout the lot that something special was happening on Stage 15 at Twentieth Century Fox. All of these performers from the studio's other productions dropped by to see the action, despite the fact that it was a closed set. I remember seeing people such as Yvette Mimieux, Mia Farrow, and Dick Van Dyke. They were all hanging out and watching us perform the 'So Long, Farewell' sequence.

"There was nothing I did not like about shooting on location. We had the most amazing time in Austria. The only downside was the weather. We would all be huddled together in a barn for hours on end waiting for the sun to come out. Then, when it finally did, we ran out of the barn to perform some of the 'Do-Re-Mi' sequence. It was freezing cold in that barn up on the mountain. But being on location was just an amazing, wonderful experience. We were so well rehearsed that we didn't need to think about what we were doing. It was the first time in my life that I had ever eaten in a restaurant or flown on an airplane. The experience sort of instilled in me my love of baking, because I had never eaten that kind of food in my life.

"Julie Andrews would sing to us during those breaks when we were huddled together in the barn, trying to stay out of the rain. She had her guitar and played along to her singing as we were all wrapped in blankets. There are times when the experience seems like it happened yesterday. I was old enough to remember it. It's comparable to a fabulous summer vacation with a bunch of cousins, something one could never forget. The memories remain engrained in my psyche. Performing in *The Sound of Music* was not 'just a job.' It was an experience. I cannot say this about the other things I have done. I feel so blessed to have been chosen by Mr. Wise and to have been a part of something that will never go away after I'm long gone. It will continue to inspire people to do what they do.

"One day, Kym Karath threw up on me. She was being talked into entering a cold, horrible, leach-infested lake. It was a freezing alpine lake, and Kym didn't know how to swim. The sequence took two days to film. Every time the boat tipped, Kym would sink to the bottom of the lake. And crewmembers were poised and ready to bring her up to the surface simply because she was not going to come up by herself. During the process, Kym ingested a lot of lake water. Wise then decided that there could not be a single shot in which everybody falls out of the boat and then comes to the shore. It couldn't be done because Kym needed to be saved every time. The editors planned to later cut around the scene, and, because of this, Wise said to me, 'Heather, just go ahead and hold on to Kym. We'll do a shot of you coming out of the lake holding on to her.' The cameras then started rolling. Julie Andrews was originally supposed to grab Kym. But she fell out of the rear of the boat. I therefore found myself holding onto Kym. And then Robert Wise said, 'Cut! Cut! Heather, just dunk down and wipe it off.' At this point, I hadn't even realized that Kym had thrown up all over me. I proceeded to dunk down and wipe off the vomit. We then continued filming. I guess the overall experience touches upon the perils of filming in an Austrian lake.

"*The Sound of Music* holds up very well in this day and age, and it has been digitally remastered. The quality is so good that you can see everybody's freckles. Nicky Hammond has remained a really good friend through the years, and I also keep in touch with others such as Angela Cartwright, Kym

Karath, Duane Chase, and Debbie Turner.[49] The experiences never really end. They're like brothers and sisters of mine. We care for each other, and we love each other. In a way, we're like an extended family. My favorite memories of performing in the film are the friendships that were made during the production. Such friendships are more valuable than anything else.

"Robert Wise was like a father figure to me. And he remained so until his death. He was the type of guy who didn't take any prisoners. If you did something that Mr. Wise did not like, he would say, 'Stop it, right now. This is not happening.' But he was so validating. And considering that he had to deal with seven kids for almost a year, I'd say that's an accomplishment in itself. He never lost his cool. The only time I remember him being somewhat agitated took place at one location, the Leopoldskron castle.[50] We were running around playing hide-and-seek and having a great time when Mr. Wise suddenly yelled, 'Stop!' He called us all inside because we were making a lot of noise. Mr. Wise then addressed us, saying, 'I need to remind all of you that we are making a movie here. I just want to remind you of that.' We got the point immediately. That was the only time Mr. Wise was ever firm with us. We were just having fun, running around singing 'Do-Re-Mi' all over the hills, but Mr. Wise was the most patient director I've ever encountered. He always referred to a desired take as 'a beauty take.' Prior to shooting, he'd sometimes say, 'I want a beauty take.' And whenever he followed the filming of a particular shot with the words, 'That's a beauty take,' you immediately knew you'd done a good job. Mr. Wise had the whole storyboard in his head because of his experience as an editor back in the day. He knew exactly what he wanted to do before he even placed the camera on you. He knew exactly what he wanted the shot to look like before we started filming.

"Robert Wise was just brilliant, but he was a director who got put out to pasture way too soon. The times I spent with him in the years prior to his

---

49 Nicholas Hammond appeared in *The Sound of Music* as Friedrich, the eldest of the von Trapp boys. Duane Chase appeared as Kurt and Debbie Turner appeared as Marta, the fourth and sixth eldest of the von Trapp children respectively.
50 The scenes representing the lakefront terrace and gardens of the von Trapp manor were filmed along the exterior of Schloss Leopoldskron (in Salzburg, Austria).

passing were valuable. Sometimes, I would meet him for lunch. He often appeared frustrated because he had so much more to offer the entertainment industry. Nobody was hiring him, and it was very discouraging. But the industry puts people out to pasture before they should be."

Upon Baroness Schraeder's arrival at von Trapp's manor, the captain makes reference to the region's scenery. "Trees, lakes, mountains . . . when you've seen one, you've seen them all," he casually tells her. Yet, for theatergoers with an appreciation for nature, the film's cinematography offers an experience unlike any other, especially during the aerial sequences of the picture's opening minutes. Ted McCord, Wise's director of photography, worked tirelessly to ensure a vivid presentation from beginning to end. *The Sound of Music* premiered in New York on March 2, 1965, and became an instant box office sensation. It ultimately earned a total of five Oscars at the 38th Academy Awards, which transpired on April 18, 1966. Wise himself received two: one for Best Picture and another for Best Director. McCord was nominated but did not win, as Freddie Young of *Doctor Zhivago* (1965) fame instead took home the award for Best Cinematography of the "Color" category.

Executives of the British Broadcasting Corporation (BBC), in particular, took a liking to Wise's film. At the time of the Cold War, paranoia became commonplace in some households, and the BBC eventually arranged for the construction of a special bunker during the mid-1960s. Inside, *The Sound of Music* was set to play on a continuous loop for one hundred days in the event of a nuclear strike. Of course, tensions subsided and a catastrophe was averted.

Regarding Wise, *The Sound of Music* served as a gateway to *The Sand Pebbles*. In fact, when the 38th Academy Awards transpired in Santa Monica, California, on that memorable Monday in 1966, he was not in attendance. Instead, Wise was on location in Taiwan working diligently on his upcoming film. When the news of his two awards was broadcast over the airwaves, a special celebration complete with firecrackers and a dragon dance was held in his honor. Wise was touched, but his focus remained strictly on *The Sand Pebbles*. Jake Hinkson, author and film aficionado, perhaps said it best when he declared, "*The Sound of Music* has become a beloved classic sure, but it's not remembered as Robert Wise's *The Sound of Music*. It's remembered as Rogers & Hammerstein's *The Sound of Music*."

32
THE SAND PEBBLES

(PRODUCED 1965-1966, RELEASED 1966)

> "The Master said, 'The gentleman understands what is right, whereas the petty man understands profit.'"
> - Confucius, *Analects 4.16*

Robert Wise became fascinated with China, a nation rich in history, primarily due to several books and films he devoured through the years. *The Sand Pebbles*, a novel by Richard McKenna, was published in 1962. It pertains primarily to the establishment of U.S. gunboats along the Yangtze River during the 1920s. Wise was given the book's galley proofs and immediately took a liking to the story. He particularly became intrigued with the character of Jake Holman, the novel's protagonist. Wise then approached Twentieth Century Fox's Richard Zanuck. The latter was not only the head of production, he was also the son of Darryl F. Zanuck, the on-again-off-again studio chief. Together, Wise and the younger Zanuck discussed the possibility of adapting *The Sand Pebbles* for the silver screen.

In due course, the proposal was approved, and preparations began shortly thereafter. Yet, it eventually became clear that a film of such magnitude would take time to develop. When Wise was in England to direct *The Haunting* (1963), he occasionally discussed the impending production of *The Sand Pebbles* with the elder Zanuck, who was living in Paris at the time. Delays, however, quickly became commonplace. Wise therefore had little choice but to put his cherished project on the back burner when, in 1964, he agreed to direct *The Sound of Music* (1965). Robert Anderson, an established playwright and screenwriter of *Until They Sail* (1957), was nevertheless afforded ample time to craft his adaptation of McKenna's novel. Following a years-long ordeal, Wise, along with his cast and crew, traveled to the island of Taiwan in November of 1965 to begin production of *The Sand Pebbles*. It was an undertaking that would ultimately prove to be both expensive and difficult.

Robert Wise: Master and Commander.

In 1926, Holman (Steve McQueen), an engineer of the United States Navy, arrives in Shanghai with orders to report to the *San Pablo*, a gunboat inherited from Spain following the conclusion of the Spanish-American War many years earlier. Upon boarding the vessel, he meets the officer of the deck,

Frenchy Burgoyne (Richard Attenborough), who refers to the ship's sailors as "Sand Pebbles." A group of Chinese laborers, also known as "coolies," work aboard the *San Pablo* to help the Americans with their day-to-day duties. It is not long before Holman clashes with Chien (Tommy Lee), the bilge coolie, over the maintenance of the ship's engine. Chien, however, is subsequently killed when a faulty jacking gear results in a freak accident. A disappointed Lieutenant Collins (Richard Crenna), the ship's commander, orders Holman to train a replacement for Chien. Po-han (Mako), an affable laborer, is chosen for the job. Meanwhile, the students of China support a new leader, Chang Kai-Shek of the Nationalist Party. He leads a fight against the warlords who have ravaged the nation. A civil war therefore appears imminent, but the Americans are blamed for much of the unrest.

Collins and his crew are ordered to avoid any confrontation with the natives, who will treat such an attack as war propaganda. The U.S. government calls for the evacuation of Americans from central China. The *San Pablo* arrives in Paoshan to rescue a group of missionaries. Two such missionaries, Reverend Jameson (Larry Gates) and Shirley Eckert (Candice Bergen), are fairly acquainted with Holman. As the ship prepares to depart with the evacuees in tow, Po-han, still ashore, is captured by an angry mob. Collins and Holman offer to pay a ransom for the coolie's safe return, but the mob, intending to provoke an incident, dares the ship to open fire. In order to avoid such an incident, Holman shoots and kills Po-han. Jameson, meanwhile, has been sentenced to death because opium was discovered to be growing on a remote piece of mission property. The *San Pablo* therefore takes him and Shirley to Changsha, where he plans to appeal his sentence to a higher court.

Burgoyne eventually falls in love with, and marries, Maily (Marayat Andriane), the one-time hostess of the Red Kettle Bar.[51] Such an establishment is the favored Changsha hangout of the sailors. In time, Holman and Shirley become close, but he figures that a relationship between a sailor and a missionary cannot thrive. The court eventually grants Jameson permission to

---

[51] Marayat Andriane also became known as Emmanuelle Arsan, a pen name used for the erotic novels she wrote.

return to China Light, his mission in Paoshan. He departs Changsha with Shirley. The natives ultimately grow tired of the gunboats. The coolies of the *San Pablo* later jump ship, but not before opium is planted aboard in an attempt to frame the Americans. Collins and company find themselves in a state of siege. Furthermore, the water in the channel is too low for the *San Pablo* to leave Changsha, and the siege persists. As a result, access to the shore becomes severely restricted. Burgoyne secretly swims ashore at night to visit Maily, enduring the river's ice-cold water in the process. As a consequence, he tragically succumbs to hypothermia. Maily, pregnant with Burgoyne's child, is later killed by the natives, and Holman is framed for the murders. Collins fears that the affair will quickly become an international incident, as Nationalist soldiers have joined the protest against the *San Pablo*. To make matters worse, word arrives that American treaty people are being killed. The water in the channel rises, and the *San Pablo* departs for China Light to make a final rescue attempt. Upon arrival, Collins and company discover Jameson to be adamant about evacuating. He and the other missionaries have declared themselves to be stateless persons. Nationalist troops, however, storm the mission and kill Jameson. Collins orders his crew to discreetly escort Shirley from China Light. He remains at the mission to delay the advancing troops but is abruptly killed. Holman continues the fight; unfortunately, he is also killed. Shirley subsequently escapes with the help of Bronson (Joe Turkel) and Crosley (Gavin MacLeod), the remaining Sand Pebbles.

Richard McKenna passed away in 1964. He therefore did not live to see *The Sand Pebbles* on the big screen. Whether McKenna would have appreciated Wise's film or not is unknown. Robert Anderson, in particular, had his own ideas regarding the novel's adaptation, often defending such ideas against those who disagreed with him. Steve McQueen, perhaps, was the greatest critic of them all. He feuded with Anderson over several of the script's details, particularly the character of Jake Holman. McQueen took exception to how such a character should be presented to audiences. Anderson was subsequently relieved of his duties as the film's screenwriter. Several theories thus abounded regarding the script's final draft, one of which asserted that Wise stepped in to make the revisions himself. Hence, differences between the novel and film, some more significant than others, are evident. For example, Wise, unlike McKenna, immediately introduces the character of Jameson upon the narrative's beginning.[52] The film opens with a bold statement, "CHINA 1926 ... RAVAGED FROM WITHIN BY CORRUPT WARLORDS ... OPPRESSED FROM WITHOUT BY THE GREAT WORLD POWERS WHO HAD BEATEN CHINA TO HER KNEES A CENTURY BEFORE ... CHINA ... A COUNTRY OF FACTIONS TRYING TO UNITE TO BECOME A NATION ... THROUGH REVOLUTION...." Shortly thereafter, as Jameson dines aboard a riverboat en route to China Light, he declares to those present, "[Gunboats] are symbols of what the great powers have done to this nation." He exits the narrative a short time later and does not reappear for at least another hour, but his immediate presence within the film's opening minutes is imperative. Through Jameson, Wise reinforces the central themes of corruption and conflict. Much is then presented to audiences over the course of a three-hour period.

A selection of Wise's later, lengthier films feature roadshow versions. Such versions were originally produced so that particular films could be showcased in designated venues prior to being released nationwide. In the case of *The Sand Pebbles*, its roadshow version includes approximately fifteen minutes of additional footage and is undeniably significant. It presents a unique perspective of Stawski (Simon Oakland), machinist's mate of the *San Pablo*. Furthermore, the roadshow version reveals important details not only of Holman's friendship with Po-han, but also of the special connection Holman makes with Shirley.

Similar to the coolies of the *San Pablo*, the otherwise bothersome Stawski is a character frequently seen in the film's first act, but rarely in its second. Nevertheless, during a scene included only in the roadshow version, he finally lives up to the crew's expectations, which is to serve as the ship's machinist's

---

52 Craddock, a tall, bearded man, is a character from Richard McKenna's novel and is also the basis for the character of Reverend Jameson.

mate. When Stawski is first introduced to the audience, he is established as a chief proponent of the coolies. He makes it clear to Holman that Clip Clip, the barber coolie, does all of the shaving on board the *San Pablo*. Shortly thereafter, problems between Holman and Chien arise. As Holman submerges beneath the floor plates of the engine room to examine the bilge side, Chien "blows the glass," thus exposing the former to incredibly hot steam. In the aftermath, Stawski comes to Chien's defense, telling Holman, "He probably didn't even know you was there."[53] Alas, the tension begins.

Stawski, whose dislike for Holman grows with each passing day, eventually targets Po-han. The trouble begins in the days following Chien's death. Stawski discovers Po-han to be drinking coffee while touching the engine's throttle. He becomes angered and attempts to assault Po-han, but Holman intervenes. Stawski later fabricates the skirmish's details, claiming he was not the instigator. As a result, the crew calls for Po-han to be permanently relieved of his duties aboard the *San Pablo*. Holman therefore proposes the idea of a boxing match to take place between Stawski and Po-han at the Red Kettle Bar. If Po-han emerges victorious, he will remain on the *San Pablo*; if Stawski is the victor, he will earn enough money to purchase a sexual escapade with Maily.[54*] Although Po-han agrees to participate in the fight, Holman does not make him aware of the issues at stake.

The fight's initial rounds come and go rather quickly. Po-han eventually learns that a loss to Stawski will result in a loss of money for Holman. Yet, upon learning he will not be allowed to return to the *San Pablo* if Stawski emerges victorious, Po-han suddenly becomes instilled with the will to see the fight through to its end. As the tide of the match turns, so, too, does that of the film. Stawski is defeated at a point when the ship's alarm begins to

---

53 Richard McKenna's novel presents a different scenario. Instead of Stawski, Wilsey, a minor character, is the one to defend Chien. Furthermore, regarding the barber coolie's presence aboard the *San Pablo*, the character of Shanahan, described by McKenna as "a little man," is the one to warn Holman against "breaking Clip Clip's rice bowl." In the role of "Red Dog" Shanahan, Robert Wise cast Joe Di Reda, whose stocky build was opposite that of the Shanahan of the novel.

54 Such an escapade is made possible by the proprietors of the Red Kettle Bar.

blare throughout the city. The crew returns to the *San Pablo* prior to the arrival of an angry mob.

During the following scene in which Collins and Ensign Bordelles (Charles Robinson) converse, the audience learns of the reason for the unrest. Earlier, up the Yangtze River, British warships engaged in battle with a local warlord, thus resulting in hundreds of casualties. As a consequence, the Americans are perceived by the Chinese as "foreign devils," and regarding the coolies' affiliation with the *San Pablo*, the beginning of the end becomes imminent. Hence, the outcome of the boxing match remains significant. Following the defeat of Stawski, the audience sees less of him, and it simply becomes a matter of time before the coolies exit the picture as they jump ship.

Later, upon the film's climax, as the *San Pablo* encounters a boom of junks blocking the Chien River, the crew prepares to fight the defending militia. Holman orders Stawski to remain in the engine room and "take the throttle." In the roadshow version, a fire breaks out aboard the *San Pablo* during the battle, temporarily bringing the ship to a standstill. Stawski is absent from the scene. He remains in the engine room, finally living up to his title of machinist's mate. His actions, or lack thereof, transpire at a point when the narrative has become quite serious. Early in the film, as theatergoers see more of Stawski, he is presented as an obnoxious, rude individual. Yet, considering the lighter tone associated with the first act of *The Sand Pebbles*, his character is also perceived as a relative source of comic relief. Such relief, however, frequently occurs at the expense of another.

Po-han, resilient amidst continuous harassment from Stawski, develops a special friendship with Holman, and the film's roadshow version essentially offers a unique perspective of their short-lived bond. Additional footage regarding the character of Chien is significant. During Holman's first morning aboard the *San Pablo*, a coolie abruptly approaches him to take measurements for a new uniform. Burgoyne, who is present at the time of the impromptu fitting, seizes the opportunity to offer an explanation to a confused Holman:

BURGOYNE: This is Sew Sew. He'll make your uniforms for you.

HOLMAN: Ah.

SEW SEW: This before time belong P'tocki. Me tinkee you little bit all same P'tocki.

HOLMAN: Who's P'tocki?

BURGOYNE: Guy you replaced ... died last winter in Changsha. Typhus.

Burgoyne then shifts his attention from Holman to Sew Sew.

BURGOYNE: Hey. He'll need shorts.

HOLMAN (to Sew Sew): Hey. Don't worry too much about the shorts. I want dungarees.

SEW SEW: Sand Pebble, any man no wanchee too much dungalee.

HOLMAN: Yeah? This sailor wanchee plenty dungalees. You understand? You makee all same, a lot of....

Holman directs his attention towards Burgoyne.

HOLMAN: A lot of good shorts'll do me down in the engine room.

BURGOYNE: Well, you don't need to get dirty down there. Old Chien'll handle that. He knows more about the plant than anybody.

Holman is clearly caught off guard at the thought of a coolie running the engine room, but before he can seek an explanation from Burgoyne, the sound of a whistle indicates the beginning of a "repel boarders starboard" drill. Shortly thereafter, Holman and Chien come face-to-face for the first time. Wise briefly cuts to a shot of Po-han, who nervously observes the tense exchange. Holman then submerges beneath the floor plates to examine the bilge side. Within the roadshow version, Chien glares at Po-han in disgust seconds before he "blows the glass." Po-han's support of Holman, in essence, meets with severe disapproval. In time, the jacking gear accident transpires and Chien is mortally wounded. The roadshow version then features an additional minute of footage as Holman and Po-han work diligently to repair the engine. In times of tragedy, their bond strengthens. Collins subsequently orders Holman to train Po-han as Chien's replacement.[55]

The roadshow version later presents a curious exchange. Immediately following Holman's proposal of the aforementioned boxing match, Burgoyne subtly requests a meeting with him to take place outside the crew's quarters. Determined to permanently relieve Maily of her duties at the Red Kettle Bar, Burgoyne cannot come to terms with the possibility that Stawski will "win" her upon successfully defeating Po-han:

BURGOYNE: What the hell are ya doing? You know what I'm trying to do for Maily.
HOLMAN: They're givin' the coolie a bad shake.
BURGOYNE: So what? You'll be rid of him and get your engine back.
HOLMAN: Hey. It was my fault 'cause he was canned.
BURGOYNE: I don't get it. You lose your money and Ski'll get Maily all on account of that slopehead.
HOLMAN: Well, what do ya call her?
BURGOYNE (livid): You shut your m....!

In a rare moment of the film during which only viewers of the roadshow version bear witness, Burgoyne becomes annoyed with Holman, whose existence aboard the *San Pablo*, Wise gradually suggests, no longer evolves entirely around the ship's engine. Po-han becomes a priority, and he is not alone.

As the narrative progresses, Holman and Shirley grow relatively close with one another, and the roadshow version includes additional footage that simply reinforces the importance of such a relationship. Upon discussing her true purpose in China, Shirley subsequently questions Holman's motives. *The Sand Pebbles* features many memorable scenes, one of which is set on a sailboat positioned in a small, serene body of water. At such a point of the narrative, Holman explains to Shirley how he came to join the U.S. Navy. Yet, the

---

55 Richard McKenna's novel provides an alternative version of the events. Holman teaches Po-han about the differences between water and steam at a point of the narrative when Chien is still alive. In the film, such a lesson transpires some time after Chien's death.

following scene, evident only in the film's roadshow version, is perhaps more significant. As Wise transitions away from the sailboat, he presents a brief image of the *San Pablo* before cutting to the interior of a quaint restaurant. Outside the window, snowflakes gently fall to the ground, and Shirley then seizes the opportunity to speak of China Light and her pupils:

SHIRLEY: I can't tell you how excited I get watching these kids learn. I guess because back home, most of us just went through the motions. Well, we got by. But here, there's a real sense of purpose. You know, they want to do something.

HOLMAN: Yeah. They want to get rid of the U.S. Navy.

SHIRLEY: Well, wouldn't you feel the same way if the Chinese had gunboats running up and down the Mississippi?

HOLMAN: Yeah. How about that?

SHIRLEY: I hope someday all people can pledge allegiance to something beyond country. To something that emphasizes not their differences but what they've got in common. Like what you found in Po-han.

HOLMAN: Go ahead.

SHIRLEY: Well, in a small way, it's what we're doing at China Light. You see, people live wonderfully together. It's only the nations that can't get along ... like Frenchy and Maily. Now, why can't they get married, Jake? Who has the right to say "No?" I'm so fed up with people always telling me how to think and what to do. I guess things have to be that way for you in the navy. I wouldn't think you'd like it.

HOLMAN: I don't.

SHIRLEY: Why don't you get out?

HOLMAN: Now, look ... I told you before, I'm in the Navy because they put me there. I didn't go out looking for it.

SHIRLEY: The judge didn't say you had to sign up forever.

HOLMAN: You're digging into me pretty good, Shirley. You know that? Ah ... I better get back to my ship.

The Sand Pebbles features several noteworthy conversations between Holman and Shirley. The aforementioned exchange, however, is of the utmost significance. For the first time of the narrative, Shirley appears to make a breakthrough, as Holman gradually develops an interest in China Light. Burgoyne eventually marries Maily. Holman and Shirley preside over the ceremony as the bride and groom exchange self-written vows. Later, upon Burgoyne's death, Maily is unsure of her future. Holman mentions China Light, suggesting she find solace in the mission. He offers to accompany her there, essentially confirming his desire to leave the service. Maily, however, is murdered in cold blood before she has the chance to make any decisions regarding the future.

Directing Steve McQueen.

Conditions go from bad to worse for the crew of the *San Pablo*, and by the time the final rescue attempt is made at China Light, Holman has confidently determined where his future lies. "You better get back to the ship, Captain . . . 'cause [the missionaries are] staying here, and so am I," he tells Collins.[56]

---

56 Although Collins is officially a lieutenant, the highest ranking officer of a naval vessel is traditionally referred to as a captain.

Nationalist troops then arrive on the scene, and the Americans are unfortunately outnumbered. Yet, it is the destiny of Holman, an engineer, to perish at China Light. Ironically, as an assassin's bullet claims his life, he is positioned between a pair of crates containing the most basic of engines.

"When Steve was getting ready to begin work on *The Sand Pebbles*," Neile Adams McQueen said regarding her husband's involvement with the production, "Paul Newman and his wife, Joanne Woodward, visited our house the night before we departed the states for Taiwan. Paul and Steve were standing near the car saying their goodbyes, and I was observing them from the other side of the vehicle when I heard Paul say, 'Okay! See you guys in nine weeks.' Well, as it turns out, we were gone for nine months! It was a hard location because of the weather. The cast and crew had a total of four call sheets. One was for foggy weather. Another call sheet was created just in case the level of the river was too high. Yet another was prepared in case of cloudy weather. And the last sheet was created for a sunny day. The weather in Taiwan was always so strange and unpredictable.

"Steve and Bob Wise got into a few fights now and then. At one point, some kind of serious verbal altercation occurred. Following the argument, Steve didn't speak to Bob for about two weeks. He would instead answer questions with a simple 'Yes' or sometimes just mumble 'No' or 'Whatever' at times when a response was expected of him. In retrospect, their disagreement was really harmless. I think it all began with Bob saying something like, 'You mustn't do that because of so and so.' Whatever it was, Steve felt put out about it.

"Overall, we had a great time in Taiwan. Pat, Bob's wife, was fabulous. They both stayed at the Grand Hotel. Steve and I opted to live in a house during the film's production. Our children, Terry and Chad, accompanied us to Taiwan. Although it was a difficult location for the cast and crew, it was kind of fun for me and the kids. I enrolled them in the local Dominican school. They rode the bus along with the Taiwanese children. Chad, however, became too much of a problem during those trips to and from school, so he eventually rode with me in the car. He was a handful.

"During a day of rest for the cast and crew, Steve took the kids on a bike ride, and Taiwan, in those days, used human excrement for fertilizer; I›m not sure if this still happens or not, but as Steve and the kids were riding in the area, they all fell in a field that had just been fertilized. A short time later, when they made it back to the house, I wouldn't let any of them inside. I had to hose everybody down! They removed all of their clothes while standing in the home's front yard. And after I sprayed water all over them, I made sure they scrubbed themselves really well once they finally made it inside.

"Around Christmas time, a group of us went to a brothel, where a sex show transpired before our very eyes. And as these women were carrying on, I specifically remember Dick Crenna standing in the background singing 'Silent Night'. He was a very funny person to be around. Bob, being such a straight-laced person, naturally did not accompany us on that particular evening.

"One day, we went to the airport to meet somebody affiliated with the production. As this person was getting off the plane, he asked, 'What's that smell?' And Dick, who happened to be with us, replied, 'That's shit!' The other person then said, 'I know! But what do they do to it?' At that point in time, Taiwan was a strange place to visit. I'm not sure what it's like these days. We were there about fifty years ago. It has undoubtedly become a more civilized nation. But during the 1960s, it was just madness. Taiwan, however, was also an R&R area for the American service people, and while *The Sand Pebbles* was being produced, a large contingent of military personnel happened to be there. With Bob's blessing, I taught dance classes to those who were interested. It turned out to be a great way for me to spend my time. In short, Bob was such a nice man, and I stayed in touch with him almost until the very end."

"A few weeks prior to the beginning of production, *The Daily Variety* listed all of the actors who had been cast in *The Sand Pebbles*," Gavin MacLeod said in regard to being chosen for the role of Crosley. "I spotted Sy Oakland's name. We'd worked together during the filming of Robert Wise's *I Want to Live!* I figured the two of us would have a great experience flying to Taiwan because it would give us time to catch up on our lives. Sometime prior to leaving the states, however, an important message was waiting for me as I arrived home one day. My wife informed me that the studio had called and said I was going to be part of the cover set. At the time, the crew hadn't given much thought to the weather. Due to the possibility of rain, I was instructed to perform in a scene with Steve McQueen earlier than scheduled. I therefore flew to Taiwan by myself.

"Somebody from the studio met me at the airport and drove me to the hotel. Steve was standing just outside its front doors. In the mid-1960s, he was a big movie star. He greeted me with the words, 'Hey, bro!' He always called me that because we had earlier played brothers on Broadway. 'Hey, bro,' he continued, 'did you ever think I'd be a big movie star?' I candidly replied, 'I'll tell you the truth. I never thought you would be, but I'm so happy for you. Whenever that camera is close to you, it reveals how fascinating of a person you are!' Steve was a strong guy. He frequently rode that motorcycle of his, although such an activity was in direct violation of his contract.

"Shortly after my arrival, I told Steve that I was starving. He then spoke of a great restaurant upstairs in the hotel. I've always been a finicky eater. I couldn't even eat turkey for Thanksgiving because I would think of the harm being done to the animal. After checking in at the front desk, I went straight to the restaurant. And the first thing on the menu that caught my attention was ox penis soup. My first thought was whether it came in its original shape or was perhaps diced. I had no idea what the chef did with it. That's when I first realized I was going to lose weight while being on location in Taiwan.

"After a while, the rest of the actors arrived from overseas. It became a wonderful experience. We were in Taiwan for a while, then we went to Hong Kong. After shooting in Southeast Asia, we went back to the lot at Twentieth Century Fox and shot a few scenes at the studio's ranch. Throughout the production, Mr. Wise had wonderful people working for him, such as Charlie

Maguire and Reggie Callow. I always felt protected while on location. But I think the Taiwanese started shooting at our boat one day. We then had no choice but to move it. Chang Kai-shek was alive at the time, and whenever he came into town during our stay, the Taiwanese soldiers, armed with guns, would pull down all of the blinds in our hotel rooms and then stand on the roof. There were about four black sedans with purple window shades; none of us could determine which of the sedans was occupied by Chang Kai-shek. On one particular day, elections took place. People either voted for Chang Kai-shek, or they didn't vote at all. There was nobody else who would dare challenge him; but Taiwan was a great location. And Robert Wise was a great leader.

"*The Sand Pebbles* provided me with the opportunity to work with all of these actors I admired. Richard Attenborough was just amazing in the role of Frenchy Burgoyne. When we were on location, he and I took the same car back to the hotel one day. He was talking about how much he wanted to film *Gandhi*, and then, about fifteen years later, he produced and directed it. Later, when the production of *The Love Boat* moved to Samuel Goldwyn Studios, I saw Attenborough on the lot and had the opportunity to catch up with him. In regard to additional cast members of *The Sand Pebbles*, I had known Dick Crenna for years. It was great to see him in the role of Lieutenant Collins, especially because he had mostly done comedy up to that point of his career. Barney Phillips, Joe Di Reda, Steve Ferry, and Gus Trikonis were others I had known prior to the production of Wise's film. We had a wonderful group of performers on that set. Shep Sanders had about two lines in the entire film. Years later, he and I worked together in Yugoslavia for the production of *Kelly's Heroes*. Again, I think he only had a couple of lines in that film, too. Much later, when I performed in a two-character play in my hometown of Rancho Mirage, Shep came to see the show. I told him that the two of us were destined to be together. We went from the Orient many years ago, to the former Yugoslavia, which is now made up of several republics, and finally back to the United States.

"In Taiwan, the cast and crew traveled to work primarily in a bus. The locals often urinated in the streets; kids would go to the bathroom in plain view for everybody to see. Taiwan was very primitive back then. And if somebody died, you'd see the body out in the open. After a full day of work, the body would still be in the same location as we headed back to the hotel. Then, we finally discovered that there was only one coroner in town who could legally declare another to be dead. But he was so busy. If a person died, the corpse would simply be exposed for a long period of time. It was a shocking thing for us to see.

"One day, we ventured away from the hotel to do some exploring. It was our day off. The people in our group were Candice Bergen, Joe Di Reda, the driver, and me. I had an old friend from high school who became a Catholic nun in Taiwan. She was caring for people who had leprosy, working in a hospital about an hour-and-a-half from where we were filming. I thought it would be nice to visit her. We therefore made arrangements for our driver to take us to the hospital, but he ran out of gas. And we suddenly found ourselves surrounded by Taiwanese soldiers. Their guns were pointed directly at us. We were subsequently placed in a holding area, and part of me figured it was the end. I thought, 'We're finally gonna die and we're not even in the movie!' After some time, however, the head guy came to our holding area. We explained that we had simply run out of gas. The Taiwanese had never seen anybody looking the way Candice Bergen had; she was gorgeous. Any director could shoot her soft palette and she'd still be divine. I figured the Taiwanese soldiers would rape her and then kill us all. But instead, they attempted to say things, then pointed and started to laugh. Nothing happened.

"Our driver eventually showed up with a car full of gas, and they let us go. All they could say in English were the words 'movie star.' We got in that car and did what we had to do. I saw my friend, the nun, for a brief period of time. As we were heading back to the hotel, we stopped for more gas and also had to use the restroom. Then, some people in a nice car arrived at the filling station. It was pulling a wagon containing four German Shepherds. We then discovered the vehicle's occupants were going to kill the dogs because they were preparing to eat the animals for dinner. Candice was furious and kept referring to the Taiwanese as savages. I'm glad they were unable to understand what she was saying. Finally, they took off, and so did we. Back on the set, an edict was put up on the board declaring that nobody was allowed to leave the location without permission, as it was too dangerous. It sort of changed everybody's mood regarding how they felt about Taiwan. That was a strange and scary experience for me. I really thought we were gonna buy the ranch.

"I think almost every film director is conscientious about what they do. Robert Wise was very caring. I've always considered him to be the best in the business because, when he directed *The Sand Pebbles*, his demeanor was similar to that of General Patton. He had so many talented people working for him. Maurice Zuberano composed some of the storyboards in order for the camera to tell the story. Furthermore, it seemed like the locals in every different county of Taiwan spoke a different dialect of the language, and whenever Wise called for the cameras to start rolling, four or five of his crew had to relay those orders in each of the various dialects. On the first day of shooting, somebody said, 'Action!' And only one person out of perhaps hundreds started to move. That's why it was necessary for those crew members to be present to speak the different dialects. Needless to say, it was sometimes challenging for them to get the action going.

"To me, Robert Wise has always been the best. Orson Welles broke a lot of rules and made some great pictures, but Robert Wise was a humanitarian. He cared about people. When we were on location for the production of *The Sand Pebbles*, and my fourth child, a girl, had just been born, it was a very difficult period of time for me because I had been away from my family for a while. But it was necessary to make some money to pay for the house, feed the kids, and all that. I unexpectedly ate a lot while on location. It was done out of frustration. And as a result, I started to get heavier and heavier. One day, as Wise was standing on a bridge, he looked down at me and said, 'Gavin, if you don't stop eating, I'm gonna have to start calling you Moby Dick.' His humor often made it easier for me to get through the tougher times of the production. Robert Wise had a wonderful laugh. It was simply one of his many amazing qualities that I'll never forget."

Composer Jerry Goldsmith.

The Sand Pebbles, a film Wise declared to be the personal favorite of his motion picture career, remains fascinating on many levels. The end of the first act depicts the *San Pablo* to be sailing away from the camera. Following the intermission, a familiar image is then presented to theatergoers. As the second act commences, the audience is again afforded a view of the *San Pablo*. Unlike before, however, the conspicuous gunboat heads directly towards the camera, preparing to encounter whatever obstacles lie ahead. The first and second acts of *The Sand Pebbles* each contain a fair amount of action. Yet, a profound difference between the two becomes evident. Up to the point of Po-han's death, not a single firearm is discharged.[57] The first act, to reiterate, is relatively lighthearted. At times, comic relief supports the narrative. The boxing match between Stawski and Po-han serves as an example. Chief Franks (Barney Phillips) officiates. Prior to the fight's first round, he confers with both individuals to make sure the rules are understood:

FRANKS (to Po-han): You savvy?
PO-HAN (hesitates): Me savvy.
FRANKS: Alright.
STAWSKI: Me no savvy!

The crowd erupts in laughter, and Franks jokingly prepares to backhand Stawski. As the fight ensues, it becomes a memorable scene of the film. Furthermore, Wise's direction of the match is noteworthy. He frequently intercuts between the fighters and spectators, thus exhibiting a technique similar to that presented in *The Set-Up* (1949) and *Somebody Up There Likes Me* (1956). The alarm of the *San Pablo* then disrupts the match, and the mood of the film begins to change. In time, the second act begins. Later, during the battle at the boom of junks, Franks is shot dead. Several others abruptly lose their lives as well, and the comical overtones of the first act suddenly become irrelevant. Ironically, at the time of Holman's first morning aboard the *San Pablo*, Burgoyne suggests that the Americans will probably never engage in any battles. However, chaos ensues and everything falls apart within the second act of *The Sand Pebbles*. It is an act during which Wise occasionally affords viewers a glimpse of the deteriorating *San Pablo*, thus symbolizing the plight of its sailors. The absence of the coolies, too, is undoubtedly significant.

One of the greatest challenges Wise faced while directing *The Sand Pebbles* was to present an accurate depiction of the Chinese culture. Fortunately, he was afforded the opportunity to collaborate with a talented group of

---

57 In the roadshow version of the film, approximately one hour prior to Po-han's death, local bandits fire shots at the passing *San Pablo* as it sails on Flag Day.

individuals, including Joseph MacDonald, the director of photography, and Jerry Goldsmith, composer of the picture's score. In addition, designer Boris Leven sketched many of the film's interior locations on paper several weeks prior to production. The end result of everybody's involvement generated a total of eight Oscar nominations, including one of the Best Picture category for Wise, who served in a dual capacity of producer and director.[58] *The Sand Pebbles* also led to the only Academy Award nomination of Steve McQueen's career.

Through the years, Wise's thirty-second film has been applauded for its depiction of American gunboat diplomacy. In 1971, *Yangtze Patrol: The U.S. Navy in China* was published. Its author, Kemp Tolley, served aboard a gunboat during the 1930s. His book offers a survey of over 150 years of Chinese history, concluding with the threat of the Japanese empire in 1942. Especially noteworthy, though, is the attention Tolley grants to the significance of the Yangtze River. Victor H. Krulak, a retired lieutenant general of the U.S. Marine Corps, contributed the book's foreword, and he perhaps said it best upon declaring, "The Yangtze River has, for two thousand years, been simultaneously the spine and the central nervous system of the Chinese society."

---

[58] Despite its eight nominations, *The Sand Pebbles* failed to earn a single Oscar at the 39th Academy Awards on April 10, 1967. Robert Wise, however, was presented with the Irving G. Thalberg Memorial Award for his hard work and dedication to the motion picture industry.

33
STAR!

(PRODUCED 1967, RELEASED 1968)

"Part of show business is magic. You don't know how it happens."
- Sammy Davis Jr.

Gertrude Alice Dagmar Klasen was born on July 4, 1898, in London, England. At ten years of age, she sang and danced in a festive pantomime, primarily to support her struggling family. It eventually became clear to those who knew Klasen that she was destined to become an all-around solid performer. In time, she changed her name to Gertrude Lawrence.[59] Later, during a stage production of *Hannele*, she met Noël Coward, the esteemed playwright and composer. A friendship gradually formed. Together, the two shared ideas for plays, musical revues, and more. While in her forties, Lawrence occasionally performed for the British and American troops who were destined for combat during World War II. In the early 1950s, she landed the role of Anna Leonowens in Rodgers and Hammerstein's *The King and I*. In addition to performing on the stage, Lawrence starred in several films throughout her storied career. To her, life was fast-paced and exciting. However, on September 6, 1952, Lawrence died of liver cancer in New York City at the age

---
[59] Klasen's father originally performed under the name of Arthur Lawrence.

of fifty-four. Years later, Twentieth Century Fox and Robert Wise arranged for the dramatization of her life story to take place on the silver screen. The undertaking appeared to be ideal, and when Julie Andrews agreed to portray Lawrence, those of the studio eagerly anticipated a major success.

A teenage Gertrude "Gertie" (Andrews) performs in small-time vaudeville shows with her father, Arthur Lawrence (Bruce Forsyth), until landing a gig at Swansea Music Hall. Yet, her clumsiness both on stage and off frustrates her peers. She departs Wales for London. Upon arrival, Gertie intrudes into a theater, where auditions for a popular musical revue transpire. She inadvertently meets André Charlot (Alan Oppenheimer), the show's producer, and also becomes reunited with Noël Coward (Daniel Massey), a childhood friend. Gertie joins Charlot's chorus and eventually marries Jack Roper (John Collin), a stagehand of the theater.[60] The marriage ends in divorce, but not before it results in the birth of a baby girl.

Gertie is later courted by Sir Anthony "Tony" Spencer (Michael Craig), a decorated veteran of the British army. Through him, she "[meets] the highest in the land and [learns] to walk with princes." Meanwhile, Coward helps to revive Gertie's theater career. In time, she travels to America to star in a new revue; critics are genuinely impressed. Spencer continues to pursue Gertie, but she remains unwilling to commit to marriage. In need of a break from the theater, she takes her daughter, Pamela (Jenny Agutter), to the south of France. It is not long before Gertie finds herself back in England performing alongside Coward in his new play. Several suitors, including Spencer, continuously present themselves to her. Following years of living beyond her means, Gertie discovers that she is deeply in debt. Spencer, in the interim, departs for India to govern a small province. As a means of repaying her creditors, Gertie earns supplemental income through the endorsement of commercial products. She also occasionally sings at dance halls.

Hospitalized due to exhaustion, Gertie receives word that she has over-

---

60 In reality, Gertrude Lawrence's first husband was dance director Francis Gordon-Howley.

come bankruptcy. Courtesy of Coward, she returns to the stage for yet another production. Upon the conclusion of the show's run, additional success follows, as the critics and general public are in awe of such talent. Gertie, however, grows further apart from Pamela with each passing day. Furthermore, a majority of the men who originally sought her hand in marriage have married. Gertie goes to Cape Cod to reacquaint herself with Richard Aldrich (Richard Crenna), a banker and theater owner whom she had earlier met at a party. Amidst difficulties and trouble, she remains detached from reality. Gertie is unsure of what she wants in life simply because she has not come to terms with who she really is. A frustrated Aldrich tells her to stop acting. In time, the two are married. Coward celebrates Gertie's union with Aldrich, proclaiming, "at last, [she is] deflowered."

Gertrude Lawrence: Star!

Star! begins with the most unique of overtures. Traditionally, when large-scale films of the era commenced in such a manner, a theater's lights remained lit and the screen's curtains remained closed. In addition, the sound of background music enhanced the feeling of a live performance. Wise, who was no stranger to overtures, did not wish for the opening minutes of *Star!* to transpire with closed curtains. The film therefore begins with the image of a theater's interior, complete with a stage and orchestra pit.[61] Lennie Hayton, the Oscar-nominated composer of *Star!*, appears as the conductor. As he leads his orchestra, the names of several Gertrude Lawrence stage productions, some of which are *Nymph Errant* and *Tonight at 8:30*, appear on a screen above the pit. The film's first act begins shortly thereafter, thus leading to the introduction of many interesting characters, but some, including "dancing sensation" Jack Buchanan (Garrett Lewis) and "revue artist" Billie Carleton (Lynley Laurence), do not appear following the intermission.

Those remaining well into the second act, particularly Gertie's suitors, are of relative importance to the narrative. Charles Fraser (Robert Reed), a New York actor, and Ben Mitchell (Anthony Eisley), an investment banker, vie for her attention. A patient Spencer, too, waits in the wings. Yet, from the get-go, it is established that the most important man in Gertie's life is Noël Coward. Their lifelong friendship is one for the ages. As Gertie endures the many tribulations of being a star, Coward is more or less with her every step of the way, and of her four suitors, he becomes inclined to endorse Aldrich over the others. Coward cautions Gertie against the perils of loneliness while imploring her to complete a journey of self-discovery, but he comes to understand that such rhetoric is best reinforced through Aldrich. Furthermore, the production of *Lady in the Dark* is symbolic of Gertie's impending union with Aldrich.

Coward, at one point, stresses to Gertie that loneliness becomes more difficult with time, but his words do not ring true until she ultimately dismisses Aldrich from a surprise birthday party held in her honor. Relation-

---

61 The overture of *Star!* was the last sequence to be filmed, transpiring well after the conclusion of principal photography.

ships, too, sometimes prove challenging. As the film's first act draws to a close, Gertie finds herself missing Spencer. Coward takes notice and declares, "Close personal relationships are bloody difficult, my darling ... but they do get easier with time. Loneliness gets harder." Later, during the surprise party at Coward's apartment, Gertie discovers that both Fraser and Mitchell have wives of their own, and Spencer has gone to India. Although the three men have clearly moved on with their lives, Aldrich has not. He patiently waits to speak with Gertie following the departure of the other guests. Coward becomes privy to Aldrich's intentions and immediately exits the room:

ALDRICH: I just wanted to ask your advice about a play we're doing. It's called *Skylark*.

GERTRUDE: I'm not interested in your amateur theatricals.

ALDRICH: I should also like to, uh, apologize for upsetting you.

GERTIE: You didn't.

ALDRICH: Clearly, Miss Lawrence, for one reason or another, I did. Perhaps, it's simply because I made the mistake of talking about myself first.

GERTIE: What do you mean?

ALDRICH: That you're a star. You expect to be treated as one.

GERTIE (scoffs): Mr. Aldrich, that kind of remark went out with Irving.

ALDRICH: However, I think it does still apply to someone as unsure of herself as you are.

GERTIE: Oh, I love playing truth games, but only with my friends.

ALDRICH: On the contrary, Miss Lawrence, I think the truth would absolutely terrify you.

GERTIE: That's enough! Who are you to talk to me like this?

ALDRICH: Oddly enough, someone who both admires and respects you.

GERTIE: Get out!

ALRICH (prepares to leave): You know, I should like to have driven you home. I hate seeing anyone ... I hate, uh, leaving anyone so completely alone.

GERTIE: Get out!

Aldrich departs. Gertie then cries out to Coward, but to no avail. Whether he hears her or not is unknown. Coward nevertheless respects Aldrich, who challenges Gertie more than any of the other suitors. At one point, as she recovers in a hospital from acute exhaustion, a period of loneliness appears imminent:

GERTIE (to Coward): Except for you, I'm alone.
COWARD: Nonsense. This hospital is constantly besieged by throngs of feverish admirers.
GERTIE: Well, I don't want them.

Gertie's respect for Coward is evident. More often than not, he knows her better than she knows herself, and Coward, in referencing Gertie's weakened condition, perhaps says it best when he declares, "It's the only time I've ever been certain you weren't acting."

Robert Wise prepares Julie Andrews for the "Limehouse Blues" sequence.

Earlier in the narrative, Coward tells Gertie, "You'll never decide what you want until you've decided who you are," thus foreshadowing Aldrich's sudden demand for her to "stop acting." Aldrich's actions are motivated in part by a rehearsal of *Lady in the Dark*. Gertie prepares for the show with a rendition of "My Ship." One verse states, "*My ship's aglow with a million pearls, and rubies fill each bin.*" When Aldrich earlier confessed to Gertie that it bothered him to leave "anyone so completely alone," she attempted to remedy her frustration with a shopping spree at Cartier, the retailer known for its expensive jewelry. Interestingly enough, an additional verse of "My Ship" affirms, "*But the pearls and such, they won't mean much, if there's missing just one thing.*" Upon the spree's completion, Gertie travels to Cape Cod to see Aldrich, but the visit ends disastrously. "*That dream need never be, if the ship I sing doesn't also bring my own true love to me,*" she later sings during the rehearsal of *Lady in the Dark*. Coward sits in the empty theater to watch Gertie perform. Also present is Aldrich, who listens to the lyrics of "My Ship" with regret for the past. Gertie's rendition concludes. The show's director then requests for her to rehearse "The Saga of Jenny", arguably the most popular number of *Lady in the Dark*, but an unmotivated Gertie subsequently storms out of the theater and into the lobby:

GERTIE: Noël! Noël, you've gotta help me!
ALDRICH (interjecting): Gertrude!
GERTIE: I can't do it!
ALDRICH: Gertrude!
GERTIE: I just can't do it!
ALDRICH: Stop it! Stop acting!
GERTIE: What?
ALDRICH: Stop acting.
GERTIE: I'm sorry, Richard. I . . . I'm just so. . . .
ALDRICH: Frightened.
GERTIE: Yes!

A silent Coward observes the exchange with nothing but admiration for Aldrich. "You don't begin to understand! I've got to do *Jenny* and I don't know how," Gertie declares. Aldrich immediately takes her and Coward to dinner, but Gertie does not realize she is headed to New York's famous Cotton Club, and it is there that she has no choice but to become the spectator of a revue. For a brief period, she ceases to be the star. Gertie is ultimately introduced to a fresh perspective of life. "You're a very clever man," Coward then says to Aldrich, thus setting the stage for the film's grand finale.

"The Saga of Jenny," a climactic sequence, is symbolic of Gertie's destiny, as her forthcoming marriage to Aldrich marks the beginning of a new chapter. The importance of such a sequence is established during the film's opening scene. Following the overture, Wise begins *Star!* with a unique presentation of newsreel footage. It features a grainy, black-and-white texture and is suggested to be a documentary of Gertie's life. Suddenly, the presentation is halted as Wise transitions to a screening room. The projector stops so that Gertie might argue with Jerry Paul (Damian London), the documentary's producer, in regard to the narration's wording. "Miss Lawrence, I need your okay to show this picture," he says and follows with a few questions. Gertie's approach to such questions is noteworthy. "I get analyzed onstage every night in *Lady in the Dark*," she declares. It eventually becomes clear that the narrative of *Star!* is presented as a flashback.[62] The newsreel nevertheless recurs throughout Wise's picture and sometimes includes authentic footage of the era. In order to ensure a sharp contrast between the film and so-called documentary, Ernest Lazlo, Wise's cinematographer, shot the documentary using the Academy standard film aspect ratio of 1.375:1. Such a technique sets the stage for the ultimate transition of the picture.

Upon the film's conclusion, viewers are presented with yet another clip from the newsreel. Gertie is revealed to be resting on a swing high above a stage as her rendition of "The Saga of Jenny" begins. Suddenly, she leaps onto a diagonal wire and swiftly rides its sharp incline directly to the floor.

---

62 A selection of Robert Wise's additional films, including *The Captive City* (1952) and *So Big* (1953), follow a similar pattern.

As Gertie bursts through the decorative paper of a covered, circular ring, the grainy texture of the newsreel wondrously transforms into the colored, seventy-millimeter format of the picture. Furthermore, the original monophonic sound becomes stereophonic. Of particular significance, however, is the image of a star. It appears on the decorative paper of the ring but is visible only for a very short while. During the aforementioned transition, Gertie destroys the image, and her actions essentially symbolize the beginning of a new chapter.

With Aldrich, Gertie is more than a star, as her existence begins to take on a different meaning. In the production of *Lady in the Dark*, she appears as Liza Elliot, the editor of a fashion magazine who occasionally undergoes psychoanalysis. Gertie can relate to the character she portrays on the stage primarily because both are often pursued by individuals of the opposite sex. During the climactic sequence, she tells the tale of a girl named Jenny, whose "*equal would be hard to find.*" It is a struggle of which Gertie is all too familiar. However, upon the film's conclusion, such is not the case. She has found Aldrich, a man who remains with her until the day she dies.

Daniel Massey.

"Prior to being cast in *Star!*, I had recently moved to Los Angeles," Alan Oppenheimer said regarding his portrayal of André Charlot. "Earlier, I spent ten years as an actor at the Arena Stage in Washington, D.C., and then, I went on the road in repertory for three plays: *The Madwoman of Chaillot*, *The Trojan Women*, and *The Rivals*. The stars of these productions were Sylvia Sidney, Eva La Gallienne, and Leora Dana, respectively. I played the leading male roles. We wound up in Hollywood, and I got a fantastic agent from the Kumin-Olenick Agency. He accompanied me to the audition for Star! Those were the days when an agent would accompany a client to an audition. Those were also the days when agents would read a script to learn more about an upcoming production. They didn't just get a breakdown of the story. I had a pretty good ear for accents, and after I read for Bob Wise, he told my agent, 'Fine! That's good!' Bob, I believe, had another actor in mind for the role of André Charlot but replaced him with me because the price was right. At the time of the film's production, a very famous drama writer from *Life* magazine visited the set. Bob introduced me to him and said, 'This is Alan Oppenheimer, who plays André Charlot, the French impresario, sometimes with a Belgian accent.' Bob was a very sweet and funny man.

"During the first day of shooting, I was involved with the first scene, which took place in the office. After about two or three takes, I asked, 'Bob, what are you looking for?' And he said, 'Better.' I immediately understood. As I recall, that was his first and last direction to me. During the rest of my time with him, everything was just wonderful. The best directors are those who cast well and then leave you alone. They cast you because they believe you can do the job well. They don't pick and pick and pick. Everything I've ever read about the best directors is that ninety percent of a great film is attributed to the casting. They trust you. Wise's direction to me was not, 'Do this. Do that.' He simply said, 'Better.' And again, I definitely understood what he meant.

"We flew to New York to film some of the scenes, such as the one where André Charlot and a few of the others fall into the river. That was done at the lake in Central Park. I was in spasms because I was so nervous. My neck and back were a mess; the make-up department made about four toupees for me. Every time I went into the water, I had to come out and all of my makeup had to be redone, and a new toupee was placed on my head. I think we did it three or four times, but it was interesting. In the scene, I'm standing on the back of a boat. I eventually give the command to move forward. The boat starts moving and then my character falls into the water. Even with the spasms, once the scene got going, I forgot about my own personal, physical pain and was able to perform well. Of course, upon emerging from the water, the pain returned. But the same kinds of things happened to me when I was performing on the stage. I could have a terrible cold or headache. But the minute I hit the stage, there was no headache. Whatever physical pains I had disappeared as I was performing. My concentration was on the work, and everything turned out very well.

"My favorite memory of performing in *Star!* is doing the scene with Julie Andrews and Daniel Massey in which our characters are waiting at the Algonquin following the premiere of *André Charlot's Revue of 1924*. We are sitting at a table in anticipation of the show's reviews. Jock Livingston, a great actor who appeared as Alexander Woollcott, was also there. On my wall at home, I have two original prints created by caricaturist Al Hirschfeld. I purchased them at Margo Feiden's art gallery in New York. One of the prints depicts that particular scene at the Algonquin. The other Hirschfeld print that I own depicts a scene in which the character of Charlot is having a conversation on the telephone. Al Hirschfeld personalized both to me.

"Regarding my fellow cast mates, I got to be fairly close to Daniel Massey during the production of *Star!*. I thought he was brilliant. He taught himself to play the piano and was actually the godson of Noël Coward; his father was Raymond Massey. The reason he taught himself to play the piano is because he didn't want the hands of a stand-in pianist to appear in the final cut of the film. All of the piano playing was therefore done by Daniel, and he studied very hard to do that. The same thing goes for the singing. He did his best to copy Noël Coward's style. Daniel was just a great guy. On a personal level, I had very little to do with Julie Andrews even though I shared some scenes with her, but I don't think we chatted much at all. Mostly, we focused on the work and would then retire to our dressing rooms to prepare for the next scene.

"I would sometimes watch the filming of other scenes that did not include me. I remember watching the music hall scenes, and then there was Garrett Lewis, a fantastic dancer who went on to become an Oscar-nominated set decorator. He was great. After *Star!*, he had a lifelong career and earned multiple Oscar nominations for his designs.

"I attended the premiere of *Star!*; we had a limousine, red carpet, and all that stuff. I was a stage actor and didn't realize its importance. *Star!* was my first big picture, and I had only been in Los Angeles a very short time. I think it's a wonderful movie. And since it first premiered, I've seen it probably twice all the way through. Early in my career, I was performing in television's *Bonanza*. After I viewed the first day's dailies, the director pulled me aside and said, 'I don't ever want you to go to dailies again!' I agreed, but asked for an explanation. He said, 'Because if you see something you like, you'll be repeating it all through the episode, and if you see something you don't like, it'll destroy your performance.' I figured his reason was a good one. I therefore never went to see my work, and whenever it was aired, I didn't make plans to watch it.

"A few years after *Star!*, I performed in *Little Big Man* and later attended its premiere. As I was watching it, I thought to myself, 'Gosh! This film is terrible!' I felt this way because I was too attached to it. I've seen *Little Big Man* about two or three times on television. It's a damned good movie. But when you're close to a project, you're critical and uncomfortable, thinking, 'I should've done this instead of that and vice versa.' Ethel Barrymore, sister of the great John Barrymore, was asked a particular question. 'Do you ever see yourself in the movies?' Her answer is the best I've ever heard. She replied, 'No. I can't see myself on stage. Why would I want to see myself on film?'"

Star! premiered in New York on October 22, 1968.[63©] It earned a total of seven Academy Award nominations, the most notable of which was Daniel Massey in the category of Best Supporting Actor. Yet, despite the nominations, Wise's film failed to earn a single Oscar. Nevertheless, the best lines of William Fairchild's script belong to Massey, whose performance as Noël Coward has remained memorable through the years. Many individuals, in short, contributed significantly to the production of Wise's film. Some performed in front of the camera, whereas others worked diligently behind the scenes. William Reynolds, the film's editor, cut the narrative's sequences with precision, allowing for the action to transpire at a steady pace.[64] Choreographer Michael Kidd, in particular, was a welcome addition to the crew. For the production of the film's musical numbers, he assumed the responsibility of setting up the cameras ahead of time. An observing Wise occasionally made suggestions when necessary, but overall, he respected Kidd's knowledge of dance and the stage.

Upon shooting a majority of the film, Wise halted the production for several weeks so that rehearsals for all remaining sequences could transpire. With the exception of the overture, "Limehouse Blues" was the final sequence to be filmed. Kidd came up with the idea to begin such a sequence with one slow, continuous take. Wise steadfastly approved, and as a result, the scene developed beautifully and remains one of the more memorable sequences of the picture. Kidd's time on the set of *Star!* was noteworthy in more ways than one. He went on to marry Shelah Hackett, his devoted assistant, several months after the film's theatrical release.

---

63 *Star!* did not perform well at the box office. With a budget exceeding fourteen million, Twentieth Century Fox hoped to recoup some of its investment. Therefore, in 1969, the studio re-released the film as *Those Were the Happy Times*. It was heavily edited, resulting in the removal of almost an hour of original footage. Robert Wise disapproved of such edits and requested that his name be removed from the credits.

64 William Reynolds and Robert Wise first worked together during the production of *The Day the Earth Stood Still* (1951). Reynolds was very much aware of Wise's expectations, having also edited *The Sound of Music* (1965) and *The Sand Pebbles* (1966).

In addition to Kidd, Donald Brooks, the costume designer, deserves his share of credit. The narrative of *Star!* transpires over the course of many years, and each represented era features various styles and fashions. Through his designs, Brooks worked tirelessly to offer an accurate depiction of such eras. He had his work cut out for him, especially in regard to the costumes that appear in the film's colorful stage productions. Julie Andrews alone wore well over a hundred outfits for the picture, and as if that was not enough, approximately 185 sets, constructed throughout seven sound stages of Twentieth Century Fox, were used during the filming of *Star!* Boris Leven, the production designer, was nominated along with fellow designers Walter M. Scott and Howard Bristol for Best Art Direction. Naturally, an attention to detail was precise. For example, Leven's design of the Brixton Music Hall, featured early in the film during the "Piccadilly" sequence, included a tin roof that was not particularly visible to theatergoers. Wise, however, encouraged its inclusion in the set, as such a feature established a sense of realism for his performers. He was, in essence, in awe of his cast and crew, but perhaps most important was the partnership Wise shared with producer Saul Chaplin. Together, both men collaborated during the productions of *West Side Story* (1961), *The Sound of Music* (1965), and *Star!*

Chaplin was an accomplished composer and songwriter. Throughout his career, he produced several musicals. In the twilight of his life, Chaplin confessed that *Star!* was his personal favorite. He took pride in selecting all of the film's musical numbers, but of special significance was his friendship with Wise. "Our tastes were exactly the same," Chaplin once said. "I was entirely in charge of the music, but I often depended on Bob, because, as a musician, I didn't have a totally objective judgment about things. And very often, I would go by Bob's reaction. Although he was very appreciative of music in general, such a reaction would be more like that from an audience than any reaction I might have had. But there was one expression of his that drove us batty. Bob, who of course started in Hollywood as a film editor, wanted everything ten percent faster. We eventually discovered that, for some reason, music slows down on the screen. If you play something slow, it's even slower when being photographed. I therefore agreed with Bob that everything should be ten percent faster. He was truly a wonderful man."

PART IV
THE SCIENCE
AND SURREALISM
OF THE SEVENTIES

34
THE ANDROMEDA STRAIN

(PRODUCED 1970, RELEASED 1971)

"The scientist is not a person who gives the right answers, he is one who asks the right questions."
- Claude Lévi-Strauss

In 1969, Michael Crichton, a physician turned novelist, celebrated the publication of his first bestseller, *The Andromeda Strain*. The narrative evolves around the scientific investigation of a deadly, extraterrestrial microorganism. Not long after the novel's publication, Robert Wise received a phone call from Universal regarding plans for a motion picture adaptation. Presented with the opportunity to direct a modern thriller, Wise gladly accepted and set forth to reunite with a familiar collaborator.

Nelson Gidding, hired by the studio to pen the film's script, decided to transform a character of Crichton's novel. Dr. Peter Leavitt became Dr. Ruth Leavitt, a female microbiologist, thus presenting a significant modification to the previously existing, all-male team of scientists. Wise, however, had reservations regarding Gidding's decision. Twentieth Century Fox's *Fantastic Voyage* (1966), released just a few years earlier, featured Raquel Welch in the role of a female scientist, and many considered her to be a sex symbol of the era. Wise essentially strived for the characters of his film to be taken seriously and wished to avoid any comparisons to Welch, but after meeting Kate Reid, a British performer ultimately selected for the role of the abrasive Dr. Ruth Leavitt, he approved of Gidding's decision. The remainder of the picture's cast was assembled shortly thereafter, and in early 1970, filming commenced.

"There's a fire, sir."

In the small town of Piedmont, New Mexico, two servicemen of the United States Air Force are mysteriously killed while attempting to recover Scoop VII, a satellite that has recently returned to Earth. In California, at Vandenberg Air Force Base, Major Arthur Manchek (Ramon Bieri) declares a state of emergency and summons a team of experts to investigate. Scoop VII is named for the Scoop Project, the chief purpose of which is to collect organisms from outer space. Dr. Jeremy Stone (Arthur Hill), a college professor, and Dr. Mark Hall (James Olson), a surgeon well-versed on the subject of blood chemistries, are airlifted to Piedmont and, upon arrival, discover many of the town's inhabitants to be dead. Shortly thereafter, Stone and Hall locate the satellite. It appears to have been opened by the town's doctor just prior to his death. Hall makes a strange find. The blood of those deceased is clotted and powdered.[65] Two survivors, a baby and a frail man, are discovered

---

[65] Some of Piedmont's dead appear to have committed suicide, an issue further explored in Michael Crichton's novel.

amongst the dead. They are evacuated from Piedmont. The entire area is then declared to be contaminated.

To avoid a worldwide epidemic, Stone requests that the president authorize the complete neutralization of Piedmont. The satellite, in addition to the survivors, is taken to Wildfire, an underground, multi-level laboratory in a remote part of Nevada. Dr. Ruth Leavitt (Reid) and Dr. Charles Dutton (David Wayne), additional members of the team, join Stone and Hall at the facility. Laboratory animals are instantly killed when exposed to the satellite, which is believed to contain a form of space germ. Others, however, suspect a living organism to be responsible for the deaths.

Through a series of tests, Dutton theorizes that the inhalation of such an organism results in the clotting of blood, which begins in the lungs and then spreads outward. Further scans of the satellite reveal the presence of green patches. Shortly thereafter, the existence of a growing organism is confirmed. Meanwhile, following a lengthy delay, the president agrees to neutralize Piedmont, but when the team learns that the organism functions like an atomic reactor, they plead for the order to be canceled. A nuclear blast could provide enough energy to spawn a gigantic supercolony.

Arthur Hill and James Olson receive direction and guidance from Robert Wise.

A seal is later broken in autopsy, causing Dutton to become contaminated. His frantic behavior leads to rapid breathing, which curiously prevents the organism, dubbed Andromeda, from killing him. Hall subsequently concludes that Andromeda struggles to exist in blood chemistries with extreme amounts of either acid or alkali, thus accounting for the two original survivors. Wildfire is equipped with a nuclear device for self-destruction that is automatically activated in a state of emergency, and as contamination begins to spread throughout the laboratory, the device becomes activated. Fortunately, Hall is able to disarm it with only seconds remaining. Andromeda mutates to a noninfectious form. The colony throughout Piedmont subsequently moves to the Pacific Ocean, and the clouds above Andromeda are seeded with silver iodide in the hopes that raindrops will carry the organism into the ocean, where the alkaline reaction from the seawater is expected to kill it.

Expo 67, the World's Fair of Montreal, Quebec, Canada, showcased a series of films in which the use of split screens was exhibited to the general public. Simultaneous events of such films were thus presented for audiences to enjoy. A year later, Norman Jewison made use of the technique in order to depict particular, hair-raising sequences of *The Thomas Crown Affair* (1968). When the time came for the production of *The Andromeda Strain*, Wise, too, incorporated the split screen effect as a means of enhancing his narrative.

For example, upon Stone and Hall's arrival in Piedmont, as both men surprisingly make one gruesome discovery after another, the audience is afforded both an objective and subjective point of view. Such a scene remains one of the most memorable of the picture. Wise, however, was not only attentive to the film's onscreen effects. He was equally observant of Gidding's script and desired to make *The Andromeda Strain* as factual as possible. Gidding believed the novel to be "highly imaginative" and "ahead of the curve, scientifically." Modifications were therefore made, but such modifications did not completely dismiss Crichton's original work.

The film's opening credits are set against an elaborate backdrop, as Wise presents his audience with a series of objects that have yet to be explained, such as a graph of the acid-alkali tolerance range and the pie chart of Wildfire's operating costs. The credits eventually come to a close, and the words "Odd Man Hypothesis" are barely visible as the screen abruptly fades to black. Crichton describes such a hypothesis as a theory used "to determine reliability of commanders in making life/death decisions." Hall, the only single male of the group, is theoretically the best candidate to disarm Wildfire's nuclear device should it be triggered in a state of emergency. He is, in essence, the odd man. The attention the film affords Hall in comparison with how such a character is presented in the novel is significant. A major difference regarding the discovery of Jackson (George Mitchell), Piedmont's adult survivor, serves as an example, but it is Hall's tense relationship with Ruth Leavitt that ultimately makes for an entertaining narrative.

In the film, Hall is the first to discover Jackson, thus presenting a much different scenario than that of the novel. Due to the omission of particular details, such a discovery essentially becomes a bold and brave encounter. A general commonality between Crichton and Wise's narratives is the chilling beginning. Jackson, whose identity is unknown at such an early point of the story, approaches the doomed servicemen just prior to the sound of a high-pitched scream. The setting is not Piedmont, but instead, a control room of Vandenberg Air Force Base. Readers and theatergoers have no choice but to derive their knowledge of the incident from a radio transmission. In the novel, the servicemen refer to Jackson as "the man in the white robe."[66] In the film, however, he is described as a "thing in white." The haunting scream then transpires. Approximately twenty-five minutes later, as Hall assists Stone with the loading of the baby onto the helicopter, he becomes alarmed as an off-screen voice suddenly shouts, "You!" Jackson is then revealed to be approaching with a cleaver. A startled Hall falls to the ground. Several seconds pass before he eventually regains his composure to boldly confront Jackson, who, as it turns out, does not pose too serious of a threat. Nevertheless, because of the method in which Jackson is initially introduced

---

66 As the novel nears its conclusion, Crichton writes of the encounter from the perspective of Jackson, who generally describes the exchange as "funny."

to audiences, the scene is not without suspense or tension, and as a result, theatergoers generally sympathize with Hall.

In the novel, Hall does not accompany Stone to Piedmont. Instead, Dutton is the one to do so.[67] Furthermore, the main discovery of Jackson is made remotely at Vandenberg, as Major Manchek views film taken from the camera of a reconnaissance aircraft. The reader then learns that the one in the white robe is "an old man, with a withered face." Later, at Piedmont, Stone, not Hall, encounters Jackson, and the exchange is simply not as tense in comparison to that of the film. Regarding the novel, Hall is absent from Piedmont because Peter Leavitt, of all characters, is in the process of transporting him to the Wildfire facility.

"I never liked red lights ... reminds me of my years in a bordello."

In Wise's film, a tense relationship emerges between Ruth Leavitt and Hall, thus enhancing the narrative. Such tension, in part, exacerbates her abrasive demeanor. Upon the scientists' arrival at Wildfire, Stone takes note of Hall's first meeting with Ruth:

---

67 The character of Dr. Charles Dutton is based on Dr. Charles Burton of the novel. Following Wise's film, David Wayne, the actor who portrays Dutton, coincidentally starred in television's *The Good Life* (1971) as Charles Dutton, a completely different character from that presented in *The Andromeda Strain*.

STONE: You two know each other, don't you?
HALL: By reputation only.
RUTH: Ah, yes. Up to now, we've had to worship from afar.
STONE: Be good, Ruth.

The exchange is puzzling. Shortly thereafter, as the men are together in a locker room of the facility, Hall remarks, "Who picked Leavitt? Talk about the Odd Man Hypothesis, which we haven't yet, she's really an oddball." Later, on the third day, the team awakens following a period of rest. Hall then arrives in the cafeteria to rendezvous with the group, and Ruth is the first to speak as she hands him a glass of brownish liquid:

RUTH: Hemlock! All for you, Hippocrates!
HALL (taking the glass): Not your own venom?

Stone proceeds to explain that the liquid is referred to as Nutrient 42-5, a dietary supplement originally developed for the astronauts. Later, as the setting shifts to the main control laboratory, located on the facility's fifth and lowest level, the tension between Ruth and Hall becomes particularly evident. In the scene, Dutton prepares to determine how the disease enters the body. Ruth seizes the opportunity to make a condescending remark pertaining to Hall:

RUTH: Dutton, be careful. Let our distinguished surgeon handle the knife.
HALL (to Ruth): Fine, but not for a while. First, I'm a pediatrician and a geriatrist.

Hall exits, and Ruth is taken aback at his retort. Although neither of the two had met prior to arriving at Wildfire, it becomes apparent that she has resented the "overpriced M.D." for some time.[68] Stone senses Ruth's anger and intervenes:

---

68 A comparison between Michael Crichton and Robert Wise's versions regarding the Leavitt-Hall relationship reveals significant differences. The Leavitt of the novel, although present in the control room at the time of the exchange, does not speak. Instead, Stone addresses Hall directly, stating, "You're the practicing physician among us. I'm afraid you've got a rather tough job right now." "Pediatrician and geriatrist?" Hall asks. "Exactly. See what you can do about [the baby and the man]," Stone replies.

STONE (to Ruth): Take it easy. Charlie will have a technician.

In the novel, Crichton writes, "For his own part, Peter Leavitt was irritated with Hall. In general, Leavitt had little patience with practicing physicians." The tension between both characters, however, is clearly more noticeable in the film. Ruth's personality features a sharp edge. Such a character, however, is intriguing, and coupled with that of Dr. Mark Hall, what originates as intriguing ultimately becomes entertaining.

Joe Di Reda.

"Robert Wise was a delightful man," Sandra de Bruin said regarding her appearance as a technician of the Wildfire facility. "Prior to being cast in *The Andromeda Strain*, I had been in Hollywood for about a year and had done a few TV shows. My agent told me about Mr. Wise's film and got me an audition. It was being shot at Universal, on the biggest sound stage I had ever seen. About six girls, including myself, were brought in to audition for the role of the cowardly technician. We all lined up in front of Bob. He went up and down the line a few times. Then, he paused to look at me and, similar to the way one might shoo a dog away, dismissed me. At least, I thought that was the case. As I started to leave, I said, 'Thank you, Mr. Wise. It was nice meeting you.' But he then said, 'Where are you going?' As a means of offering an explanation, I imitated the gesture he had earlier made towards me. He paused and said, 'Oh. Well, I meant. . . .' Then, he did the reverse of his previous gesture and indicated that he wanted me to come to where he was seated; I complied. Wise then turned to his assistant director and said, 'You can let the rest of the girls go.' And that's how I came to be cast in *The Andromeda Strain*.

"Following that meeting, I was sent a copy of the entire script. I was given a small part that consisted of very few lines. During one scene, my character runs away from Kate Reid, who is collapsing in front of a laboratory door, and I'm yelling, 'She's got the germ! She's got the germ!' The other scene in which I appeared takes place towards the end of the film as James Olson's character is climbing to a higher level of the complex to deactivate the self-destruct mechanism. I see him and, like the cowardly technician I portray, back away in the opposite direction.

"When the cameras were not rolling, Kate Reid didn't really interact much with anyone. She had an aura about her that appeared to say, 'Stay clear!' James Olson was the nicest man. He and I would walk to the chuck wagon together to get something to eat. Of all the performers on the set, I definitely liked him the best. In regard to the filming of that scene when I run away from Kate Reid, I was very nervous, and the sound stage was so enormous. There I was suddenly working with Robert Wise, the director of *West Side Story*, *The Sound of Music*, and all of these amazing pictures. In fact, during the production of *West Side Story*, as a young teenager, I lived a couple of blocks away from where the cast and crew were filming in New York City. Several times, I would walk over to the closed set and watch the filming.

"At the time of *The Andromeda Strain*, I thought it was amazing that I had come full circle. On my first day of filming, one of the extras didn't show up, and due to matching issues, the scene could not be filmed. Mr. Wise said, 'Come back tomorrow.' So I returned the following day. It came to the point where I was getting ready to do my big lines. But I was just a nervous wreck. So, I did it a couple of times and then started running, as my character was supposed to do. Mr. Wise would say, 'Come back and do it again.' And we did it about two or three more times. Then, Mr. Wise said, 'Okay, this time, I want you to do it, but I want you to keep running until you hear the word CUT.' I asked him, 'Why do you want me to run all that distance?' And he said, 'Keep running. I want to hear the foot steps.' Well, I ran and ran and ran. I ran all the way around that enormous sound stage and back to Mr. Wise. The entire crew cheered. Mr. Wise smiled and said, 'Okay. We got rid of the nervous energy. Now, let's do it again!'; and so we did it again, and it was fine. Following the conclusion of shooting that scene, I returned to the set another day to film the scene with James Olson. There really wasn't much to it. The special effects team was doing their part to integrate a lot of fog into the tower, so that things would appear somewhat blurry to the viewer. My job was to just act frightened and back away from James Olson. After the filming of that scene, that was it for me.

"She's got the germ!"

"Later, Bob invited me to the premiere of *The Andromeda Strain*. Of course, I was thrilled, and spent days trying to figure out what to wear. It took place in Hollywood - I think it was held at Grauman's. The premiere was a benefit for the Inner City Cultural Center, in order to raise money for the organization. It turned out that a good friend, C. Bernard Jackson, who played the bongo drums for my dance class at UCLA, was head of the whole Center. It was so incredible running into him at the premiere.

"Bob and I remained friends for a long time following the production of *The Andromeda Strain*. I guess he was somewhat amused by me, or perhaps, it was just his deep sense of loyalty. Whenever I had an audition or was working at a studio and knew Bob had an office on the lot, I would stop by to visit with him. If he was not in his office, I would leave a note. One time, I had a late evening audition with some producer doing an independent film at Universal. Before the audition, I stopped by Bob's office, which was directly across from where I was to audition. I told Bob there was no specific part mentioned but that the producer wanted to meet me. I dashed off across the way and was greeted by this well-dressed but sleazy producer who immediately offered – insisted – that I have a glass of wine. A half hour or so went by as this producer complimented me, told me he could make me a star and offered more wine. I was very uncomfortable.

"Suddenly, there was a knock on the door and Reuben Cannon, Head of Casting, was standing there. Reuben said he was checking on me and that I had to be off the lot before he could go home. I jumped up and rushed out the door with Reuben, but then out of the corner of my eye, I spotted Bob. He was standing in front of his office, hands in his pockets. He then waved and called out 'Good Night.' As Reuben and I walked, I asked him why he was checking on me. (It's not the norm!) He said, 'Mr. Wise called my office and said that he was concerned and thought someone should check on you as it was getting late.' Actually, this was not surprising, as I found out later. Bob had an aversion to producers and super stars taking sexual advantage of starlets and studs. He was disgusted with the reputation of Tinsel Town in the 1960s and 1970s.

"Sometime after *The Andromeda Strain*, Bob's wife, a lovely woman named Pat Doyle, passed away from cancer. It was obviously devastating to him, as the marriage was a happy one. In 1976, Bob was at MGM prepping for *Audrey Rose*. I stopped by the studio to say hello and asked if I could buy him a hot dog; it cracked him up. He suggested we go to the commissary, which we did – the executive commissary. We dated for about nine months after that. I was quite a bit younger than Bob, by about twenty years; but going back to Pat, apparently she was just wonderful, and she had a twin sister, Mimi, who was married to Wells Root, a screenwriter and one of the original founders of the Writers Guild of America, West. We all were very fond of one another. As a director, Bob was tenacious, loyal, methodical, patient, and very detailed right down to his storyboards. He also had the bluest eyes you ever saw. I was with him throughout the production of *Audrey Rose*, and it was interesting to watch him work.

"For the most part, he worked with the same people behind the scenes. Maurice Zuberano is an example. They all stayed together and worked well together. Bob always kept his distance from the crew but was very loyal to them. One day, during the production of *Audrey Rose*, I called the set because I was going to meet him for lunch. I said, 'Can I speak to Bob Wise?' The gentleman who answered the phone, some sort of an assistant, replied, 'Bob Wise?' And I said, 'Yes, Bob Wise.' He then said, 'We don't have a Bob Wise here.' So, I then said, 'How about a Mr. Robert Wise?' And the gentleman immediately said, 'You mean the director, Mr. Wise. Yes, I'll get him.' This guy had been working with Bob for the past five films, but he just didn't recognize the name 'Bob.' On the set, Bob was patient but insisted that everyone follow his direction. He would say to his performers, 'Let's just follow the storyboard and hit the marker.' His editing background was very evident when he was directing actors.

"Bob used to have a home along Broad Beach, near Malibu. It seemed that anybody who was anybody lived on Broad Beach. Many Friday nights, he would host special screenings. A wide variety of folks were invited for these special occasions. Bob would show whatever film was popular at that time, and a lavish buffet was presented for all of the guests. Bob, however, was not much of a social man, with the exception of those Friday nights at the beach home. He enjoyed going out to dinner, but that was about it. Sometimes, on select evenings, he and I went out with other people. For example, if a new film or show was opening and it interested him, we would attend.

Later in his life, Bob moved to an apartment in one of the Century City towers with his second wife, Millicent, but I know he loved that beach home and his Irish setter. It must have been very hard for him to leave it all behind.

James Olson, Arthur Hill, David Wayne, and Kate Reid.

"When the Motion Picture Academy paid tribute to Bob at the Academy Awards, following his death, it was very brief. His picture was not even on the screen two seconds. It was confusing to me because, back in the 1960s and 1970s, he was one of the most important film directors in town, having won multiple Oscars. Bob truly was an enormous presence in Hollywood and a lovely man."

The Andromeda Strain premiered in New York on March 21, 1971. Nine days later, it debuted in Los Angeles. The film's theatrical trailer declares, "The picture runs over 100 minutes! The story covers 96 of the most critical hours in world history! The suspense will last through your lifetime!" *The Andromeda Strain* was presented to the general public as the story of the globe's first space age crisis, and theatergoers, in general, reacted positively to Wise's picture. Approximately twenty minutes into the narrative, during the flight to Piedmont, Hall remarks, "I never went in much for science fiction." "Nor do I," Stone retorts. The exchange is ironic, as Wise considered *The Andromeda Strain* to be more "science fact" than science fiction. Crichton, however, believed his story contained a fair balance between the two, but his attention was essentially directed elsewhere.

"The story is a howdunit, a variation of a whodunit with scientists playing detective and tracking down the killer, then trying to remove its lethal sting," Crichton said regarding the film adaptation. Crichton, in short, was quite supportive. He often visited Wise's set and was also permitted to star in a brief cameo. Upon the film's beginning, as Hall stands in an operating room immediately prior to departing for Vandenberg Air Force Base, Crichton, in the role of a bearded surgeon, appears just outside of the room. It is from that moment that *The Andromeda Strain* becomes extraordinary. The aforementioned trailer advertises it as a G-Rated picture but openly acknowledges that the film "MAY BE TOO INTENSE FOR YOUNGER CHILDREN." Some of the film's elements, particularly the mild nudity and horrific animal testing, caught many by surprise. One particular sequence set in the Wildfire laboratory depicts the death of a rhesus monkey, but it was photographed under the supervision of the Society for the Prevention of Cruelty to Animals (SPCA). In order for such a sequence to appear realistic, the monkey's cage, prior to being sealed, was filled with oxygen. The crew then exposed the monkey to an environment of pure carbon dioxide. As it went into convulsions and subsequently became unconscious, resuscitation was immediately provided without incident. In short, Wise surrounded himself with a crew that worked wonders behind the scenes.

The Andromeda Strain marked Wise's sixth collaboration with designer Boris Leven. Excluding *The Haunting* (1963), the two had worked together since the production of *West Side Story*. Wise appreciated Leven's eye for detail, particularly when it came to the design of the Wildfire facility. Leven's creativity more or less substantiated Crichton's ideas. Coincidentally, Wise's professional association with Leven came to an end following the release of *The Andromeda Strain*. Nevertheless, as one chapter concludes, another begins. In June of 1971, Wise was elected as the tenth president of the Directors Guild of America. Some figured his career behind the camera was nearing its end, but such was not the case. It was simply Wise's desire to become more active within the industry, and for a man of fifty-six years of age, plenty of juice remained in the tank.

35
TWO PEOPLE

(PRODUCED 1972, RELEASED 1973)

"Nobody has ever measured, not even poets, how much the heart can hold."
- Zelda Fitzgerald

In 1971, Robert Wise and friend Mark Robson formed an independent production company by the name of The Filmakers Group. Twenty years earlier, both men accomplished a similar feat with their establishment of Aspen Pictures. In specific regard to The Filmakers Group, *Happy Birthday, Wanda June* (1971), a Robson-directed drama, marked the corporation's debut. Wise served as an uncredited producer of the picture. The Filmakers Group followed with *Limbo* (1972), starring Kate Jackson. It addressed the turmoil of the Vietnam War, a conflict Wise, in addition to many others, opposed.

Enter Richard De Roy, a screenwriter who first broke into the industry while serving in the military. Originally a serviceman of the United States Army Reserve, he was one day called to active duty and stationed in Astoria, New York, the location of the army's film studio. It was there that De Roy became involved with the production of training films for American troops, but he did not always support the policies of his country or its military. In time, De Roy wrote *Two People*, a screenplay pertaining to a deserter of the

Vietnam War who finds love while traveling the globe. Wise considered the adaptation of De Roy's script to be an ideal undertaking for The Filmakers Group, and production subsequently began during the latter half of 1972.

Evan Bonner (Peter Fonda), an American, seeks refuge in the Moroccan city of Marrakech. He meets with Fitzgerald (Alan Fudge), a representative of the U.S. Embassy, regarding his imminent departure for the states. Shortly after boarding a train for Casablanca, thus marking the first leg of the journey home, Bonner meets Deirdre McCluskey (Lindsay Wagner), a popular fashion model, and the two become acquainted through conversation. Deirdre, however, is more forthcoming. She eventually attempts to engage Bonner in mild sensual contact, but he does not reciprocate. Upon arrival in Casablanca, they go directly to the airport and prepare to catch a Paris-bound plane. Bonner, however, is detained by the authorities, thus arousing the curiosity of both Deirdre and Barbara Newman (Estelle Parsons), the fashion editor with whom Deirdre travels. Bonner mentions Fitzgerald's name to the supervising police agent and is subsequently released. Bonner then confesses to Deirdre that he is a deserter of the Vietnam War. On an honor system, he intends to fly to France and then the states, where, following a court-martial, he will be sent to a military prison. Their plane departs Casablanca.

During the flight, Deirdre speaks not only of her personal opposition to the war, but also of the demonstrations in which she has actively participated. Much to her disappointment, however, Bonner declares that he is tired of running from the government. Following their arrival in Paris, he breaks from the group, as the ladies are registered at a hotel different from his. Later that evening, after several lonely hours of being apart from one another, Bonner and Deirdre meet by chance at a nightclub. Without hesitation, they kiss passionately. Although both find comfort and peace in each other, it becomes clear that their time together is limited. As Bonner prepares to depart for America, Deirdre suggests that he remain in Paris with her. He decides against it. Deirdre ultimately accompanies Bonner to the states. She introduces him to her mother (Frances Sternhagen) and young son, Marcus

(Brian Lima). Bonner and Deirdre, along with the boy, enjoy a final outing at the park before he begins the next chapter of his life.

Prior to Bonner's departure from Marrakech, Fitzgerald treats him to dinner at a fancy Moroccan restaurant. Deirdre and Barbara, too, dine at the establishment. Fitzgerald, the audience learns, is acquainted with Barbara. Both acknowledge one another, albeit briefly. Deirdre and Barbara are accompanied by Ron Kesselman (Geoffrey Horne). He is not only a business associate of Deirdre's, he is also her ex-lover and Marcus's father. Despite having been away from the states for an extended period of time, Kesselman is in no hurry to return. He would rather traverse the Sahara than go to New York. Deirdre, however, longs to see Marcus. Bonner's mindset is similar in the sense that he does not wish to delay his departure for the states. Fitzgerald informs him that the next direct flight from Casablanca to New York will not transpire for a few days. Bonner nevertheless wishes to proceed with his journey out of Africa as soon as possible, and because he chooses an alternative itinerary, such actions have a significant impact on his return home.

On the train prior to departure from Marrakech, Deirdre becomes acclimated to the compartment she shares with Barbara. Bonner, meanwhile, approaches the train from the railway platform. Deirdre immediately recognizes him and remarks, "There's that boy who was with Mr. Fitzgerald last night." Wise's method of bringing his two leads into contact with one another is indeed most interesting. During the previous scene at the Moroccan restaurant, Wise does not allow theatergoers to observe Deirdre laying eyes on Bonner for the first time. Instead, the focus is on the trivial interaction between Barbara and Fitzgerald. Throughout a majority of the narrative, Deirdre and Bonner bond through conversation, but similar to the scene at the restaurant, Wise occasionally limits what the audience is allowed to see. Important details, however, are not completely omitted regarding Deirdre and Bonner's conversations. Two separate voice-overs, transpiring at key points of the narrative, essentially paint the picture of a budding, unique relationship between two people.

The initial voice-over, occurring en route to Casablanca, presents a conversation during which Deirdre and Bonner learn of their separate backgrounds, thus setting the stage for what is to follow. At first, she considers him to be aloof, but he eventually proves to be relatively inquisitive. Upon their departure from Marrakech, Deirdre struggles to make a breakthrough. She attempts to engage Bonner in conversation until finally confessing, "I think I've used all my openers." During the following sequence, however, Wise presents the voice-over, and it consists of a conversation during which Bonner strives to learn more about Deirdre:

BONNER: Where are you from?
DEIRDRE: Originally? A town in Ohio called Steubenville.
BONNER: What do you know? We might have dated. I'm from West Virginia ... Fayette.
DEIRDRE: Ah, well, I haven't been back there for years.
BONNER: Where's your family?
DEIRDRE: My mother lives with me in New York.
BONNER: Your father dead?
DEIRDRE: I don't know. He took off when I was thirteen.
BONNER: That's nice.
DEIRDRE: Well, he got tired or something ... the coal mine ... or Steubenville ... or Mom. I used to think he got tired of me.

As the audience is afforded the opportunity to hear Deirdre and Bonner converse, the events presented onscreen depict his purchase of cactus fruit from a vendor on the train. Bonner then slices the fruit in preparation for it to be consumed. Meanwhile, Deirdre watches him with the utmost curiosity. Regarding the aforementioned voice-over, Bonner eventually remarks, "Our paths would not have crossed," and later, sometime after their arrival in Paris, such appears to be the case until a most important revelation.

As Deirdre and Barbara decide whether or not to attend the opening of a prestigious art gallery, Bonner himself visits the most unique of galleries, one that prominently features oil paintings of nude figures, and as he wanders from one exhibit to the next, Wise presents a voice-over with far-reaching consequences. The time two people spend apart essentially proves to be just as significant as the time they spend together. Although Bonner's eyes remain transfixed on the gallery's individual paintings, his thoughts are confirmed to be elsewhere as the first traces of Deirdre's voice are heard:

DEIRDRE: I suppose Mother felt the name Deirdre made up for something. There was an Irish princess named Deirdre . . . Deirdre of the Sorrows. Now, according to the legend, when she was born, someone prophesied that she would make a lot of people unhappy. She did. A prince fell in love with her and died because of it.

Through Deirdre's words, Bonner curiously finds himself missing her and ultimately ventures to the nightclub as a remedy for his lonely heart. Yet, such an action is meant to be. The paths of Deirdre and Bonner may not have crossed during the course of their early lives in the states, but as they rendezvous at the Paris nightclub, both come to the realization that things happen for a reason. Their time together, however, is severely limited. "I really had myself convinced I could be a better person with you," she later confesses to him. Bonner nevertheless has learned to accept and appreciate Deirdre for who she is. At one point, he says, "I don't want to kill time with you," and later, as Deirdre sleeps in a Paris hotel room, Bonner cherishes every waking moment he spends at her side. Because in the end, he knows he will be compelled to go his own way.

"Robert Wise actually moved the production of *Two People* from Columbia to Universal so that I could be cast as the lead in the picture," Lindsay Wagner said. "To be honest, I don't know how I came to his attention. But I met with him to do a reading. Robert had obviously seen something I had done, which wasn't much at such an early stage of my career. At that point, I had only been in the business for about six months, having performed in approximately nine or ten guest starring roles on episodic television. *Two People* was my first feature. Following some screen tests, Robert was insistent that I play the lead. But Columbia wanted someone else for the role. So, Robert basically picked up his marbles and went to the next game. I was under contract to Universal and that turned out to be the perfect place for him to move his production.

"I was quite familiar with Robert Wise prior to meeting him. I'd seen *The Sound of Music* many times. In addition, *West Side Story* and *Run Silent Run Deep* were films of his with which I was the most familiar. The whole experience of being cast in *Two People* was just shocking. For 'Robert Wise' to insistently want me in his film when, at the time, he could have cast anybody he wished, was just so moving. Not only was it amazing to be working with him, but starring alongside Peter Fonda, who was huge at the time, was an experience in itself.

"Shooting on location was amazing. *Two People*, and I'm sure this isn't necessarily true with other films that Robert or many others ever made, was literally shot in sequence. Being new to the business, I thought to myself, 'This is so easy! After a day of filming, you get up the following morning and do the next logical thing.' Shooting in the story's chronological order definitely simplified things from a performer's standpoint. At the time, I didn't realize that something like this would not happen for the remainder of my career. It was very rare to follow such a schedule.

"We started off in Morocco. In the early seventies, Morocco, although beautifully exotic, wasn't terribly modern. We had a lot of people helping out and taking us from one place to the next. It was nice and they made us feel comfortable. We would get on the train in the morning; the storyline called for us to travel from Marrakech to Casablanca. Robert would then film the first few miles of the Marrakech Express as we traveled. The background that one sees when viewing *Two People* is quite accurate when compared to what an actual tourist traveling the same route would have seen. In order to resume filming the following day, we were driven to the general area of where the train stopped the previous day. Sometimes, the location was so far we would take the train. It blew my mind that Robert was so meticulous with this aspect of his picture; he really enjoyed it. Then, we traveled to Paris to shoot for the next couple of months. The locations were spectacular. When we flew from Morocco to Paris, we actually filmed on the plane. We had the whole first class cabin to ourselves. Once again, Robert was filming the story in the exact sequence in which it was supposed to transpire. That was a once in a career experience, thus far anyway.

"Peter Fonda was quite the prankster, which made the production even more fun, but sometimes admittedly a little annoying. I say that adoringly. He was constantly throwing firecrackers around and kind of terrorizing people. As much of a prankster as Peter was, he won my heart when we were filming in Paris. During the scene in which I wear the long, evening gown with an ankle-length cape, our characters decide to rush back to the hotel and consummate our relationship and let ourselves have these last twenty-four hours together. At that point, the script indicates our characters 'begin to run.' So, as we started to run, he stepped on the corner of my cape, and because we were moving so fast, I couldn't catch my balance. I began to fall face down on the sidewalk. Peter then literally threw his body under mine and broke my fall. I landed on him and completely escaped injury. That was quite impressive.

Peter Fonda, Robert Wise, and Lindsay Wagner.

"Robert to this day remains one of the nicest, most gracious film directors I've ever encountered. He was just a spectacular role model. Consequently, my indoctrination into the business was that power, success, and kindness can all coexist, because to me, those are the characteristics that defined Robert Wise. He treated the crew the same way he treated the stars; it was brilliant. Robert did a majority of his directing during the casting process. From my experience, Robert kept digging until he found the person who, to him, naturally represented the character. He didn't cast major stars just for the purpose of enhancing his project and then try to make them fit into his vision of the part. Being so new in the business, I was obviously a good example of that. One day during the production of *Two People*, I said to Robert, 'Are you sure there's nothing you want to tell me?' My reason for asking was that he didn't direct our performances a whole lot. Robert replied, 'No, you showed me who this character was the day we did the screen test.' Following the production, I had heard others say the same thing about him. 'Yes, he did most of his directing during the film's casting,' they'd tell me.

During the screen tests and readings, Robert provided me with some direction here and there, and once I nailed it, he essentially set me free. Of course, every now and then, he would speak to me about my performance, but again, he rarely did much directing outside of the casting. He did help us integrate our instincts into his desired blocking. It was one of Robert's unique qualities. He was extremely prepared with his storyboards, and the relationships he shared with his performers were very special."

Two People was released on March 18, 1973. Despite the film's bold stance against the Vietnam War, it did not fare particularly well with the American public, even with those who opposed the war. Some compared Wise's picture with *Love Story* (1970), starring Ali MacGraw and Ryan O'Neal. Although both films present a relatively entertaining narrative of two lovers from different backgrounds, *Two People* was dismissed as lackluster and unimaginative. Roger Ebert of the *Chicago Sun-Times* wrote, "What we have here, potentially, is a sort of bittersweet, radicalized *Love Story*, and that must have been what sold the director, Robert Wise, on the project. The movie sounds superficially as if it might have a comment to make on the effect of the war on its warriors. Well, that may be true, but true of a movie they didn't make. What we're left with is an awfully awkward journey into banality." Wise and Robson, in general, were unaffected by such criticism, choosing instead to focus on future endeavors. In the wake of *Two People*, The Filmakers Group produced a select few of the decade's "disaster" films. Robson in particular enjoyed much success at the box office with his direction of *Earthquake* (1974), and Wise, too, had something special in mind for the most avid of theatergoers.

36
THE HINDENBURG

(PRODUCED 1974-1975, RELEASED 1975)

"Whether outwardly or inwardly, whether in space or time, the farther we penetrate the unknown, the vaster and more marvelous it becomes."
- Charles A. Lindbergh

May 6, 1937, marked the end of an era. The LZ 129 Hindenburg, an immense Zeppelin carrying thirty-six passengers and sixty-one crew members, caught fire and crashed while attempting to land in Lakehurst, New Jersey. Such a tragedy irrevocably damaged the airship's reputation. At the time of the incident, the Hindenburg was on the verge of completing a three-day journey from Frankfurt, Germany. Tragically, more than a third of its occupants were killed. Where and how the fire originally started was unknown. Some cried sabotage; others, however, were reluctant to believe such theories. It was not until 1962 when a credible hypothesis began to receive worldwide attention. A. A. Hoehling's book, *Who Destroyed the Hindenburg?*, declared crew member Eric Spehl, a rigger, to be the saboteur. The hypothesis developed into a solid theory and was eventually accepted as an historical fact. Years later, Michael MacDonald Mooney based his 1972 novel, *The Hindenburg*, on Hoehling's findings. Such a topic, in time, garnered interest from several film studios. Universal Pictures, however, proved to be the most enthusiastic, ultimately securing the rights to Mooney's novel and tapping Robert Wise to direct its upcoming production.

Colonel Franz Ritter (George C. Scott) of the Luftwaffe, or Nazi air force, is summoned to the Ministry of Propaganda in Berlin, where he is informed of a suspected plot to sabotage and destroy the LZ 129 during an upcoming flight to America. An order for him to guard the aircraft's safety is given. Ritter makes an urgent request for the flight to be canceled so that the Gestapo is afforded ample time to foil the plot, but such a request is denied. Upon boarding the Zeppelin, he meets Martin Vogel (Roy Thinnes), his cabinmate. Together, the two discuss the varied backgrounds of the passengers and crew. It is not long before Ritter deduces that Vogel is an undercover agent of the Gestapo.

Meanwhile, Karl Boerth (William Atherton), rigger of the LZ 129, arouses suspicion. He detects an investigating Ritter along the keel's walkways and becomes startled. In the process, a steel control cable is inadvertently unfastened and rips the fabric cover on the ship's port fin. The damage initially goes unnoticed. Ritter openly questions Boerth's status as a Hitler Youth leader, but the latter claims he is no longer active in such a capacity because of his dedication to the Hindenburg. Due to intense winds, the condition of the torn fabric becomes worse. Boerth is ultimately able to repair the damage despite risking his life. Ritter, however, continues to monitor the shady rigger and communicates his suspicions to Captain Lehmann (Richard A. Dysart), an off-duty Zeppelin pilot.

Freda Halle (Lisa Pera), Boerth's mistress, is later arrested in Germany. Ritter informs Boerth of the news and seizes the opportunity to ascertain the existence of a bomb onboard the aircraft. He intimidates Boerth, declaring that the authorities will eventually coerce Freda into confessing the plot's details. The existence of a bomb is subsequently confirmed. Boerth reveals his intention to destroy the ship as a means of protesting Nazi Germany, but he plans for the explosion to transpire around the time of the mooring mast when nobody is expected to be aboard. Ritter concludes that arresting his suspect will not keep the bomb from detonating. He therefore conducts a search of the ship, but Vogel intervenes and takes Boerth into custody, thus complicating matters. Ritter locates the bomb but accidentally triggers it. A massive explosion ensues. In the aftermath, the final report of the board of inquiry states that the most plausible theories for the Hindenburg disaster are structural failure, static electricity, Saint Elmo's fire, and sabotage. Chancellor Hitler publicly declares the catastrophe to be an act of God.

George C. Scott as Colonel Franz Ritter.

The Hindenburg marked screenwriter Nelson Gidding's fifth and final collaboration with Wise. Gidding's adaptation of Mooney's novel is complete with hair-raising sequences and shady, untrustworthy characters. Some aspects of the film's plot, however, are simply less interesting than others. By way of illustration, Edward Douglas (Gig Young), an advertising executive, occasionally arouses suspicion. Throughout the journey, he appears anxious and cannot bear any delays. Yet, the mystery surrounding Douglas quickly becomes trivial when the audience learns he is intent only on racing a competitor, who travels by sea, to America. Both vie for the coveted General Motors account, nothing more, nothing less.

Other elements of the film naturally warrant more attention. For example, shortly after Ritter uncovers Vogel's true identity, the picture fades to black, a cinematic technique not often used by Wise. Nevertheless, such a technique essentially separates *The Hindenburg* into a total of three segments, or acts.[69] The aforementioned fade marks both the conclusion of the first act and beginning of the second. Later, as Wise repeats his use of the technique in order to transition into the third act, the circumstances of the story are similar. Because just prior to the conclusion of the second act, yet another exchange between Ritter and Vogel transpires. Yet, the manner in which the first and second acts conclude is not as important as how they begin. The issue of hydrogen vs. helium, as the audience comes to discover, is paramount. Furthermore, such an issue justifies Captain Lehmann's consequent presence aboard the aircraft.

As the first act of the film commences, Wise presents an era in which hydrogen has contributed to "the climax of man's dream to conquer the air." An authentic three-minute newsreel, spanning the course of 150 years, attributes the evolution of air travel to a supposed newfound power. Theatergoers are first exposed to an original logo of Universal Pictures.[70] The newsreel, produced by Universal in 1937, is then presented in its original black-and-white format, and it is not long before the audience becomes familiar with the fanciful invention of Joseph-Michel and Jacques-Étienne Montgolfier, two brothers from France. An unseen narrator refers to their hot air balloon as a "rock-a-bye baby perkin' along with a new gas: hydrogen."

The newsreel continues, as several different machines capable of flight are revealed to have been developed through the years. It then culminates with the birth of the Hindenburg, featuring "sixteen giant cells containing over seven million cubic feet of hydrogen, which lifts her 242 tons of luxury into the clouds." As the newsreel concludes, Wise transitions to a color format as a proper beginning to his motion picture. Hydrogen is initially touted as a prized commodity of air travel, but shortly thereafter, Major Napier (René Auberjonois), a passenger of the Hindenburg, encounters Ritter and says, "I say, you must be the special security officer. It's a good thing, too. You know

---

69 A selection of Robert Wise's films, some of which are *West Side Story* (1961) and *The Sound of Music* (1965), include an intermission, partially as a means of concluding the narrative's first act. On each occasion, the picture fades to black.

70 Universal officially used the logo from 1936 to 1946.

this ruddy blimp is filled with hydrogen?" Hence, the disadvantages become evident. Hydrogen is believed to be efficient, but unlike its counterpart, it is dangerously flammable.

The Hindenburg.

Upon the beginning of the second act, the narrative has acknowledged helium as an efficient alternative suitable for air travel, but an important exchange at the headquarters of the U.S. State Department reveals the cons of such a gas. Dr. Luther (Rolfe Sedan), the German ambassador, declares the American monopoly of helium to be a "chief danger" to the Hindenburg. The U.S. Helium Act of 1925 forbade the export of helium to foreign countries, and Congress was reluctant to reverse such a policy. Some believed helium would be used by foreign leaders, namely Hitler, primarily for military reconnaissance instead of commercial air travel. Hence, the embargo remained in effect by 1937. Furthermore, several theorists blamed such an embargo for the Hindenburg disaster. Luther's visit to the U.S. State Department serves a chief purpose. He calls for the embargo to be lifted, ultimately pleading his case on behalf of a key individual.

Captain Lehmann, aboard the Hindenburg as an observer, travels across the Atlantic to meet with representatives of the U.S. government regarding the use of helium in German airships. His journey is motivated in part by the letter of a fanatic, but Captain Fellows (Stephen Elliot) of the Lakehurst Naval Air Station believes Lehmann's mission to be a worthy cause. Following the film's opening credits, Wise rapidly shifts from one location to the next (i.e., the German Embassy in Washington to the Staaken Airfield in Berlin, the Ministry of Propaganda to the Zeppelin Company in Frankfurt). He does so in order to establish conflict, but perhaps the most important setting of the sequence is Milwaukee, the city in which such conflict begins.

Mrs. Kathie Rauch (Ruth Schudson), a civilian in the confines of her own home, frantically writes a letter. The audience eventually learns of its contents, disclosing "how and where the zeppelin will be destroyed." Should a catastrophe befall the Hindenburg, Dr. Luther fears it could be blamed on the Americans. Mrs. Rauch, however, is eventually exposed as a fraud. "A crank letter has been made into a matter of state. The purpose of exaggerating the bomb scare was to get helium. I went along with that," Lehmann later confesses to Ritter. Fellows, meanwhile, understands the dangers of hydrogen all too well. On more than one occasion, Wise transitions to the Naval Air Station in Lakehurst. Fellows is not only revealed to be a clear proponent of helium, he is also against America's monopoly. Later, he declares, "I hope Washington gives Lehmann the helium." The bomb's detonation, however, ends such hope. As the explosion rips through the Hindenburg, Wise transitions to a black-and-white format, the very method used to begin his picture.

William Atherton.

"I read in the trades that Robert Wise was going to be directing *The Hindenburg*," Alan Oppenheimer said regarding his involvement with the film. "Since he and I had already worked together during the production of *Star!*, I wrote him a letter which basically asked, 'I hear you are doing a German picture, how could you not hire a performer by the name of Oppenheimer?' Bob got back to my agent with a message stating that he would consider casting me in his film. He put my name and picture up on his bulletin board. Every day, he would walk by it. And finally, Bob decided to give me the part of Albert Breslau.

Anne Bancroft as the Countess.

"When it came time to film the Hindenburg's explosion, Bob had about twelve cameras rolling to capture as much of the action as he could. We were on the set at Universal. The ship's model was immense, but it only represented a section of the Hindenburg. The cast and crew were waiting to hear the word 'action' in order to begin the scene, but suddenly, the explosion, along with the accompanying special effects, ignited prematurely. Bob could only do one take. Otherwise, there'd be nothing left. Then, I heard somebody yell, 'Roll 'em, roll 'em, roll 'em!' And all twelve cameras started rolling. Miraculously, Bob got it all, but he was really panicked in the heat of the moment.

"In the film, my character and his spouse burn up. A scene depicting the fleeing passengers was filmed to intercut with the footage containing the explosions. Bob used vertical strips in the doorways, and these strips contained lit gas. It was awfully hot. I think I may have been wearing asbestos clothing. Then, after the first take, Bob said, 'Okay, we have to do it again.' And unbeknownst to me, he told the special effects crew to turn the gas up higher. When I reacted to that flame the second time around, I was convinced I was on fire. 'Sorry, I had to do that,' Bob later confessed. I told him that it felt very real to me. I thought my head was going to explode. Sometimes, directors have little tricks up their sleeves. It was very clever.

"In regard to working with George C. Scott, I loved that man. On the first day of filming, we were in between shots, and I noticed George walking away from the set. At the time, I was such a novice. I walked over to him and said, 'George, I. . . .' But then he cut me off, 'No, no, please, I have to concentrate.' I immediately apologized and left him alone. Therefore, he and I never schmoozed between shots. George was very concentrated, often thinking about his upcoming scenes. We had a good relationship following the production of *The Hindenburg*. Years later, he did a Noël Coward play on Broadway called *Present Laughter*, which I attended. After the show, I went back to the dressing room and received a very warm welcome from him and his wife, Trish. George and I had great admiration for each other. I wish I'd worked with him again. He was a hell of an actor."

"Robert Wise was a pro," according to René Auberjonois. "He was aware of the technical challenges he faced with *The Hindenburg*, and I believe he cast well-trained theater actors in the major roles so that he could focus more on the technicalities and less on the acting. In the 1970s, it was very complicated for one to direct and produce a big film like *The Hindenburg*. It was shot on the biggest sound stage at Universal. The crew may have even combined two stages together in order to have more space. But Wise was not an actor's director for that film. I think he was mostly concerned with the logistics of making such a big film under those kinds of circumstances; and so my memory of him as a director is that he was a gentle-seeming, low-key, and respectable man. He didn't really talk to us much about our performances. It was all about getting this big film produced.

Crossing the Atlantic.

"Working with Burgess Meredith was incredible. As a child, I grew up in a community outside of New York City near Nyack. Actors and artists, as well as cartoonists of *The New Yorker* magazine, lived in the area. A fair number of these people were blacklisted. I lived in this area from the time I was eight until I was about sixteen. A friend and neighbor of ours was Alan Jay Lerner. During the two summers when I was fourteen and fifteen years old, I took care of his and Nancy Olson's kids by the swimming pool. Their neighbor was Burgess Meredith, who had two kids of his own. Stationed around the pool, I was somewhat of a glorified babysitter and lifeguard. At that time in my life, I was hoping to become an actor. In my mind, Burgess was mythological because of 1935's *Winterset*, but also because of his performances in other films and stage plays. I didn't really know him personally. I was just a kid who took care of his kids.

"One time, I pulled one of Burgess's kids out of the water by his hair when he was drowning. I guess that didn't make me much of a lifeguard; but many years later, Burgess and I had the opportunity to work together on *The Hindenburg*, and by then, due to a measure of success, acting had become my profession. Being paired with Burgess Meredith was unbelievable. I just couldn't believe my good fortune. We weren't yet living on the West Coast. I was still a New York actor. We were renting a house near Malibu - it belonged to another actor and was located along the Pacific Coast Highway. I would carpool with Burgess and essentially drove him to work every day because he also lived in the colony. Our scenes were always together. We'd go for coffee, drive to Universal, go to our little trailers, and then go to sleep. Eventually, we would be called to the set. Our trailers were in close proximity to one another; my door faced his. We would emerge from our trailers to begin work, sort of yawning in the process, and I remember him looking at me as we were walking to the stage, saying, 'There's nothing like the sleep that you have when you're being paid to sleep.'

Richard A. Dysart as Captain Lehmann.

"In addition to Burgess Meredith, *The Hindenburg* also provided me with the opportunity to reunite with Annie Bancroft. My first show in New York City was *King Lear*. It starred Lee J. Cobb and took place at the Lincoln Center. The show was in repertory with a production called *A Cry of Players*, written by William Gibson. It was about Shakespeare as a young man. Bancroft played Shakespeare's wife and Frank Langella was Shakespeare. I played Ned Alleyn, the head of an acting troupe that inspires Shakespeare. He was an historical character that became one of Shakespeare's leading actors. It was during the production of this show that I got to know Annie through Frank. He and I were good friends and had the same agent. Frank knew Annie and Mel Brooks very well, so the four of us usually went out in the evening for dinner and dancing. When Annie was cast in *The Hindenburg*, it was a serendipitous and wonderful kind of continuation of a typical relationship that happened in the theatre. Sometimes, you do plays and never see your fellow colleagues once the performances have finished, and on some occasions, you are lucky enough to run into them again. That was the case with Annie.

"I didn't know George C. Scott prior to the production of *The Hindenburg*, but he was a New York actor. The one thing we had in common is that we knew a lot of the same people. As a comradely group of actors, we were all very comfortable together. Richard Dysart and I had been founding members of a theatre company called the American Conservatory Theatre. We had performed together in the past and were good friends. Although our characters didn't interact much in *The Hindenburg*, we ate lunch together everyday. Peter Donat, another cast member, was also involved with our theatre. Bill Atherton, like me, attended Carnegie Tech (These days, it's called Carnegie Mellon). Bill and I had a lot of things in common and were friends. During many weekends, we would end up on the beach, either at the home of Burgess Meredith or Larry Hagman, both of whom were neighbors.

Alan Oppenheimer.

"I remember the filming of the card game scene, but it's almost like a childhood memory in the sense that I'm not sure whether it's from a photograph, or that I actually remember performing in the scene. My recollection is that we were up in a room playing the game, as if we were in a ship. Of course, this all transpired on the Universal sound stage. The set was huge and very impressive for its time. Somebody linked me to a picture of a bunch of us sitting around the table during the game. Major Napier was cheating at cards. I felt like a character from Pinocchio. Burgess Meredith and I were comic relief.

"Regarding the exterior shots of the zeppelin, I'm sure we filmed them somewhere in Los Angeles, perhaps at the airport. I have a pretty clear memory of shooting the scene in which Burgess and I flee the wreckage and survive the crash because, candidly, I didn't want to be there. The production schedule of *The Hindenburg* went long, and as a result, I lost a part that I wanted very badly in another film called *Hard Times* with Charles Bronson. The role of Poe instead went to Strother Martin. He was a wonderful actor, but we were very different. At the time, I was much younger than him. It was one of those painful experiences where I was grateful to be cast in *The Hindenburg*, but at the same time, I really didn't want to be in it anymore. I wanted to go on to my next job, like some contractor on a building. I remember my agent saying, 'They're not going to be able to do it. The schedule is not going to work out because we went longer. My advice would be for you to speak with Robert Wise personally. If an agent called on your behalf and asked for you to be excused from the picture, it wouldn't be a classy way for the issue to be handled. That's why you should probably talk to Robert Wise yourself.' But I was very shy and terribly uncomfortable. When Wise wasn't busy doing a lot of other things, I suppose I could have tried to say something about it, but my presence was important for the resolution of the film.

"I think the only piece of creative input I brought to the crash scene was that Major Napier was missing a shoe. I remember suggesting to Wise, 'Maybe my character should lose a shoe during the process of escaping the wreckage.' But I don't know if that actually happened or not. I may have pitched the idea and it didn't happen, or maybe it did happen. Nevertheless, it's unnoticeable to viewers during the chaos of the scene. It was a big, busy shoot. And when I was anticipating the role in *Hard Times*, there was only one more day of filming that remained on *The Hindenburg*, but as I remember, I then had to wait around for an additional three weeks just to do that little thing of running away from the burning ship. And again, I would have preferred not to have been there for that shot. That's just an example of one not always getting what he or she wants in this business. It's not that working on *The Hindenburg* was a terrible experience; it was a perfectly wonderful experience. I was a young actor and I had two young children. It was a job and I was glad to have it because it meant that I wouldn't have to worry about how I was going to pay bills for the next six months or so.

Burgess Meredith and René Auberjonois.

"I have vivid memories of working with directors such as Robert Altman (*MASH*), John Guillermin (*King Kong*), and Irvin Kershner (*Eyes of Laura Mars*). But I have very little recollection of Robert Wise directing me as an actor. And that is unique, really. I didn't have much of a director-actor relationship with him. He was just busy doing what he had to do in order to get that huge film made. But my overall impression of Robert Wise is that he was a very intelligent and reserved gentleman."

The 1970s were popular in regard to the production of "disaster" films, beginning with the release of Universal's *Airport* (1970). *The Poseidon Adventure* (1972), produced by Twentieth Century Fox, later captivated the nation's attention. *Earthquake* (1974) and *The Towering Inferno* (1974) accomplished the same feat and continuously played to sold-out crowds. Wise's opportunity to partake in the excitement transpired during the summer of 1974, when he began work on *The Hindenburg*. He coined the term "Zeppelin Fever," which referred to the public's eager anticipation of what the future of air travel had in store for society. Many wondered if the spectacular airships would ever make a comeback. Prior to its premiere, *The Hindenburg* aroused the public's curiosity with an appealing tagline that declared, "THE TRUTH AT LAST? WHO DESTROYED THE HINDENBURG? Of 97 aboard, eight had a motive. One had a plot. By some miracle, 62 survived."

The Hindenburg premiered on Christmas Day in 1975. For Wise, however, the occasion was not particularly festive. Although his time with the cast and crew was memorable, 1975 ultimately became a trying year. Wise's term as the president of the Directors Guild of America came to an end, but whether he was emotional or not regarding his disassociation with the union is unknown, because more poignant was a tragedy that occurred on September 22nd of that year. Patricia Doyle, Wise's wife of thirty-three years, passed away following a battle with cancer. She was his most ardent supporter and did everything to ensure her husband's success. In fact, upon tying the knot in the early 1940s, Patricia gave up a career in entertainment to become fully committed to her marriage and family. Without a doubt, the latter part of 1975 and beyond was clearly a period of mourning for Wise, and only time, if anything, could heal his grieving heart.

Albert Whitlock was in charge of creating the special visual effects for *The Hindenburg*. Robert Wise did not commit himself to directing the film until Whitlock guaranteed that such effects could be produced successfully.

37
AUDREY ROSE

(PRODUCED 1976, RELEASED 1977)

> "Each night, when I go to sleep, I die. And the next morning, when I wake up, I am reborn."
> - Mahatma Gandhi

Once upon a time, a six-year-old boy named Raymond De Felitta experienced the most unusual of phenomena. Having never touched a piano in his life, he was suddenly overcome with a rush of confidence. Young Raymond approached the family's piano and began to play a complex, yet melodious, tune of the ragtime era. His father, Frank, immediately took note of the bizarre incident. Raymond then declared, "My fingers are doing it all by themselves, Daddy! Isn't it wonderful?" Frank De Felitta, a writer, was overcome with astonishment and particularly questioned if an unseen force was at work. Hence, the idea of a new book pertaining to the concept of reincarnation eventually became a reality. In 1975, De Felitta's novel, *Audrey Rose*, was published. Shortly thereafter, United Artists expressed an interest in acquiring the story's rights for motion picture production. De Felitta accepted the studio's proposal and also agreed to pen the script of what would ultimately become Robert Wise's thirty-seventh film.

New Yorkers Janice (Marsha Mason) and Bill Templeton (John Beck), a happily married couple, experience the greatest joys of life while spending quality time with Ivy (Susan Swift), their daughter and only child, but things take an unusual turn when Elliot Hoover (Anthony Hopkins), a man who has been stalking the family for weeks, delivers startling news. Years earlier, Hoover's five-year-old daughter, Audrey Rose, was killed in a car accident. Hoover's wife also perished in the crash. Yet, according to psychics, Audrey Rose was reincarnated. Through a process of elimination, Hoover concludes that the soul of his late daughter is trapped inside of Ivy's body. Templeton becomes skeptical. Janice, however, is not quick to dismiss Hoover's theory. She is mindful of the annual nightmares that transpire around the time of Ivy's birthday. Hoover wishes for the soul to be mended. He demands Janice's support but later goes to extremes and abducts Ivy, thus complicating matters. The police arrive on the scene and take Hoover into custody. At the ensuing trial, Janice ultimately comes to his defense, declaring he is Ivy's only hope for survival. An unsatisfied Templeton allows for Dr. Steven Lipscomb (Norman Lloyd), a reputed psychiatrist, to conduct an experiment that is "unique in the annals of psychiatry." Ivy undergoes hypnosis. Lipscomb attempts to take her back to the time before she was born. However, memories of the accident resurface. As Ivy is brought out of hypnosis, she becomes unaware of her surroundings. Audrey Rose takes control of the body, and a loss of consciousness transpires. All attempts at reviving Ivy fail, and she dies shortly thereafter. Hoover nevertheless declares that "her soul is free."

Wise's directorial debut with *The Curse of the Cat People* (1944) began a peculiar pattern of sorts. In time, the theatrical release of *The Body Snatcher* (1945) suggested that a potential career in horror films was swiftly becoming a reality, but Val Lewton was responsible for the production of such films, and Wise eventually chose a different path to success. Coincidentally, following *The Body Snatcher*, Wise did not direct another film of the horror genre for nearly twenty years. When the time came, *The Haunting* (1963) was produced as a tribute to Lewton. The production of *Audrey Rose* transpired the following decade and thus marked Wise's fourth and final foray into the realm of horror. The film, however, has also been categorized by some as a mystery, but such a classification merely serves as the backdrop to a more significant theme.

Early in the film, Templeton is persuaded by Russ Rothman (Stephen Pearlman), his good friend and attorney, to make direct contact with Hoover so that the mystery behind the latter's motives might be unraveled. A formal invitation is subsequently extended. Hoover visits the Templeton residence to further discuss the connection between Ivy and Audrey Rose. Rothman, meanwhile, eavesdrops from an upstairs corridor, but he is unable to make sense of the situation. Hoover, in short, does not bear ill will towards the Templetons. His visit nevertheless remains significant, as it is linked with the ensuing trial. Throughout the proceedings, Wise presents three separate individuals on the witness stand, and not only do the testimonies of such characters lead to Hoover's exoneration, they better justify the spiritual concept of reincarnation.

Robert Wise and Susan Swift.

Maharishi Gupta Pradesh (Aly Wassil), a Hindu sage and first presented witness of the trial, offers testimony regarding "the difference between matter and spirit." Through his rhetoric, in addition to a montage of ritualistic practices, the audience is able to better understand Hoover's previous journey to India. At the time of the earlier meeting at the Templeton residence, reincarnation becomes the subject of conversation. Hoover explains that he did not always believe in life after death. His trek to the Indian subcontinent, however, ended many years of seeking and searching:

HOOVER: I went to India where I learned of a way of life that was totally alien to mine. But in time, with the help and the wisdom of simple people, I came to know the reality of their religious convictions and to know the truth of reincarnation.

Later, at the trial, the Maharishi explains that death is not the end to life. As he speaks, Wise presents an image of Hoover, who appears stoic while listening to such testimony. The camera slowly zooms in on its subject, and the faint sound of Hindu music grows louder as Wise transports his audience to India. An ensuing montage of cremation and imminent rebirth accompanies the Maharishi's rhetoric, which declares that death is merely "a momentary separation, a fragile respite in the astral cosmos, where the soul must wait and, through meditation, seek to clothe itself in the highest spiritual garment before attempting rebirth in the next Earth life." As the montage ends and a transition back to the courtroom is made, Hoover's demeanor remains unchanged. His firm belief in reincarnation is justified through the preceding montage. The trial continues and, in time, audiences come to understand Hoover's pain.

Mary Lou Sides (Ivy Jones), the motorist who crashed into Audrey Rose's vehicle years earlier, takes the stand to describe the accident from her perspective, but her recollection of the impact's immediate aftermath is perhaps the most haunting, as a connection between her testimony and Hoover's initial visit to the Templeton residence is eventually made. During such a visit, Ivy awakens suddenly, startling everybody in the household. She approaches her bedroom window and raises her arms. Following a brief period of hesitation, Ivy presses the palms of her hands against the window, shrieking in pain amidst the chaos. Later that night, despite Templeton's protests to the contrary, Janice declares, "I saw her burn her hands on a cold window!" In court, as the wheelchair-bound Mary Lou Sides painfully recounts the accident's details, she says, "All at once, [Audrey Rose's] car went up in flames. It was horrible. And I could see the girl ... screaming ... and beating her hands against the window ... and screaming, 'Hot! Hot! Hot! Hot! Hot! Hot!'" As such testimony is offered, Wise's camera remains fixed on Janice, who, with each passing day, better understands the connection between Ivy and Audrey Rose. Mary Lou Sides contributes significantly to the case, but even before she takes the stand, Hoover makes a special request of his attorney, Brice Mack (Robert Walden), asking that a key individual be called to testify.

Janice is the last of the presented witnesses to take the stand, and it ultimately becomes clear that Hoover's initial visit to her apartment factors into the trial and its overall outcome. She openly admits to Judge Harmon Langley (Philip Sterling) and the others, her belief that Ivy has been reincarnated from Audrey Rose's soul, thus worsening the strain on her marriage to Templeton. Following such a revelation, as court adjourns for the day, Scott Velie (John Hillerman), the prosecuting attorney, takes note of Janice's exit from the courthouse. Templeton is nowhere in sight, as he has departed separately from his spouse. Yet, the turning point in their relationship does not transpire during the trial, but instead, during Hoover's aforementioned visit. At such a point of the narrative, Templeton remains convinced that Ivy burned her hands on the heater and refuses to accept any alternative theories. Janice is devastated and eventually deems Hoover to be "the only chance [Ivy] has of living."

Following Janice's testimony at the trial, Velie and Mack meet with Judge Langley in the latter's chambers. Lipscomb's proposed experiment, a test of which Templeton approves, becomes the subject of their discussion. In time, Velie convinces Langley to authorize it. Tragically, in the aftermath of the experiment, Ivy is dead. Furthermore, Janice's marriage to Templeton remains in doubt. "[Templeton] still cannot accept the idea that while Ivy's body is gone, her soul continues to exist," she confesses in a letter to Hoover, who has returned to India to attain peace for the deceased's soul. Shortly thereafter, Wise concludes his picture with a significant passage from the Bhagavad Gita, which states, "There is no end. For the soul there is never birth nor death. Nor, having once been, does it ever cease to be. It is unborn, eternal, ever-existing, undying and primeval...."

"Through my agent, Robert Wise called and asked me to read the script of *Audrey Rose*, which I did," Marsha Mason said. "At the time, I was very interested in karma and reincarnation. The script particularly appealed to me, so I was hired very quickly. Everything else fell into place as Tony Hopkins, John Beck, and Susan Swift were then cast in the picture.

"I didn't read Frank De Felitta's novel in its entirety. I may have read parts of it, but I often find that it isn't particularly helpful for me to read a book on which a film is based unless an historical context is presented within the narrative, and since *Audrey Rose* pertained to a specific subject matter, I didn't feel that the book would necessarily inform me any more than the script did.

Marsha Mason.

"Mr. Wise's choices in regard to the film's production were all very conscious. In some of my scenes, the weather is rainy. And this is how he wanted it to be in order to achieve a particular mood for the film. I did spend some time asking questions about his directing and about his history. Wise was a very methodical, easy-going, and relaxed kind of director, but everything was done in pre-production. He showed me the storyboards, which really gave me a good perspective of how he approached the work.

"Wise was gentle and soft-spoken when it came to directing the young Susan Swift for her scenes. It was the way he was in life. Wise was terrific, but firm, with Susan. She was also easy-going and very much enjoyed performing in the film. Given the nature of the subject matter, we actually had a very relaxed set.

"If I had to choose a favorite memory of performing in *Audrey Rose*, it would have to be the filming of the hypnotism sequence. In the scene, I'm looking through a window and seeing my daughter become somebody else. I'm the only one in the shot. It was very challenging for me to try to infuse that moment with all of my feelings. Of all the people in this world, who has honestly had the experience of seeing a child transform into a being similar to what is portrayed in *The Exorcist*? It was the most complicated scene for me to do. I had to make decisions regarding the meaning of the internal monologue. I appreciate difficult challenges and tend to respond really well to such challenges, and these are the moments I tend to remember when it comes to performing in various films. I also recall the times during which I have a vivid idea upon initially reading a script and then being able to realize and implement the idea weeks later when it comes time for the actual shooting. Those are the two key aspects that really make the work worthwhile for me.

"Any film set reflects the personality of its director. Paul Mazursky's set [of 1973's *Blume in Love*] was more jocular than that of Robert Wise's; it was a reflection of Paul's personality. The same goes for Mark Rydell (1973's *Cinderella Liberty*) and Herb Ross (1977's *The Goodbye Girl* and 1983's *Max Dugan Returns*). Bob Wise's set was professional and low-key, like him. He was a solid, practiced artist and cared a great deal about film. By the time I had met him, it was late in his career. He had nothing to prove. I found it intriguing that Wise was interested in the subject matter of *Audrey Rose*. He must have had an idea of what would challenge him.

"Wise was always extremely and excruciatingly kind to his crew. He maintained long relationships with those who worked behind the scenes. For example, Dorothy Jeakins was the film's costume designer. She also served in the same capacity during the production of *The Sound of Music*. According to Dorothy, Bob Wise tapped into the personal profits he received from that particular film and distributed a fair share to every crew member. He enjoyed close, personal relationships with many people. Some directors do not; instead, they're more demanding, or perhaps more complicated.

"Regarding Tony Hopkins and John Beck, they were great. I was particularly taken with Tony in the sense that he was British and had a heavy theatrical background. I also came from the theatre. And because of such experience, Tony and I wound up working together in a New York play for the Roundabout. It was Harold Pinter's *Old Times*. Jane Alexander also starred in that production. Tony and I had an affinity for the theatre, and each other. John, on the other hand, came more from television and was not so much from the theatre, but we had a really nice mix of personalities on Wise's set. And regarding Susan Swift, I stayed friends with her for quite awhile following the production of *Audrey Rose*. She would send me cards and we'd talk on the phone. Susan's mother, a very nice lady, stayed in touch with me for a few years following the picture.

"I don't recall if there was a special premiere for the film. In the 1970s, things were not the same as they are in modern times. The business has changed dramatically. The marketing and packaging of a picture today is much different from the way things were handled back then. Even the Academy Awards were low-key; we didn't have a big red carpet. Nobody asked me what I was wearing. It was simply a very different business then. During the production of *Audrey Rose*, I enjoyed viewing the dailies. Some directors, like Tony Richardson, didn't want the actors to see a film's dailies, but I insisted because I always felt that I knew enough to be objective, and invariably, the director and I always agreed on which take worked best. I can be very objective about my work, which is not necessarily the case with actors in general. However, by seeing through the dailies, then the rough cut, then the finished cut, and then doing ADR (Automatic Dialog Replacement), I'd pretty much gone past it, meaning that if the studio wasn't planning a film premiere, it didn't matter too much to me. I rarely, if at all, watch myself perform. One time, I was at home when I heard a familiar voice coming from the television in the distance. I got up from my chair, went around a corner, and then entered the room in which the television was located and discovered that the voice belonged to me. I watched for about five minutes and then decided I was satisfied with what I had seen and went back to whatever it was I was doing at the time.

"I believe part of Robert Wise's success in the industry can be attributed to the fact that he started as a film editor. His storyboards were created by Maurice Zuberano, a skilled artist. Each individual shot was drawn by hand, which is something that Martin Scorsese has also done for his films. In an odd way, the entire production of *Audrey Rose* was already laid out for us in a series of pictures. They were presented as little small squares on a big page. Wise was different from other directors. Herb Ross, for example, worked on his feet. If he believed what he saw, then he was satisfied. Perhaps, he may have used a shot list and storyboards, but if he did, I don't remember seeing them. Wise, on the other hand, essentially knew his film inside out, and I was fascinated."

The filming of *Audrey Rose* concluded during the latter part of 1976. As Wise's picture underwent post-production, most of his attention became transfixed on his personal life. Over a year had passed since the death of his wife, Patricia. Wise essentially sought happiness in the bonds of matrimony once more. On January 29, 1977, he married Millicent Franklin. Shortly thereafter, on April 6th of that same year, *Audrey Rose* premiered nationwide. It did not, however, fare well with a majority of theatergoers. Some were quick to make comparisons with William Friedkin's *The Exorcist* (1973). Vincent Canby of *The New York Times* was blunt in his criticism, openly declaring, "The soul of [*Audrey Rose*] is that of *The Exorcist* instantly recycled." Frank De Felitta eventually opted to write a sequel. It was entitled *For Love of Audrey Rose*. Published in 1982, De Felitta's novel further chronicled Janice Templeton's search for meaning. Wise himself took a modest approach when reflecting on the production of *Audrey Rose*, ultimately claiming, "I don't think we're going to prove reincarnation in this picture, but I'm very open to the whole possibility of the supernatural, the paranormal, [and] the possibility of dimensions out there."

38
STAR TREK: THE MOTION PICTURE

(PRODUCED 1978-1979, RELEASED 1979)

"The cosmos is within us. We are made of star-stuff. We are a way for the universe to know itself."
- Carl Sagan

During the latter half of the 1960s, an imaginative, science fiction television program aired on the network of the National Broadcasting Company (NBC). The program developed a loyal fan base and, from an allegorical perspective, "boldly" explored social issues of the era. It held a special place in the hearts of science fiction fanatics across the country, and many watched it religiously. The program's name consisted of two simple words: *Star Trek*. Yet, on June 3, 1969, much to the disappointment of its viewers, the show's final episode hit the airwaves. Poor ratings ultimately led to the program's cancellation. A reincarnation of the show, *Star Trek: The Animated Series* (1973), was later presented to the American public. Its success, however, was short-lived. Gene Roddenberry, the creator of *Star Trek*, was nevertheless determined to keep his beloved franchise alive.

Roddenberry and his closest associates believed that a live-action, spin-off television series of the original program could be developed. The project was given a working title of *Star Trek: Phase II*, but Paramount executives became skeptical, believing such a project would ultimately prove to be a financial failure. Coincidentally, the latter part of the 1970s marked a rising popularity in science fiction films. *Star Wars* (1977) and *Close Encounters of the Third Kind* (1977) continuously played to sold-out crowds, and Paramount wanted to reap the full advantages of the sci-fi market. Hence, plans for *Star Trek: Phase II* were ultimately scrapped and replaced with a new project, the production of a full-length motion picture.

Roddenberry was chosen by the studio to be the film's producer. One by one, members of the original cast committed themselves to such a venture, but Leonard Nimoy, best known for his portrayal of the alien Captain Spock, had reservations about joining the others. Enter Millicent Wise, the newly-wed spouse of Robert Wise. She had been an ardent supporter of *Star Trek* since its inception in 1966, and Wise himself had recently become attached to Roddenberry's project. Millicent eventually told her husband, "You can't possibly do *Star Trek* without Spock! It just won't work, because he and Captain Kirk have such a thing going!" Wise agreed with his wife and later relayed her thoughts to the studio, and from that special moment, it was simply a matter of time before Nimoy changed his mind and reunited with his fellow castmates.

An alien, cloud-like object of "unbelievable destructive power" is on a direct course for Earth, and the only starship in interception range is the *USS Enterprise*. The ship has been redesigned under the constant supervision of Captain Decker (Stephen Collins), but Kirk (William Shatner), Chief of Starfleet Operations, assumes command of the *Enterprise* due to his experience. Decker reluctantly accepts a temporary grade reduction to the rank of Commander. Epsilon 9, a space station, transmits friendship messages to the cloud but is subsequently destroyed. Shortly before the *Enterprise* embarks on its mission, Lieutenant Ilia (Persis Khambatta), a Deltan, joins the crew. Decker was previously stationed on Ilia's home planet, where the two were in a relationship. The *Enterprise* departs. A short time later, Spock (Nimoy) unexpectedly arrives on the scene via shuttlecraft and is appointed science officer of the ship. The *Enterprise* eventually encounters the cloud, and Kirk avoids any actions that could be misinterpreted as hostile. The cloud attempts to communicate with the *Enterprise* by way of a peculiar, telepathic-like transmission. The crew, however, is initially unsure of how to respond to such a transmission. As a result, the cloud attacks using a form of plasma energy. Mirroring the invader's frequency and rate of speed used during its previous transmission to the *Enterprise*, Spock replies with a message of friendship, thus thwarting the attack and saving the ship from destruction.

Later, however, a probe infiltrates the bridge and attempts to take control of the main computer. Spock destroys the terminal's console. The probe therefore responds by abducting Ilia. A tractor beam seizes the *Enterprise* and begins to transport it towards the cloud's center. Ilia suddenly reappears on the ship, but not as a human. Instead, she reappears as a mechanism. Such a mechanism is programmed by an entity known only as V'Ger, which, the crew learns, travels to Earth on a mission to find, and join with, its creator. Spock attempts to establish a mind-meld, or telepathic link, between him and "the aliens" but sustains neurological trauma in the process. He later confirms that V'Ger is an "evolving, instinctively needing" child and should be treated as such. The tractor beam pulls the *Enterprise* closer to the heart of the cloud, which has dissipated to reveal an immense vessel.

Deep within the vessel's interior, Kirk and crew discover V'Ger to be Voyager 6, a late-twentieth century probe originally designed to collect data and transmit it back to Earth. Voyager 6 is believed to have landed on a machine-inhabited planet, where it was accepted as a "primitive, yet kindred" object of its own kind. The cloud, or vessel, was then built so that V'Ger could travel to Earth to "learn all that is learnable," and then return such information to its creator. In the process, however, V'Ger amassed so much knowledge that it achieved consciousness itself and became a living thing. V'Ger demands to evolve and requires a human quality, or "a capacity to leap beyond logic." Decker sacrifices himself and physically joins with the mechanism formerly known as Ilia. As a consequence, V'Ger is given the ability to create its own sense of purpose out of human weaknesses, thus becoming empowered with the drive that compels people to overcome such weaknesses.

Wise's involvement with *Star Trek: The Motion Picture* essentially began during a 1978 meeting with Michael Eisner, Paramount's then head of production. Jeffrey Katzenberg, an up-and-coming executive with the studio, was also in attendance. Wise immediately expressed to both men his unfamiliarity with *Star Trek*. He was subsequently provided with several episodes of the original series for his viewing pleasure. Wise was no stranger to the genre of science fiction, as *The Day the Earth Stood Still* (1951) and *The Andromeda Strain* (1971) have remained among his most memorable pictures. Yet, both films present a setting that is essentially limited to the confines of the Earth. With *Star Trek: The Motion Picture*, Wise was afforded the opportunity to venture into the universe. Upon the production's completion, however, he concluded that the overall experience was not particularly pleasant. For instance, as filming began, the script was not complete, as much of its content had yet to be determined. Alas, extensive revisions were made by screenwriter Harold Livingston and several others.

According to Wise, many of the rewrites transpired during the film's final week of production. Those of the original cast apparently had certain ideas regarding their characters' dialogue. Hence, the end result is a satisfactory, yet relatively complex, work of fiction. The proverbial leap from television to the silver screen proved to be a difficult undertaking for the cast and crew alike, but upon its world premiere on December 7, 1979, Wise's picture presented a tale of which "there is no comparison." Theatergoers were generally pleased, and some returned for multiple viewings in order to better understand the film's story. Certain subtleties initially went unnoticed by select theatergoers. For example, following Ilia's abduction, the *Enterprise* encounters a closing orifice while traversing the interior of the cloud, or vessel. Kirk and Spock ponder their next move:

KIRK: What do you make of all this?
SPOCK: I believe the closed orifice leads to another chamber, undoubtedly part of the vessel's inner mechanism. I suspect it may be necess-....

Kirk stares at Spock in confusion, unable to make sense of the abrupt pause. The blaring sound of the ship's alarm suddenly breaks the silence as the crew is alerted to the presence of an intruder. Unbeknownst to those viewing Wise's film for the first time, the mechanism formerly known as Ilia has begun its infiltration of the *Enterprise*. In retrospect, however, a core-deep connection between Spock and V'Ger is essentially confirmed upon such an infiltration. Together, Spock and V'Ger come to discover that logic is not without its limits. In addition, both engage in a relentless search for answers. Furthermore, their actions are influenced by a peculiar, intellectual curiosity.

Spock and V'Ger initially perceive logic as a constant of the universe, but it eventually becomes clear that such is not the case; imperfections are evident. Prior to entering the cloud, the *Enterprise* barely escapes destruction. As members of the crew breathe a sigh of relief, Kirk addresses Spock:

KIRK: It would seem our friendship messages have been received and understood, Mr. Spock.
SPOCK: I would say that was a logical assumption, Captain.

Ironically, Spock senses "pure logic" from what he refers to as a "highly advanced mentality." Yet, he cannot perceive any form of emotion. Those of the *Enterprise* detect a similar demeanor from Spock and often struggle to understand the stoicism that defines him. "It's how we all feel," Lieutenant Uhura (Nichelle Nichols), the ship's communications officer, declares in an attempt to explain why the crew is overjoyed at his earlier, sudden arrival. Spock nevertheless remains focused on V'Ger and comes to realize that logic is not the solution to self-fulfillment. Kirk later ponders the execution of a Starfleet order to self-destruct the *Enterprise* in the hopes of eliminating the alien threat. Everyone onboard, however, will be sacrificed. As Kirk considers the pros and cons of such a decision, he makes an unexpected find. Tears flow from Spock's eyes, and Kirk is quick to discover that it is not the crew for whom his science officer grieves:

KIRK: Not for us.
SPOCK: No, Captain, not for us ... for V'Ger. I weep for V'Ger as I would for a brother. As I was when I came aboard, so is V'Ger now ... empty, incomplete, and searching. Logic and knowledge are not enough.

Later, at V'Ger's center, Kirk comes to the realization that its evolution is dependent on a human quality, or a "capacity to leap beyond logic."

Throughout a majority of the film, Spock is preoccupied with his own, separate search for answers, as is V'Ger. Yet, both do not necessarily receive timely responses to their so-called questions. As Spock is first seen on his home planet of Vulcan, he undergoes Kolinahr, the ritual to purge all emotion.[71] The rite of passage, however, does not transpire as planned. The Vulcan Master (Edna Glover) presents Spock with a ceremonial necklace. Such an adornment is essentially a symbol of pure logic. Unbeknownst to first-time viewers, however, Spock senses the coming of V'Ger and abruptly halts the ritual. The master then establishes a mind-meld with him:

VULCAN MASTER: I sense the consciousness calling to you from space. Your human blood is touched by it, Spock.

Later, on the *Enterprise*, Spock recounts the experience, thus indicating that such a consciousness is a source more powerful than anything he has ever encountered. "I believe it may hold my answers," he declares. Yet, following Spock's mind-meld with V'Ger, it becomes clear that V'Ger struggles to comprehend "simple" emotions and is persistently in search of meaning,

---

[71] In 2001, a Director's Edition of the film was released on DVD, thus enabling Robert Wise to present the general public with a motion picture more consistent with his original vision. The Vulcan sequence, among others, includes additional footage absent from 1979's theatrical presentation.

continuously inquiring, "Is this all that I am? Is there nothing more?" Despite V'Ger's inability to identify certain feelings of warmth and endearment, it exhibits a particular human quality often reflected within additional characters of the narrative.

Viewing the dailies.

Spock and V'Ger are driven by an intellectual curiosity in their separate quests for meaning, and such curiosity ultimately works to the advantage of both. As the *Enterprise* travels within the vessel's interior, Decker questions the alien's motives:

DECKER: Why bring us inside? Not to destroy us. They could have done that outside.
KIRK: They still can.
SPOCK: Curiosity, Mr. Decker. Insatiable curiosity.

Had V'Ger been successful during its earlier attempt to destroy the *Enterprise*, it would have ultimately failed to join with "the creator." Instead, Kirk and his crew are drawn to the cloud's interior, where they continue their investigation. Eventually, Spock exhibits an intellectual curiosity of his own as he steals a thruster suit in search of answers. He makes a significant find during his mind-meld with V-Ger, thus becoming aware of its profound desire to understand its place in the universe. Upon the film's conclusion, courtesy of Decker, the alien entity accomplishes its objective. Spock casually suggests that the new life form must learn to deal with foolish human emotions. Yet, the answers to his questions are made clear, as his calling in life has essentially been discovered. Spock belongs on the *Enterprise*, thus affirming, "My task on Vulcan is completed," and Wise, shortly thereafter, concludes his film with one of the most memorable proclamations of *Star Trek* lore, which boldly declares, "THE HUMAN ADVENTURE IS JUST BEGINNING."

"Following the cancellation of *Star Trek: The Original Series*, Norway Productions and Paramount Pictures went back and forth for years regarding whether to produce another television series or a feature film," Alan Dean Foster said as he reflected on his contribution to the script of *Star Trek: The Motion Picture*. "They were in the process of bringing back the concept as a television series. When *Star Wars* and *Close Encounters of the Third Kind* were released in theaters and grossed loads of money, the twelve-year-old daughter of Charles Bluhdorn supposedly said, 'Daddy, why can't we have a *Star Trek* movie?' Bluhdorn, of course, was the CEO of Gulf & Western, which owned, among other things, Paramount. Whether Bluhdorn's daughter really approached him with this question or not, it's a good story.

"Eventually, the decision came down from on high that the studio was not going to produce another television series, but instead, a big-budget movie. Prior to that, Norway and Gene Roddenberry had solicited dozens of story ideas for the proposed, revived television series. I submitted three stories. I was asked to come in as one of many writers. Roddenberry and everybody knew I was very familiar with the *Star Trek* universe based on my novelizations (the *Star Trek Logs*) of the Saturday morning animated TV series. Of the three story ideas I submitted, one was based on a two-page, typed, and double-spaced outline called *Robot's Return*, by Roddenberry. He gave it to me and said, 'See if you can make anything out of this.' Using that as a starting point, I came up with a story idea called *In Thy Image*, which I was then asked to develop as a full-scale treatment for a one-hour television program as part of the new *Star Trek* series.

"Subsequent to that, it was decided that the studio wanted to open the series with a two-hour movie for television. *In Thy Image* was selected. Next thing I heard was that the studio had changed its mind again and was now planning to do a big-budget film and not a television series. Suddenly, real money, real prestige, and real ego became involved. I reckon that the folks at Norway started running around saying, 'We've got to reach the Paramount corporate heads before they change their minds again.' Somebody then likely said, 'Hey, we've got this treatment for a two-hour show.' Because at this point, I had been asked to expand my treatment for a one-hour show into a treatment for a two-hour show. 'Let's throw this treatment at them and see what happens.' Whereupon Michael Eisner supposedly read it and said, 'This is our movie.' And that's how the treatment for *In Thy Image* came about, after which I became a complete non-person at both Norway Productions and Paramount, and was not asked to work on the script or contribute anything else to the movie, even though I would have done so for free, because I'm a fan as much as I am a writer.

"When the project became a big-budget film, I ceased to exist as far as the production was concerned. I was a young guy and had no pull in the business. If you don't know somebody, or if you don't have a long string of credits, you are sent off into purgatory, and that's the end of it. That's how it works a lot of times with big-budget, Hollywood films. I just accepted the conditions as they were and moved on with my life. My uncle, Howie Horowitz, was a well-known producer in Hollywood. I therefore had some idea of how the business worked even though I wasn't deeply involved in it. So, I just kind of shrugged the whole thing off and went back to writing my novels. Was I unhappy about it? Sure. I had my own ideas for the film, but they were never solicited, not even for free. Maybe that was my mistake. When you offer something for free to somebody in the motion picture business, they immediately get suspicious of you. People may have said, 'What does he really want?' Nobody could probably fathom the notion that I just wanted to see as good a *Star Trek* movie as possible simply because I was a fan of the original show. But it never came up and nothing ever happened. I wasn't even invited to visit the set. Perhaps, my presence was discouraged because the studio was concerned I might have had something to say regarding the structure of the story. The last thing people want on a set is another writer, much less a science fiction writer on a science fiction film. I'm not bitter but I was certainly disappointed.

"The first five minutes of *Star Trek: The Motion Picture* are all mine. I'll take credit for the Klingon sequence, because it's presented exactly the way I wrote it. After that, things go all over the place and get changed. Not entirely because the screenplay was written by different people, but because different events transpired. Originally, Leonard Nimoy wasn't committed to the film, so he wasn't in the original treatment. There was a young, pure Vulcan character named Lieutenant Xon. And then, of course, Nimoy finally did commit and everything had to be changed. Nevertheless, I still wasn't asked to contribute anything else. But again, I will take credit for the first five minutes of the film. And I'm also the one who made Kirk an admiral. Considering many years had passed, I figured he was long overdue for a promotion.

"I think *Star Trek: The Motion Picture* is a good film. Everybody knows that it was rushed because of a Christmas release date. If the studio had taken more time, it would have been a better film. A subsequent director's cut by Robert Wise certainly improved it, as story elements that are critical to understanding the plot are restored. I think the film was a very brave attempt to do something that people generally just don't do in Hollywood. Today, if one went into the offices of Universal or Disney or Sony or any of the other majors and said they wanted to make a film about the next step up in human evolution, and if a big budget is sought, it's just not going to happen. That's basically the idea of *Star Trek: The Motion Picture*. It's much harder to make a good film about an idea than it is to make a good film about people shooting at each other. That's probably an oversimplification, but it's so much easier to sell a story of ships shooting at each other in space where bad aliens with horrendous masks fill the roles of the antagonists.

"In retrospect, I certainly wish I'd had more involvement with *Star Trek: The Motion Picture*. It's kind of a sad situation. There are people in the business who will listen to suggestions, and then there are people who are only interested in self-aggrandizement and their own ego and their own money. I'm proud of what I did on the film. I think it's a good film. It's not a great film. But if it hadn't been quite so rushed, if Doug Trumbull, the second unit director and special photographic effects director, had been given more time to work on the effects, and if Wise, who was a great editor, hadn't been rushed so much in the editing process, the studio would have ended up with a better picture, which is why a director's cut was later released.

Isaac Asimov was credited as a special science consultant during the production of *Star Trek: The Motion Picture*.

"My wife and I were invited to the film's premiere at the Smithsonian in Washington, D.C. Paramount was going to pay for everything. However, since I had such a bad experience with the whole process, we declined. I had never been to a major movie premiere before and it would have been kind of fun, but I was afraid I would end up sitting next to people to whom I would probably say discourteous, tactless things. Too many people had too much involved personally in the film, so I just stayed away from it.

"After I was not asked to work on the screenplay, the pre-release credits came out. Credits are filed with the various guilds. If anybody has an objection to how the credits are going to appear in the final cut of a film, he or she is expected to speak up. When I viewed these pre-release credits, the words 'Story by Gene Roddenberry, Screenplay by Gene Roddenberry and Harold Livingston' were displayed. I wondered why my name didn't appear. It was listed on the shooting script as 'Story by Alan Dean Foster and Gene Roddenberry.' I therefore called my agent and asked for an explanation. She said, 'Don't get excited. They filed their set of credits. Now, we'll file ours.' And so I said, 'You know . . . I wrote ninety-eight to ninety-nine percent of this treatment, or story. And if they're going to be this way, I'm going to file for sole story credit.' So, I did. Time passed, and I eventually received a phone call from Livingston. He said, 'Just because Roddenberry's being a son-of-a-bitch doesn't mean you have to be one, too.' I thought about it and said, 'You know what? We'll just file for the credits the way they should've been filed in the first place, which was story by me and Roddenberry.' I called my agent and told her this. She said, 'Okay. If that's what you want, then that's what we'll do.' I got a call from her a little while later and she told me, 'I've just talked to Roddenberry's people. He's in La Costa recovering from overwork and can't be bothered with this sort of thing.' At that point, I threw my hands up into the air and went to my wife, who is a very down-to-earth person, and said, 'I understand the business now. It's run by a bunch of twelve-year-old boys!' I called my agent back and said, 'Look, whatever!' And that's why I have sole story credit on the film. Because at that point, Roddenberry was too busy to be bothered with objecting to my credit refiling. It's not that I feel bad about having sole story credit, because I did write ninety-eight percent of the treatment and I can prove it. Roddenberry and his people knew I could prove it. It was simply a very unpleasant experience after doing the actual writing work. My name was on the shooting script that the actors were carrying around with them. How could the studio possibly take it off of the film? My agent, who represented Charles Bronson among others, said, 'That's just the way the business works.' I replied, 'If that's the way the business works, then I don't want to be a part of that business.' I found out many years later that apparently it was Livingston who went to Roddenberry and said, 'This guy Foster has no experience writing screenplays, except in college, and he shouldn't be writing a script for a film this big. I'll do it.' I have no idea if this is true. I only came across this information by casually perusing various *Star Trek* websites through the years.

"At one point during the ordeal, shortly after filing for sole story credit, I was walking around my Los Angeles home in a blue funk. My wife, JoAnn, who's from a small town in Texas, looked at me and said, 'Are you sure you want to live here and be near these people?' Being a very low-key sort of person, I thought about it and said, 'No. Let's go live someplace we both like.' My wife didn't like Los Angeles, and I couldn't live in central Texas. I figured I could find a place to quietly write my books and nobody would bother me. So, we moved. And if I had stayed in Los Angeles, where I grew up, and continued in the movie business, I would probably have a lot more money and I'd get a one-sixteenth shot of myself on the back of *People* magazine once a year. But I would be a much less pleasant human being. So, I have my wife to thank for leaving Los Angeles. It turned out to be a wise decision."

Upon the theatrical release of *Star Trek: The Motion Picture*, the critical reception was average. *Variety* referred to the film as "a search-and-destroy thriller that includes all of the ingredients the TV show's fans thrive on: the philosophical dilemma wrapped in a scenario of mind control, troubles with the space ship, the dependable and understanding Kirk, the ever-logical Spock, and suspenseful take with twist ending." Wise essentially did what he could to stay true to the original series. For example, throughout the picture, William Shatner's narration periodically recurs in the form of the Captain's Log, a traditional feature of the television episodes, and on such occasions during Wise's film, theatergoers can hear the familiar notes belonging to the music of Alexander Courage, who scored the original series. Courage served as an uncredited orchestrator of *Star Trek: The Motion Picture*, collaborating with Jerry Goldsmith, the film's composer, to add a touch of authenticity to the production. Yet, the greatest commonality between the original series and its silver screen adaptation is the cherished cast.

Upon the film's climax, as the *Enterprise* nears its final destination within the alien vessel, Wise presents an image of Lieutenant Pavel Chekov (Walter Koenig), the ship's tactical officer, positioned on the bridge at his console. The image marks the beginning of a memorable camera shot. Following Chekov, Wise pans left to reveal Lieutenant Uhura. An image of Doctor Leonard "Bones" McCoy (DeForest Kelley), chief medical officer of the *Enterprise*, is then presented. Wise continues his shot of the crew as he pans to the ship's helmsman, Lieutenant Commander Hikaru Sulu (George Takei). An image of Chief DiFalco (Marcy Lafferty), Ilia's replacement on the bridge, follows. The camera then moves upward to present a concerned Decker before gradually panning right to reveal Kirk. Finally, the focus shifts to Spock, and the shot concludes shortly thereafter. Hence, within the space of a single minute, Wise individually presents each principal member of the original cast during a most noteworthy scene.[72]

Despite Wise's efforts to direct a quality motion picture, the film was ultimately criticized for its slow pace. Some made comparisons to Stanley Kubrick's *2001: A Space Odyssey* (1968), released a decade earlier. Evidently, upon the release of Wise's film, the slow movement of ships through space, although popular with audiences during the 1960s, was "no longer surprising and elegant." Early in the narrative, as Scotty transports Kirk via shuttlecraft to the *Enterprise*, the journey transpires over the course of six minutes. The scene appears lengthy to theatergoers. Yet, a sense of realism regarding the elapsed time is evident. Decades earlier, Wise directed *The Set-Up* (1949) using a similar technique, as the onscreen action takes place within the

---

[72] James Doohan, another key member of the original cast, does not appear in the scene. His character, Montgomery "Scotty" Scott, chief engineer of the *Enterprise*, naturally spends most of his time in the ship's engine room. Furthermore, Marcy Lafferty and Stephen Collins, although present in the shot, were not members of the original cast.

actual running time of the film. Despite the reintroduction of such a clever technique in *Star Trek: The Motion Picture*, it did not fare particularly well with audiences, and the film, in short, essentially marked the beginning of the end for Wise. It was the last of his big-budget productions, and another ten years would pass before his return to the director's chair.

The *Star Trek* franchise itself underwent considerable change as preparations for a sequel, *Star Trek II: The Wrath of Khan* (1982), began during the early 1980s, but Gene Roddenberry, Paramount decided, was unfit to reprise his role as producer. Over $45 million had been spent on *Star Trek: The Motion Picture*, and Roddenberry's constant demands for rewrites affected the overall production of the film. Harve Bennett, a television producer with Paramount, was hired as the executive producer of *Star Trek II: The Wrath of Khan*, which became an instant success upon its premiere on June 4, 1982. The well-liked sequel, budgeted at just over $11 million, ultimately earned $97 million at the box office. Sometime later, an interviewer questioned Bennett about Roddenberry and the franchise. "I am his replacement," Bennett said. "[Roddenberry] alienated some really creative people who were doing the very best to make his show a hit."

On October 24, 1991, tragedy struck the *Star Trek* universe when Gene Roddenberry died of heart failure. A few weeks later, *Star Trek VI: The Undiscovered Country* (1991), the final *Star Trek* film to feature each principal member of the original cast, premiered in theaters nationwide. It was fittingly dedicated in memory of Roddenberry. In the following years, *Star Trek* continued to thrive with the development of additional motion pictures and television programs. On February 25, 2015, Harve Bennett passed away at the age of eighty-four. Coincidentally, only two days later, Leonard Nimoy died at his home in Bel Air, Los Angeles, but their legacies, in addition to those of Gene Roddenberry and *Star Trek*, have continuously endured and will ultimately do so forever.

PART V
TWILIGHT

39
ROOFTOPS

(PRODUCED 1988, RELEASED 1989)

> "If you obey all the rules, you miss all the fun."
> - Katharine Hepburn

Throughout the 1980s, Robert Wise spent very little time in the director's chair, instead dedicating his time to the preservation of the motion picture industry. To begin the decade, he returned to the Directors Guild of America following a lengthy absence, to serve as the chairman of a special projects committee.[73] Wise was welcomed with open arms, as many valued his solemn advice and considerable range of expertise. Years later, in 1984, he became the president of the Academy of Motion Picture Arts and Sciences, serving in such a capacity until 1987. In 1988, he received the D.W. Griffith Award as a tribute to his lifetime achievements in cinema, but Wise, at seventy-four years of age, was not ready to abandon the director's chair just yet. During that same year, he reported to Silvercup Studios, located in the New York borough of Queens, in order to begin production of his thirty-ninth film. *Rooftops*, based on a story by Allan A. Goldstein and Tony Mark, was written

---

[73] Robert Wise served as the president of the Directors Guild of America from 1971 to 1975.

for the screen by Terence Brennan. The film evolves around the troubling times of distressed youths living on New York's east side. Wise had earlier captured the nation's attention with his production of *West Side Story* (1961), and almost thirty years later, it essentially became time for him to shift focus to the other side of town.

Jason Gedrick as T.

A parentless rebel in his mid-twenties known only as T (Jason Gedrick) makes his residence on a New York City rooftop within the confines of an empty water tower. Squeak (Alexis Cruz), a troubled teenager from a broken home, finds solace in his graffiti and frequently seeks companionship with T. Lobo (Eddie Vélez), a local drug pusher, plans to take control of the neighborhood in order to expand his territory. He demands T's cooperation but is met with resistance. One evening during a party, T meets the beautiful Elana (Troy Beyer). The two begin a romantic relationship. Shortly thereafter, T learns that Elana is a cousin of Lobo's. Her father happens to be very ill, and due to mounting medical bills, Elana acts as an accomplice to Lobo's drug deals, thus earning supplemental income to pay such bills.

Lobo is arrested during a police raid but is eventually released due to insufficient evidence. He believes T to be the whistleblower and sees to the destruction of the water tower. Fortunately, nobody is hurt or killed. Lobo orders Elana to stay away from T and forbids any relationship between the two. His demands, however, are ignored. Squeak, too, refuses to back down from any of Lobo's threats, but he is subsequently pushed from a building and dies. T seeks to avenge his fallen friend; he confronts Lobo and a fight ensues. As a result, the latter is killed while plunging to his death through an unstable rooftop.

As *Rooftops* begins, a group of skinheads initiates a confrontation with Squeak, and a chase ensues. The official poster of *Rooftops* features the names of four performers in starring roles: Jason Gedrick, Troy Beyer, Eddie Vélez, and Tisha Campbell. Yet, throughout the film's opening credits, as the chase intensifies, the name of an additional performer, along with the other four, is displayed. As Squeak evades his assailants while simultaneously racing along the streets of Manhattan, the words "Alexis Cruz" fittingly appear next to him. He is an important part of the story. Wise's attention to such a character is therefore noteworthy. Also, with the exception of T and Elana, Squeak is the only individual to appear on the aforementioned poster.[74] In addition, he is revealed to be flaunting a most prized possession. Squeak's glaring overcoat, covered entirely with graffiti, is a true reflection of its artistic owner. It is also the most significant element of the narrative. The coat plays an integral part in the development of a supporting character and is additionally reflective of Squeak's expansive mural. Furthermore, it becomes beneficial in times of peril.

Kadim (Allen Payne), a supporting character of the film, learns to overcome adversity primarily because of Squeak's overcoat. Additionally, Kadim's feud with Raphael (Rafael Báez), Lobo's henchman, is an obstacle to self-fulfillment. The tension between the two begins during an argument over the coat. In the scene, Raphael abruptly takes the coat from Squeak and then taunts Kadim, who is present. Raphael baits Kadim into retrieving the coat

---

74 A rare, alternate poster of the film features only Jason Gedrick and Troy Beyer.

for the defenseless teen. Yet, the exchange does not transpire as planned. Instead, Kadim is repeatedly punched in the face. Throughout the film, he is presented as one who endures several hardships. For example, as his friend, Amber (Tisha Campbell), is berated by an unruly man on a busy Manhattan sidewalk, Kadim watches the events unfold from a distance. Amber's mother is a prostitute, and the man happens to be her mother's pimp. The abuse is partly verbal, partly physical, and Kadim is not compelled to take action. He simply lacks motivation. Regarding his home life, Kadim must care for his ailing father, an ex-boxer suffering from permanent brain damage due to a prolonged career in the ring. A son, in essence, discovers himself to be virtually powerless in all attempts to improve his father's standard of living.

Kadim is defeated during the first, aforementioned encounter with Raphael, and to reiterate, Squeak's coat is the cause of their scuffle. Without the coat's inclusion in the narrative, such a feud most likely would have been nonexistent. Later, when Kadim and Raphael meet again, the latter is overpowered. Not only does Kadim exact revenge, he overcomes an important obstacle, as the conflict's resolution ultimately leads to his self-fulfillment. He will no longer be deterred in the face of adversity. For the remainder of the narrative, a significant improvement in Kadim's life is evident, but sadly, such is not the case with Squeak. In the aftermath of Kadim's first encounter with Raphael, Squeak is hung by his ankles several stories above the pavement following an unsuccessful attempt at retrieving the coat. T intervenes and a tragedy is avoided, albeit temporarily. As Squeak is released, he immediately reclaims his coat. It is a work of art, and the coat's value, to Squeak, is priceless. Yet, as he places the finishing touches upon another artistic piece that is important to him, his actions lead to an unfortunate demise.

Squeak's expansive mural, which covers a building's exterior brick wall and spans multiple stories, is not only a reflection of the overcoat, but its mere existence contributes to the pace of the narrative. It is essentially indicative of the passage of time. Approximately thirty minutes into the film, as Wise intercuts between scenes, he reveals Squeak, from a distance, to be hard at work on the unfinished mural. The image is brief, but significant. The audience is henceforth exposed to occasional shots of the mural, thus indicating its closeness to completion. Although it eventually becomes defaced by Lobo's crew, such actions do not deter Squeak. The latter's will to persevere, however, ultimately results in his murder at the hands of Lobo himself. Squeak's death transpires approximately twenty minutes prior to the narrative's conclusion, but throughout the remainder of the film, his memory remains significant. As *Rooftops* comes to an end, T and Elana embrace each other on an outdoor dance floor. They pause to honor the mural. It is positioned above, and in the distance from, their location. T and Elana then share a passionate kiss, and Wise concludes his film. Squeak's memory, however, lives on not only through the mural, but also through the one object without which he is rarely seen.

Squeak's mural.

The overcoat proves advantageous when trouble is at hand, thus affirming its significance to the narrative and its characters. Curiously enough, it is utilized by T as a defense mechanism. Within the narrative's opening minutes, as he is first introduced to the audience, he makes a request of Squeak for the coat. The latter is being pursued by the skinheads. T then uses the coat to trick the assailants into thinking he is Squeak. They ultimately plunge through an unstable roof, never to be seen again.

Upon the film's conclusion and following the death of Squeak, an unidentifiable individual, wearing the overcoat, is presented as one who flees Lobo's henchmen. The audience then discovers the mystery man to be T. For the second time, he uses the overcoat as the ideal disguise. Then, from out of nowhere, T suddenly leaps onto Lobo, simultaneously wrapping the coat around the head of his victim. Minutes later, history repeats itself. Lobo, like the skinheads before him, finds himself in the wrong place at the wrong time. The roof on which he stands is unstable and therefore cannot withstand the pressure. Lobo falls to his death. The tagline of *Rooftops* states, "It's the only place to be." Such a catchphrase is naturally applicable to T and his circle of friends, but those who pose a threat to the community literally become victims of the unstable, unpredictable rooftops.

"My favorite memory is the dancing," Troy Beyer said in regard to her appearance as Elana. "I was reminded of what transpired on the set of *West Side Story* simply because Robert Wise knew what he was doing in terms of creating opposition to dance. And when the time came for *Rooftops* to be produced, I enjoyed watching how he was able to do that with us, as actors. Wise and his wife, Millicent, were valued people, and I had the privilege of having dinner with them on several occasions. He did not speak of his previous films. Instead, he appeared to be concerned about what the future had in store for him. I thought it was interesting. There was such a legacy, such an impressive resume. And during those dinners, Wise basically conveyed to me that the times were changing.

"Regarding the cast, I was especially grateful to Jason Gedrick. He's a great guy and we had a memorable experience together. Having known each other prior to filming made it really fun. We've always had a nice rapport through the years. I didn't have much interaction with others, like Eddie Vélez, simply because I was focused on my scenes with Jason, but Eddie was great. Alexis Cruz was another of whom I didn't see much, but he was a cute kid and a joyful person to be around. Tisha Campbell-Martin and I became really close during the production of *Rooftops*. In 1989, she and I were at a formative period in our lives in terms of our careers and becoming young ladies.

Troy Beyer.

"Although some critics were unkind upon the theatrical release of *Rooftops*, I thought the film was fantastic. I really loved what Robert Wise, as well as producers Howard Koch Jr. and Taylor Hackford, did with the story, and I appreciated what it was they were trying to create. The experience was quite an opportunity for me. It was a privilege to have such an important role and to be directed by Robert Wise. Therefore, regardless of the criticism, I'm honored to have been a part of this film."

New Visions Pictures, a small corporation formed during the 1980s by Hackford and filmmaker Stuart Benjamin, produced and distributed *Rooftops*. Wise's penultimate film, the only R-rated picture of his career, premiered on March 17, 1989. In Roger Ebert's column for the *Chicago Sun-Times*, he wrote, "*Rooftops* comes alive during the passages of music and dance, which feel like those moments in a musical when the characters burst into song, but then it tries to fit those flights of fantasy into a melodrama about drugs. It's too tight a squeeze." Wise indeed faced several challenges with the direction of his picture. Although *Rooftops* presents a basic, straightforward story to its viewers, some aspects of the film are relatively complex. Combat, a unique consolidation of dancing and sparring, is periodically featured throughout the narrative, and Wise faced the challenge of integrating such a consolidation into his film while also comparing and contrasting it with the Brazilian martial art of Capoeira.

On other occasions throughout the production, however, expectations were not as demanding. For example, while directing a steamy love scene between Jason Gedrick and Troy Beyer, Wise did not concern himself with censorship issues. The infamous Hays Code had been defunct since the late 1960s. Hence, along with an R-rating came a particular degree of latitude. Times had clearly changed since Wise first became involved with the motion picture industry. Some figured his career was at its end, but such an end was yet to come.

Alexis Cruz and Jason Gedrick.

40
A STORM IN SUMMER

(PRODUCED 1999, BROADCAST 2000)

> "Many receive advice, only the wise profit from it."
> - Harper Lee

Hallmark Hall of Fame, an anthology series of motion pictures, first aired on television in 1951. It was named after Hallmark Cards, the well-known greeting card company. For the first time in the history of home entertainment, a major corporation had developed and sponsored a television program as an effective means of advertising and marketing its products to the public. *Hallmark Hall of Fame* persevered through the years and, almost seventy years later, remained on the air at the time of this book's publication. Rod Serling, in addition to being the producer and narrator of the beloved *Twilight Zone* (1959), was a creative writer of sorts. In the late 1960s, he penned a teleplay entitled *A Storm in Summer*. It tells the story of an elderly Jewish man's relationship with an underprivileged Black child from Harlem. At a time of extreme racial prejudice in America, Serling's teleplay addressed the ongoing issues of such prejudice on the heels of the Civil Rights Movement. *Hallmark Hall of Fame* ultimately produced *A Storm in Summer*, and the film, or episode, aired in February of 1970. Decades later, as the dawn of a new millennium neared, Showtime, in association with Hallmark Entertainment, adapted the story for its cable television network, and Robert Wise, a man many believed to be retired from the industry altogether, returned to the director's chair one last time to fitly conclude a memorable career in motion pictures.

The year is 1969. The setting is Fairview, New York. Abel "Abe" Shaddick (Peter Falk), the aging owner of a delicatessen, receives an unexpected visit from Gloria Ross (Nastassja Kinski), an employee of the local country club. She oversees the Fresh Air Vacation Plan, a program that affords disadvantaged children from New York City the opportunity to spend two weeks with families in the Fairview community. Gloria informs Shaddick that his nephew, Stanley Banner (Andrew McCarthy), has volunteered his services. Shaddick, furthermore, learns that he has been made a co-sponsor of the engagement. The news of hosting a never-before-seen child is not taken lightly, and when the young Herman D. Washington (Aaron Meeks) arrives in town, the often-irresponsible Banner makes preparations for an impromptu departure for Atlantic City. The two encounter each other at the bus depot; Banner sends Herman to the deli and then leaves town. Shaddick and Herman initially clash over the arrangement's details, but tensions subside when a mutual decision to go fishing at a nearby lake is made.

Herman eventually becomes acclimated to his host and vice versa. Later, Gloria invites them to the country club. Mrs. Parker (Gillian Barber), a bigoted member, objects to Herman's presence and gets into a verbal altercation with Shaddick. Gloria's attempt to address the issue is cut short when she receives an important telephone call. Herman's brother, Bill, a sergeant with the U.S. Army, has been killed in Vietnam. Shaddick regretfully breaks the news a short time later. A devastated Herman struggles to cope with his emotions. Shaddick speaks of his son, Benjie, who was killed in action during the Second World War. He explains that although the sorrow of losing a loved one is unbearable, the crying comes to an end. Shaddick becomes emotional while pondering the irony of life. Gloria arrives at the deli to take Herman back to the city. Upon departing, he and Shaddick share a tearful embrace. Herman vows to one day return to Fairview.

Arrival in Fairview.

At the Fairview bus depot, as Banner prepares to flee for Atlantic City, he issues a warning to Herman, declaring, "Don't let my, uh, my uncle turn you off. He's not a bad egg. He's just a little odd ... set in his ways." Shortly thereafter, Shaddick's impetuous nephew departs, never to be seen for the remainder of Wise's film. In time, Herman arrives at the deli and comes face-to-face with Shaddick. It is not long before both discover their differences from one another. Herman says, "I come on a bus just a couple of minutes ago." Shaddick then replies, "I came on a boat fifty-five years ago." Yet, despite being a resident of Fairview for a lengthy period of time, Shaddick remains withdrawn, and his reclusive nature severely limits his interactions with the town and its residents. Herman, prior to leaving Harlem, gives thought to the very things he will experience during his two-week vacation. His grandmother (Ruby Dee) is enthusiastic as she speaks of swimming, fishing, and fresh air. Through such things, as fate would have it, Shaddick and Herman essentially discover Fairview together.

"You're the only nine-year-old on Earth that acts like Humphrey Bogart."

As a result of Gloria's invitation to the country club, Shaddick finds himself interacting with the establishment's employees and patrons while Herman enjoys the swimming pool. Prior to such an invitation, Shaddick was barely aware of the club's existence despite being a longtime resident of Fairview. Earlier, when Gloria visits the deli to introduce herself to him, she speaks of her first meeting with Banner:

GLORIA: My name is Gloria Ross and I met your nephew at the club last night.
SHADDICK: At the club?
GLORIA: Yeah, at the country club.
SHADDICK: Oh, the country club. Wonderful.

Shaddick is privy to the club's existence primarily because of his nephew. Just prior to Gloria's arrival, he comments, "[Banner] commutes between his bed and the country club." To the casual observer, Shaddick would appear to be talking to himself. Yet, through Wise's direction, the audience is aware that such is not the case. Shaddick spends a fair amount of his time addressing Benjie's portrait as a means of communicating with his late son. He is relatively more concerned with the dead than the living. At the time of Shaddick's visit to the club, it becomes clear that he would rather be elsewhere. Fairview, in essence, is of little interest to him. Naturally, his only reason for visiting the club is so that Herman can experience the joys of swimming. Shaddick is then exposed to the supercilious behavior that exists among some of the town's residents, namely Mrs. Parker. Such behavior, however, becomes trivial when news of Bill's death arrives via telephone, and Shaddick deems it best to avoid informing Herman of the tragedy until the two are together at the lake.

Through the cherished pastime of fishing, Shaddick and Herman experience Fairview's natural surroundings and ultimately grow close. As they reminisce about Benjie and Bill, certain commonalities become evident. Although Shaddick and Herman do not see eye to eye during their first encounter at the deli, an assortment of fresh salmon, visible within a refrigerated display case, eventually catches Herman's attention and thus marks a turning point of the narrative:

HERMAN: You got a lake here?
SHADDICK: Yeah, I got a small lake.
HERMAN: Do you ever fish in it?
SHADDICK: No, I don't fish. My son and I, we used to fish.

As Herman learns of Benjie's demise, he mentions Bill, who is still alive at such a point of the narrative. Herman boldly declares that his brother, a "real tiger," is going to take him fishing upon returning from Vietnam, but in the meantime, he visits the lake with Shaddick to try his luck. "Between a seventy-year-old Jew and a nine-year-old Black boy, there is not, Miss Ross, what you would call a mutuality of interest," Shaddick later tells Gloria. Nevertheless, his visit to the lake marks the beginning of something special with Herman, who eventually becomes instilled with respect for Shaddick and at one point refers to the latter as a tiger. Hence, a comparison with Bill is clearly apparent. Yet, Herman remains guarded when relating to those outside of his community:

SHADDICK: Once two guys go fishing, or even to the movies, all they should care about is that they enjoy. That's fundamental.
HERMAN: We equal, huh?
SHADDICK: Yeah ... yeah, maybe more than we both realize.
HERMAN: There's rats where I live ... great big ones! And the johns stink, ugh! You could smell 'em all over the building. If we equal, how come I gotta live there?

For one who appears to detest such stench, Herman has undoubtedly traveled to the ideal location.

Ruby Dee.

The country club's Fresh Air Vacation Plan offers more to Fairview than Herman and Shaddick initially realize. As a change in the weather becomes evident, so, too, does a resolution. Upon the film's beginning, as Gloria discloses the details of Herman's imminent arrival, Shaddick does not appear to be accommodating. She nevertheless does what she can to sell him on the plan. All attempts, however, appear futile:

SHADDICK (to Gloria): I'm supposed to have a breakdown because some nameless little mumser doesn't get his fresh air? I got my own problems. So you go back and you tell your members I got no time for children, no sympathy for their social charities, and no place for my nephew, Stanley Banner. This is my final word.

Of course, things do not go as planned for Shaddick. Herman arrives, but the two eventually bond through thick and thin. Later, Shaddick learns of Bill's death. Shaddick then delays his decision to notify Herman until they are alone together, and when the news is ultimately delivered, Wise presents an image of heavy clouds moving into Fairview. Hence, the storm in summer officially begins. Although Shaddick initially opposed Herman's visit, it becomes clear that Fairview is the key to uniting both individuals. Shortly thereafter, the narrative concludes on the most positive of notes. As Shaddick stands alone in his delicatessen, he addresses the late Benjie, solemnly declaring, "[The storm will] end the heat and cleanse the Earth."

"Just prior to being cast in *A Storm in Summer*, I was working quite a bit," Gillian Barber said regarding her appearance as Mrs. Parker. "It was a very busy period in my career. The film's casting director, Sid Kozak, had initially been my agent. When he first notified me of the audition, I just about fell out of my chair because I'm a big musical aficionado. And the fact that Bob Wise had directed both *The Sound of Music* and *West Side Story* made me so excited. I really wanted the role of Mrs. Parker. It didn't matter to me how big or small the role was, I just really wanted to work with Bob. *A Storm in Summer* was filmed in Vancouver, BC. To my great surprise, my scenes were filmed in North Vancouver, which wasn't very far from where I lived at the time.

Gillian Barber as Mrs. Parker.

"I have one word to describe Robert Wise: gentleman. I cannot stress that enough. He had a sparky relationship with Peter Falk, sparky in the sense that it was friendly but it was intensely about the work. They sometimes had arguments, or rather, creative discussions at a louder pitch, about specific moments of the film. My scenes were finished over the course of five days. The experience wasn't long at all because all of the scenes were compressed into a shorter period. Normally, those of us with smaller parts were scheduled in a manner where we were used for the least amount of time. This way, the studio didn't have to pay us as much as the leads. But for me, it was a lot of work per day. The summer was very hot that year, and I can't stand the heat so I was a bit miserable. If my facial expressions ever conveyed any negativity, Bob would get this look on his face that appeared to say, 'Suck it up, Princess! Get out there and do it!' So, that was a nice little lesson for me to learn, to just shut up and commit myself to the job regardless of the conditions. Of course, Bob never said those words because he was such a gentleman. But if an eyebrow was raised, or if he began sighing at something, I understood immediately that Bob was a director who had worked with all the big names in the industry, and I just needed to get the job done. It was understood that it wasn't about me and how hot I was. It was about telling the story in the best way possible.

"Having worked quite a bit over the last thirty years, my favorite thing to do on a film set is observe the relationship between a director and an actor. And because Bob and Peter had such lively discussions going on between them about the way Peter's character should move through life, I couldn't take my eyes off of them. It appeared to me that Bob was intensely invested in telling the story using the best method possible. Therefore, my favorite memory of appearing in *A Storm in Summer* is having the opportunity to be a fly on the wall and listen to the discussions between Bob and Peter.

"Regarding my fellow castmates, I didn't have much of a chance to work with Nastassja Kinski, but she was present on the set the same day as me. In regard to Peter Falk, because I had seen him discuss things with Bob Wise, I felt that, as an actor, he was very much in control of what he was doing. I found myself being fairly acquiescent to anything Peter and I discussed in terms of what the scene should look like. I thought Aaron Meeks was an incredibly mature young man. He was an old soul, for sure. As a Canadian working with such big stars, it's always such a tightrope to walk because you want to do your best work, but you feel awkward about asking them to do something for you. I just tried to make things work using the best method possible. I found Peter Falk to be very exciting, intelligent, intense, and private. All of those qualities just made me admire him all the more. I really wanted to make sure I connected with him during the filming of our scenes together.

"There have been rumors that Bob did not feel honored towards the end of his career. But regarding such rumored feelings, he did not seem sad or dejected during the production. At least, it didn't appear that way to me. I felt as if he was still very much in control of what he wanted from an actor and knew how to get it. I am saddened to know that Robert Wise, somebody who had such a great body of work, did not feel honored at such a stage of his life, because I found him to be truly invested in telling the story of his picture. To me, that is the highest praise I could have for a film director. Regarding *A Storm in Summer*, I not only hope he was proud of the work that we all did for him, but I also hope that he carried the experience with him for the rest of his life."

"I've tasted more hate in my life than I have wine."

A Storm in Summer premiered at the Palm Springs International Film Festival in January of 2000 and debuted on Showtime the following month. The film's reception was generally positive. The experience not only provided Wise with the opportunity to collaborate with an outstanding cast, but through the narrative, he reminisced about a selection of his previous motion pictures to some extent. Upon arrival in Fairview, Herman openly draws a comparison between the inept Stanley and the withdrawn Shaddick, thus prompting the latter to ask, "Do you know what an Achilles' heel is?" Coincidence or not, Wise's *Helen of Troy* (1956) features a modest depiction of the mighty Greek hero. Later within the narrative of *A Storm in Summer*, as Herman and his semi-amiable host prepare to take in a screening of *Butch Cassidy and the*

Sundance Kid (1969), Shaddick comments, "This [film is] supposed to be pretty good . . . Paul Newman and, uh, that other fella." Robert Redford, a performer with whom Wise never collaborated, is not referred to by name. The significance, however, is in regard to Newman, who starred in Wise's *Somebody Up There Likes Me* (1956) and *Until They Sail* (1957). Interestingly enough, upon the beginning of *A Storm in Summer*, the local sheriff (Keith Martin Gordey) says to Shaddick, "Somebody up there doesn't like you much, huh?" Without a doubt, Paul Newman's Rocky Graziano is quite different from Peter Falk's Abel Shaddick. Nevertheless, to general audiences, both characters are indeed likeable and ultimately garner sympathy.

Peter Falk and Robert Wise.

On May 18, 2001, *A Storm in Summer* earned the Daytime Emmy Award of the "Outstanding Children's Special" category. The award was split between *A Storm in Summer* and Showtime's *Run the Wild Fields* (2000). Rod Serling, despite having been dead for over twenty-five years, posthumously earned an Emmy nomination of the "Outstanding Writing in a Children's Special" category. For Wise, the experience was memorable. Although he had to work within the confines of a limited, three-week shooting schedule, his project was completed on time. "[*A Storm in Summer*] took me back to when I was making those B pictures at RKO with this marvelous producer, Val Lewton," Wise said upon the film's premiere. "We were making those in eighteen days, so I knew this could be done in twenty-one days. It was not a long script. We didn't have that many different sets or locations. I am very proud of it as a film. I think it's very good. This is my fortieth film, and probably, that's it. I'm eighty-five years old now. I feel I have done my bit. I am very happy it is going to be my last film."

BIBLIOGRAPHY

BOOKS

Agee, James. *Agee on Film: Reviews and Comments by James Agee*. New York: Grosset & Dunlap, 1969.

Beach, Edward L. Jr. *Run Silent Run Deep*. New York: H. Holt & Co., 1955.

Confucius, & Waley, Arthur. *The Analects of Confucius*. London: G. Allen & Unwin, 1938.

Crichton, Michael. *The Andromeda Strain*. New York: A.A. Knopf, 1969.

De Felitta, Frank. *Audrey Rose*. New York: Putnam, 1975.

De Felitta, Frank. *For Love of Audrey Rose*. New York: Warner Books, 1982.

De Maupassant, Guy. *The Collected Novels and Stories of Guy de Maupassant*. New York: A.A. Knopf, 1922.

Dickens, Charles. *The Old Curiosity Shop*. London: Dent, 1907.

Ferber, Edna. *So Big*. New York: Doubleday, Page, & Co., 1924.

Fisher, Joe. *The Case for Reincarnation*. New York: Bantam, 1985.

Graziano, Rocky, & Corsel, Ralph. *Somebody Down Here Likes Me, Too*. New York: Stein & Day, 1981.

Gunn, James. *Deadlier than the Male*. New York: Duell, Sloan, & Pearce, 1942.

Hawley, Cameron. *Executive Suite*. Boston: Houghton Mifflin, 1952.

Hemingway, Ernest. *Men Without Women*. New York: C. Scribner's Sons, 1927.

Hoehling, A.A. *Who Destroyed the Hindenburg?*. Boston: Little Brown, 1962.

Homer, & Lattimore, Richmond. *The Iliad*. Chicago: University of Chicago Press, 1951.

Jackson, Shirley. *The Haunting of Hill House*. New York: Viking Press, 1959.

Leeman, Sergio. *Robert Wise on His Films*. Los Angeles: Silman-James, 1995.

Longfellow, Henry Wadsworth. *The Poems of Henry Wadsworth Longfellow*. New York: Heritage Press, 1943.

Lyon, Dana. *The House on Telegraph Hill*. New York: Mercury Publications, 1948.

March, Joseph Moncure. *The Set-Up*. New York: Covici Friede Publishers, 1928.

McGivern, William P. *Odds Against Tomorrow*. New York: Dodd, Mead, & Co. 1957.

McKenna, Richard. *The Sand Pebbles*. New York: Harper & Row, 1962.

Mooney, Michael M. *The Hindenburg*. New York: Dodd, Mead, & Co., 1972.

Schaefer, Jack. *Collected Stories of Jack Schaefer*. Boston: Houghton Mifflin, 1966.

Short, Luke. *Gunman's Chance*. New York: Sun Dial Press (reprint), 1942.

Stegner, Wallace. *The Sound of Mountain Water*. New York: Doubleday & Co., 1969.

Stevenson, Robert Louis. *A Child's Garden of Verses*. New York: Scribner, 1905.

Stevenson, Robert Louis. *The Short Stories of Robert Louis Stevenson*. New York: C. Scribner's Sons, 1923.

Tolkien, J.R.R. *The Two Towers*. London: G. Allen & Unwin, 1954.

Tolley, Kemp. *Yangtze Patrol: The U.S. Navy in China*. Annapolis: Naval Institute Press, 1971.

Trapp, Maria A. *The Story of the Trapp Family Singers*. Philadelphia: Lippincott, 1949.

Wickes, Frances G. *The Inner World of Childhood: A Study in Analytical Psychology*. New York: D. Appleton & Co., 1927.

Williams, Blanche C. *Best American Stories: 1919-1924*. New York: Doubleday, Page, & Co., 1926.

Woolf, Virginia. *Jacob's Room*. London: Hogarth Press, 1960.

ARTICLES, ESSAYS, AND SHORT STORIES

Austin, Bruce. "An Interview with Robert Wise." *Literature/Film Quarterly*, Vol. 6, No. 4, 1978.

Barber, Lester E. "This Rough Magic: Shakespeare on Film." *Literature/Film Quarterly*, Vol. 1, No. 4, 1973.

Bates, Harry. "Farewell to the Master." *Astounding Science Fiction*, October 1940.

Bodger, Lowell A. "A Modern Approach to Film Titling." *American Cinematographer*, Vol. 40, No. 8, 1960.

Buhle, Paul. "The Last of the Hollywood Ten." *The Progressive*, Vol. 65, No. 1, January, 2001.

Connell, Richard. "The Most Dangerous Game." *Collier's*, January 19, 1924.

Cooledge, Dean R. "Dames in the Driver's Seat: Rereading Film Noir." *Literature/Film Quarterly*, Vol. 35, No. 1, 2007.

Dunn, Linwood G. "Effects and Titles for *West Side Story*." *American Cinematographer*, Vol. 42, No. 12, 1961.

Gabhard, Krin. "Religious and Political Allegory in Robert Wise's *The Day the Earth Stood Still*." *Literature/Film Quarterly*, Vol. 10, No. 3, 1982.

Gross, Cordelia Baird. "Protection for a Tough Racket." *Harper's Magazine*, December 1954.

King, Susan. "'Storm' Breaks the Calm." *Los Angeles Times*, February 4, 2000.

Love, Edmund G. "Ninety Saddles for Kengtu." *Collier's*, September 6, 1952.

Lovecraft, H.P. "Supernatural Horror in Literature." *The Recluse*, August 1927.

Sobchack, Thomas. "Genre Film: A Classical Experience." *Literature/Film Quarterly*, Vol. 3, No. 3, 1975.

Sloane, Judy. "Callsheet." *Film Review*, June 1995, pp.21-24.

Welsh, Jim. "Postmodern Shakespeare: Strictly Romeo." *Literature/Film Quarterly*, Vol. 25, No. 2, 1996.

Wodehouse, P.G. "The Adventures of Sally." *Collier's*, October 8, 1921.

ONLINE RESOURCES

AMERICAN FILM INSTITUTE. WWW.AFI.COM

CLASSIC IMAGES. WWW.CLASSICIMAGES.COM

INTERNET BROADWAY DATABASE. WWW.IBDB.COM

INTERNET MOVIE DATABASE. WWW.IMDB.COM

TURNER CLASSIC MOVIES. WWW.TCM.COM

INDEX

Numbers in **bold** indicate photographs

Abbott, George 234
Adams, Neile 217-218, **232**, 233-235, 352-353
Adventures of Sally, The 35
Agee, James 33
Alamo, The 205-206
Alcott, Louisa May 163
Allen, Edward 170
Alvin and the Chipmunks 153
Anderson, Robert 239, 342, 344-345
Andrews, Julie 329, 335-336, 362, **366**, 371-372, 374
Andromeda Strain, The 377-390, **378**, **379**, **382**, **384**, **386**, **389**, 430
Angeli, Pier 211, **214**, 217-218, **218**, 225
Angelou, Maya 227
Anthony, Ray 227-228, **232**
Asimov, Isaac **437**
Atherton, William 402, **406**, 411
Attenborough, Richard 343, 355
Auberjonois, René 404, 408-413, **413**
Audrey Rose 387, 388, 417-426, **419**

Bagdasarian, Ross 153
Ball, Lucille 137
Bancroft, Anne **407**, 410-411
Barber, Gillian 454, 459-462, **460**

Bardot, Brigitte **191**, 194
Barrymore, Ethel 372
Basehart, Richard 95, 107-108, 114, 115, 116
Bates, Harry 117, 120-121
Bau, Gordon 170
Beach Jr., Edward Latimer 254
Beatles, The 335
Beck, John 418, 422, 424
Beetley, Samuel E. 65
Begley, Ed 280, **284**
Bel Geddes, Barbara 68, **70**
Belafonte, Harry 280, **280**, **283**
Benjamin, Stuart 451
Bennett, Harve 441
Bennett, Joan 268
Bergen, Candice 343, 356, 357
Bernstein, Leonard 293, 294, 305, 307
Berry, Chuck **237**
Beyer, Troy 446, 447, 450-451, **451**, 452
Beymer, Richard 164, 169, 294, 302, 304
Blaustein, Julian 117
Blondell, Joan **230**, 234
Blood on the Moon 67-74, **70**, **73**, 309
Bloom, Claire 318, **323**, 324
Bluhdorn, Charles 434
Blume in Love 423
Bodeen, DeWitt 4, 8, 9, 15
Body Snatcher, The 25-33, **28**, **30**, **32**, **33**, 418
Bolton, Muriel Roy 57
Born to Kill 49-56, **50**, **51**, **53**, **55**, **56**, 116
"Boule de Suif" 22
Breen, Joseph I. 49
Brennan, Terence 446
Brooks, Donald 374
Burke and Hare 28-29, 30, 32
Burton, Richard 156, **157**, 185
Butch Cassidy and the Sundance Kid 462-463

Cagney, James 198, **198**, 199, 203-204, 205, 207
Campbell, Tisha 447, 448, 451
Canby, Vincent 426
Cannon, Reuben 387
Capone, Al 129
Captive City, The 129-136, **136**, 137, 368
Carter, Ann 3, **14**, **15**
Cartwright, Angela **218**, 332, 336
Cat People 4, 5, 10, 12, 13, 15

Chakiris, George 295, 301-306, **305**
Chaplin, Saul 374
Charlot, André 362, 370, 371
Citizen Kane 1, **2**, 2, 114, 126, 129, 135, 171, 196, 305
Cohn, Art 75, 82
Collins, Stephen 428, **433**, 440
Connell, Richard 35, 38, 39, 40
Coolidge, Philip 268, **270**
Cortesa, Valentina 107, 108, **110**, 114-115, 116, 276
Cortez, Ricardo 58, 63, **65**
Cotten, Joseph 2, 90, **91**, 95, 276
Courage, Alexander 439-440
Coward, Noël 361, 362, 363, 364, 365, 366, 367, 368, 371, 373, 408
Cravat, Nick 254, **264**
Crenna, Richard 343, 353, 355, 363
Crichton, Michael 377, 378, 380, 381, 383, 384, 389-390
Criminal Court 41-48
Crowther, Bosley 169
Cruz, Alexis 446, 447, 450-451, **452**
Curse of the Cat People, The 1-15, 4, **5**, **7**, **10**, **11**, **12**, **13**, **14**, **15**, 17, 22, 418

Damone, Vic 217-218
Daniell, Henry 26, **30**, 32
Dante, Michael 218-224, **226**
Davis Jr., Sammy 361
Davis, Elmer 127
Day the Earth Stood Still, The 117-127, **119**, 156, 373, 430
De Bruin, Sandra 384-389, **386**
De Corsia, Ted 103, **104**, **105**
De Felitta, Frank 417, 422, 426
De Maupassant, Guy 17, 19, 22
De Roy, Richard 391-392
Deadlier than the Male 49
Dean, James 209
Dean, Julia 3, **11**
Dee, Ruby 455, **458**
Dee, Sandra **240**, 240, 247, **249**
Desert Fox, The 155, 156, 161
Desert Rats, The 155-162, 248
Destination Gobi 145-153, **146**, 157
Di Reda, Joe 346, 355, 356, **384**
Diamond, I.A.L. 137, 143
Dickens, Charles 41
Dmytryk, Edward 276
Donen, Stanley 328
Doohan, James 440
Douglas, Paul 177, 228, 234, **234**

Doyle, Mimi **184**, 388
Doyle, Patricia xiv-xv, xvi, 64, **326**, 352, 387, 388, 414, 425
Dubbins, Don 198, 204, **208**
Dysart, Richard A. 402, **410**, 411
Earhart, Amelia 155
Ebert, Roger 398, 451
Edwards, James 78
Einstein, Albert 266, 327
Eisner, Michael 430, 435
Executive Suite 171-184, **172**, **174**, **176**, **177**, **179**, **180**, **183**, **184**, **277**, 328
Exorcist, The 423, 426

Fairchild, William 373
Falk, Peter 454, **456**, 460, 461, **462**, 463, **463**
Fantastic Voyage 377
"Farewell to the Master" 117, 120-121
Father Knows Best 125
Feather, William 208
Fellig, Arthur "Weegee" **83**
Felton, Earl 43
Ferber, Edna 163, 164, 170
Fiscus, Barbara 97
Fiscus, Kathy 97
Fitzgerald, Zelda 391
Foch, Nina 173, 182
Folsey, George 181
Fonda, Peter 392, 396, 397, **397**
Fontaine, Joan **240**, 240, **245**
Foster, Alan Dean 434-439
Foy III, Eddie 259-264
Franciosa, Anthony 228, **230**, 234-235
Francis, Robert 204

Gable, Clark 198, 252, **252**, 259, 260-261
Game of Death, A 35-40
Gandhi, Mahatma 417
Garland, Judy 209
Garmes, Lee **132**
Gay, John 254
Gebert, Gordon xix, 108, 113-115
Gedrick, Jason **446**, 446, 447, 450, 452, **452**
Gersh, Phil 151
Gibson, William 309, 316, 410
Gidding, Nelson xx, 268, 271, 279, 280, 317-318, 377, 378, 380, 403
Godfather, The 225
Goldsmith, Jerry **358**, 360, 440
Goldstein, Allan A. 445

Goldstone, Richard 75
Good Life, The 382
Gormé, Eydie 248
Goya, Francisco **12**, **13**, 13-14
Graham, Barbara 109, 267-277
Gray, Billy 118, **119**, 122-126
Graziano, Rocky 209-225, **211**, 262, 463
Greene, Eve 49, 55
Gross, Cordelia Baird 227
Gunman's Chance 67
Gunn, James 49, 55
Gwenn, Edmund 137-138, **141**

Hackett, Shelah 373
Hackford, Taylor 451
Hagman, Larry 411
Hammond, Nicholas 336, 337
Hard Times 412, 413
Hardwicke, Sir Cedric 186, **188**, 193
Harline, Leigh 157
Harris, Julie 318, **319**, 324
Hathaway, Henry 155-156, 161
Haunting of Hill House, The 317-318, 320-321, 322, 324
Haunting, The 317-325, **318**, **319**, **321**, **323**, **324**, 342, 390, 418
Hawley, Cameron 171
Hayden, Sterling 164, 169
Hayton, Lennie 364
Hayward, Lillie 67-68
Hayward, Susan ix-x, **268**, 268, **273**, 276, **277**, 305
Hecht, Harold 240, 251, 252
Helen of Troy 185-196, **186**, **187**, **188**, **191**, **194**, **195**, 197, 462
Helmore, Tom 229, **235**
Hemingway, Ernest 309
Hepburn, Katharine 445
Hermann, Bernard 126
Heymann, Werner 19
Hickok, James Butler "Wild Bill" 67
Higher and Higher 41
Hill, Arthur 378, **379**, **389**
Hill, James 251, 252, 265
Hindenburg, The 109, 401-415, **403**, **405**, **406**, **407**, **409**, **410**, **411**, **413**
Hinkson, Jake 339
Hirschfeld, Al 371
Hoehling, A.A. 401
Holden, William 173, **176**, **179**, 180, 181, 182, **183**
Holiday Affair 115
Holliman, Earl 151-152

Hopkins, Anthony 418, 422, 424
Horowitz, Howie 435
House on Telegraph Hill, The xix, 107-116, **110**, 276
Houseman, John 171, 172, 181
Hughes, Howard 84
Hunchback of Notre Dame, The **32**

I Want to Live! ix-x, 109, 267-277, **268**, **269**, **270**, **273**, **275**, **277**, 279, 305, 354
Indrisano, John 84
Ingster, Boris 143-144
Inside Story, The 171
It's Hard to Find Mecca in Flushing 227
Iyer, Pico 107

Jackson, C. Bernard 386-387
Jackson, Shirley 317-318, 320-321, 322, 324, 325
Jacob's Room 25
Jeakins, Dorothy 424
Jewell, Isabel **50**, 50
Jewison, Norman 380
Johnson, Richard 318, **321**
Josephy, Alvin M. 130, 137, 143

Kafka, Franz 279
Kaltenborn, H.V. 127
Kaplan, Sol 147, 148, 153
Karath, Kym 332, 336, 337
Karloff, Boris 25, 26, 27, 28, **28**, 32-33
Katzenberg, Jeffrey 430
Kefauver, Estes 129, 130, 131, 135-136
Keith, Carlos see Lewton, Val
Keller, Helen 1
Kelly, Gene 328
Kelly, Grace **202**
Kennedy, Arthur 152
Kennedy, Burt 205
Kenyon, Curtis 90
Kidd, Michael 373, 374
Kimble, Lawrence 43, 57
King Lear 410-411
Kinski, Nastassja 454, 461
Knox, Dr. Robert 28, 31, 32
Koch Jr., Howard 451
Koerner, Charles 17
Kozak, Sid 459
Kreuger, Kurt **19**
Krulak, Victor H. 360

Lafferty, Marcy 440
Lancaster, Burt 240, 251, 252, **254**, 261, **264**, 265
Lang, Fritz 126, 195
Langella, Frank 410-411
LaRoche, Mary 259
Laurents, Arthur 293-294
Laurie, Piper 240, **246**
Lawrence, Gertrude 361-374, **363**
Lazlo, Ernest 368
Lee, Harper 453
Lehman, Ernest xx, 171, 181, 182, 209, 306, 307, 328, **333**
Leigh, Janet 115
Lennart, Isobel 227, 309, 316
Lerner, Alan Jay 409
LeRoy, Ken 301
Letter to Three Wives, A 99
Leven, Boris 360, 374, 390
Lévi-Strauss, Claude 377
Lewis, Flora 57
Lewis, Garrett 364, 372
Lewton, Val 4, 5, 10, 11, 15, 17, 23, 25, 26, **26**, 31, 33, 129, 172, 325, 418, 464
Lincoln, Abraham 89
Lindbergh, Charles A. 401
Livingston, Harold 430, 438, 439
Livingston, Jock 371
Loder, John 35, 39
Loggia, Robert 210, **219**
Long, Audrey 36, 39, 50
Longfellow, Henry Wadsworth 145
Love Story 398-399
Love, Edmund G. 145
Lovecraft, H.P. 317
Lugosi, Bela 25, 27, **33**
Luna, BarBara 301
Lundigan, William 58, **61**, 64, 108, **110**, 115, 171
Lyon, Dana 109, 115
Lyon, Gus 97

Macaulay, Richard 49, 55, 56
MacDonald, Archer 144
MacDonald, Joseph 360
MacDonald, Philip 26
MacLaine, Shirley 306, 309-310, **311**, **315**, 316
MacLeod, Gavin ix-xi, **269**, 344, 353-358
Mademoiselle Fifi 17-23, **19**, 39, 106
Magnificent Ambersons, The 2, 126

Mankiewicz, Don 268, 271
March, Fredric 173, **180**
March, Joseph Moncure 75, 78
Mark, Tony 445
Marlowe, Hugh 119, 124
Maross, Joe **254**, 258, **261**
Martin, Lock 119, 123
Martin, Strother 412
Mason, James 156, 161
Mason, Marsha 418, 422-425, **422**
Massey, Daniel 362, **369**, 371, 373
Mature, Victor 94, 138, **139**, 144
Mazursky, Paul 423
Mazzola, Anthony 125
McCarthy, Joseph 143
McCartney, Paul 335
McCauley, Danny xv
McCord, Ted 338
McCrea, Joel 35, 39
McGivern, William P. 279
McKenna, Richard 341, 342, 344, 345, 346, 349
McNally, Stephen 198, 203, 204, **204**
McQueen, Steve x, 217-218, 219-222, 235, 342, 344, **351**, 352-353, 354, 360
Meeks, Aaron 454, 461
Meisner, Sandy 302
Menzies-Urich, Heather 334-338
Meredith, Burgess 409-410, 411, 412, **413**
Michener, James A. 239
Mineo, Sal 217, 220, 225, **226**
Mirisch, Harold 294, 304
Mischel, Josef 22
Mister 880 137-138
Mitchum, Robert 68, **70**, 74, 115, 306, 309-310, **315**, 316
Montgomery, Edward S. 267-268, 269, 270, 272, **275**, 276
Mooney, Martin 47
Mooney, Michael MacDonald 401-402, 403
Moross, Jerome 131
Morrow, Vic 204, **206**
Most Dangerous Game, The 35, 37, 38, 39, 40
Muhammad Ali 75
Murphy, Richard 155
Musuraca, Nicholas **73**
My Uncle Sosthenes 17
Mystery in Mexico 57-65, **59**, **61**, **65**

Neal, Patricia **98**, 98, 118, 123, 124, 138, 144
Newman, Alfred 147

Newman, Paul 210, **210**, 217, 220, 222, **223**, 225, 235, 241, **243**, **247**, 352, 463
Nimitz, Chester W. 251
Nimoy, Leonard 428, 436, 441
North, Edmund H. 117, 120, 121, 123, 125
Nugent, Frank S. 89-90

O'Driscoll, Martha 41, 42, **43**
Oakes, Susan 302
Oakland, Simon 269, **275**, 294, 345, 354
Odds Against Tomorrow 279-289, **280**, **281**, **283**, **284**, **286**, **288**, **289**, 316, 317
Old Curiosity Shop, The 41
Olson, James 378, **379**, 385, 386, **389**
Olson, Nancy 164, 169, 409
Oppenheimer, Alan 362, 370-372, 407-408, **411**

Paarlberg, Antje 163, 169, 170
Pajama Game, The 234
Papas, Irene 198, **202**, 204, **208**
Parker, Eleanor 98, 329
Pearson, Drew 121, 127
Petracca, Joseph 143
Phipps, William 180-181
Pichel, Irving 35, 40
Pitti, Carl 205
Podestà, Rossana **186**, 186, **191**, 193
Polonsky, Abraham 279-280, 286
Powell, Dick 234
Preminger, Otto 263
Present Laughter 408
Protection for a Tough Racket 227
Provost, Jon 334

Raimi, Sam 40
Raines, Claude 118
Randolph, Jane 3, 4, **10**, **12**
Redford, Robert 463
Reid, Kate 377-378, 379, 385, **389**
Rennie, Michael 118, **119**, 123, 124, 156
Reynolds, William 373
Rickles, Don ix, 255, **261**, 261-262
Robbins, Jerome 293, 294, **295**, 297, 301-302, 305, 306
Robe, The 185
Robinson, Casey 90
Robson, Mark 129, 239, 391, 399
Roddenberry, Gene xvi, 427-428, 434-435, 438, 439, 441
Rodgers and Hammerstein 327, **328**, 339, 361
Rogell, Sid 73-74

Rogers, Wayne 287
Roman, Ruth 98, **101**, **105**
Romero, Pepe 65
Rooftops 445-452, **446**, **449**, **451**, **452**
Roosevelt, Eleanor 267
Rope 82
Ross, Herb 423, 425
Run for the Sun 39
Run Silent Run Deep ix, 161, 240, 251-266, **252**, **254**, **257**, **259**, **261**, **265**, 396
Ruric, Peter 22
Russell, Elizabeth 3, **7**
Russell, Kurt 334
Ryan, Robert **76**, 76, 78, **80**, 84, 262, 280, **281**, 289

Sabrina 182
Sagan, Carl 427
Sand Pebbles, The x, 328, 338, 339, 341-360, **342**, **351**, 373
Sanders, Shep 355
Sands, Danny 203
Schoedsack, Ernest B. 35, 40
Scorsese, Martin 425
Scott, George C. 402, **403**, 408, 411
Scott, Janette 190, 192-195, **195**
Secret of the Sea, The 145
Selznick, David O. 25, 95
Serling, Rod 453, 464
Sernas, Jack 186, **191**, 194
Set-Up, The 75-84, **76**, **77**, **79**, **80**, **83**, 209, 262, 325, 359, 440
Seventh Victim, The 129
Shakespeare, William 293, 307, 410
Shatner, William 428, **433**, 439
Short, Luke 67
Shorter, Baxter 271
Shumate, Harold 67
Simmons, Jean 185, 228, **230**, 234, 236, **240**, 240, 247, **247**
Simon, Simone 3, **4**, 4, 9, 10, 11, 15, 18, **19**
Sinatra, Frank 41
Sir Lancelot **5**
Skouras, Spyros P. 185
Slezak, Walter 51, **55**
Smith, Kent 3, 4, **10**
So Big 163-170, 368
Somebody Up There Likes Me 208, 209-226, **210**, **211**, **214**, **216**, **218**, **219**, **223**, **224**, **226**, 227, 235, 262, 359, 463
Something for the Birds 137-144, 225
Sondheim, Stephen 293, 307
Sound of Hunting, A 251, 252

Sound of Music, The 106, 109, 162, **218**, 262, 327-339, 342, 373, 374, 385, 396, 404, 424, 459
Stanford, Thomas 305
Stanwyck, Barbara 164, 173, **177**, **183**, **277**
Star Trek II: The Wrath of Khan 441
Star Trek: The Motion Picture xv, xvii, 135, 146, 196, 266, 427-441, **433**, **437**
Star! 196, 316, 328, 361-374, **366**, 407
Stegner, Wallace 197
Stevenson, Robert Louis 6, 25, 26, 28, 30, 31
Storm in Summer, A 453-464, **455**, **456**, **458**, **460**, **462**
Stranger on the Third Floor 144
Surtees, Robert 207
Swift, Susan 418, **419**, 422, 423, 424

Taylor, Elizabeth 304
Taylor, Robert 227
Tea and Sympathy 246
This Could Be the Night 227-237, **229**, **230**, **232**, **234**, **235**, **237**, 331
Thomas Crown Affair, The 380
Three Secrets 97-106, **98**, **100**, **101**, **104**, **105**, 316
Tierney, Lawrence **50**, 50, **51**
Tolkien, J.R.R. 239
Tormé, Mel 41
Totter, Audrey **76**, 77, **79**, **85**
Tracy, Spencer 107, 197-198, 207
Trap, The 152
Trapp Family, The 327
Trapp Family in America, The 327
Trevor, Claire 50, **53**, **56**
Tribute to a Bad Man 197-208, **198**, **200**, **202**, **203**, **204**, **206**, **208**
Trumbull, Doug 437
Trumbull, John 297, **299**
Tully, Tom 68, **70**
Turner, Debbie 337
Turner, Ted 325
Twain, Mark 49
Two Flags West 89-95, **91**, 104, 276
Two for the Seesaw 306, 309-316, **311**, **315**
Two People 391-399, **397**
Two Towers, The 239
Tyson, Cicely 286-287

Until They Sail 239-248, **240**, **242**, **243**, **245**, **246**, **247**, 342, 463

Vadim, Roger 194
Vélez, Eddie 446, 447, 450
Vidaurreta, Emilio Azcárraga 57

Von Fritsch, Gunther 3
Votrian, Ralph 246-248, **249**

Wagner, Lindsay 392, 395-398, **397**
Wanger, Walter ix, 267-268, 270, 275, 276, **278**
Warden, Jack 256, 259, **259**, 261, 262
Warth, Theron 67-68, 129
Waxman, Franz **263**
Wayne, David 379, 382, **389**
Wayne, John 205
Webb, Roy 29
Welch, Raquel 377
Welles, Orson 1, **2**, 2, 263, 357
Wellman, William A. 164
Welsh, Bill **100**
West Side Story xv, 162, 169, 196, 262, 263-264, 293-307, **305**, 328, 374, 385, 390, 396, 404, 446, 450, 459
White, Jacqueline 58, **59**, 61, 62-64
Whitlock, Albert **415**
Who Destroyed the Hindenburg? 401
Wickes, Frances G. 7
Widmark, Richard 39, 146, 152
Wild Wild West Revisited, The 205
Wilder, Billy 137, 182, 309
Wilson, Earl 236
Wilson, Julie 235, 236
Winters, Shelley 177, 283, **289**
Wise, Douglas E. xiii-xviii
Wise, Millicent 389, 425, 428, 450
Wodehouse, P.G. 35
Wood, Natalie 294, 302, **303**, 304, 307
Woodward, Joanne 352
Woolf, Virginia 25
Wray, Fay 35, 39
Wyler, William 328
Wyman, Jane 164, **165**, 169, 170

You Can't Buy Luck 47
Young, Jack 203-207

Zanuck, Darryl F. 95, 117, 118, 327, 328, 341, 342
Zanuck, Richard 327, 328, 341
Zuberano, Maurice 135, 196, 357, 388, 425